D0948818

ERIC GILL
A Bibliography

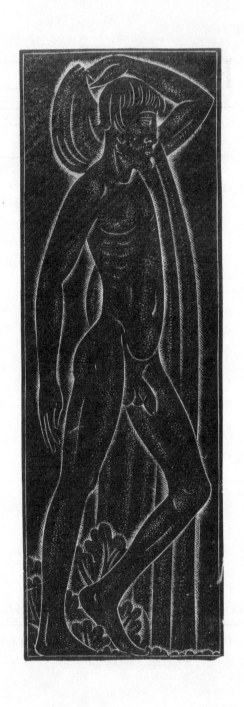

ERIC GILL

A Bibliography

by
EVAN GILL
Second edition
revised by
D. STEVEN COREY
AND
JULIA MACKENZIE

ST PAUL'S BIBLIOGRAPHIES · WINCHESTER

OMNIGRAPHICS INC · DETROIT

1991

The *Bibliography of Eric Gill* was originally published in 1953
by Cassell & Co. Ltd. The Revised Edition under the title of
Eric Gill: A Bibliography was first published in Great Britain
in 1991 by St Paul's Bibliographies,
1 Step Terrace, Winchester, Hampshire and in the United States by
Omnigraphics, Penobscot Building, Detroit, Michigan.

British Library Cataloguing in Publication Data
Gill, Evan
Eric Gill: a bibliography.
1. English engravings. Gill, Eric. Bibliographies
I. Title   II. Corey, D. Steven   III. MacKenzie, Julia
016.76992

ISBN 0–906795–53–2

Library of Congress Catalog No. 90 53251

Frontispiece. This wood-engraving of Mellors (P727) by Eric Gill,
who used himself as the model, was intended for a new edition of
Lady Chatterley's Lover, but was in fact used as the frontispiece to
Clothing Without Cloth, published in 1931.

Designed by John Mitchell
Set in Linotype Plantin Light
by Nene Phototypesetters Ltd, Northampton

Printed in Great Britain on long-life paper ∞
by the Redwood Press, Melksham

CONTENTS

PREFACE
TO THE SECOND EDITION

In 1983 Mr Robert Cross first asked me to undertake a second edition of this book, the first edition of which will be referred to as E R G. He knew that the Albert Sperisen collection of Eric Gill at the Gleeson Library, University of San Francisco, where I am the Special Collections Librarian, is particularly strong in the printed material, including bibliographical variants, just as the Clark Library is known for Gill manuscript material and the Harry Ransom Humanities Research Center (H R H R C) for its holdings of Gill sculpture and drawings. Even with the fine Sperisen collection of Gill at hand, neither of us had any idea how much work lay ahead or how long it would take. There were a couple of shelves in our collection of items which had appeared since 1953. These needed to be added and of course there would be corrections and additions to the original text. The Clark Library and the H R H R C would also have to be visited. A year's worth of work, perhaps, when worked into a full-time job and a busy life out of the library. Simple, really, or so it seemed.

I began by listing all the new material in our collection to be added. Julia MacKenzie made a similar list in England. We compared lists and I began making full entries following the patterns and precedents in E R G. One of our earliest tenets was to keep E R G as intact as possible. Then I went through our holdings of items already in E R G, comparing our copies with the entry and noting variants and discrepancies. This was the point at which it was clear our task would not be so simple. Evan had worked on his own and, as he admitted, he was not trained in bibliography. As a result he had missed many variants and discrepancies abounded. On my first visit to the Clark Library it was clear that their holdings would have much to contribute and would have to be visited several times.

I have examined closely both our collection, for which I have adopted the location symbol G L, and the holdings of the Clark Library in Los Angeles, for which I have used the location symbol C L C, which they themselves use in their copy of E R G. I have also been helped by the printed catalogue of the

Samuels' collection at the HRHRC (no. 636.91). One of our earliest decisions was to keep the ERG numbering system intact. It had been used for thirty years and was essentially sound. For new material we have used a letter sequence following on from ERG's number, e.g. 406, 406*a*. Due to the amount of new material in Section IV entries following no. 636 have been given a new sequence, starting at 636.1, and the same system has been used in Section V. Comments in the first person are by ERG.

SECTION I. We decided not to make any additions to this section although later books could logically be added, for instance Christopher Skelton's *The Engravings of Eric Gill*. But the two earlier works devoted to Gill's wood-engravings (nos. 17 and 27) were published during Gill's life with his collaboration. The possible candidates for Section I will be found in Section IV instead, which has been considerably enlarged. Although there are no new entries in Section I a number of entries have been significantly enlarged. For identifying Gill's wood-engravings, however, we have dropped the old numbering in ERG, the Cleverdon/Gill system which ERG had supplemented in an appendix, and have adopted the now universally used Physick numbers, supplemented by Skelton (*see* Cross Reference List of Engraving Numbers, below, pp. 337–43). The St Dominic's Press entries presented many problems. Fr Brocard Sewell's checklists (nos. 636.76 and 636.126) have been of considerable help. But there is still no adequate bibliography of the press so I have described all the variants I could find, which I hope will provide a better view of these titles; but much remains to be done. I have also mentioned dust jackets which perhaps had not the importance thirty years ago that we attach to them now. Elsewhere, I have mentioned dust jackets only selectively. Finally, for the sake of consistency, we have reproduced the few title pages in Section I which, for whatever reason, were not reproduced in ERG.

MEASUREMENTS. The dimensions for some items are straightforward as the wrappers are the same size as the text pages. When bindings begin to appear, ERG usually gives the page dimensions, not that of the binding, but not consistently. For the second edition we have used page dimensions consistently. Following the practice in ERG measurements are listed height by width, in inches, to the nearest $\frac{1}{8}$th inch.

SECTION II. The symbol CPI at the end of an entry means that the *Catholic Periodical Index* was my only source of information for that entry. The Clark Library owns a large number of Gill's manuscripts, notes and drafts of the periodical articles in this section.

SECTION III. I have not included every book with a Gill illustration. We have included all books done during his lifetime and shortly after. Evan Gill did not have Renate Muller-Krimbach's excellent checklist of the Cranach

Press (no. 636.52), which enabled us to include all known work done by Gill for this press. I was also happy to be able to describe two interesting St Dominic's Press items not in E R G, the *Proprium Missarum Dioecesis Westmonasteriensis* (no. 271a), unrecorded anywhere and with an unrecorded Gill wood-engraving in *Cantica Natalia* (no. 391a). The copies of *Cantica Natalia* at G L and C L C enabled me to discover that Physick and Skelton were mistaken in describing the Gill wood-engraving on p. 24a as (P158) instead of (P269).

SECTION IV. This section presented the greatest problems in new numbering but we hope the system adopted will be usable. E R G usually listed undated periodical appearances at the beginning of each year. Entries new to the second edition are grouped at the end of each year. Dated periodicals have been integrated in chronological order by month and day throughout the year's entries. This does lead to a lot of additional a and b entries but this follows the practice of E R G. We have not seen a copy of every item listed in E R G, particularly in Section IV, so doubtless some errors have crept through.

SECTION V. This section has not grown as much as it might, because we have not included every possible ephemeral item – where would it end? (Indeed, Sections IV and V have had to be necessarily selective.) A number of typographical items fit comfortably in this section, however.

SECTION VI. This new section was added to handle a small but interesting aspect of Gill work, his posters. The posters printed by St Dominic's Press with Gill wood-engravings are all rare. I have listed those found in Sewell as well as those I myself have seen.

APPENDIX. This has been eliminated in the second edition since Physick and Skelton have completely supplanted this very preliminary listing of Gill's wood engravings from 1934 to 1940.

POSTSCRIPT. This has been eliminated in the second edition and has been moved to Section I where it is the last item (no. 54a).

INDEX. The index has been corrected and considerably augmented.

It only remains for me to add my grateful thanks to a number of people: to Robert Cross who has given me unfailing patient support even when we went years past our initial optimistic deadline; Julia MacKenzie who helped with every stage of the revision and the index; and Mr Paul E. Birkel, Dean of the University Library at U S F whose approval and support were essential. Thanks must also go to David McKitterick, Librarian, Trinity College, Cambridge, for his informed guidance. For information found in the second edition I owe a great debt of gratitude to the following: Judy Beresford of Ayer Pub. Co., Salem, New Hampshire; John Bidwell, Reference/Acquisitions

Librarian at the William Andrews Clark Memorial Library, UCLA, for his unfailing friendly help and intelligent advice; Carol Briggs, Manuscripts Librarian at the Clark Library; John P. Chalmers, Librarian, Harry Ransom Humanities Research Center, Austin, Texas; James Davis, Rare Book Librarian, University Research Library, UCLA for his checklist of Hague & Gill and much other useful information; Christopher Skelton for his superb 'illustrated Physick' which made my own work so much easier and for his informative and encouraging correspondence, and for allowing us to use the cross reference list of engraving numbers; Robert N. Taylor of the HRHRC; Decherd Turner, then Director of the HRHRC; and Judith Wainwright, Reference Librarian at the Gleeson Library, USF. For general support and encouragement I would like to thank David Chapman and David Berryman who gave me pleasant accommodations while I was researching at the Clark Library; Mr & Mrs Norman H. Strouse who changed the course of my life in the direction of rare books; and my supportive and long-suffering San Francisco friends, particularly David Forbes and Dorothy Whitnah.

Finally I would like to dedicate this second edition to Mr Albert Sperisen of San Francisco, the great Gill enthusiast and collector who waited more than thirty years for a revised edition of ERG and without whose collection and constant help this revision would not have been possible.

D. STEVEN COREY

PREFACE
TO THE FIRST EDITION

Everything has a beginning – be it bibliographies or battleships. The keel-plate of the present work was laid down some years ago when I set out to make a simple, straightforward catalogue of my own collection of my brother's books, of books or journals containing reference to his work and of some volumes of press cuttings. As time went on my collection grew and with it the conviction that there was need of a more thoroughgoing, comprehensive work, in short, a full-dress bibliography. I am well aware that in my attempt to meet this need I have laid myself open to the charge of showing an astonishing lack of discrimination; of setting a disproportionate value upon anything in which my brother had a hand or moved other hands to write about him; of overloading the work with minutiae; and so forth. I doubt not that I lack the Boswellian quality of knowing what to retain and what to abandon and seek consolation in the thought that everything is valuable to those who are interested in this or that personality. Where the book's omissions and imperfections are concerned I draw no little comfort from the words of one whose wide knowledge and experience in such matters pre-eminently fit him to pronounce a judgement: 'If the bibliographer is to await perfection he will probably never publish his work at all' (P. H. Muir, *Points, 1874–1930*, Constable, 1931).

I now turn to the general arrangement of this book. It is divided into five sections; in the first of these and in a portion of the third I have given, in as much detail as I have found possible, the actual bibliographical structure of Eric's writings in book form and of the books he illustrated. Broadly speaking, I suppose I have no right to claim that any more than this section (I) and subsection (III*a*) fall within the term 'bibliography' in the strictest sense, for in those alone have I attempted to analyse each entry uniformly under the set headings, Size, Collation, Pagination and Contents, etc. I am aware that division by *form of publication* should, if possible, be avoided; that a book, an article in a journal or a pamphlet is of equal status, bibliographically.

Nevertheless, in dealing with Eric's written work I have felt it desirable to make a distinction between his books and his other writings; hence Sections I and II. Similarly in Section III I have drawn a distinction between books illustrated by him and books which, though of no less importance in themselves (indeed many of them are of far greater importance as books), contain no more than a decorated title-page or initial letters engraved by him. Thus we have the subdivisions (*a*) and (*b*) of Section III. In the former we include, for example, the Golden Cockerel edition of *The Song of Songs* but record in the latter the same Press's edition of Plato's *Phaedo* because, though containing a title-page and floreated initial letters engraved by E. G., it can hardly be described as a book 'illustrated' by him. Of perhaps even greater importance is the need for my third subdivision of this section, namely (*c*). I hold that a clear distinction should be drawn between a book containing an engraving executed specifically for that book and with *that book alone in the mind of the engraver*, and another, of perhaps quite a different character, which through the printer's whim contains the same engraving but used this time to fill an odd space or serve as a tail-piece. At the risk of labouring the point it might be mentioned that in the thirty-seven entries which fall within this subdivision (*c*) there are altogether 128 engravings (excluding the imprint engravings, e.g. *D P and Cross*) and that only one of these had *not* been used in an earlier publication. (Ironically enough that one was *Crucifix, Chalice and Host* (D44) engraved for *The Devil's Devices* but discarded.)

Section IV calls, I think, for no special comment.

Section V: *Miscellanea*. The inclusion of such a section may be a confession of weakness; it may be objected that any item which is worth including in a bibliography should be appropriate to some division of the subject and therefore have a right of entry in one or other of the earlier sections. This notwithstanding I cannot but think that if these entries serve a useful purpose this is the best place for them.

St Dominic's Press. This is not the place for a history of this hand-press which was set up in a Ditchling stable in January 1916. I do think, however, that in view of Eric's close association with it from its beginnings and for several years thereafter it calls for special mention. And it will be seen from these pages that as regards both writing and engraving, his own earliest work, and the best part of his work for some time to come, first saw the light in the little publications Hilary Pepler printed and published at this Press. From the bibliographical standpoint I cannot do better than quote Will Ransom who, in his excellent Check List of St Dominic's Press, writes: 'This press is at once the despair of collectors and an exciting field of research. It is certain that no complete and accurate bibliography can ever be compiled, particularly if variant bindings and dates are recorded' (*Selective Check Lists of Press Books, Part Two*. New York: Philip C. Duschnes, 1946).

Now, as to the subheadings in the two major sections, namely, I and III (*a*).

Size. This has been given in inches. I have deliberately refrained from the use of the forms fol., 4to, 8vo, etc., holding, on unquestionable authority, that the terms denoting folding or format should not be used to indicate height or shape.

Pagination and Contents. At the risk of breaking up the continuity of this paragraph I have described in full the contents of each volume of collected essays (or lectures), e.g. *Art-Nonsense, Beauty Looks After Herself* or *Work and Leisure.* Exceptions to this rule exist where the List of Contents is combined with a title-page which has been reproduced as, for example, in *Work and Property &c* (no. 33). Where the essay has been published previously it will be found as an independent publication in the appropriate Section. It will then have two index references, one as a publication in its own right (usually shown as the Editio Princeps) and another as a collected essay. *Songs Without Clothes,* for example, is indexed under no. 8 as an independent publication and again, under no. 18, as one of the essays appearing in *Art-Nonsense.*

Illustrations. Two comprehensive iconographies of Eric's wood-engravings have been published and to them reference is made wherever a wood-engraving (w-e.) has been mentioned, by the file number which appears in parentheses immediately after the title of the engraving. The first of these two volumes was published by Douglas Cleverdon (Bristol) in 1929 (cf. no. 17) and covers the period 1908–27 and the engravings DI to D241 and 1 to 214. (The prefix 'D' denotes engravings finished at Ditchling before 1924.) The second volume, published by Faber and Faber in 1934 (cf. no. 27), covers the period 1928–33 and the engravings numbered 215 to 543. A third and last volume, to cover Eric's engravings from 1934 until his death in 1940 (nos. 544 to 679), has yet to be compiled. To fill that gap for the time being I have added, as an Appendix to this work, what we might call a Short-Title Catalogue of this last group.

I do not think the other subheadings require any special comment, save perhaps that entitled *Reviews,* the inclusion of which I justify by quoting Mr J. D. Cowley's invaluable book *Bibliographical Description and Cataloguing* (London: Grafton and Co. 1939) where he writes (p. 136): '... the resources available for estimating contemporary opinion on the book should be recorded, including reviews, criticisms and allusions.' Much else that has been included (notably in Section IV) may, I hope, be justified on similar grounds if only that it may be rescued, in the words of Master Richard Hakluyt, 'from the vasty maw of oblivion'.

EVAN R. GILL

Liverpool
22 February (Eric's birthday in 1882)
1952

ACKNOWLEDGEMENTS
to the First Edition

I wish, in the first place, to acknowledge my indebtedness to Mr S. Samuels of Liverpool. Without his encouragement and support this work could never have been undertaken, and I also owe much to his kindness in giving me access to his extensive and almost complete collection of my brother's books and engravings.

The compilation of this book gave me several happy visits to Pigotts where Eric lived and where Mary Gill always smoothed my way to Eric's book-room and shelves. These peeps into his workshop were of inestimable inspiration and value and provided me with many 'chippings' without which I should have been greatly handicapped.

To Mr Walter Shewring I shall ever be grateful for his criticism and advice on many points, for his help in a variety of ways, and more particularly for his bringing to my notice several items of the distant as well as the more recent past which, but for him, would doubtless have been missed altogether.

I am specially indebted to Mr P. H. Muir and to Mr D. I. Masson, of the University Library, Liverpool, whose expert knowledge solved many of the knotty problems of format and collation. Here, however, let me hasten to absolve them from blame for any mistakes which, notwithstanding their advice, may have found their way into Sections I and III (*a*).

I am grateful to Barbara Beresford (Mrs J. K. Harrison) for the help she gave me in 'plating' (to borrow a philatelic term) the scores of engravings in the *Troilus and Criseyde* and *Canterbury Tales* volumes. To find the duplications and to note them as well as the variants called for much care and she did this work to my great satisfaction.

My thanks are due to my wife for her patience during the time this book has been in the making. For her help, too, notably in the compilation of the Indexes where her skill at Patience was turned to good account in the sorting, shuffling and re-sorting of my index cards.

Lastly, the printer, without whom all the efforts of those mentioned in the preceding paragraphs would have been of no avail. The skilful use he has made of the *Perpetua* roman and *Felicity* italic type faces would, I feel sure, have warmed the heart of the designer. His work throughout the following pages, maintaining as it does the highest standards of accuracy and clarity, shows how admirably he upholds the traditions of the University Press, Cambridge.

E.R.G.

ACKNOWLEDGEMENTS:
Illustrations in the Revised Edition

The following illustrations in the Revised Edition were supplied by Mr D. Steven Corey as Librarian of the Richard A. Gleeson Library:

3*a* second state, 6 C L C copy, 8 (wrapper), 16 (P556 Intaglio), 29 (title page and dust jacket, 33 (cover), 34 (cover), 37 (cover), 38 (cover), 45 (cover), 46 (cover), 52 (dust jacket), 54*a* (three versions of the title page), 269, 271*a* (first page and illustration on p. 65), 285 (original and finished drawing for binding), 302*a*, 302*b*, 309 (sketch and final cover), 340 (wood-engraving), 388*b*, 391*a* (page 24a), 664.43, 664.45, 664.46 (two pages,) 664.50.

The frontispiece is reproduced from a photograph of the original supplied by the Harry Ransom Humanities Research Center, University of Texas at Austin. The remaining items originated from Evan Gill's *Bibliography of Eric Gill*, though many were rephotographed from the original editions of the books in the Eric Gill collection at Chichester by courtesy of the West Sussex Record Office and Mrs P. Gill, the County Archivist. Mary Gill and Walter Shewring, Eric Gill's executors, visited Chichester in 1950, with a view to establishing a permanent collection of the works of Eric Gill in the city. The basis of the collection was to be formed from bequests by Mary Gill, Walter Shewring, Evan Gill and Fr. Desmond Chute, and it was hoped that once the collection was established, other owners of works by Eric Gill would take the opportunity of adding to the collection. The collection, which has been looked after by the West Sussex Record Office since 1967, has continued to grow, and has already been the subject of two published catalogues.

I

BOOKS AND PAMPHLETS, ETC
WRITTEN BY ERIC GILL

Numbers 1– 54*a*

SERVING AT MASS

BEING INSTRUCTIONS AND
DIRECTIONS FOR LAYMEN
AS TO THE MANNER OF
SERVING AT LOW MASS.

Printed and Published
BY DOUGLAS PEPLER
at Ditchling Sussex
1916   [1]

1916

1 SERVING AT MASS

[Compiled by Eric Gill]

TITLE-PAGE: Reproduced. Shows title-page device: *Chalice and Host with Ω and A* (P54).

SIZE: $4\frac{1}{2} \times 3\frac{3}{4}$.

COLLATION: [A]⁴, B–C⁸, [D]⁴. Pp. 5–6 are pasted on the stub [B3] of pp. 11–12 and are not included in the signatures. [D4] is a stub behind the pasted-down [D3].

PAGINATION AND CONTENTS: Pp. viii + 38; [i]–[iv] blank, of which the first leaf is pasted down as the front end-paper but forms an integral part of the book; [v] [vi] title-page, verso Imprimatur dated: 21 SEPTEMBRIS 1916; [vii] [viii] Note by the compiler, verso blank; 1–35 text; [36] Colophon worded: COMPILED BY ERIC GILL | PRINTED AND PUBLISHED | BY DOUGLAS PEPLER | HAMPSHIRE HOUSE | HAMMERSMITH | AND DITCHLING SUSSEX | A.D. 1916.; printer's device: *D P and Cross* (P64); [37] [38] blank and pasted down as end-paper, also forming an integral part of the book. Printed from *Caslon O.F.* on hand-made paper.

ILLUSTRATIONS: In addition to the engraving on the title-page there is a wood-engraving: *Chalice and Host with Candles* (P53) used as a tail-piece on p. 35.

BINDING: Stiff dark grey paper wrappers, sewn, printed on front, in silver: SERVING | AT | MASS | [w-e. *Device: Chalice and Host* (P65)] The whole set within a frame of plain rules. Copies are known without the device on cover (see below). All edges trimmed.

DATE OF PUBLICATION: 1916.

3

PRICE: 6*d*., later increased to 1*s*., cf. advertisement in *Sculpture* (no. 5).

NOTE: This is no. 10 of S. Dominic's Press publications.

VARIANTS: GL copy has black paper wrappers with the lettering printed in gold, without the device on cover.

PENNY TRACTS
No. 1

SLAVERY & FREEDOM
Reprinted from the Easter number of *The Game*.

Respondeo dicendum	I reply by saying ....
Liber est causa sui, servus autem ordinatur ad alium.	The freeman is an end in himself but the slave is for another.

S. Thomas Aquinas, Summa 1A Qu. 96 *Art.* 4   *Trans. V. M. Nabb*

That State is a State of Slavery in which a man does what he likes to do in his spare time and in his working time that which is required of him. This State can only exist when what a man likes to do is to please himself.

That State is a state of Freedom in which a man does what he likes to do in his working time and in his spare time that which is required of him. This State can only exist when what a man likes to do is to please God.

A man is a Slave when between him and God who is the *final* cause is interposed another man as an *efficient* cause.

A man is free who is subject only to those causes which are called *final*.

[2]

1917

2 SLAVERY AND FREEDOM

COVER-TITLE: Reproduced.

SIZE: $8\frac{1}{4} \times 5\frac{1}{2}$.   COLLATION: A quarter-sheet folded as two leaves.

PAGINATION AND CONTENTS: Pp. 4; [1] title and first page of text; 2–3 rest of text and list of books published by Douglas Pepler; 4 continuation of publisher's list. Printed from *Caslon O.F.* on Batchelor hand-made paper. All edges trimmed.

ILLUSTRATIONS: None.

DATE OF PUBLICATION: n.d. [1917]

PRICE: One penny.

NOTES: This leaflet, no. 1 of the *Penny Tracts*, was reprinted from the Easter 1917 number of *The Game*, Vol. 1, no. 3, pp. 33–5 (no. 69). It was reprinted in *Art-Nonsense* (1929) (no. 18) and, along with *Essential Perfection*, as a $9\frac{1}{4} \times 6$ 4-page single-fold, 'Number One of the Series LOQUELA MIRABILIS', August 1936, of 'A series of reprints and original writings printed by hand by Guido Morris and published by him at The Latin Press, Langford, East Somerset, and later in the 30-page magazine *Loquela Mirabilis*, Vol. 1, no. 1, November 1936, also published by Guido Morris. See 'The Quest for Guido' by Anthony Baker, *The Private Library*, Vol. 2, no. 4, Winter 1969, pp. 139–76. The *Penny Tracts* are not listed in S. Dominic's Press book list (1930) but reference to them appeared in the advertisement pages of various publications of the Press, e.g. *The Mistress of Vision* (1918).

GOD SAVE THE KING
PENNY TRACTS
No. 3

THE NEXT STEP

A stable condition of society more approximate to FREEDOM than the one in which we live, is desirable. This can be achieved by:

THE RESTORATION OF THE MONARCHY

And the appointment, for the duration of the war and one year, of a Regency Council consisting of:

JELLICOE

AND

ROBERTSON

E.G.   D.P.

[3] *Printed by 'Douglas Pepler, Ditchling Sussex. 10 oi 17*

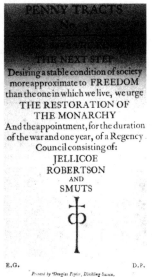

[3a.
Second
state]

3 THE RESTORATION OF THE MONARCHY

[Written in collaboration with D.P[epler]]

TITLE AND TEXT: Reproduced.

This is a single sheet printed from *Caslon O.F.* on Batchelor hand-made paper. The wording: G O D S A V E T H E K I N G and the printer's device: *D P and Cross* (P64) are printed in red. 1917.

SIZE: $7\frac{1}{2} \times 4\frac{7}{8}$.

PRICE: One penny.

NOTES: Cf. Note concerning the *Penny Tracts* under No. 2, above.

VARIANTS: G L has a copy without the date at bottom and there is no rule after NO. 3 (a proof?).

SUBSEQUENT EDITIONS: 3a. This leaflet was later reprinted (n.d.); the text was then rearranged and the name Smuts added to those of Jellicoe and Robertson. The imprint at foot is without date. G L has two states of this reprint. In one GOD SAVE THE KING and the printer's device are printed in brown ink and it measures $6\frac{3}{4} \times 4\frac{3}{8}$. In the other these are printed in red and there is an exclamation point (!) after the word KING. It measures $7\frac{3}{4} \times 5\frac{1}{4}$. Both states are printed on Batchelor hand-made paper.

ESSENTIAL PERFECTION
AN ESSAY BY ERIC GILL
[REPRINTED FROM "THE GAME" JANUARY NUMBER A.D. 1918.]

[4]

1918

4 ESSENTIAL PERFECTION

COVER-TITLE: Reproduced.

SIZE: $7\frac{1}{2} \times 5\frac{1}{2}$.   COLLATION: A quarter-sheet folded as two leaves.

PAGINATION AND CONTENTS: Pp. 4; [1] cover-title; 2–4 text, signed at foot of p. 4: 'E.G. 8. 12. '17.'

ILLUSTRATIONS: None.

DATE OF PUBLICATION: n.d. [1918]

PRICE: n.p. [2d.]

NOTES: This is no. 20 of S. Dominic's Press publications. It was first published in *The Game*, Vol. II. no. 1, January 1918, pp. 21–3 (no. 69) and revised and reprinted in *Art-Nonsense* (1929) (no. 18). The revised text was reprinted along with *Slavery and Freedom* as 'Number One of the Series LOQUELA MIRABILIS' by Guido Morris, August 1936 (cf. note under No. 2, above). C L C has the manuscript of the text as written for *The Game*.

VARIANTS: Both G L and C L C have copies $7\frac{3}{4} \times 5\frac{1}{2}$.

5 SCULPTURE

TITLE-PAGE: Reproduced. Shows publisher's device: *D P and Cross* (P64).

SIZE: $8 \times 5\frac{1}{2}$.   COLLATION: [Unsigned: 1^2, $2–3^4$, 4^2 enclosing 5^2.]

PAGINATION AND CONTENTS: Pp. iv + 24; [i] [ii] blank; [iii] [iv] title-page, verso blank; [1]–21 text; [22] printer's imprint: PRINTED BY DOUGLAS PEPLER, DITCHLING, SUSSEX.; [23] [24] blank. Four pages of the pub-

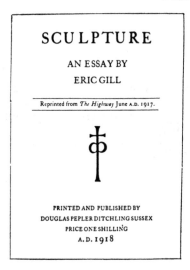

SCULPTURE

AN ESSAY BY
ERIC GILL

Reprinted from *The Highway* June A.D. 1917.

PRINTED AND PUBLISHED BY
DOUGLAS PEPLER DITCHLING SUSSEX
PRICE ONE SHILLING
A.D. 1918

[5]

lisher's advertisements are inserted between pp. [22] and [23]. Printed from *Caslon O.F.* on hand-made paper.

ILLUSTRATIONS: None.

BINDING: Brown paper wrappers; worded on front as on title-page but without the frame of rules and with the price reading: PRICE ONE SHILLING & 6D., the '& 6D.' being crossed out by pen-stroke. Top edges trimmed, others untrimmed.

DATE OF PUBLICATION: July 1918.

PRICE: 1s.

PRINTING: 400 copies.

NOTES: This is no. 21 of S. Dominic's Press publications. The essay originally appeared in *The Highway*, June 1917 (no. 70).

VARIANTS: Two variants are known, viz. (*a*) Price on cover is printed: PRICE ONE SHILLING, the 'ONE' being crossed out by pen-stroke. The pagination '5', which is absent in the copy described above, is here present. The outsize measurements are $7\frac{5}{8} \times 5\frac{1}{4}$. In the second variant (*b*) the price on front cover is unaltered. There is no frame of plain rules on the title-page and there are no pages of advertisements, the collation thus being: [Unsigned: 1^2, $2-4^4$.] Outsize measurements: $7\frac{7}{8} \times 5\frac{3}{8}$. In all three impressions the word 'full' in line 4, p. 10 is misspelt 'fnll'.

SUBSEQUENT EDITIONS: This essay was reprinted (1924) in book form with considerable additions and alterations, a Preface and three wood-engravings (no. 10). It was subsequently reprinted in *The Architectural Review*, Vol. LIX, no. 353, April 1926, pp. 128–9 as *The Carving of Stone* and again in *Art-Nonsense* (1929) (no. 18), under the title *Stone-carving*.

Welfare Handbook. No. 5 BIRTH CONTROL PRINTED AND PUBLISHED AT S. DOMINIC'S PRESS, DITCHLING, SUSSEX. A.D. MCMXIX.	*Welfare Handbook* No. 5. **BIRTH** CONTROL PRINTED AND PUBLISHED AT S. DOMINIC'S PRESS, DITCHLING, SUSSEX

[6]   [6. CLC copy]

1919

6 BIRTH CONTROL

TITLE-PAGE: Reproduced.

SIZE: $5\frac{1}{4} \times 4\frac{1}{4}$.

COLLATION: Three unsigned gatherings of 4, 8 and 4 leaves respectively.

PAGINATION AND CONTENTS: Pp. viii + 24; [i]–[iv] blank, of which the first leaf is pasted down as the front end-paper but forms an integral part of the book; [v] [vi] title-page, verso blank; [vii] [viii] Preface by Vincent McNabb, O.P., verso blank; [1]–21 text; [22]–[24] blank, of which the last leaf is pasted down as an end-paper also forming an integral part of the book. Printed from *Caslon O.F.* on Batchelor hand-made paper.

ILLUSTRATIONS: None.

BINDING: Stout dark grey paper wrappers, sewn, lettered in gilt on front as on title-page but for rearrangement of the words BIRTH CONTROL, which are on separate lines. Edges trimmed. The device on the title-page and cover: *Dog and flaming torch* is from a wood-engraving by Desmond Chute.

DATE OF PUBLICATION: 1919.

PRICE: This book, like the others of the series (*Welfare Handbooks*), was published at 1*s*.

REVIEW: *The New Witness*, 21 November 1919.

NOTE: This is no. 28 (5) of S. Dominic's Press publications.

VARIANTS: The CLC copy is lettered in black on front cover. Reproduced. GL copy has variant cover which measures $6 \times 4\frac{1}{2}$, red paper wrappers printed in black, with the device of a rampant lion, not by Gill (6a).

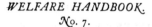

WELFARE HANDBOOK.
№. 7.

DRESS

Being an Essay in Masculine Vanity
and an Exposure of the UnChristian
Apparel favoured by Females.

PRINTED AND PUBLISHED AT S. DOMINIC'S PRESS,
DITCHLING, SUSSEX. A.D. MCMXXI.

[7]

1921

7 DRESS

TITLE-PAGE: Reproduced.

SIZE: $5\frac{3}{4} \times 4\frac{1}{2}$.   COLLATION: A single unsigned gathering of 14 leaves.

PAGINATION AND CONTENTS: Pp. vi + 22; [i]–[iv] blank; [v] [vi] title-page, verso quotation from *A Modern Utopia* by H. G. Wells; [1] [2] illustration, verso blank; [3]–13 text; [14] blank; [15] [16] illustration, verso blank; [17] [18] colophon worded: PRINTED AT S. DOMINIC'S PRESS, | [device: *Dog and flaming torch* (Chute)] | DITCHLING, SUSSEX., verso blank; [19]–[22] blank. Printed from *Caslon O.F.* on Batchelor hand-made paper.

ILLUSTRATIONS: There are two wood-engravings, placed:

Dress, 1920 (P186), p. [1]

Dress, 1860 (P187), p. [15]

BINDING: Stout dark grey paper wrappers, sewn, lettered in gilt on front as on title-page and, on back: PRICE ONE SHILLING. Edges trimmed. The device on the title-page and cover (a peacock) is from a wood-engraving by Desmond Chute.

DATE OF PUBLICATION: 1921.

PRICE: One shilling.

NOTES: This is no. 28 (7) of S. Dominic's Press publications. This essay originally appeared in *Blackfriars*, Vol. I, no. 9, December 1920, pp. 524–9 (no. 79). It was revised and reprinted in *Art-Nonsense* (1929) (no. 18).

VARIANTS: I have seen a copy wherein the device on title-page is printed in

9

red. The make-up of this copy is in a gathering of ten leaves, sewn through the middle, the blanks at either end being omitted. The edges of this copy were trimmed. The CLC copy of the regular edition measures $5\frac{3}{8} \times 4\frac{1}{4}$. The GL copy of the variant has twelve leaves, i.e. with one set of blanks. The illustration leaves are conjugate and are printed on stiffer, whiter paper.

SUBSEQUENT EDITIONS: In 1986 Neil Shaver of the Yellow Barn Press, Council Bluffs, Iowa, reprinted the essay. 200 copies. $7 \times 5\frac{1}{4}$. 15 numbered pages. Handset in 14 point Joanna. Blue cloth boards with printed paper title label on front cover, no dust jacket. Frontispiece wood-engraved portrait of Gill by John De Pol who also designed the decorated endpapers. Contains line engravings of (P186) on p. [3] and (P187) on p. [9].

1922

8 SONGS WITHOUT CLOTHES

TITLE-PAGE: Reproduced. Shows publisher's device: *S D P and Cross* (P145).

SIZE: $8 \times 4\frac{1}{2}$.   COLLATION: [Unsigned: 1^4, $2-3^8$, $4-5^4$.]

PAGINATION AND CONTENTS: Pp. viii + 48; [i] [ii] blank; [iii] [iv] title-page, verso blank; [v]–[vii] Preface; [viii] blank. [1]–46 text; [47] [48] blank. Printer's imprint at foot of p. 46: PRINTED AT S. DOMINIC'S PRESS, DITCHLING, SUSSEX. Printed from *Caslon O.F.* on hand-made paper watermarked with a device *Bible & Crown*.

ILLUSTRATIONS: None.

BINDING: Cream paper wrappers, sewn, lettered on front: SONGS | WITHOUT CLOTHES Top and fore-edges trimmed, others un-trimmed.

DUST JACKET: Issued in a tissue paper jacket. GL copy is in a glassine jacket.

DATE OF PUBLICATION: November 1921.

PRICE: Five shillings.

PRINTING: 240 copies.

NOTES: This is no. 34 of S. Dominic's Press publications. This book comprises two essays the first of which (pp. [1]–40) originally appeared in *The Game*, February, March, May, July and August 1921 (no. 69) under the title *The Song of Solomon and Such-like Songs*. It was revised and reprinted, under its present title, in *Art-Nonsense* (1929) (no. 18). The second (pp. 41–6) is a reprint of the essay *Of Things Necessary and Unnecessary* which first appeared in *The Game*, October 1921. This, also, was revised and reprinted in *Art-Nonsense*.

VARIANTS: I have two other issues of this book which appear to be contemporary with that described above, viz. (*a*) In grey-brown paper boards, unlettered, $\frac{1}{4}$ linen, size $7 \times 4\frac{3}{4}$. All edges cut. (*b*) The so-called 'large paper'

SONGS
WITHOUT CLOTHES

BEING A DISSERTATION ON THE SONG
OF SOLOMON AND SUCH-LIKE SONGS, BY
ERIC GILL TOGETHER WITH A PREFACE
BY FR. VINCENT MᶜNABB, O.P.

PRINTED AND PUBLISHED AT S. DOMINIC'S PRESS
DITCHLING SUSSEX ON THE FEAST OF
THE PRESENTATION OF OUR LADY
A.D. MCMXXI.

SONGS WITHOUT CLOTHES

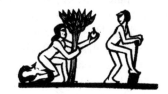

FIVE SHILLINGS
S. DOMINIC'S PRESS

[8]

[8. Wrapper]

edition, light grey paper boards, $\frac{1}{4}$ linen, with paper label on front worded: SONGS | WITHOUT CLOTHES, the whole set within a frame of plain rules. Size: 8 × 5. Top and fore-edges trimmed, others uncut. From internal evidence it would appear that the copy first described and that lettered (*b*) were printed from the same setting of type, for they are printed on the same watermarked paper and, further, the letter 'c' in 'McNabb' on the title-page is skied. The copy described under (*a*) is printed on paper watermarked with a garter device (Batchelor's hand-made) and in this the letter 'c' is not skied.

It is clear from the gatherings in an unopened copy of the regular issue (G L) that the two watermarks occur in the same sheet of paper; the garter device is simply the countermark. The preliminary leaves including the preface are formed from a folded half-sheet which can show either the watermark or the countermark, which probably led to Evan's confusion. There are five copies of this title in the G L, each one different in size and because of the confusion about the paper, none of them matches Evan's descriptions in that regard. In addition they show no connection between the paper and the skied or unskied 'c', nor could any other pattern be detected from the copies at hand. The term unskied must be qualified. In this context it only means that the top of the 'c' is level with the top of the 'M' as opposed to being above the 'M' as the title-page

11

depicted shows. No copy has been seen in which the 'c' is where one would expect to find it, at the foot of the 'M'.

But the G L has copies that match, with some variations, the three issues that Evan identified. A copy of the regular issue in the G L is 8×5, no edges are trimmed and the 'c' is not skied. Another copy of the regular issue in the G L is $7\frac{1}{2} \times 4\frac{3}{4}$, trimmed at the fore-edge and bottom but not at the top, with an unrecorded separate grey-brown cover around the wrappers. Reproduced. Shows *Adam and Eve*, (P87). In the G L copy of the (a) variant, the 'c' is skied. The G L copy of the (b) variant is $7\frac{7}{8} \times 5\frac{1}{2}$, is completely untrimmed and the 'c' is not skied. The C L C copy of the (b) variant is $8 \times 5\frac{1}{4}$ and only the top edge is trimmed. The H R C copy of the (b) variant had no edges trimmed and has a plain green wrapper around the boards.

The C L C has Gill's proofs with MS. corrections in his hand. G L has a copy of the regular issue, $7\frac{3}{4} \times 5$, with MS. revisions by Gill in pencil throughout for its appearance in *Art-Nonsense*.

1923

9 WAR MEMORIAL

TITLE-PAGE: Reproduced.

SIZE: $6\frac{1}{4} \times 5$.   COLLATION: An unsigned folded sheet of 8 leaves.

PAGINATION AND CONTENTS: Pp. 16; [1] [2] blank; [3] [4] title-page, verso note concerning the wood-engraving *Money-changers*; 5–14 text; [15] [16] blank. Printed from *Caslon O.F.*

ILLUSTRATION: There is one wood-engraving: *Christ and the Money-changers* (P152), p. 5.

BINDING: Stout greyish paper, sewn, lettered on front precisely as on title-page but with: PRICE ONE SHILLING added at foot. The w-e. on title-page and cover was engraved by David Jones. Printed on the back cover is a list of books published by S. Dominic's Press. Edges untrimmed.

DATE OF PUBLICATION: 1923.

PRICE: One shilling.

NOTES: This is no. 28 (10) of S. Dominic's Press publications. This essay was revised and reprinted in *Art-Nonsense* (1929) (no. 18). The design on the title-page and cover: *Domini canis*, is from a wood-engraving by David Jones. Cf. nos. 407, 632 and 634.

10 SCULPTURE

TITLE-PAGE: Reproduced. Shows w-e. *Sculpture* (P228).

SIZE: 7×5.   COLLATION: [Unsigned: 1^2, 2–6^4, 7^2.]

PAGINATION AND CONTENTS: Pp. iv + 44; [i] [ii] blank; [iii] [iv] title-page,

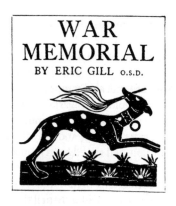

WAR
MEMORIAL
BY ERIC GILL O.S.D.

PRINTED & PUBLISHED AT S. DOMINIC'S PRESS
DITCHLING SUSSEX A. D. MCMXXIII [9]

SCULPTURE
*An Essay on Stone-cutting,
with a preface about God, by*
Eric Gill, T.O.S.D.

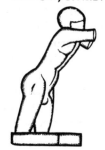

At Saint Dominic's Press,
Ditchling, Sussex [10]

verso blank; [1]–41 text; [42] blank; [43] [44] blank and though pasted down as end-paper form an integral part of the book. Printed from *Caslon O.F.* on Batchelor hand-made paper.

ILLUSTRATIONS: In addition to the w-e. on title-page there are two wood-engravings, placed:

Crucifix (P259), p. 20.
S. Cuthbert's Cross (P261), p. 41.

BINDING: Canvas boards, sewn, lettered on front: SCULPTURE | AN ESSAY ON STONE-CUTTING | ERIC GILL | [w-e. *Sculpture* (P228)] | AT SAINT DOMINIC'S PRESS | FIVE SHILLINGS Top edges cut, others uncut. Variant binding: A few copies in (limp) blue leather, lettered on front SCULPTURE.

DATE OF PUBLICATION: n.d. CLC copy is dated '23 xi 23', printed immediately above the tail-piece on p. 41. GL copy is inscribed 'A.T.G. & C.E.G. from E.G. on December 2nd. 1923.'

PRICE: Five shillings.

NOTES: This book comprises two essays previously published separately. The first (pp. [1]–20), here called: *Preface: Quae ex Veritate et Bono*, was originally published in *The Game* (1922) (no. 69) under the title: *Quae ex Veritate Bonoque*. The second, here entitled *Stone-carving* (pp. 21–41), is a revision of the pamphlet *Sculpture* (1918) (no. 5). Both were further revised and reprinted as separate essays in *Art-Nonsense* (1929) (no. 18) under the titles given in the present book though each is incorrectly attributed to 1921.

13

1926

11 ID QUOD

TITLE-PAGE: Reproduced. Shows author's device: *S. Thomas' hands* (P382).

SIZE: $7\frac{3}{4} \times 4\frac{1}{2}$.

COLLATION: Three unsigned gatherings of 4, 8 and 8 leaves respectively.

PAGINATION AND CONTENTS: Pp. xiv + 26; [i]–[viii] blank; [ix] [x] title-page, verso: PRINTED AND MADE IN GREAT BRITAIN.; [xi] Dedication: TO J. MCQ.; [xii] Imprimatur dated: I, SEPT., 1926; [xiii] [xiv] Prologue, verso blank; [1]–19 text; [20] Colophon worded: THIS BOOK WAS PRINTED BY ROBERT | GIBBINGS AT THE GOLDEN COCKEREL | PRESS, WALTHAM SAINT LAWRENCE, | FOR ERIC GILL, CAPEL-Y-FFIN, ABER- | GAVENNY, AND COMPLETED ON THE | XVII DAY OF SEPTEMBER, MCMXXVI. | COMPOSITORS: A. H. GIBBS & F. YOUNG. | PRESSMAN: A. C. COOPER. THE EDITION | IS LIMITED TO 150 COPIES, OF WHICH | THIS IS NO.   [Signed: *Eric Gill TSD*] [Printer's device, in black: *Cockerel* (Chute)]; [21]–[26] blank. Printed from 11 pt. *Caslon O.F.* on Batchelor hand-made paper with oak leaf watermark. The front end-paper forms a part of the first half-sheet and is reckoned in the above pagination.

ILLUSTRATIONS: There are two full-page copper-plate engravings, printed separately, and placed:

> *David* (P372), frontispiece.
> *Flying Buttresses* (P373), facing p. 10.

The two illustrations are conjugate and folded round the first complete gathering.

BINDING: $\frac{1}{4}$ canvas, blue paper boards, sewn, with paper label on front lettered: ID QUOD | VISUM PLACET | BY ERIC GILL T.O.S.D. All edges untrimmed.

DATE OF PUBLICATION: October 1926. MS. dated September 1926. CLC has MS. draft dated 14 Nov. 1925.

PRICE: Fifteen shillings.

PRINTING: 150 signed and numbered copies.

REVIEW: *The Times Literary Supplement*, 16 December 1926.

NOTES: The title-page device: *S. Thomas' hands* (P382) was designed for use on the title-pages of books containing his writings. *Id Quod* was the first book for which it was used. The engraving *David* is after a photograph, *Flying Buttresses* is after a drawing of S. Pierre, Chartres. This essay was revised and reprinted in *Art-Nonsense* (1929) (no. 18). CLC has a group of illustration proofs, text revisions signed and dated, and letters and notes about the book plus Gill's galley proofs with corrections and three pages of MS. additions.

ID QUOD
VISUM PLACET
A practical test of the beautiful

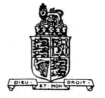

ROYAL MANCHESTER INSTITUTION

ARCHITECTURE AND SCULPTURE

BY
ERIC GILL
T.O.S.D.

A LECTURE BY ERIC GILL, T.S.D.
DELIVERED AT THE UNIVERSITY
OF MANCHESTER ON WEDNESDAY
FEBRUARY 16TH 1927

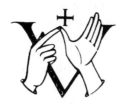

[11]

MANCHESTER
GEORGE FALKNER & SONS LIMITED
PRINTERS
191 DEANSGATE

[12]

1927

12 ARCHITECTURE AND SCULPTURE

TITLE-PAGE: Reproduced.

SIZE: $8\frac{1}{2} \times 5\frac{1}{2}$.   COLLATION: One unsigned gathering of 18 leaves.

PAGINATION AND CONTENTS: Pp. 36; [1] [2] title-page, verso list of officers of the Royal Manchester Institution, 1926–7; 3–34 text; [35] [36] blank.

ILLUSTRATIONS: None.

BINDING: Light brown paper wrappers, sewn, printed on front exactly as on title-page.

DATE OF PUBLICATION: n.d. [1927]

PRICE: n.p.

REVIEW: By F. S., *Blackfriars*, November 1927.

NOTES: This Lecture was delivered under the auspices of the Royal Manchester Institution, the Manchester Society of Architects and the Institute of Builders (Manchester Branch). It was revised and reprinted in *Art-Nonsense* (1929) (no. 18). G L copy is in a mailing envelope.

1928

13 CHRISTIANITY AND ART

TITLE-PAGE: Reproduced. Shows w-e. *S. Thomas' hands* (P382).

SIZE: $7\frac{3}{4} \times 4\frac{1}{2}$.   COLLATION: [ ]⁴, [ ]⁴, b–d⁸, [ ]⁴.

PAGINATION AND CONTENTS: Pp. xvi + 56; [i]–[x] blank; [xi] [xii] half-title: CHRISTIANITY AND ART, verso blank; [xiii] [xiv] title-page, verso blank; [xv] [xvi] blank, verso frontispiece; 1–42 text; [43] colophon: THIS ESSAY WAS FIRST PRINTED IN BLACKFRIARS, THE | REVIEW OF THE ENGLISH DOMINICANS. IT HAS BEEN REVIS- | ED BY THE AUTHOR AND IS NOW PUBLISHED WITH THE PERMIS- | SION OF THE EDITOR OF BLACKFRIARS. THIS EDITION | WAS PRINTED AT THE SHAKESPEARE HEAD PRESS AT | STRATFORD-UPON-AVON FOR FRANCIS WALTERSON, | CAPEL-Y-FFIN, AND IS LIMITED TO 200 COPIES OF WHICH | THIS IS NO.   [Signed: *Eric Gill* | *David Jones*]; [44]–[56] blank. Both end-papers are pasted down and form an integral part of the book. Printed from 11 pt. *Caslon O.F.* on Batchelor hand-made paper with oak leaf watermark.

ILLUSTRATIONS: There are two wood-engravings, placed:

A full-page engraving by David Jones, frontispiece.

Tail-piece: Lovers (P166 2nd state), p. 35.

BINDING: Full bound blue buckram; lettered in gilt on spine, reading downwards: CHRISTIANITY AND ART. All edges untrimmed.

DATE OF PUBLICATION: January 1928.

PRICE: 12s. 6d.

PRINTING: 200 numbered copies signed by both author and artist.

NOTES: Notwithstanding the date on the title-page this book was not published until January 1928. It comprises two essays which originally appeared in *Blackfriars*, viz. *The Church and Art* (Feb. to May 1926, cf. no. 102) and *An Essay in Aid of a Grammar of Practical Aesthetics* (April 1921, cf. no. 82) here printed as an Appendix (pp. 36–42). Both were revised for the present publication and again revised and reprinted in shortened form and as separate essays in *Art-Nonsense* (no. 18).

14 ART & LOVE

TITLE-PAGE: Reproduced. Shows w-e. *S. Thomas' hands* (P382).

SIZE: $7\frac{3}{4} \times 4\frac{1}{2}$.   COLLATION: [Unsigned: 1–2⁴, 3–4⁸.]

PAGINATION AND CONTENTS: Pp. xvi + 32; [i]–[viii] blank of which the first leaf is pasted down as the front end-paper but forms an integral part of the book; [ix] [x] blank, verso printer's imprint: PRINTED AND MADE IN GREAT BRITAIN; [xi] [xii] title-page, verso blank; [xiii] [xiv] Dedication: M.E.G. | ETSI DILECTISSIMUS CHRISTUS | TU IN CHRISTO DILECTIS-SIMA | E.P.J.G., verso blank; [xv] [xvi] Author's Note dated: SALIES-DE-

CHRISTIANITY AND ART

By ERIC GILL T.O.S.D.

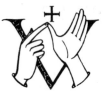

The frontispiece engraved by
DAVID JONES T.O.S.D.

ART & LOVE
BY ERIC GILL

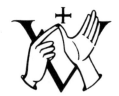

FRANCIS WALTERSON
CAPEL-Y-FFIN
ABERGAVENNY
1927

DOUGLAS CLEVERDON
BRISTOL
1927

[13]

[14]

BEARN, FEB. 1927, verso list of illustrations; [1]–26 text; [27] [28] blank, verso colophon: THIS BOOK WAS PRINTED BY ROBERT | GIBBINGS AT THE GOLDEN COCKEREL | PRESS, WALTHAM SAINT LAWRENCE, | BERKSHIRE, FOR DOUGLAS CLEVERDON, | BRISTOL, AND COMPLETED ON THE | 30TH DAY OF JUNE, MCMXXVII. | COMPOSITORS: A. H. GIBBS & F. YOUNG. | PRESSMAN: A. C. COOPER. THE EDITION | IS LIMITED TO 260 COPIES, OF WHICH | NOS. 1–35 CONTAIN AN EXTRA SET OF | THE ENGRAVINGS. THIS IS NO.   [Signed: *Eric Gill T.S.D.*] Printer's device, in black: *Cockerel* (Chute) at foot; [29]–[32] blank. The back fly-leaf and end-paper are of the same substance as the book. Printed from 11 pt. *Caslon O.F.* on Batchelor hand-made paper with oak leaf watermark.

ILLUSTRATIONS: There are six full-page copper-plate engravings, printed separately, and placed:

Adam and Eve in Heaven, or the Public-House in Paradise (P480), facing p. [1]

The Artist: Man's peculiar and appropriate activity (P481), facing p. 5.

With ritual chant (P482), facing p. 12.

Clothes: For dignity and adornment (P483), facing p. 16.

A Symbol of Divine Love (P484), facing p. 23.

Bread of these stones (P485), facing p. 26.

The first and fourth illustrations are conjugate and folded round the first

17

ART & PRUDENCE
an essay
by ERIC GILL, T.O.S.D.

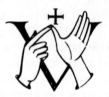

THE
GOLDEN COCKEREL PRESS
MCMXXVIII

[15]

complete gathering. The second and third are conjugate and folded around ff. 3–6 of the same gathering. The fifth and sixth are conjugate and folded around ff. 4–5 of the second complete gathering. There are also six initial letters from wood-engravings.

BINDING: Ordinary edition: Full-bound black buckram, lettered in gilt on spine, reading upwards: ART AND LOVE. Special edition: Full-bound vellum. All edges untrimmed.

DATE OF PUBLICATION: March 1928.

PRICE AND PRINTING: Ordinary edition: 225 signed and numbered copies at 21s. Special edition: thirty-five signed and numbered copies containing an extra set of the engravings, at 2 guineas. Note: twenty-five of the Ordinary edition and five of the Special edition were not for sale.

REVIEW: *The Times Literary Supplement*, 15 March 1928.

NOTES: The substance of this essay was first published in *Blackfriars*, Vol. V, no. 55, October 1924 (no. 90). It was reprinted in *Rupam: Journal of Oriental Art—chiefly Indian*, no. 21, January 1925 and again in *Art-Nonsense* (1929) (no. 18). Notwithstanding the date on the title-page this book was not published until March 1928.

15 ART & PRUDENCE

TITLE-PAGE: Reproduced. Shows w-e. *S. Thomas' hands* (P382).

SIZE: $7\frac{3}{4} \times 4\frac{1}{2}$.   COLLATION: [Unsigned: 1–2⁴, 3⁸.]

PAGINATION AND CONTENTS: Pp. viii + 24; [i] [ii] blank; [iii] [iv] blank, verso printer's imprint: PRINTED AND MADE IN GREAT BRITAIN; [v] [vi] title-page, verso blank; [vii] [viii] Publisher's Note, verso blank; 1–18 text; [19] colophon: THIS BOOK WAS PRINTED BY ROBERT GIBBINGS AT THE | GOLDEN COCKEREL PRESS, WALTHAM SAINT LAWRENCE, | AND COMPLETED ON THE 12TH DAY OF JUNE, 1928. | COMPOSITORS: A. H. GIBBS & F. YOUNG. PRESSMAN: A. C. COOPER. THE EDITION IS LIMITED TO 500 COPIES, | OF WHICH THIS IS NO.   Printer's device, in black: *Cockerel* (Chute) at foot; [20]–[24] blank. Printed from 11 pt. *Caslon O.F.* on Batchelor hand-made paper with oak leaf watermark.

ILLUSTRATIONS: There are two full-page copper-plate engravings, printed separately and placed:

>   *The Bird in the Bush* (P505), facing p. 1.
>   *Crucifix* (P506), facing p. 8.

The two illustrations are conjugate and folded round the second half-sheet.

BINDING: Full-bound red buckram, lettered in gilt on spine, reading upwards: ART & PRUDENCE: ERIC GILL. All edges untrimmed.

DUST JACKET: Red paper, printed on front exactly as on title-page.

DATE OF PUBLICATION: September 1928.

PRICE: 17s. 6d.

PRINTING: 500 numbered copies.

REVIEWS: *The Times Literary Supplement*, 15 November 1928. *The Observer*, 20 January 1929.

NOTES: This essay was delivered as a lecture at Manchester University, 7 February 1928. It was originally published in *The University Catholic Review*, Vol. I, no. 3, May 1928 (no. 115). It was revised and the plates were engraved specially for this edition. This book is no. 61 of the Golden Cockerel Press publications. The essay was further revised and reprinted in *Beauty Looks After Herself* (1933) (no. 24).

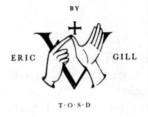

[16]

16 THE FUTURE OF SCULPTURE

TITLE-PAGE: Reproduced. Shows w-e. *S. Thomas' hands* (P382).

SIZE: $7\frac{7}{8} \times 5\frac{1}{8}$.

COLLATION: Unsigned: Two gatherings of four leaves each, one leaf (pp. 15–16) pasted on to previous gathering, and two conjoint leaves.

PAGINATION AND CONTENTS: Pp. ii + 20; [i] [ii] blank; [1] [2] title-page, verso blank; [3] [4] Author's Note dated: CHRISTMAS 1928, verso blank; 5–[18] text; [19] [20] blank, verso colophon: PRINTED IN THE OFFICE OF THE LANSTON MONOTYPE CORPORATION LIMITED, 43 FETTER LANE, LONDON, E.C.4, | FOR ERIC GILL, PIGOTTS, NORTH DEAN, HIGH | WYCOMBE, BUCKS. DECEMBER 20, 1928. Beneath this, printed in red, is the wood-engraving: *Map: Pigotts Roads* (P556). Printed from Monotype *Baskerville roman*. Reproduced.

BINDING: Full-bound black cloth, lettered on spine, reading upwards: ERIC GILL: THE FUTURE OF SCULPTURE. All edges cut.

20

PRINTED in the office of the Lanston Monotype
Corporation Limited, 43 Fetter Lane, London, E.C.4.
FOR ERIC GILL, Pigotts, North Dean, High
Wycombe, Bucks.   December 20, 1928

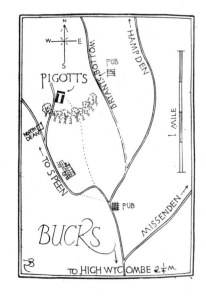

[P556. Intaglio]

DATE OF PUBLICATION: Christmas 1928. MS. dated 1 December 1927.
PRICE: n.p. This book was printed for private distribution.
PRINTING: Fifty-five copies.
NOTES: This essay was delivered as a lecture at the Victoria and Albert
Museum, London, in December 1927 and first published in *Artwork*, Spring
1928 (no. 113). It was reprinted in *Art-Nonsense* (1929) (no. 18) and in *The
American Review* (New York: The Bookman Publishing Co., Inc. Price 40c.),
Vol. 5, no. 3, Summer 1935, pp. 257–86, under the title *Sculpture in the
Machine Age*. It is entered as no. 22 in the Great Britain section of the catalogue
of an exhibition of books illustrating British and Foreign Printing, 1918–29,
held at the British Museum in April 1929 (no. 642).
VARIANTS: GL has a copy with PIGOTTS ROADS (P556) on p. [20] printed
intaglio in black. Other copies have been reported but not seen; perhaps five
were so printed. Not recorded in Physick or Skelton. GL has also an ordinary
copy with a paper guard sheet tipped in after the colophon [20].

21

1929

17 ENGRAVINGS BY ERIC GILL

TITLE-PAGE: Reproduced. Shows w-e. *S. Thomas' hands* (P382).

SIZE: $13 \times 9\frac{3}{4}$. G L covers $13\frac{3}{4} \times 10\frac{3}{4}$.

COLLATION: [Unsigned: $1-8^4$, 9^6, $10-35^4$.] The first leaf of the ninth gathering is cut off, leaving a stub only.

PAGINATION AND CONTENTS: Pp. xxii + 260; [i]–[viii] blank (the first two pages are pasted down as end-papers but form an integral part of the book); [ix] [x] blank, verso frontispiece [*Self-portrait* (P497)]; [xiii] [xiv] title-page, verso imprint: PRINTED AND MADE IN ENGLAND: [xv] [xvi] publisher's acknowledgements, verso blank; [xvii]–[xxii] Contents and list of engravings reproduced in the book; [1] [2] half-title: PREFACE BY ERIC GILL, verso blank; 3–21 text of Preface; [22] blank; [23] half-title: CHRONOLOGICAL LIST OF ENGRAVINGS | 1908–1927; 24 statement by the publisher concerning the chronological list; 25–49 text of chronological list; [50] blank; [51] [52] half-title: SELECTED ENGRAVINGS, verso blank; [53]–[257] the engravings (foliated '1' to '103'); [258] blank; [259] [260] colophon: PRINTED FOR DOUGLAS CLEVERDON | AT THE FANFARE PRESS, LONDON | MCMXXIX set within a cartouche: *D.C. E.G.* (P613) designed specially for this book, verso blank.

ILLUSTRATIONS: There are one hundred and forty-seven engravings as numbered and described on pp. xvii–xxii.

BINDING: Ten copies full-bound vellum by Sangorski and Sutcliffe, g.e. Gold stamped on front with device: *Tree and Burin* (after P189), lettered on spine, in gilt: ENGRAVINGS | BY | ERIC GILL and, at foot: 1929. Eighty copies $\frac{1}{4}$ vellum by Wood, t.e.g., other edges trimmed. Gold-stamped on front and lettered on spine as above. Four hundred copies black cloth, t.e.g., other edges cut. Gold-stamped on front as above but lettered on spine, in gilt: ENGRAVINGS | BY | ERIC | GILL and, at foot: DOUGLAS | CLEVERDON.

DATE OF PUBLICATION: 1929. MS. of Preface dated 10–17 September 1928.

PRICE: Vellum edition: Thirty guineas ($250). Hand-made paper edition: Ten guineas ($75). Ordinary edition: Five guineas ($40).

PRINTING: Ten copies (eight of which were for sale) on Japanese hand-made vellum numbered I to X, signed by Eric Gill, containing an extra set of the engravings on Japanese paper and proofs of the self-portrait in the first, second, third and final states. Plates 83, 89, 90, 94, 96 and 103 were hand-coloured by Eric Gill. Eighty copies on Batchelor hand-made paper, numbered 1 to 80, and signed by Eric Gill, containing an extra set of the engravings on Japanese paper. Four hundred and ten copies (of which four hundred were for sale) on paper manufactured for this edition, numbered 81 to

ENGRAVINGS BY ERIC GILL

A SELECTION

of Engravings on Wood and Metal
representative of his work to the end
of the year 1927 with a complete
Chronological List of Engravings
and a Preface by the Artist

BRISTOL
DOUGLAS CLEVERDON
1929

[17]

480. One half of each number of the copies offered for sale was reserved for sale in America through Walter V. McKee, 32 University Place, New York City.

NOTES: The original 13 × 10 french-fold prospectus issued by Cleverdon in 1928 lists an introduction by Desmond Chute. A one-page $8\frac{1}{4} \times 5\frac{1}{2}$ later announcement, laid into the G L copy, states that, 'Through prolonged illness, the Rev. Desmond Chute is unable to complete the introduction to "Selected Engravings of Eric Gill." The publisher has been fortunate enough, however, to persuade Mr. Eric Gill to write it in his place. As stated in the original prospectus, it will consist of an exposition of the artist's intellectual and moral position; and though it may not be so full an appreciation of his achievements, it will be at least an authentic exposure of his aims. Douglas Cleverdon.' The McKee prospectus is similar to Cleverdon's but it is sewn into printed paper wrappers which omit reference to Chute.

REVIEWS: By Owen Rutter, *The Observer*, 15 September 1929. *The Print Collector's Quarterly*, January 1930. By K.P., *Apollo*, March 1931.

ADDENDA AND CORRIGENDA:

P. 13   Correct spelling of 'iniquitousness' (l. 19) by deleting fourth 'i'.

P. 25   D10 [P11] *Bookplate: Domine Jesu . . . .* Add: *Two blocks: one for black and one for red.*

P. 26   Insert: D17a [P17] *Device: 1895 B A C, w-e.* $1\frac{3}{8} \times 1\frac{3}{8}$*. For Brighton Arts Club.*

P. 27   D34 [P35] *Decoy Duck.* Size should read '$2\frac{3}{8} \times 1\frac{1}{2}$'.

P. 28   Insert: D54a [P56] *Another bookplate: From the Library of Charles Lambert Rutherston.* $2\frac{1}{8} \times 1\frac{1}{8}$.

P. 29   D67 [P70] *Child and Spectre.* Size should read '$1\frac{1}{2} \times 1\frac{3}{8}$'.

P. 30   D78 [P83] *Christmas Gifts.* Size should read '$1\frac{5}{8} \times 2\frac{3}{8}$'.

Insert: D83a [P90] *Device: S. George and the Dragon. w-e.* $1\frac{3}{4} \times 1\frac{3}{4}$*. For S. Dominic's Press. Engraved partly by John Beedham, finished by E.G.*

P. 32   *Diagrams for Carpentry Tools.* This group of engravings should be numbered 'D107a-v' [P114–P134]. For 'eighteen' read 'twenty-two' and add: *including an extra one not used in the book.*[1]

D112 [P71] *Lettering with nib.* This should be recorded under 1916 not 1918. It was used in the text of lettering sheets of 'Formal Writing' by Edward Johnston, published by Douglas Pepler, 1916, cf. 'Copy Sheets' (no. 311).

D115 [P141] *Entire Dragon.* Insert size: '$2 \times 2\frac{1}{4}$'. Delete whole of note as

---

[1] The engraving *Madonna and Child: with gallows* (D106 [P82]) should follow D77 [P81] (not, as here, under late 1917). I received from my brother Eric one of the Christmas cards for which it was designed and this was sent to me for Christmas 1916. That year, viz. 1916, should be added to the marginal note concerning this engraving.

printed and substitute: *Published in Saint George and the Dragon and Other Stories (S. Dominic's Press, 1919). Also printed in 'Health', Welfare Handbook No. 1 (S. Dominic's Press, 1919). ('Entire' so entitled because of his unusual virility.)*

P. 33   D131 [P160] S. Cuthbert's Cross. Size should read '$1\frac{1}{2} \times 1\frac{5}{8}$'. Add to note: *Also used in 'Sculpture' (S. Dominic's Press, [1923]).*

       D132 [P161] *Device: Hand and Cross.* Add: *Published in 'Autumn Midnight' (S. Dominic's Press, 1923).*

       Insert: *D132a [P162] Device: Hand and Cross.* $1\frac{1}{4} \times \frac{3}{4}$. *A variant of* D132 [P161]. *For use by members of the Spoil Bank Association, Ditchling, but not much used.*

       D133 [P163] *New England Woods.* Add, in fifth column: *D133–4 [P163–4] were printed . . . .*

P. 34   D138 [P168] *Woodcutter's Knife.* Add, in fifth column: *D138–9 [P168–9] were printed in 'Wood Engraving' (S. Dominic's Press, 1920).*

       D141 [P65] *Chalice and Host.* Add, in fifth column: *Used in 'Serving at Mass' (S. Dominic's Press, 1916).*[2]

       D146 [P177] Add: *Device for Bookplate:* . . .

       Insert: *D146a [P175] Bookplate: JOHN MAURICE ROTHENSTEIN Text: IN MORTALIBUS . . . on border, EX LIBRIS in middle.* $2\frac{3}{4} \times 1\frac{3}{16}$. *For J. M. Rothenstein.*

P. 35   Insert: *D169a [P199] Woman with arms up and across her chest.* In fifth column: *Block subsequently carved into statuette.*

P. 36   D174 [P204] and D175 [P205] Add: *Device for Bookplate:* . . .

       D180 [P210] Bookplate: *S. Luke.* Add to words: 'In two blocks' *with alternative block for base.*

       D185 [P216] *Bookplate: Madonna and Child.* Add in fifth column: *Printed on dust-wrapper of 'The Mistress of Vision' (S. Dominic's Press, 1918).*

P. 37   D192 [P224] *The Holy Ghost as Dove.* Size should read '$1\frac{1}{4} \times 1\frac{1}{2}$'.

P. 38   D230 [P260] *Rosary Crucifix.* Size should read '$2\frac{1}{8} \times 1\frac{1}{4}$'. Add to note in fifth column: *except those in E.G.'s reference collection.*

       D231 [P261] *Rosary Crucifix.* Size should read '$1\frac{1}{4} \times \frac{3}{4}$'.

       D238 [P268] *Madonna and Child.* Add in fifth column: *For Christmas poem.*

P. 39   10 [P281] *Flower-piece.* For '*1924*' read '*1925*'.

---

[2] The engraving *Chalice and Host* (D141 [P65]) is wrongly placed here (under 1920). As stated above, it was used in *Serving at Mass* published in 1916, cf. no. 1. It was also used in the funeral 'card' for Olof Alice Johnston (1917) (no. 317) and again in *The Order of the Burial of the Dead* (1917) (no. 361). From this it is, I think, fair to assume that it was engraved in 1916 at about the same time as the other engraving of *Chalice and Host*, cf. D53 [P54].

P. 40   18 [P289] *Deposition.* Add to notes in fifth column: *Nos. 19–21 [P290–2] were used in 'Clothing Without Cloth' (Golden Cockerel Press, 1931).*

P. 44   104–5 [P385–6] *Devices: Girl on Carpet and Girl in Leaves.* Add to note in fifth column: *Used in 'Uncle Dottery' (Cleverdon, 1930).*

110 [P391] *Tailpiece: Spray of Leaves.* The size of the first of the two smaller blocks referred to in the Notes should read $\frac{1}{4} \times \frac{5}{8}$. Delete the words: 'the two smaller were not used' and substitute: *the first of the two smaller blocks was used as a line-filling in the half-title of 'Troilus and Criseyde' (Golden Cockerel Press, 1927) as well as in the title-pages of all four volumes of 'The Canterbury Tales' (Golden Cockerel Press, 1929–31).*

111 [P393] *Device: Cockerel and Printing-Press.* For *Autumn 1927* read *Winter 1926.*

P. 45   119 [P401] *Initials: I T.* Delete the words '. . . but not used' and substitute *but used for 'Lamia' (Golden Cockerel Press, 1928).*

18 ART-NONSENSE AND OTHER ESSAYS

TITLE-PAGE: Reproduced. Shows w-e. *Belle Sauvage, IV: girl standing* (P623).

SIZE: Ordinary edition: $9 \times 5\frac{1}{2}$; Large Paper edition: 10×6.

COLLATION: [ ]^6, 1–20^8, 21^4.

PAGINATION AND CONTENTS: Pp. $2 + x + 328$ of which the first leaf forms a fly-leaf; [i] [ii] half-title: ART-NONSENSE AND OTHER ESSAYS, verso blank; [iii] title-page; [iv] quotation from *Progress and Religion* by Christopher Dawson; v-vi Apology; vii Author's acknowledgements; [viii] blank; ix-x Contents: 1. SLAVERY AND FREEDOM (1918); 2. ESSENTIAL PERFEC-TION (1918); 3. A GRAMMAR OF INDUSTRY (1919); 4. WESTMINSTER CATHEDRAL (1920); 5. DRESS (1920); 6. SONGS WITHOUT CLOTHES (1921); 7. OF THINGS NECESSARY AND UNNECESSARY (1921); 8. QUAE EX VERITATE ET BONO (1921); 9. STONE-CARVING (1921); 10. WOOD-ENGRAVING (1921); 11. INDIAN SCULPTURE (1922); 12. A WAR MEMORIAL (1923); 13. THE REVIVAL OF HANDICRAFT (1924); 14. THE PROBLEM OF PARISH CHURCH ARCHITECTURE (1925); 15. RESPONSI-BILITY, AND THE ANALOGY BETWEEN SLAVERY AND CAPITALISM (1925): 16. ID QUOD VISUM PLACET (1926); 17. ARCHITECTURE AND SCULPTURE (1927); 18. ART AND LOVE (1927); 19. CHRISTIANITY AND ART (1927); 20. ESSAY IN AID OF A GRAMMAR OF PRACTICAL AESTHE-TICS (1927); 21. THE ENORMITIES OF MODERN RELIGIOUS ART (1927); 22. THE CRITERION IN ART (1928); 23. THE FUTURE OF SCULPTURE (1928); 24. ART-NONSENSE (1929). [N.B. The dates given in parentheses

ART-NONSENSE
AND OTHER ESSAYS
BY ERIC GILL

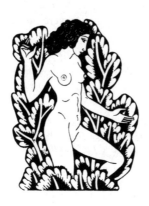

LONDON
CASSELL & CO., LTD. & FRANCIS WALTERSON
1929

[18]

indicate, in several instances, the year the essay was published in its revised form, not when it was first published.] 1–324 text; [325] [326] colophon: PRINTED BY THE CAMBRIDGE UNIVERSITY | PRESS FOR MESSRS CASSELL & CO. LTD, AND | MR FRANCIS WALTERSON. THE TYPE, OF | WHICH THIS IS THE FIRST USE, IS THE | 'PERPETUA,' DESIGNED BY THE AUTHOR | AND CUT BY THE LANSTON MONOTYPE | CORPORATION LIMITED, LONDON; verso blank; [327] [328] blank. [The colophon in the Large Paper edition is the same except for the words: 'In addition to | the ordinary (unlimited) edition one | hundred copies were printed on large | paper of which this is no. . . .' inserted between '. . . Walterson' and 'The type . . .'.] The Large Paper edition was printed on hand-made paper and signed, beneath the colophon, *Eric Gill*. The title-page device in this edition is w-e. P622 which is the same as P623 but engraved in white line on black instead of black line on white.

ILLUSTRATIONS: None.

BINDING: Ordinary edition: full-bound blue buckram, lettered in gilt on spine: ART | NONSENSE | at top and CASSELL | WALTERSON at foot. Top edges trimmed, others uncut. Large Paper edition: full-bound red buckram; lettered in gilt on spine as for the 'ordinary' edition. Top edges gilt,

27

others uncut.

DATE OF PUBLICATION: 5 December 1929.

PRICE: Ordinary edition: one guinea. Large Paper edition (boxed): five guineas.

REVIEWS: By Joseph Thorp, *Spectator*, 8 October 1929. By H. E. W., *Apollo*, March 1930. By the Rev. John O'Connor, *Blackfriars*, April 1930. By Richard F. Russell, *The London Mercury*, May 1930. By A. K. Coomaraswamy, *International Studio*, May 1930. By Peter Quennell, *Architectural Review*, June 1930. By J. G. Noppen, *Burlington Magazine*, June 1930. By G. K. Chesterton, *The Studio*, 1930, reprinted in *A Handful of Authors* edited by Dorothy Collins, London & New York, 1953 and *Chesterton Review*, Vol. VIII, no. 4, November 1982. By D. H. Lawrence, *The Book-Collector's Quarterly*, Oct.–Dec. 1933.

Notes: It will be noted that certain passages in the text were underlined, e.g. on p. 12; this denotes italicization, the italics for this fount not having been available when the book was printed.

SECONDARY EDITION: CASSELL'S POCKET LIBRARY.

TITLE-PAGE: ART-NONSENSE | AND OTHER | ESSAYS | BY | ERIC GILL | [Publishers' device: *Woman kneeling with bow in hand*] CASSELL | & COMPANY, LTD. | LONDON, TORONTO, MELBOURNE | AND SYDNEY.

SIZE: $6\frac{3}{4} \times 4\frac{1}{4}$.   COLLATION: [ ]⁶, 1–20⁸, 21⁴.

PAGINATION AND CONTENTS: Pp. 2 + x + 328 of which the first leaf forms a fly-leaf; [i] [ii] half-title: CASSELL'S POCKET LIBRARY | [decorative rule] ART-NONSENSE AND OTHER ESSAYS, verso Statement of Editions: FIRST PUBLISHED 1929 | SECOND EDITION (FIRST CHEAP EDITION) 1934; [iii] [iv] title-page, verso quotation from *Progress and Religion* by Christopher Dawson; v–vi Apology; vii Author's and Publishers' acknowledgements; [viii] blank; ix–x Contents [as already described]; 1–324 text; [325] [326] printers' imprint: PRINTED IN GREAT BRITAIN BY | LOWE & BRYDONE PRINTERS LTD., LONDON, N.W.1 | F. 20. 334, verso blank; [327] [328] blank.

ILLUSTRATIONS: None.

BINDING: (*a*) Brick-red cloth, lettered in gilt on spine: ART | NON-SENSE | AND | OTHER | ESSAYS | [small diamond] ERIC | GILL | [abstract ornament] and, at foot, CASSELL with double cross-bands at head and foot. Top edges blue, all edges cut. (*b*) Maroon leather; Publishers' device blind-stamped on front, lettered in gilt on spine as for (*a*) above. Top edges gilt, all edges cut.

DATE OF PUBLICATION: 1934.

PRICE: Cloth edition: 3*s*. 6*d*. Leather edition: 5*s*.

NOTE: This was no. 17 of Cassell's Pocket Library.

```
┌─────────────────────────────────────────┐
│                                          │
│  Handworkers' Pamphlets         No. 4    │
│            1s. od.                       │
│  ────────────────────────────────────── │
│                                          │
│              Art and                     │
│           Manufacture                    │
│                                          │
│                                          │
│             ERIC GILL                    │
│  ────────────────────────────────────── │
│                                          │
│     NEW HANDWORKERS' GALLERY             │
│        14 PERCY STREET                   │
│              W. 1                        │
│                                          │
└─────────────────────────────────────────┘
```

[19]

19 ART AND MANUFACTURE

TITLE-PAGE: Reproduced. Shows w-e. *S. Thomas' hands* (P382).

SIZE: $7\frac{3}{4} \times 5\frac{1}{4}$. G L and C L C copies $7\frac{5}{8} \times 5$.

COLLATION: One unsigned gathering of eight leaves.

PAGINATION AND CONTENTS: Pp. 16 (N.B. the pagination of the text runs from 43 to 56); [41] Author's note; [42] frontispiece; 43–56 text; inside back cover printers' imprint: PRINTED IN LONDON AT THE FANFARE PRESS, | NOVEMBER 1929. | THE PUPPETS ARE ENGRAVED AFTER DESIGNS | BY THE AUTHOR. On verso of back cover is printed a list of Handworkers' Pamphlets.

ILLUSTRATIONS: There are two engravings on wood after designs by Gill. A note by Evan in his own copy of the bibliography (C L C) reads: 'Engraved by John Beedham – blocks touched up by E.G. cf. Diary Oct 16, 1929.'

> *An advertisement hoarding with puppets*, frontispiece.
> *A puppet*, p. 56.

BINDING: White paper wrappers, sewn, printed on front as shown in reproduction.

29

DATE OF PUBLICATION: n.d. [December 1929]. MS. dated October 1929.
PRICE: 1s. There were also 60 copies numbered and signed by the author and
sold at 5s. each.
REVIEW: By Herbert Read, *The Listener*, 29 January 1930 (cf. no. 440).
NOTES: This essay was originally delivered as a lecture entitled *Art in Relation
to Life* to the Pangbourne Arts & Crafts Society, 26 November 1928. It was
re-written and re-named for the present pamphlet. It was revised and given as
a lecture to the Design and Industries Association, 30 March 1933, under the
title *Art and Industrialism* and published under that title in *Design for To-Day*,
May and June 1933 and reprinted under the same title in *Beauty Looks After
Herself* (no. 24). As *Art and Manufacture* this essay must not be confused with a
lecture bearing the same title which was given at University College, Bangor,
in November 1934, and was published as the first of a series of three lectures
under the title *Work and Leisure* (cf. no. 31).

1931

20 CLOTHING WITHOUT CLOTH
TITLE-PAGE: Reproduced. Shows w-e. *S. Thomas' hands* (P382).
SIZE: $9 \times 4\frac{1}{2}$.
COLLATION: One unsigned gathering of fourteen leaves.
PAGINATION AND CONTENTS: Pp. vi + 22; [i]–[iv] blank; [v] [vi] title-
page, verso printer's imprint and statement of edition: PRINTED AND MADE
IN | GREAT BRITAIN | BY THE | GOLDEN COCKEREL PRESS | AND
LIMITED TO 500 | COPIES, OF WHICH | THIS IS NO. | ... [Author's
signature: *Eric G*]; 1–16 text; [17]–[22] blank. Printed from 11 pt. *Caslon O.F.*
on Batchelor hand-made paper watermarked BATCHELOR & SON.
ILLUSTRATIONS: There are four full-page wood-engravings, printed separately and placed:

> *Mellors* (P727), frontispiece.
> *Venus* (P290, 2ND STATE), facing p. 4.
> *The Bee Sting* (P292, 2ND STATE), facing p. 12.
> *The Dancer* (P291, 2ND STATE), facing p. 20.

The frontispiece is conjugate with a blank leaf as also is the title-page conjugate
with the fourth illustration. The two pairs are folded round the gathering. The
second and third illustrations are conjugate and folded round ff. 3–6. The
printer's device: *Cockerel* (David Jones) is printed, in black, on the verso of the
fourth illustration.
BINDING: Scarlet buckram, lettered in gilt on front from the author's design:
G C P and on spine, reading downwards: CLOTHING WITHOUT
CLOTH: GILL. Top and fore-edges gilt, bottom edges uncut.
DATE OF PUBLICATION: June 1931. MS. dated 3–7 March 1931.

CLOTHING WITHOUT CLOTH

AN ESSAY ON THE

NUDE

BY ERIC GILL O.S.D.

WITH ENGRAVINGS ON
WOOD BY THE AUTHOR

AT THE GOLDEN
COCKEREL PRESS

WALTHAM SAINT
LAWRENCE
BERKSHIRE

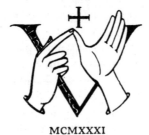

MCMXXXI   [20]

PRICE: 16s.

PRINTING: 500 signed and numbered copies.

REVIEWS: *The Times Literary Supplement*, 1 October 1931.

ARTWORK: Winter 1931.

NOTES: This is no. 75 of the Golden Cockerel Press publications and their first 'saddle-back'. This essay was reprinted in *In A Strange Land* (1944) (no. 51), American edition *It All Goes Together* (1944) (no. 52). Gill altered the text of two sentences near the bottom of page eight of his copy, now in the GL, to read: 'If prudery and the wantoness of which it is commonly the cloak or the accompaniment, be rampant let there be naked bathing in parks. If sexual frigidity be rampant let nakedness be restricted for clothes are the best aphrodisiac.'

21. TYPOGRAPHY

AN ESSAY ON TYPOGRAPHY by Eric Gill, comprising
a Composition of Time & Place (p. 3) and chapters as
follows: on Lettering (p. 25), on Typography (p. 61),
on Punch cutting (p. 77), on Paper & Ink (p. 83), on
the Compositor's 'Stick', here called "the Procrus-
tean Bed" (p. 90), on the Instrument (p. 97) and a
final chapter on the Book (p. 105).   [21]

21 TYPOGRAPHY

TITLE-PAGE: Reproduced.

SIZE: $7\frac{3}{4} \times 5$.   COLLATION: [ ]^4, a–g^8, h^4, [ ]^2.

PAGINATION AND CONTENTS: Pp. viii + 124; [i]–[iv] blank; [v] [vi] recto
blank, verso imprint: PRINTED & MADE IN GREAT BRITAIN; [vii] [viii]
title-page and list of contents, verso blank; 1–2 *The Theme* [of the book]; 3–120
text; [121] [122] printers' imprint; PRINTED BY RENÉ HAGUE & ERIC
GILL, AT PIGOTTS, | NEAR HUGHENDEN, BUCKINGHAMSHIRE, 1931.
| PUBLISHED BY MESSRS. SHEED & WARD, 31 PATER- | NOSTER ROW,
LONDON. | *Press mark: Dog and tree with flames* (P759) | [Signed] *René Hague* |
Eric Gill | (4) JUNE 1931. 500 PRINTED; verso blank; [123] [124] blank.
Printed from 12 pt. *Joanna* on hand-made paper specially made for Hague and
Gill watermarked E R (the letters joined, the E being in reverse after P723).
Note: the numeral '4' in 'round' brackets preceding the date in the imprint
denotes that this was the fourth book printed by Hague and Gill.

ILLUSTRATIONS: There are twenty-five figures in the text, four of which, viz.
nos. 21, 23, 24 and 25 are from wood engravings, placed:

Fig. 1. *Brush and pen strokes*, p. 29.
   2. *Examples of the letter A*, p. 30.
   3. *Examples of the letter G*, p. 32.
   4. *Caslon's Blackletter*, p. 35.
   5. *The Subiaco type*, p. 35.
   6. *Jenson's type*, p. 36.
   7. *Caslon's Old Face, 1734*, p. 37.
   8. *Caslon's Bodoni Modern Face, 1780*, p. 37.
   9. *Baskerville Old Face, 1768*, p. 39.
  10. *Miller & Richard's Old Style* p. 39.
  11. *Perpetua Roman and other type faces*, p. 41.
  12. *Reduced copy of a 'John Bull' poster*, p. 44.
  13. *A poster letter*, p. 45.
  14. *The letters O & D*, p. 47.
  15. *Gill Monotype Sans-serif*, p. 48.
  16. *Examples of the letter A*, p. 51.

17. *Examples of the letter R*, p. 53.
18. *Examples of the letters D, B, P & S*, p. 55.
19. *Examples of the numerals 2, 4, 3, 6 & 9*, p. 57.
20. *Examples of the letter r*, p. 59.
21. *Examples of the letter Q* (P732*b*), p. 59.
22. *Examples of the letter A*, p. 66.
23. *Examples of the letters a, e, f & g* (P732*a*), p. 62.
24. *Alphabets: Capitals, Lower-case and Italics, upright sans-serif* (P731), p. 64.
25. *Alphabets: Capitals, Lower-case and Italics, with serifs and slope* (P732), p. 65.

BINDING: Red buckram, lettered in gilt on spine, reading upwards: GILL: TYPOGRAPHY. Twenty-five copies were specially bound by Donald Attwater full leather (Welsh sheepskin), blind-tooled front and back and blind-lettered on spine, reading downwards: GILL TYPOGRAPHY. The blind tooling on front and back was not uniform in design. All edges untrimmed.

DUST JACKET: Cream paper printed in black and red. Worded: *Printing & Piety* | [long rule] *An essay on life and works in the* | *England of 1931, & particularly* | TYPO | GRA | PHY | [the letters 'TYPOGRAPHY' in red] [long rule] *By Eric Gill* | [long rule] *Sheed & Ward*. On back: *Printed by* | [*Press Mark: Tree and dog* (P733) with *Flames for tree and dog* (in red), (P733a)] *René Hague & Eric Gill*.

DATE OF PUBLICATION: June 1931. MS. dated October 1930–February 1931.

PRICE: 25*s*.

PRINTING: 500 copies signed by René Hague and Eric Gill.

PART PUBLICATION: The chapter on the compositor's stick, 'The Procrustian Bed' was printed in the Three Ridings Journal, Vol. 4, no. 5, January 1933, pp. 50–83. The chapter on lettering appeared under the title 'But Why Lettering' in the Three Ridings Journal, Vol. 6, no. 2, November 1934, pp. 24–9. Something less than one-half of this book was reprinted under the title *Two Worlds of Typography* in *The Fine Book: A Symposium*, Pittsburgh: The Laboratory Press, 1934. Chapter three was reprinted as *Typography* in *Books and Printing a Treasury for Typophiles* edited by Paul A. Bennett, Cleveland: The World Publishing Co., 1951. Chapter six was reprinted separately as *The Procrustian Bed* in Philadelphia by The Pickering Press, 1957.

REVIEWS: *The Times Literary Supplement*, 17 March 1932. By Desmond Flower, *The Book-Collector's Quarterly*, no. vi, April–June 1932. By R. E. Roberts, *New Statesman and Nation*, 7 May 1932. *Three Ridings Journal* Vol. 4, no. 4, December 1932.

NOTE: This book incorporates a lecture delivered at the Victoria and Albert

Museum in December 1929.

SECOND EDITION:

TITLE-PAGE: AN ESSAY ON TYPOGRAPHY | BY ERIC GILL | [Contents] SECOND EDITION | LONDON/SHEED & WARD/1936. [Note: The diagonal strokes printed between 'LONDON' and 'SHEED' and again between 'WARD' and '1936' are not the compiler's line-end strokes but were used by the printer as commas.]

SIZE: $6\frac{3}{4} \times 4\frac{1}{8}$.   COLLATION: [a]^4, b–i^8, k^4.

PAGINATION AND CONTENTS: Pp. viii+136; [i] [ii] blank; [iii] [iv] title-page and contents, verso printers' imprint: PRINTED AND MADE IN GREAT BRITAIN | BY HAGUE & GILL, HIGH WYCOMBE | PUBLISHED BY | SHEED AND WARD | 31 PATERNOSTER ROW, LONDON E.C. | FIRST PUBLISHED IN 1931 | SECOND EDITION 1936; [v]–[viii] *The Theme*; [1]–133 text; [134]–[136] blank. Printed from 12 pt. *Joanna*.

ILLUSTRATIONS: As in the first edition (above).

BINDING: Green cloth, lettered on spine in blue, reading downwards: GILL TYPOGRAPHY Top edges coloured green to match the casing. All edges cut.

DATE OF PUBLICATION: August 1936. Reprinted 1939.

PRICE: 5s.

PRINTING: 1193 copies.

REVIEWS: *The Times Literary Supplement*, 15 August 1936 (cf. no. 518.) *Sunday Times*, 30 August 1936. By B. H. Newdigate, *The London Mercury*, September 1936. By Bernard Glemser, *Typography* 1, November 1936. By Holbrook Jackson, *The New English Weekly*, 31 December 1936 (cf. no. 523). By B. H. Newdigate, *The Dublin Review*, January 1937. By F.P.A., *Pax*, February 1937. By F. Meynell, *Signature*, no. 5, March 1937.

NOTE: The text, revised and reset, contains a new chapter, *But Why Lettering?*

THIRD EDITION:

This edition, published by J. M. Dent & Sons in November 1941, is in all respects, e.g. size, price and binding, similar to the second edition save in the pagination which runs from '6' (the second page of *The Theme*) to 141. The top edges are uncoloured.

SUBSEQUENT EDITIONS: Fourth edition, reset, 1954, 127pp. Reprinted 1960. Fifth edition, facsimile of the second edition with new introduction by Christopher Skelton, London: Lund Humphries. 1988. Boston: David Godine. 1988. 133pp. Reviewed in *Graphics World* [Maidstone], no. 74, September–October, 1988. A Dutch translation, *Over Typografie*, was published in Amsterdam by N. V. de Arbeiderspers, 1955. Reviewed in *Drukkers-weekblad*, no. 49, 3 December 1955.

CLOTHES

AN ESSAY UPON THE NATURE AND
SIGNIFICANCE OF THE NATURAL AND
ARTIFICIAL INTEGUMENTS WORN BY
MEN AND WOMEN

By
ERIC GILL

*With ten diagrams engraved
by the Author*

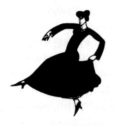

LONDON
JONATHAN CAPE, BEDFORD SQUARE
AND AT TORONTO
1931

[22]

22 CLOTHES

TITLE-PAGE: Reproduced. Shows w-e. *Woman Dancing* (P712).

SIZE: $7\frac{1}{2} \times 4\frac{1}{8}$.   COLLATION: [ ]^4, [1]–12^8, 13^4.

PAGINATION AND CONTENTS: Pp. viii + 200; [i] [ii] blank; [iii] [iv] title-page, verso: PRINTED IN GREAT BRITAIN; [v] [vi] dedication worded: TO | PRUDENCE, verso blank; [vii] Contents; [viii] quotations from D. H. Lawrence, Siegfried Sassoon and Baudelaire; [1] half-title; [2] illustration; 3–[197] text; [198] blank; [199] tail-piece and colophon worded: WRITTEN AT WEIMAR AND SALIES-DE- | BÉARN, JULY 1930, AND PRINTED BY | WALTER LEWIS AT THE UNIVERSITY | PRESS, CAMBRIDGE, JUNE 1931; [200] blank. Printed from 13 pt. *Perpetua*. In addition to the 'ordinary' copies there was an edition limited to 160 copies printed on laid paper and signed (at the foot of the colophon) by the author, of which 153 were for sale. Note: In the special edition, on p. ii of the preliminary pages, is printed a Statement of Editions worded: OF THIS SPECIAL EDITION OF CLOTHES | 160 COPIES HAVE BEEN PRINTED OF WHICH | 153 COPIES ARE FOR SALE | followed by NUMBER [. . .] (both in MS).

ILLUSTRATIONS: In addition to the title-page device there are three full-page, five half-page illustrations and an ornamental device, all from wood-engravings by the author, placed:

> *Art and Prudence* (P714) (full-page), p. [2]
> *Clothes as Houses* (P715) (half-page), p. 26.
> *Clothes as Workshops* (P716) (half-page), p. 51.
> *Clothes as Churches and Town Halls* (P717) (half-page), p. 79.
> *Clothes for special parts* (P718) (half-page), p. 110.
> *The Tyranny of Tailors* (P719) (full-page), p. [132]
> *Nature and Nakedness* (P720) (full-page), p. [162]
> *Trousers* (P721) (half-page), p. 186.
> *Tail-piece: (Trousers and Spats)* (P722), p. [199]

BINDING: (*a*) Special edition: ¼ bound pigskin; fawn Cockerell boards, lettered in gilt on spine: CLOTHES | [device] ERIC GILL | and, at foot: JONATHAN | CAPE. Cross bands at head and foot. Top edges gilt, other edges trimmed. (*b*) Ordinary edition: green cloth; lettered in gilt on spine (the letters placed one above the other): CLOTHES | ERIC | GILL, with the publishers' device at foot. Top edges cut and coloured green to match the casing, other edges trimmed. Copies of this edition are known with the lettering, etc. on spine in black. Top edges uncoloured and with the publishers' device in black on back cover.

DUST JACKET: Buff paper printed in black and red with *Woman dancing* (P712). Printed in red on front. In G. F. Sims Catalogue 58, item 107 offers three original drawings by Gill for the dust jacket which were not used. One of them is reproduced as plate 2 in the catalogue, p. 15.

DATE OF PUBLICATION: 1931 [6 July] MS. dated July–August 1930.

PRICE: Special edition: one guinea. Ordinary edition: 10s. 6d.

REVIEWS: By Gerald Heard, *The Week-end Review*, 11 July 1931. By D. B. Wyndham Lewis, *Sunday Referee*, 12 July 1931. By Frank Swinnerton, *Evening News*, 17 July 1931. By Richard Sunne, *New Statesman and Nation*, 18 July 1931. By Osbert Burdett, *The Saturday Review*, 18 July 1931. By T. Charles Edwards and Bernard Delany, O.P., *Blackfriars*, July 1931. By J. C. Flugel, *The Listener*, 5 August 1931. *Architectural Design & Construction*, September 1931. *The Times Literary Supplement*, 1 October 1931. *Southport Guardian*, 4 May 1932. CLC has a file of 46 additional reviews.

NOTES: An edition in German was contemplated, but though an 8-page prospectus containing a specimen page was issued by *Der Deutsche Buch-Club*, Abt. Verlag, Hamburg 1, Monckebergstr. 21, it never materialized. Printed on the back of this prospectus are extracts, in German, from reviews which appeared in five British journals.

VARIANT: GL has a copy of the ordinary edition with an advertisement sheet (verso blank) tipped in between pp. 196–197 for another Cape book, *Eric Gill: Mason – Sculptor* by Joseph Thorpe. Cf. no. 435. This book is also advertised on the back of the dust jacket.

By Eric Gill

with an engraving by the author

SCULPTURE
AND
THE LIVING
MODEL

Sheed & Ward   [23]

1932

23 SCULPTURE AND THE LIVING MODEL

COVER-TITLE: Reproduced. There is no title-page as such.

SIZE: 7 × 4.   COLLATION: [ ]⁴, a⁸, [ ]⁴.

PAGINATION AND CONTENTS: Pp. ii + 22; [i] [ii] recto blank, verso illustration; [1]–[21] text; [22] printers' imprint worded: PRINTED BY | HAGUE & GILL, HIGH WYCOMBE | PUBLISHED BY | SHEED & WARD | 31 PATERNOSTER ROW, LONDON, E.C. 4 | MCMXXXII. Printed from 8 pt. *Gill Extra Light Sans-Serif.*

ILLUSTRATION: There is one full-page wood-engraving, placed:

Artist and Mirror (P837) p. [ii]

BINDING: Yellow paper wrappers with overlaps, printed on front from *Gill Sans-serif* type, in black and red, as reproduced. On back of wrapper press-mark: *Tree and Dog* (P733) and *Flames for tree and dog* (P733a) and imprint: 500 COPIES | PRINTED BY | HAGUE & GILL, HIGH WYCOMBE | PUBLISHED BY | SHEED & WARD | 31 PATERNOSTER ROW | LONDON, E.C. 4 and, at foot: PRICE 2*s.* 6*d.* Top edges cut, others trimmed.

DATE OF PUBLICATION: September 1932. MS. dated 8–11 February 1932.

PRICE: 2*s.* 6*d.*

PRINTING: 500 copies.

REVIEW: By the Rev. Mark Brocklehurst, *Blackfriars*, June 1933.

NOTES: This essay was originally delivered as a lecture at Oxford on 29 February 1932 to the Oxford Arts Club according to an editor's note in the May 1932 issue of *The Oxford Outlook* in which this essay first appeared, pp. 101–120. Reprinted in *Beauty Looks After Herself* (1933) (no. 24).

37

BEAUTY
LOOKS AFTER
HERSELF

Essays by ERIC GILL, t.o.s.d.

London SHEED & WARD New York
MCMXXXIII   [24]

1933

24 BEAUTY LOOKS AFTER HERSELF
TITLE-PAGE: Reproduced. Shows w-e. *S. Thomas' hands* (P382).
SIZE: $7\frac{3}{4} \times 5$.   COLLATION: [B]⁸, C-R⁸.
PAGINATION AND CONTENTS: Pp. 256. [i] half-title: BEAUTY LOOKS
AFTER HERSELF; [2] Quotation; [3] [4] title-page, verso printers' imprint:
FIRST PUBLISHED MAY 1933 | and, at foot: PRINTED BY HAZELL,
WATSON & VINEY, LTD., LONDON AND AYLESBURY, | FOR SHEED &
WARD, | 31 PATERNOSTER ROW, E.C.4.; 5–7 Preface; [8] blank; 9
Contents: I. *Art and Prudence.* II. *Repository Art.* III. *Twopence Plain, Penny
Coloured.* IV. *Art and Sanctification.* V. *Architecture as Sculpture.* VI. *Paintings
and Criticism.* VII. *Sculpture and the Living Model.* VIII. *Architecture and
Machines.* IX. *Art and the People.* X. *Plain Architecture.* XI. *Painting and the
Public.* XII. *Art and Industrialism.* XIII. *Beauty Looks after Herself.*; [10]
blank; 11–253 text; [254]–[256] blank. Printed from 13 pt. *Perpetua.*

ILLUSTRATIONS: There are six line-drawings by the author, printed in the text of the essay *Plain Architecture*, thus underlined and placed:

1. *Tomb of Cheops*, p. 155.
2. *Roman Aqueduct*, p. 156.
3. *Church in Asia Minor*, p. 159.
4. *S. Pierre, Chartres: Buttresses*, p. 160.
5. *English Railway Viaduct*, p. 163.
6. *Church near Paris*, p. 164.

BINDING: Black cloth; lettered in silver on spine: B E A U T Y | L O O K S | A F T E R | H E R S E L F | [stop] G I L L | and, at foot: S & W Top edges dark green. All edges cut.

DUST JACKET: Cream paper, printed in blue and red.

DATE OF PUBLICATION: May 1933. MS. of Preface dated February 1933.

PRICE: 7s. 6d. (In U.S.A. $2.)

REVIEWS: *Architectural Design & Construction*, June 1933. By G. K. Chesterton, *Illustrated London News*, 10 June 1933. By Lorna Rea, *Liverpool Daily Post*, 21 June 1933. By Hugh de Selincourt, *New Britain*, 28 June 1933. By H. C. M. *Sunday Times*, 2 July 1933. By K. C. MacDonald, *G.K.'s Weekly*, 20 July 1933. *New English Weekly*, 27 July 1933. By Eric Gillett, *The London Mercury*, August 1933. By Herbert Read, *The Listener*, 2 August 1933. *The Times Literary Supplement*, 7 September 1933. By Austin Clarke, *The Observer*, 8 October 1933. By A. J. Penty, *Criterion*, April 1934. By G. J. P., *Burlington Magazine*, May 1934. C L C has a file of 9 additional reviews.

NOTES: Letters prompted by the reviews by Herbert Read and A. J. Penty were reprinted in *Letters of Eric Gill*, under nos. 240 and 216 respectively.

SUBSEQUENT EDITIONS: A cheap edition (3s. 6d.) was published in March 1935. It was reprinted in 1966, with a second printing in 1968, by Books for Libraries Press of Freeport, N.Y. as one of their Essay Index Reprint Series. The firm's stock and titles were subsequently purchased by the Arno Press of New York. In 1983 both B F L and Arno were acquired by Ayer Co. Pubs. of Salem, New Hampshire.

25 UNEMPLOYMENT

COVER-TITLE: Reproduced. There is no title-page as such.

SIZE: $6\frac{7}{8} \times 4\frac{1}{2}$.

COLLATION: A single gathering of sixteen leaves signed 'a' within a conjugate blank pair.

PAGINATION AND CONTENTS: Pp. 32; 1–32 text. Printed from 12 pt. *Perpetua* and 8 pt. *Joanna*.

ILLUSTRATIONS: There is one wood-engraving: *The Leisure State* (P850); p. 1 (reproduced).

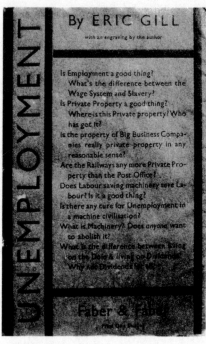

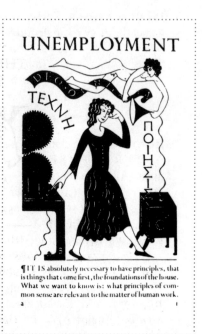

[25. Cover-title]   [25. Page 1]

BINDING: Red paper wrappers with overlaps, sewn; printed on front in black as reproduced and on back: PRINTED BY | HAGUE & GILL, HIGH WYCOMBE | PUBLISHED BY | FABER & FABER LTD. | 24 RUSSELL SQUARE, LONDON | 1933 All edges cut.

DATE OF PUBLICATION: May 1933. MS. dated 14 February 1933.

PRICE: 1s.

PRINTING: 2000 copies.

REVIEWS: By J. B., *Everyman*, 20 May 1933. *New Britain*, 31 May 1933, under the caption: *An Artist Attacks Unemployment*. *The Listener*, 31 May 1933. By R. C. K. Ensor, *The London Mercury*, July 1933. By H. C. M., *Sunday Times*, 2 July 1933. By Philip Mairet, *The New English Weekly*, 13 July 1933. *Scrutiny*, March 1934. CLC has a file of 3 additional reviews.

NOTES: This was a lecture entitled *Catholic Principles & Unemployment* delivered at High Wycombe 14 February 1933. It was revised and extended for the present pamphlet.

VARIANT: CLC has what is perhaps a proof copy, unsewn, laid in yellow wrappers printed in blue.

40

THE LORD'S
SONG

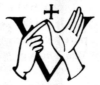

A Sermon
By
ERIC GILL

THE GOLDEN
COCKEREL
PRESS
1934

[26]

1934

26 THE LORD'S SONG

TITLE-PAGE: Reproduced. Shows w-e. *S. Thomas' hands* (P382).
SIZE: $9 \times 4\frac{1}{2}$.   COLLATION: One unsigned gathering of twelve leaves.
PAGINATION AND CONTENTS: Pp. iv + 20; [i]–[iv] blank; [1] [2] title-page,
verso printers' imprint worded: PRINTED AND MADE | IN GREAT

BRITAIN; [3] colophon worded: PRINTED & PUBLISHED BY | CHRISTOPHER SANDFORD, | FRANCIS J. NEWBERY & | OWEN RUTTER AT THE | GOLDEN COCKEREL PRESS, | 10 STAPLE INN, LONDON. | THIS BOOK IS THE FIRST | IN WHICH THE PRESS HAS | MADE USE OF ERIC GILL'S | PERPETUA ROMAN AND | FELICITY ITALIC TYPES. | LIMITED TO 500 COPIES | OF WHICH THIS IS | NUMBER [number filled in by hand]; [4] frontispiece; 5–[16] text; [17]–[20] blank. Printed from 14 pt. *Perpetua* and *Felicity* on Arnold & Foster's pure rag paper.

ILLUSTRATIONS: There is one full-page wood-engraving and a decorated initial letter, placed:

The Lord's Song (P856), frontispiece [p. 4]

A four-line initial letter *T* with leaves, p. 5.

BINDING: Full-bound white buckram, lettered in gilt on front from the author's design: G C P and on spine, reading upwards: THE LORD'S SONG: GILL. Top edges cut, other edges trimmed.

DATE OF PUBLICATION: January 1934. MS. dated May 1932.

PRICE: 12s. 6d.

PRINTING: 500 copies.

REVIEWS: *Morning Post*, 8 June 1934. *The Times Literary Supplement*, 13 September 1934.

NOTES: This essay, which is no. 92 of the Golden Cockerel Press publications, was reprinted in *In A Strange Land* (1944) (no. 51), American edition *It All Goes Together* (no. 52). There is a $9 \times 4\frac{3}{8}$ french-fold prospectus with a reproduction of the title page on the front.

27 ENGRAVINGS 1928–1933 BY ERIC GILL

TITLE-PAGE: ENGRAVINGS | 1928–1933 | BY ERIC GILL | FABER & FABER LTD | 1934

SIZE: $12\frac{1}{2} \times 9\frac{3}{4}$. COLLATION: [Unsigned: $1–15^8$.]

PAGINATION AND CONTENTS: Ff. xvi + 104; sheets printed on one side only, verso and recto alternately (actually pp. 240 joined at top); [i] [ii] title-page, verso printers' imprint worded: PRINTED BY HAGUE AND GILL, HIGH WYCOMBE | AND PUBLISHED BY FABER AND FABER LTD. | 24 RUSSELL SQUARE, LONDON W C, 1934 | and, at foot: PRINTED AND MADE IN GREAT BRITAIN; [iii]–iv Contents; [v]–vi Preface by the engraver and Publishers' Note; [vii]–xv Chronological List of Engravings 1928–1933; [xvi] blank; 1–102 illustrations; [103] [104] blank. Printed from 12 pt. *Perpetua*.

ILLUSTRATIONS: There are one hundred and thirty-three wood-engravings placed as described in the Contents. Of these the following seven had not previously been published in books: *Safety First* (P295), *Bookplate: From the books of Philip Hofer* (P502), *Sculpture* (P629), *The Chinese Maidservant* (P577), *Christmas Card: Ex te ortus est sol justitiae* (p827), *Bookplate: In latitudinem ex libris A. H. Tandy* (P839) and *Bookplate: Sola deus salus ex libris Desmond Flower* (P848).

BINDING: Green linen, lettered in gilt on spine: ERIC GILL | ENGRAVINGS | 1928–1933.

DATE OF PUBLICATION: April 1934. MS. of Preface dated 23 October 1933.

PRICE: Three guineas.

PRINTING: 400 copies.

REVIEWS: By Campbell Dodgson, *The Listener*, 2 May 1934 and in *The Print Collector's Quarterly*, Vol. 21, no. 3, July 1934. By L. H. *Manchester Guardian*, 17 May 1934. By J. G., *Morning Post*, 1 June 1934, *The Times Literary Supplement*, 26 July 1934. By Jan Gordon, *The Observer*, 7 October 1934. By C. R. G., *Connoisseur*, January 1935.

NOTE: There is a $12\frac{1}{2} \times 10$ french-fold prospectus featuring *Initials H and O* (with Venus and Cupid) (P582) from *The Canterbury Tales* on [p. 2] and *The Deposition* (P788) from *The Four Gospels* on [p. 3].

ADDENDA AND CORRIGENDA: The following may be noted:

P. viii. No. 270. [P554] The words 'of inset' should be added after 'page 15', and '274a' [P559] should be added after '274' [P559].

No. 271. [P555] The words 'of inset' should be added after 'p. 20'.

No. 271a. [P555] For 'oranges' read 'apples' and add, after 'No. 271' [P555], 'and halo'.

Insert: *272 a* [P557] *A target for miniature rifle range.* 6×6.

Nos. 274 & 274a. [P559] The words 'of inset' should be added after 'p. 29'.

P. ix. Insert: *302 a* [P591] *Border: spray of ten pointed leaves* $4\frac{1}{4} \times 1$ II *CT*

No. 308. [P598] Add: *This engraving was also used as a border for the specimen of Perpetua Italic on p. 48 of The Fleuron, No. 7.*

P. x. No. 331. [P628] The reduced version referred to in the marginal note was used on the title-page of *XXth Century Sculptors* (1930) by the same author, not on that of *Some Modern Sculptors* as is stated.

P. xi. For '368' (*Tailpiece: Chaucer writing*) read '363' [P660].

P. xii. No. 390. [P688] Insert an asterisk before the engraving number.

P. xiii. No. 427. [P727] Add to marginal note: *Also used as frontispiece for Clothing Without Cloth (Golden Cockerel Press, 1931).*

P. xv. No. 523. [P827] For 'JVSITITAE' read 'JVSTITIAE'.

Insert: *524* [P828] *Coat of Arms for Cambridge University Press* $2\frac{1}{8} \times 1\frac{7}{8}$ *Designed by E. G. Engraved by John Beedham, finished off by E. G.*

No. 526. [P833] Add to marginal note: 'Act I, p. 1.'

No. 533. [P840–3] The description should read: *Fifteen initial letters, W, T, M, T, &c.*

MONEY & MORALS / BY ERIC GILL

with nine illustrations by Denis Tegetmeier

FABER & FABER LTD / MCMXXXIV

[28

28 MONEY & MORALS
TITLE-PAGE: Reproduced.
SIZE: $7\frac{1}{2}\times 4\frac{3}{4}$.   COLLATION: $[A]^4$, a–h^8.
PAGINATION AND CONTENTS: Pp. viii + 128; [i] [ii] blank; [iii] [iv] blank,
save for signature 'A2', verso blank; [v] [vi] title-page (which includes the
Contents and List of Illustrations), verso printers' imprint worded: PRINTED
BY HAGUE AND GILL, HIGH WYCOMBE | AND PUBLISHED BY FABER
AND FABER LTD. | 24 RUSSELL SQUARE, LONDON WC, 1934 and, at
foot: PRINTED AND MADE IN GREAT BRITAIN; [vii] Author's note; [viii]
frontispiece; [1]–[125] text; [126]–[128] blank. Printed from 12 pt. *Joanna*.
ILLUSTRATIONS: There are nine illustrations from drawings by Denis
Tegetmeier, reproduced by line-block, underlined and placed as shown on
title-page.
BINDING: Pink cloth, lettered in gilt on spine: MONEY | AND |
MORALS [short rule] ERIC | GILL and, at foot: FABER | AND |
FABER All edges cut.
DUST JACKET: White paper printed in black.
DATE OF PUBLICATION: July 1934. MS. of *Money and Morals* dated 19
October 1933.
PRICE: 6s.
PRINTING: 1413 copies.
REVIEW: By A. R. B., *Colosseum*, December 1934.
NOTES: Two of the essays, viz. *Money & Morals* and *Men & Things* were first
given as lectures to the Link Society at Manchester and the Edinburgh School
of Art respectively. The third, *The Politics of Industrialism*, was first published
in *Blackfriars*, February 1934 (no. 153). A letter to the *Catholic Herald*, 1
December 1934, in which E. G. replies to criticisms by the Rev. J. B. Reeves
(printed in the previous issue) was reprinted in *Letters of Eric Gill* under no.
221.
SECOND EDITION: An enlarged edition similar in format but with a
redesigned dust jacket was published by Faber & Faber in September 1937.
This contains one additional essay, viz. *Unemployment* (first published
separately in 1933—not 1932 as is stated in the author's note, cf. no. 25) and
one additional drawing by Denis Tegetmeier, viz. *Machinery does in fact save
labour*, p. 140. The binding of this edition was in grey cloth lettered on spine in
black, reading downwards: GILL: MONEY & MORALS.
DUST JACKET: Buff paper printed in black and red.
REVIEWS: *The Times*, 4 September 1937. *The Times Literary Supplement*, 4
September 1937. By Liam O'Laoghaire, *Ireland To-Day*, October 1937. *New
English Weekly*, 18 November 1937. CLC has a file of 22 additional reviews of
the above editions.

ART

and a changing civilisation

by

ERIC GILL

JOHN LANE THE BODLEY HEAD LTD.
LONDON

[29]

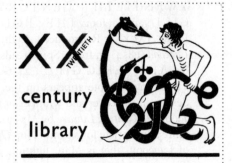

XX
century
library

ART

Eric Gill

HALF-A-CROWN NET

[29. Dust Jacket]

29 ART AND A CHANGING CIVILISATION

TITLE-PAGE: Reproduced.

SIZE: $7\frac{1}{4} \times 4\frac{3}{4}$.   COLLATION: $[A]^8$, $B-L^8$.

PAGINATION AND CONTENTS: Pp. xiv + 162; [i] [ii] half-title to series worded: THE TWENTIETH CENTURY LIBRARY | EDITED BY V. K. KRISHNA MENON | ART, verso blank; [iii] [iv] list of other volumes in the *Twentieth Century Library*, verso blank; [v] [vi] title-page, verso printers' imprint worded: FIRST PUBLISHED IN 1934 | and, at foot: PRINTED IN GREAT BRITAIN | BY WESTERN PRINTING SERVICES LTD., BRISTOL; vii–x Preliminary; xi–[xii] Contents, verso blank; [xiii] [xiv] half-title worded ART, verso quotations from Ecclesiasticus and A. K. Coomaraswamy; 1–138 text; [139] [140] blank, verso author's and publishers' acknowledgements; 141–5 Appendix I *The Question of Anonymity* by Rayner Heppenstall; 146–51 Appendix II *The School of Baudelaire* by G. M. Turnell; 152 Bibliography; 153–8 Index; [159] [160] publishers' announcements concerning the *Twentieth Century Library*; [161] [162] blank.

ILLUSTRATIONS: None.

BINDING: Red cloth, lettered on front, at top, in black: THE TWENTIETH CENTURY LIBRARY with a design by Gill, *Laocoon* (P854) blocked in black. Lettered in black on spine:

46

TWENTIETH | CENTURY | LIBRARY | ART | ERIC | GILL | and, at foot: THE | BODLEY HEAD All edges cut.

DUST JACKET: Reproduced. Light rose paper printed in black and red, with *Laocoon* (P854) on front. Spine reads: XXth | CENTURY | LIBRARY | 8 | ART | ERIC GILL | 2s 6d NET | THE | BODLEY HEAD. The following note appears on the lower inner flap of the dust jacket: 'The design on the cover and wrapper of this book has been specially made for *The Twentieth Century Library* by Mr Eric Gill, who writes: "I can think of nothing more appropriate for a symbol for *The Twentieth Century Library* than a version of Laocoon, that is Man, fighting with the twin snakes of War and Usury. These are the powers of evil with which man in the twentieth century will have to settle, or perish."'

DATE OF PUBLICATION: 1934. MS. dated 8 December 1933–6 January 1934.

PRICE: 2s. 6d.

REVIEWS: By Philip Henderson, *New Britain*, 25 July 1934. By Herbert Read, *The Spectator*, 10 August 1934. By Wyndham Lewis, *The Listener*, 26 September 1934. By Harold Nicolson, *Daily Telegraph*, September 1934. C L C has a file of 15 additional reviews.

SUBSEQUENT EDITIONS: Reprinted in 1935 with binding of beige cloth, lettered in black on front: ART with *Laocoon* (P854) in red. Lettered in black on spine: ART | ERIC | GILL | and, at foot in red: XX | CENTURY | LIBRARY | THE BODLEY HEAD. Price 3s. 6d. A new edition entirely re-set in a smaller format, was published by John Lane, The Bodley Head, under the title ART, in 1946, and again in 1949. E.G.'s *Laocoon* (P854) was not used in these two. Price 5s. Reprinted in *Literary Taste, Culture and Mass Communication* edited by Peter Davison, Rolf Meyersohn, Edward Shils, in Vol. 4 *Art and Changing Civilization* pp. 135–281, Cambridge: Chadwyck-Healey. 1978.

30 THREE BOOK TYPES

TITLE-PAGE: Reproduced.

SIZE: $7\frac{1}{2} \times 4\frac{7}{8}$.   COLLATION: Two unsigned gatherings of eight leaves.

PAGINATION AND CONTENTS: Pp. 32; [1] [2] title-page, verso blank; [3] [4] 'Advertisement' by Eric Gill; 5 Synopsis of Characters; 6–31 specimen pages of the three type faces; [32] index.

ILLUSTRATIONS: None.

BINDING: Light blue cloth, lettered in gilt on front: THREE BOOK TYPES | HAGUE & GILL All edges trimmed.

DATE OF PUBLICATION: 1934. MS. of 'Advertisement' dated 23 December 1933.

A SPECIMEN OF

THREE BOOK TYPES

designed by Eric Gill

Joanna
Joanna Italic
Perpetua

Printed by Hague & Gill
High Wycombe
MCMXXXIV   [30]

PRICE: n.p. Printed for private distribution.
REVIEW: *Caxton Magazine*, April 1934.

1935
31 WORK AND LEISURE
TITLE-PAGE: Reproduced. Shows w-e. *S. Thomas' hands* (P889), see note
below.
SIZE: $7\frac{1}{2} \times 5$.   COLLATION: A–I⁸.
PAGINATION AND CONTENTS: Pp. 144; [1] [2] blank; [3] [4] half-title
worded: WORK AND LEISURE, verso blank; [5] title-page; [6] imprint, etc.,
worded: FIRST PUBLISHED IN SEPTEMBER MCMXXXV | BY FABER AND
FABER LIMITED | 24 RUSSELL SQUARE LONDON W.C. I | PRINTED IN
GREAT BRITAIN | AT THE BOWERING PRESS PLYMOUTH | ALL RIGHTS
RESERVED | THE THREE LECTURES HERE PRINTED | WERE GIVEN AT |
UNIVERSITY COLLEGE BANGOR | IN NOVEMBER, 1934; Contents: *I Art
and Manufacture. II Art and Commerce. III Art and Holiness*; [8] blank; [9] [10]
half-title for first lecture, worded: I | ART AND MANUFACTURE | ART AS
THINGS TO BE MADE, verso blank; 11–142 text; [143] [144] blank.
ILLUSTRATIONS: None.
BINDING: Pink cloth, lettered in blue on spine, reading downwards: ERIC
GILL—WORK AND LEISURE Top edges cut, other edges trimmed.
DATE OF PUBLICATION: September 1935. MS. dated October–November

WORK AND LEISURE

by

Eric Gill

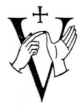

London
Faber and Faber Limited
24 Russell Square

[31]

1934.
PRICE: 5*s*.
REVIEWS: By 'Roderick Random', *Time & Tide*, 14 September 1935. By R. A. Scott-James, *The London Mercury*, October 1935. By H. F., *Apollo*, October 1935. By Bernard Kelly, *Blackfriars*, November 1935. *Spectator*, 15 November 1935. By the Rev. Thomas Gilby, O.P., *Catholic Herald*, 29 November 1935 (to which E. G. replied in the issue of 6 December). By M. R[eckitt], *The Colosseum*, December 1935. By S. John Woods, *Decorator*, December 1935. *The Christian Science Monitor*, 15 February 1936 under the caption *The Freeman has Joy in His Work*. By F. D. Klingender, *Burlington Magazine*, April 1936. Cf. issue for June 1936 for E. G.'s reply to this last review (no. 185). By F. Q. P., *The Christian Front*, June 1936. 'The sculptor shivers a lance', *Punch*, 11 September 1936.
NOTES: The title-page of this book shows the first use of the device: *S. Thomas' hands: V | ER | ITAS* (P889) a variant of the similar device (P382) previously used.

1936
32 THE NECESSITY OF BELIEF
TITLE-PAGE: Reproduced. Shows w-e. *S. Thomas' hands* (P889).
SIZE: 7½ × 4¾.   COLLATION: [A]⁸, B–X⁸, Y¹⁰.
PAGINATION AND CONTENTS: Pp. 356; [1] [2] blank; [3] half-title: THE

49

THE NECESSITY OF BELIEF

an enquiry into the nature of human certainty, the causes of scepticism and the grounds of morality, and a justification of the doctrine that the end is the beginning

by ERIC GILL

LONDON, FABER AND FABER LIMITED
24 RUSSELL SQUARE

[32]

NECESSITY OF BELIEF; [4] List of works by the same author; [5] [6] title-page, verso imprint: FIRST PUBLISHED IN APRIL MCMXXXVI | BY FABER AND FABER LIMITED | 24 RUSSELL SQUARE, LONDON W.C. I | PRINTED IN GREAT BRITAIN BY | R. MACLEHOSE AND COMPANY LIMITED | THE UNIVERSITY PRESS, GLASGOW | ALL RIGHTS RESERVED; 7–[8] Contents, verso blank; [9] [10] quotation from *The Documents in the Case by D. Sayers and R. Eustace*, verso blank; 11–354 text; [355] [356] blank. Printed from 12 pt. *Perpetua*.

ILLUSTRATIONS: None.

BINDING: Red cloth, lettered in gilt on spine: THE | NECESSITY | OF | BELIEF [the device: *S. Thomas' hands* blocked in gold] ERIC | GILL | and, at foot: FABER AND | FABER All edges cut.

DUST JACKET: Blue paper printed in black and red with *S. Thomas' hands* (P889) printed in red on front. Thirty titles of The Faber Library listed on the back.

DATE OF PUBLICATION: 2 April 1936. MS. dated 27 July–December 1935.

PRICE: 7s. 6d.

REVIEWS: By Basil de Selincourt, *The Observer*, 5 April 1936. *Tablet*, 11 April 1936. By the Dean of Exeter [Dr W. R. Matthews], *Sunday Times*, 19 April 1936. *Punch*, 29 April 1936. *Guardian*, 8 May 1936. By Paul Bloomfield, *New Statesman and Nation*, 9 May 1936. *Scotsman*, 25 May 1936. *The Times*

Literary Supplement, 6 June 1936. By H. G. Wood, *British Weekly*, 11 June 1936. By Olaf Stapledon, *The London Mercury*, June 1936. *The Studio*, June 1936. By Bernard Kelly, *Blackfriars*, June 1936. By Rayner Heppenstall, *The Criterion*, July 1936. By Holbrook Jackson, *The New English Weekly*, 31 December 1936 (cf. no. 523). By R. H. W[ilenski], *Apollo*, July 1937.

ERRATA: p. 7   Contents. For '372' (Tragedy and Comedy) read '312'.

        p. 162   Fifth line from end for 'China' read 'china'.

        p. 285   Second line for 'company' read 'category'.

        p. 299   Eighth line from end insert 'no' before 'being'.

        p. 317   At end of first line of footnote insert 'less'.

        p. 336   Sixth line for 'scarcely' read 'hardly'.

NOTES: Writing to me from Pigotts, 7 July 1936, E. G. said: 'Re N. of B. Title chosen by F. & F. much remonstrance & endeavours to get them to let me call it *Believe it or Not*. No luck.'

The chapter entitled 'Belief and Law' was reprinted in *The Examiner* (New York: Published quarterly. Price 50 cents), Vol. 1, no. 1, Winter 1938, pp. 11–27 and no. 2, Spring 1938, pp. 217–32. With a biographical sketch of the author on p. [2].

1937

33 WORK & PROPERTY &c

TITLE-PAGE: Reproduced.

SIZE: $7\frac{3}{8} \times 4\frac{3}{4}$.   COLLATION: [ ]⁴, a–i⁸.

PAGINATION AND CONTENTS: Pp. viii+144; [i] [ii] blank; [iii] [iv] title-page and Contents, verso: PRINTED & MADE IN GREAT BRITAIN; [v] [vi] list of illustrations, verso blank; [vii] [viii] author's note, verso frontispiece; [1]–141 text; [142]–[144] blank. Printed from 12 pt. *Joanna*.

ILLUSTRATIONS: There are twelve full-page illustrations from line-drawings by Denis Tegetmeier, reproduced by line-block, underlined and placed as described on page [v]. (The pagination of the eighth illustration should be 75 not 74 as shown in the list of illustrations.)

BINDING: Maize buckram, lettered in gilt on spine, reading downwards: ERIC GILL: WORK & PROPERTY All edges cut.

DUST JACKET: Reproduced. Cream paper printed in red.

DATE OF PUBLICATION: March 1937.

PRICE: 7s. 6d.

PRINTING: 1450 copies.

REVIEWS: *The Bookseller*, 21 April 1937. By G. A. F., *G.K.'s Weekly*, 3 May 1937. By Geoffrey Grigson, *Morning Post*, 11 May 1937. *The Manchester Guardian*, 12 May 1937. *John O'London's Weekly*, 20 May 1937. By Victor White, O.P., *Catholic Herald*, 21 May 1937. By T. D., *Irish Independent*,

WORK & PROPERTY &c / by ERIC GILL

containing

Man & politics   page 1

Art in relation to industrialism   7

Art & revolution   39

What is art & does it matter?   55

The value of the creative faculty in man   77

Architects & builders   93

Work & property   99

The end of the fine arts   119

Printed by Hague & Gill Ltd, High Wycombe, & published
for them by J. M. Dent & Sons Ltd, 10-13 Bedford Street
London WC2, 1937

WORK and

TEXT BY

Gill

PICTURES BY

Teg

PUBLISHED BY

Dent

PROPERTY

[33]   [33. Dust Jacket]

25 May 1937. By F. Carter, *New English Weekly*, 10 June 1937. By V. S. Pritchett, *Fortnightly Review*, June 1937. By Ceolfric Heron, O.P., *Blackfriars*, August 1937. (An extensive review to which E. G. replied in the issue of the following November.) By D. R., *Pax*, September 1937. *The Times Literary Supplement*, 4 September 1937. By L. E., *Dublin Review*, April 1938. Cf. *Bread and Roses* by Ethel Mannin (no. 596). C L C has a file of 27 additional reviews.

NOTES: The lecture *Work and Property* first appeared under the title *Art and Property* in *G.K.'s Weekly*, 16 July 1936 (cf. no. 188). The substance of the lecture *Art and Revolution* (delivered to the Artists' International Association at Christ Church Hall, Shadwell, London, E., 2 December 1936) was subsequently published in *The Catholic Worker* (U.S.A.), Vol. IV, no. 12, April 1937. MS. dated 30 October 1936 *et seq*. The lecture was reported in the *East London Advertiser*, 19 December 1936. *Art in Relation to Industrialism*, a lecture to London County Council school teachers, was first printed in *Blackfriars*, January 1936 (cf. no. 181). *The Value of the Creative Faculty in Man*, a lecture to the Aquinas Society of Leicester, was first printed in *Blackfriars*, September 1935 (cf. no. 174). *Architects and Builders* first appeared in *Catholic Herald*, 6 April 1935 (cf. no. 168).

VARIANT: G L has a copy bound in thinner boards covered in beige cloth but otherwise identical.

52

SCULPTURE ON
MACHINE-MADE BUILDINGS
A Lecture delivered to the Birmingham and Five
Counties Architectural Association in the Royal
Birmingham Society of Artists Galleries, Nov. 1936
BY
ERIC GILL

City of Birmingham School of Printing
Central School of Arts and Crafts
Margaret Street
1937

[34]

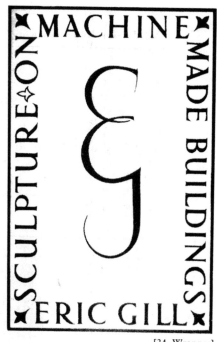

[34. Wrapper]

34 SCULPTURE ON MACHINE-MADE BUILDINGS

TITLE-PAGE: Reproduced.

SIZE: $8\frac{1}{2} \times 5\frac{1}{2}$.

COLLATION: [One unsigned gathering of twenty-two leaves.]

PAGINATION AND CONTENTS: Pp. ii + 42; [i] [ii] blank; [1] [2] title-page, verso blank; 3–[37] text; [38] colophon worded: PRINTED UNDER THE DIRECTION OF LEONARD JAY, AT THE | CITY OF BIRMINGHAM SCHOOL OF PRINTING, WHICH IS A | DEPARTMENT OF THE CENTRAL SCHOOL OF ARTS AND CRAFTS, | MARGARET STREET. THE TYPE, 12-PT. BASKERVILLE, SET AND | CAST ON 'MONOTYPE' MACHINES BY STUDENTS ATTENDING | CLASSES: TEACHERS, T. GILL AND H. BRACEY. COMPOSITORS' | WORK BY BOYS IN THE PRE-APPRENTICE CLASSES: TEACHERS, | H. C. PAGE AND F. G. MOSELEY. PRINTED BY STUDENTS | ATTENDING THE LETTERPRESS MACHINE CLASSES: TEACHERS, | A. HOYLE AND V. S. GANDERTON | 1937 | and, at foot: COVER DESIGN BY OLGA GARNER: TEACHER, A. MICHAEL | FLETCHER; [39]–[42] blank. Printed from 12 pt. *'Monotype' Baskerville*.

ILLUSTRATIONS: None.

BINDING: Cream paper wrappers, blue corded; printed on front in blue, the wording reads round the four sides, beginning at bottom left:

SCULPTURE [*ornament*] ON [*ornament*] | MACHINE [*ornament*] | MADE BUILDINGS | [*ornament*] ERIC GILL [*ornament*]. In the centre is a version of Eric Gill's monogram *E G*. The whole within a frame of plain rules. Reproduced. Cover design by Olga Garner. All edges cut.

DATE OF PUBLICATION: 1937. MS. dated 23 October 1936.

PRICE: n.p.

NOTES: This lecture was also delivered to the Dublin Metropolitan School of Art under the auspices of the Architectural Association of Ireland in March 1937. It was reprinted in *In A Strange Land* (1944) (no. 51), American edition, *It All Goes Together* (no. 52). This lecture must not be confused with a contribution, under precisely the same title, to *Industrial Arts*, Summer 1936 (no. 184).

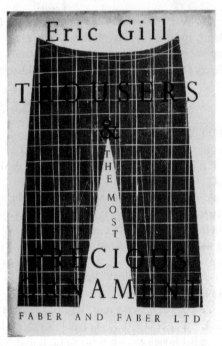

[35]

35 TROUSERS

COVER-TITLE: Reproduced. The title is super-imposed on the wood-engraving (P921), a pair of trousers, which is printed in red. There is no title-page as such but the following appears on the inside of the front wrapper:

TROUSERS & THE MOST | PRECIOUS ORNAMENT | WRITTEN BY | ERIC GILL | ILLUSTRATION BY | DENIS TEGETMEIER | PRINTED BY | HAGUE & GILL LTD | HIGH WYCOMBE | PUBLISHED BY | FABER &

FABER LTD. | 24 RUSSELL SQUARE | LONDON WC 1 | 1937 | PRICE | ONE SHILLING NET

SIZE: $7\frac{1}{2} \times 4\frac{5}{8}$.

COLLATION: b^8 with two unsigned conjugate pairs.

PAGINATION AND CONTENTS: Pp. ii + 22; [i] [ii] blank, verso frontispiece; 1–[22] text. Printed from 12 pt. *Joanna*.

ILLUSTRATION: There is one full-page line-drawing (as frontispiece) by Denis Tegetmeier reproduced by line-block, underlined: *Who minds what the masters wear?*

BINDING: Cream paper wrappers, sewn. All edges cut. CLC has Gill's original design for the front wrapper.

DATE OF PUBLICATION: 1937. MS. dated 15 February 1937.

PRICE: 1*s*.

REVIEWS: *The New English Weekly*, 1 July 1937. By J. M. Bulloch, *Daily Record & Mail*, 19 July 1937. By 'Gabriel', *The Daily Worker*, 18 August 1937. By C., *Connoisseur*, August 1937. *The Times Literary Supplement*, 4 September 1937. By Henry O. Davray, *Mercure de France*, October 1937.

1938

36 AND WHO WANTS PEACE?

TITLE-PAGE: PAX PAMPHLETS NO. 1 | AND WHO | WANTS PEACE? | BY ERIC GILL | JAMES CLARKE & CO LIMITED.

SIZE: $8\frac{3}{8} \times 5\frac{1}{2}$.   COLLATION: One unsigned gathering of eight leaves.

PAGINATION AND CONTENTS: Pp. ii + 14; [i] [ii] title-page, verso imprint worded: PRINTED BY HAGUE & GILL LTD, HIGH WYCOMBE | FOR JAMES CLARKE & CO LTD | 5 WARDROBE PLACE, LONDON E C 4 | FIRST PUBLISHED IN 1938 | and, at foot: PRINTED & MADE IN GREAT BRITAIN; 1–[13] text; [14] blank. Printed from 13 pt. *Perpetua*.

ILLUSTRATIONS: None.

BINDING: Yellow paper wrappers, stapled; printed on front in black: PAX PAMPHLETS, NO. 1 | GENERAL EDITOR: DONALD ATTWATER | [*long rule*] | ERIC GILL | AND WHO | WANTS | PEACE? | [*long rule*] | PUBLISHED BY | JAMES CLARKE & CO LTD, 5 WARDROBE PLACE, E.C. 4 | PRICE SIXPENCE.

DATE OF PUBLICATION: March 1938.   PRICE: 6*d*.

REVIEWS: By T. S. Gregory, *Tablet*, 26 March 1938. By Michael de la Bedoyere, *Catholic Herald*, 29 April 1938. By Gerald Vann, O.P., *Blackfriars*, May 1938. By C. L., *The Colosseum*, July 1938. *Church Times*, 16 September 1938. By Christopher Hollis, *Tablet*, 29 April 1939. For correspondence arising out of the last-named review see the issues of *Tablet* 6 and 13 May 1939. NOTES: The following appears on the inside of the front cover: THE FOLLOWING IS THE TEXT OF A SPEECH MADE BY MR GILL AT THE KINGSWAY HALL, LONDON, ON ARMISTICE DAY, 1936, AT A PEACE MEETING ORGANISED BY THE COUNCIL OF CHRISTIAN PACIFIST GROUPS; IT IS NOW PRINTED BY ARRANGEMENT WITH THAT COUNCIL. On the inner side of the back cover appear particulars of the series of pamphlets published in collaboration with the Pax Society.

VARIANT: HRC has a copy, perhaps never issued, of this pamphlet, similar in appearance but which varies as follows: the imprint on the title-page reads: PUBLISHED FOR THE COUNCIL OF CHRISTIAN PACIFIST GROUPS | 16 VICTORIA STREET, LONDON SW. 1, BY | STANLEY NOTT LIMITED and a rearrangement of this wording also appears on the front cover. The verso of the title-page reads, after the first line: FOR STANLEY NOTT LTD | 69 GRAFTON ST, FITZROY SQUARE, LONDON W1 | FIRST PUBLISHED IN 1937. The CLC has an unbound set of proof sheets with this Stanley Nott imprint.

SUBSEQUENT EDITIONS: This speech was reprinted in *It All Goes Together* (U.S.A. 1944) (no. 52) and was published in U.S.A. by *The Catholic Worker*, Easton, Pa., as a pamphlet. In June 1948 the Greenwood Press of San Francisco published a 12-page folio edition ($13\frac{3}{4} \times 10\frac{1}{4}$) of 100 copies handset in Perpetua and printed on Tovil handmade paper. It was designed by Jack Stauffacher and Adrian Wilson with two woodcuts by Mary Fabilli. It sold for $3.75 bound in paper covered boards or $4.75 in a handwoven fabric binding. Issued with binding covered by plain brown wrappers.

37 UNHOLY TRINITY
TITLE-PAGE: Reproduced.
SIZE: $8\frac{1}{4} \times 6\frac{5}{8}$.
COLLATION: One unsigned gathering of fourteen leaves.
PAGINATION AND CONTENTS: Pp. 28; [No pagination] [1] [2] blank; [3] title-page; [4]–[27] text and illustrations; [28] imprint worded: PRINTED BY HAGUE & GILL LTD., HIGH WYCOMBE | & PUBLISHED FOR THEM BY J. M. DENT & SONS LTD | ALDINE HOUSE, BEDFORD STREET, LONDON, WC2 | MCMXXXVIII Printed from 14 pt. *Bunyan*.
ILLUSTRATIONS: There are eleven full-page illustrations from line drawings by Denis Tegetmeier reproduced by line-blocks.
BINDING: Pink paper wrappers, sewn; printed on front in blue from type and reversed block: ERIC GILL AND | DENIS TEG | UNHOLY TRINITY | TEXT BY ERIC GILL [dot] PICTURES BY DENIS | TEGETMEIER [dot] PUBLISHED BY DENTS FOR | HAGUE & GILL LTD AT 2 SHILLINGS NET (reproduced)

UNHOLY TRINITY by ERIC GILL

Pictures by Denis Tegetmeier

1. Unholy Trinity
2. Unholy Alliance
3. Work and Leisure
4. Paradox of Plenty
5. Wheels within Wheels
6. Yes, we have no Bananas
7. Europa and the Bull
8. Swine
9. Cannon Fodder
10. Safe for Christianity
11. Melancholia

LONDON: J. M. DENT & SONS LTD
(FOR HAGUE & GILL LTD)

Eric Gill and Denis Teg

UNHOLY TRINITY

Text by Eric Gill • Pictures by Denis Tegetmeier • Published by Dents for Hague & Gill Ltd at 2 Shillings net

[37]

[37. Dust Jacket]

Issued in a pink paper slip-in case printed in blue on front: GILL AND TEG | [*long rule*] | UNHOLY | TRINITY | [*long rule*] 2 SHILLINGS [*dot*] DENT | FOR HAGUE AND GILL LIMITED and, on back: UNHOLY TRINITY | CONTAINS 11 SHORT ESSAYS BY | ERIC GILL WITH 11 PICTURES BY | DENIS TEGETMEIER. PRINTED | BY HAGUE & GILL LTD, HIGH | WYCOMBE, IT IS PUBLISHED FOR | THEM BY J. M. DENT & SONS | LIMITED AT TWO SHILLINGS NET All edges cut.
DATE OF PUBLICATION: 1938.
PRICE: 2s.
REVIEWS: *Glasgow Herald*, 18 August 1938. By F. MacM., *The Irish Press*, 20 September 1938. By E. C., *Literary Guide*, November 1938. *The Times*, 24 December 1938.

38 TWENTY-FIVE NUDES
TITLE-PAGE: TWENTY-FIVE NUDES | ENGRAVED BY ERIC GILL | WITH AN INTRODUCTION | LONDON: | J. M. DENT & SONS LTD | FOR HAGUE & GILL LTD
SIZE: $8\frac{3}{4} \times 5\frac{1}{2}$.   COLLATION: Eight unsigned gatherings of four leaves.
PAGINATION AND CONTENTS: Pp. 64; (no pagination); [1] [2] blank; [3] [4] title-page, verso imprint worded: PRINTED & MADE IN GREAT BRITAIN BY | HAGUE & GILL LTD, HIGH WYCOMBE | AND PUBLISHED FOR THEM BY | J. M. DENT & SONS LTD, ALDINE HOUSE | BEDFORD

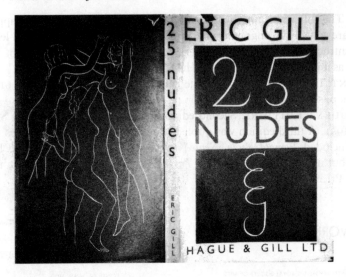

[38. Dust
Jacket]

STREET, LONDON, W.C. 1938; [5]–[8] Introduction 'signed' E.G. 12TH
SEPTEMBER 1938; [9] [10] blank; [11] [12] half-title reproduced: 25 (P969)
NUDES (P970) E G (P971), the letters printed in red, reading downwards, and
the whole superimposed on a drawing of three nude female figures (P968),
verso blank; [13]–[63] illustrations; [64] blank. Printed from 12 pt. *Joanna.*
ILLUSTRATIONS: In addition to the four wood-engravings described above,
there are a decorated initial letter '*I*' (P974) and twenty-six white line
wood-engravings. These full-page illustrations are printed on one side of the
page only and are placed in the following order: (P936) p. 13, (P938) p. 15,
(P942) p. 17, (P939) p. 19, (P941) p. 21, (P945) p. 23, (P937) p. 25, (P940) p.
27, (P958) p. 29, (P944) p. 31, (P946) p. 33, (P950) p. 35, (P948) p. 37, (P952)
p. 39, (P949) p. 41, (P947) p. 43, (P943) p. 45, (P953) p. 47, (P957) p. 49,
(P959) p. 51, (P960) p. 53, (P954) p. 55, (P955) p. 57, (P961) p. 59, (P962)
p. 61, (P963) p. 63.
BINDING: Red cloth; facsimile of Eric Gill's 'signature' *E G* blocked in gold,
on front. Lettered in gilt on spine: 25.NUDES ERIC GILL the figures
and letters placed one beneath the other, reading downwards. All edges cut
and coloured black.
DUST JACKET: Cream paper printed in red. The nudes (P968) also on the
half-title are reproduced on the back in white line on a red background.
Reproduced.
DATE OF PUBLICATION: 20 October 1938. MS. dated 5 June 1938.
PRICE: 6s.
REVIEWS: *The Times,* 24 December 1938. By C. R. C., *Connoisseur,* March
1939.

NOTE: The following note by the publishers appears inside front wrapper: 'There are actually 26 engravings by Eric Gill (27 if you count the initial letter to the introduction) in this book. The 26th does not belie the title of "25 Nudes" as it is simply an engraving of hands thrown in for good measure.'

VARIANT: In the GL copy the image is upside-down on p. 25 and (P961) is found on p. 53 while (P960) is found on p. 59.

SUBSEQUENT EDITIONS: Second edition published by J. M. Dent & Sons Ltd in 1951. A third edition was published in 1988 by Cassell Publishers Ltd which included *Female Nude, Seated* (P951) originally drawn for the first edition but discarded, but excluded *Three Hands* (P963) included in the first edition. Price £8.95.

WORK AND CULTURE

A LECTURE

GIVEN BEFORE THE ROYAL SOCIETY OF ARTS

LONDON, APRIL 1938

BY ERIC GILL

PUBLISHED BY JOHN STEVENS
29 THAMES STREET, NEWPORT,
RHODE ISLAND. MDCCCCXXXVIII

[39]

WORK AND CULTURE

A LECTURE

GIVEN BEFORE THE ROYAL SOCIETY OF ARTS

LONDON, APRIL 1938

BY ERIC GILL

PUBLISHED BY JOHN STEVENS
29 THAMES STREET, NEWPORT,
RHODE ISLAND. MDCCCCXXXXIV

[39. Second edition]

39 WORK AND CULTURE

TITLE-PAGE: Reproduced.

SIZE: $9 \times 6\frac{1}{4}$.   COLLATION: One unsigned gathering of nine leaves.

PAGINATION AND CONTENTS: Pp. vi + 30; [i] [ii] blank; [iii] [iv] title-page, verso publisher's note; [v] [vi] illustration, verso blank; 1–25 text; [26] blank; [27] [28] colophon worded: FOUR HUNDRED COPIES OF THIS BOOK | WERE PRINTED BY | THE WARD PRINTING COMPANY | NEWPORT | RHODE ISLAND, verso blank; [29] [30] blank.

ILLUSTRATION: There is one illustration, the wood-engraving *The Leisure State* (P850), placed on p. [v] and thus underlined: *Machinery releases the worker* | *for 'Higher Things'* | *Contemplation while you work.*

BINDING: Orange paper wrappers, stapled; printed on front in black, exactly as on title-page. Top and bottom edges cut, fore-edges uncut.
DATE OF PUBLICATION: 1938.
PRICE: 50 cents.
PRINTING: 400 copies.
NOTES: This is No. 2 of *John Stevens Pamphlets (Second Series)* and a reprint, with minor emendations, of the lecture given to the Royal Society of Arts, London, 27 April 1938 (cf. no. 217). It provoked a spirited correspondence in *The Examiner* (Bethlehem, Conn.) (cf. no. 546). See also Vol. II, no. 4, Autumn 1939 of *The Examiner* for E. G.'s reply (pp. 399–402) reprinted in *Letters of Eric Gill* under no. 305. MS. dated 26 July 1939.
SECOND EDITION: A second edition of 400 copies was printed by Ward in 1944. It is similar to the first edition in appearance. The date has been changed and the publisher's device has been redrawn on the title-page and front wrapper. Reproduced. The illustration on p. [v] is *The Madonna and Child with an Angel: Madonna knitting* (P60). In the colophon there is a rule under the text and the wording SECOND PRINTING.
SUBSEQUENT EDITION: A third edition of 1000 copies was printed in March 1949 in buff paper wrappers.

1939

40 SOCIAL JUSTICE & THE STATIONS OF THE CROSS
TITLE-PAGE: Reproduced. Shows w-e. *The Way of the Cross* (P985).
SIZE: $6\frac{1}{2} \times 4\frac{1}{8}$.   COLLATION: [a]², b–d⁴.
PAGINATION AND CONTENTS: Pp. iv + 24; [i] [ii] half-title worded: SOCIAL JUSTICE & THE STATIONS | OF THE CROSS, verso a note worded: THE ILLUSTRATION ON THE | TITLE-PAGE IS ENGRAVED | ON WOOD BY THE AUTHOR; [iii] [iv] title-page, verso printers' imprint worded: PRINTED & MADE IN GREAT BRITAIN BY | HAGUE & GILL LTD, HIGH WYCOMBE | FOR JAMES CLARKE & CO LTD | 5 WARDROBE PLACE, LONDON E C 4 | FIRST PUBLISHED IN 1939; 1–21 text; [22]–[24] blank. Printed from 11 pt. *Joanna*.
ILLUSTRATIONS: None, save for that on the title-page reproduced.
BINDING: Green paper boards, lettered and with wood-engraving on the front in blue exactly as on the title-page except for the substitution of ONE SHILLING NET for MCMXXXIX. Issued in a cellophane wrapper. All edges cut.
DATE OF PUBLICATION: 1939.
PRICE: 1s.
REVIEW: *Catholic Herald*, 19 May 1939.

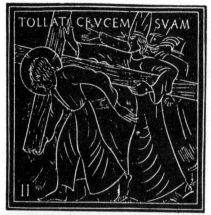

SOCIAL JUSTICE & THE STATIONS OF THE CROSS, BY

ERIC GILL, T.O.S.D.

LONDON: JAMES CLARKE & CO LTD   MCMXXXIX

[40]

ℭhe Stations of the Cross

Some Meditations on their Social Aspects

BY ERIC GILL, T.O.S.D.

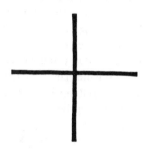

The Sower Press
UNION VILLAGE, NEW JERSEY
1944

[40. American edition]

AMERICAN EDITIONS
TITLE-PAGE: Reproduced.
SIZE: $7\frac{3}{4} \times 5\frac{3}{8}$.
COLLATION: One unsigned gathering of ten leaves, wove paper.
PAGINATION AND CONTENTS: Pp. 20; (no pagination); [1] [2] blank, verso frontispiece w-e. *Self-portrait* (P497); [3] [4] title-page, verso imprint worded: COPYRIGHT 1944—THE SOWER PRESS | PRINTED IN THE U.S.A.; [5]–[17] text; [18] [20] blank.
ILLUSTRATIONS: None, save for the frontispiece described above.
BINDING: Dusty pink paper wrappers, sewn; with the Cross, as used on the title-page, printed on front in red. This edition may also be found printed on laid paper in bright yellow wrappers.
DATE OF PUBLICATION: 1944.
PRICE: n.p.
SUBSEQUENT EDITION: There is also a small paper edition (white paper wrappers, sewn) printed by The Collins Press, Wilkes-Barre, Pa. and sold by *The Catholic Worker*, Easton, Pa. This sixteen-page booklet is entitled *Stations of the Cross by Eric Gill*.

41 SACRED AND SECULAR IN ART AND INDUSTRY

TITLE-PAGE: Reproduced.

SIZE: $9 \times 6\frac{1}{4}$.   COLLATION: One unsigned gathering of twenty leaves.

PAGINATION AND CONTENTS: Pp. iv + 36; [i] [ii] blank; [iii] [iv] title-page, verso publisher's note; [1] illustration; [2] Thesis; 3–5 Introduction; 6–31 text; [32] blank; [33] [34] colophon worded: FOUR HUNDRED COPIES OF THIS BOOK | WERE PRINTED BY | THE WARD PRINTING COMPANY | NEWPORT | RHODE ISLAND, verso blank; [35] [36] blank.

ILLUSTRATIONS: There is one illustration, the wood-engraving *David and Goliath* (P982), placed on p. [1] and underlined by a quotation from the *First Book of Samuel*.

BINDING: Green paper wrappers, stapled; printed on front in black exactly as on title-page. Top and bottom edges cut, fore-edges uncut.

DATE OF PUBLICATION: 1939.

PRICE: 50 cents.

PRINTING: 400 copies.

NOTES: This is one of the *John Stevens Pamphlets*. This lecture, with minor emendations by the author, was originally given before the Royal Institution, London, 4 February 1939. It was reprinted under the title *Sacred & Secular in Modern Industry*, in *Sacred & Secular &c.* (1940) (no. 45), and in *Last Essays* (1942) (no. 50). Extract from a letter to Graham Carey, Cambridge, Mass., from the author, dated 11 April 1939: 'I am extremely glad that you & Mr Benson approve of & wish to publish the Secular & Sacred lecture. I am truly honoured by what you say & quite agree with your suggestion to change the title to SECULAR & SACRED IN INDUSTRY & ART, though I think it would run better off the tongue if you said SACRED & SECULAR IN ART & INDUSTRY. I put it the other way round merely to temper the wind to the shorn goats at the Royal Institution.'

SECOND EDITION: A second edition was printed in 1949. It is similar to the first edition in appearance. The wrappers are blue-green and the title-page and front wrapper lettering is slightly thinner. The colophon reads: SECOND EDITION | ONE THOUSAND COPIES PRINTED | MARCH 1949

42 SOCIAL PRINCIPLES & DIRECTIONS

[Compiled by Eric Gill]

TITLE-PAGE: The title-page reproduced is of the (second) edition (see below). The first edition did not have the w-e *The Pelican and her young* (P987); the line 'Compiled by Eric Gill, T.O.S.D.' was ranged left under 'gestions', and the date was MCMXXXIX.

SIZE: $9 \times 5\frac{3}{4}$.   COLLATION: One unsigned gathering of sixteen leaves.

PAGINATION AND CONTENTS: Pp. 32; [1] [2] blank; [3] [4] title-page,

SACRED AND SECULAR IN ART AND INDUSTRY

A LECTURE

GIVEN BEFORE THE ROYAL INSTITUTION

LONDON, FEBRUARY 1939

BY ERIC GILL

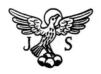

PUBLISHED BY JOHN STEVENS
29 THAMES STREET, NEWPORT,
RHODE ISLAND. MDCCCCXXXIX

[41]

SOCIAL PRINCIPLES & DIRECTIONS
extracted from the three Papal Encyclicals
RERUM NOVARUM
QUADRAGESIMO ANNO
DIVINI REDEMPTORIS
arranged according to subject matter, giving
all positive statements of doctrine, and sug-
gestions for a programme of social reform.
Compiled by Eric Gill, T. O. S. D.

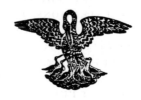

PRINTED BY HAGUE GILL & DAVEY
HIGH WYCOMBE   MCMXL

[42]

verso blank; 5 [6] Preface 'signed' E. G.; 7–30 text; [31] [32] blank. Printed from 12 pt. *Perpetua*.

ILLUSTRATIONS: None.

BINDING: Grey paper wrappers, stapled; printed on front in black: SOCIAL PRINCIPLES | & DIRECTIONS | and, at foot: COMPILED FROM THE PAPAL ENCYCLICALS All edges cut.

DATE OF PUBLICATION: 1939.

PRICE: n.p. [6*d*.]

NOTE: C L C has a proof copy measuring $7\frac{5}{8} \times 5\frac{1}{8}$.

SUBSEQUENT EDITIONS: This pamphlet was revised and reprinted in 1940. Size: $7\frac{3}{4} \times 5$. In this printing the device *The pelican and her young* (P987), which is one of the last wood-engravings Eric Gill executed, appears on the title-page. Reproduced. The wrappers are brown paper printed on front as in the earlier printing but in blue. On the back is printed: COPIES OF THIS PAMPHLET MAY BE OBTAINED FROM | ERIC GILL, PIGOTTS, HIGH WYCOMBE, BUCKS | PRICE 6*d*., POSTAGE EXTRA

VARIANT: Both the C L C and G L copies are in grey wrappers and are printed in black. On the back of the G L copy the last line reads: PRICE 6d., BY POST $6\frac{1}{2}$d

63

THE BOND OF PEACE

I

THE HUMAN PERSON
AND SOCIETY
BY ERIC GILL

THE PEACE PLEDGE UNION
DICK SHEPPARD HOUSE
ENDSLEIGH STREET
LONDON

[43]

1940

43 THE HUMAN PERSON AND SOCIETY

TITLE-PAGE: Reproduced.

Size: $8\frac{1}{2} \times 5\frac{1}{2}$.   COLLATION: One unsigned gathering of twelve leaves.

PAGINATION AND CONTENTS: Pp. 24; [1] [2] title-page, verso printers' imprint worded: PRINTED BY | HAGUE GILL & DAVEY, HIGH WYCOMBE | AND PUBLISHED BY | THE PEACE PLEDGE UNION | DICK SHEPPARD HOUSE | ENDSLEIGH STREET, LONDON, W.C. 1 | FIRST PUBLISHED 1940 | and, at foot: PRINTED AND MADE IN GREAT BRITAIN; [3] [4] the aims of The Peace Pledge Union, verso blank; 5–23 text; [24] blank. Printed from 13 pt. *Perpetua*.

ILLUSTRATIONS: None.

BINDING: Blue paper wrappers, stapled; printed on front: THE BOND OF PEACE | [*long rule*] | THE | HUMAN | PERSON | AND | SOCIETY | [*long rule*] | ERIC GILL | [*long rule*] | THE PEACE PLEDGE UNION | DICK SHEPPARD HOUSE | ENDSLEIGH STREET | LONDON, W.C. 1 3*d*. On the back is information about and a list of three other titles in The Bond of Peace series.

DATE OF PUBLICATION: 1940. MS. dated 21–4 December 1939.

PRICE: 3*d*.

REVIEWS: *Adelphi*, March 1940. *Friend*, 22 March 1940.

NOTE: This lecture was reprinted in *In A Strange Land* (1944) (no. 51), American edition *It All Goes Together* (1944) (no. 52).

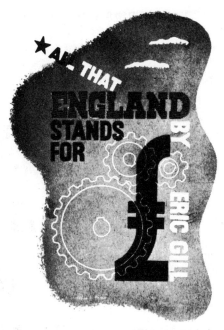

ONE PENNY   [44]

44 ALL THAT ENGLAND STANDS FOR

COVER-TITLE: Reproduced. The cover design printed in blue and black, symbolizing money and the machine, was the work of Clive Latimer.

SIZE: 8 × 5.   COLLATION: One unsigned gathering of four leaves.

PAGINATION AND CONTENTS: This pamphlet comprises five unnumbered pages. Printed in blue and black it bears the following imprint at foot of p. [5]: DESIGNED BY CLIVE LATIMER FOR THE PEACE PLEDGE UNION, DICK | SHEPPARD HOUSE, ENDSLEIGH STREET, LONDON, W.C. I, AND PRINTED | BY UNWIN BROTHERS LTD., LONDON AND WOKING.

ILLUSTRATIONS: None.

BINDING: White paper wrappers, stapled. On back are the initials PPU in white on a blue circular background.

DATE OF PUBLICATION: [n.d.] MS. dated 5 January 1940.

PRICE: 1d.

SUBSEQUENT EDITIONS: Hague Gill & Davey printed an edition of this title but as a 4-page single-fold, also undated but with no cover wrapper. The types are Gill Sans titling and Joanna text. Caption title: ALL THAT ENGLAND | STANDS FOR | BY ERIC GILL. HRC has a copy measuring $8\frac{3}{4} \times 5\frac{1}{8}$. The imprint at the bottom of p. [4] reads: PRINTED BY HAGUE GILL & DAVEY, HIGH WYCOMBE. GL and HRC also have copies measuring $8\frac{3}{4} \times 4\frac{7}{8}$ with the

65

fuller imprint: PUBLISHED BY THE ACTIVIST GROUP, 15 STANHOPE STREET, MANCHESTER 19, & THE FORWARD │ MOVEMENT, 4 DOUGHTY MEWS, LONDON W.C.1 │ PRINTED BY HAGUE GILL & DAVEY, HIGH WYCOMBE. The HRC copy of this issue has the price 1d stamped in red at the bottom of p. [1].

SACRED & SECULAR &c / by ERIC GILL	ESSAYS BY ERIC GILL
containing	
Sacred & Secular — page 11	**sacred**
Sculpture — 61	**and**
Work & Culture — 85	**secular**
St Teresa of Lisieux — 125	
Mass for the Masses — 143	
Ownership & Industrialism — 157	
and eight illustrations by Denis Tegetmeier	
LONDON / J. M. DENT & SONS LTD FOR HAGUE & GILL LTD / 1940	8 PICTURES BY TEG

[45]   [45. Dust Jacket]

45 SACRED & SECULAR &c
TITLE-PAGE: Reproduced.
SIZE: $7\frac{5}{8} \times 4\frac{3}{4}$.   COLLATION: $[\ ]^4$, $[a]b–m^8$.
PAGINATION AND CONTENTS: Pp. 200; [1]–[3] blank; [4] frontispiece; [5] [6] title-page, verso printers' imprint worded: PRINTED & MADE IN GREAT BRITAIN BY │ HAGUE GILL & DAVEY, HIGH WYCOMBE │ FOR HAGUE & GILL LTD │ BEDFORD STREET, LONDON, W.C.2 │ FIRST PUBLISHED 1940; [7] list of illustrations; [8] author's acknowledgements 'signed' and dated *EG 14.4.39*; [9] blank; [10] illustration; 11–[198] text; [199] [200] tail-piece, verso blank. Printed from 12 pt. *Joanna*.
ILLUSTRATIONS: There are seven full-page illustrations and a tail-piece from line-drawings by Denis Tegetmeier underlined and placed as described on p. [7].

BINDING: Red cloth, lettered on spine in silver, reading downwards: SACRED & SECULAR BY ERIC GILL All edges cut.

DUST JACKET: Reproduced. Grey paper printed in red. On back is an advertisement for *Work and Property* (no. 33).

DATE OF PUBLICATION: April 1940.

PRICE: 7s. 6d.

REVIEWS: By Rev. A. J. McIver, *The Oscotian*, Vol. 11, no. 1, May 1940. By D. B. Wyndham Lewis, *The Weekly Review*, 2 May 1940. *The Times Literary Supplement*, 11 May 1940. By G. MacE., *Irish Independent*, 28 May 1940. By Peter Thompson, *Catholic Herald*, 31 May 1940. *Public Opinion*, 14 June 1940. *John O'London's Weekly*, 28 June 1940. For correspondence between the author and the writer of the review in *The Oscotian* see the October issue of that journal, pp. 85–8. The two letters from E. G. there printed were reprinted in *Letters of Eric Gill* under no. 339.

NOTES: Two of the above essays, viz. *Work & Culture* and *Sacred & Secular in Modern Industry* (the latter as *Sacred and Secular in Art and Industry*) were published separately as *John Stevens Pamphlets* in 1938 and 1939 respectively (cf. nos. 39 and 41). The essay *Sacred & Secular* was reprinted in a revised and substantially shortened form in *Last Essays* (1942) (no. 50) under the title *Secular and Sacred in Modern Industry*. References to and quotations from this volume were made by Ethel Mannin in *Bread and Roses* (cf. no. 596).

46 CHRISTIANITY AND THE MACHINE AGE

TITLE-PAGE: Reproduced.

SIZE: $7\frac{1}{4} \times 4\frac{7}{8}$.   COLLATION: [A]B–E^8.

PAGINATION AND CONTENTS: Pp. viii + 72; [i] [ii] half-title worded: THE CHRISTIAN NEWS-LETTER BOOKS, NO. 6. [*underlined*] | CHRISTIANITY AND | THE MACHINE AGE | GENERAL EDITOR: | ALEC R. VIDLER, WARDEN OF ST. DEINIOL'S LIBRARY, HAWARDEN, verso General Preface; [iii] [iv] title-page, verso list of books uniform with this one and, at foot, imprint worded: FIRST PUBLISHED 1940 | MADE IN GREAT BRITAIN; v–[vi] Contents, verso blank; vii–[viii] Apology 'signed' and dated: E G JANUARY 29, 1940, verso blank; 1–72 text. Printers' imprint at foot of p. 72 worded: PRINTED AND BOUND IN GREAT BRITAIN BY RICHARD CLAY AND COMPANY LTD., | BUNGAY, SUFFOLK.

ILLUSTRATIONS: None.

BINDING: Cream paper boards; printed on front in blue with reversed lettering: CHRISTIAN NEWS-LETTER BOOKS | CHRISTIANITY | AND THE | MACHINE AGE | ERIC | GILL Lettered on spine, in blue, reading upwards: CHRISTIANITY AND THE MACHINE AGE All edges cut.

CHRISTIANITY AND
THE MACHINE AGE

BY
ERIC GILL

LONDON
THE SHELDON PRESS
NORTHUMBERLAND AVENUE, W.C.2
NEW YORK : THE MACMILLAN COMPANY

[46]

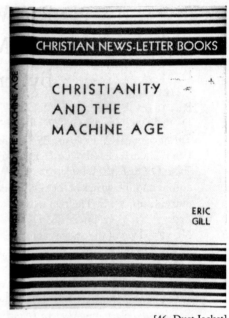

[46. Dust Jacket]

DUST JACKET: Reproduced. Cream paper printed in blue. Wording and design identical to binding. On back the words Sheldon Press are printed in blue at the bottom.
DATE OF PUBLICATION: 1940. MS. dated 22 January 1940.
PRICE: 1s. 6d.
REVIEW: *Church Times*, September 1940.
AMERICAN EDITION: This book was published in New York by The Macmillan Company, 1940.

47 ON SOCIAL EQUALITY

A pamphlet of a single sheet ($10\frac{3}{4} \times 8$ in.) being a statement specially written by Eric Gill for The Activist Group and published by them from 15 Stanhope Street, Levenshulme, Manchester. MS. dated 6 August 1940.

48 DRAWINGS FROM LIFE

TITLE-PAGE: Reproduced. Shows w-e. *S. Thomas' hands* (P889).
SIZE: $8\frac{3}{4} \times 5\frac{1}{2}$.   COLLATION: [Unsigned: 1^4, $2-6^8$, 7^4.]
PAGINATION AND CONTENTS: Pp. xxiii + 73; [i] [ii] half-title worded: DRAWINGS FROM LIFE, verso blank; [iii] [iv] title-page, verso printers'

DRAWINGS
FROM LIFE
by Eric Gill

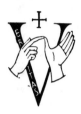

London : Hague & Gill Ltd   [48]

imprint worded: PRINTED AND MADE IN GREAT BRITAIN | BY HAGUE
GILL & DAVEY, HIGH WYCOMBE | AND KIMBLE & BRADFORD | FOR
HAGUE & GILL LTD | AND PUBLISHED BY THEM | AT 10–12 BEDFORD
STREET, LONDON W.C. 2 | FIRST PUBLISHED 1940; [v] [vi] half-title:
Introduction, verso blank; [vii]–[xxi] Introduction, paged i–xv; [xxii] blank;
[xxiii] half-title: DRAWINGS FROM LIFE; 1–[72] the Drawings; [73] blank.
Printed from 12 pt. *Joanna*.

ILLUSTRATIONS: There are thirty-six full-page reproductions of drawings
from life of the nude female figure. These are reproduced on unnumbered
pages facing those which are numbered 1 to 36 respectively.

BINDING: Dark violet-blue cloth; silver blocked on front with the author's
device: *S. Thomas' hands* (P889), lettered on spine in *Gill Sans-Serif* in silver,
reading downwards: DRAWINGS FROM LIFE ERIC GILL
All edges cut.

DUST JACKET: Blue paper printed in red. GL has a preliminary proof copy
on brown paper printed in blue and rose. Spine reads downwards: ERIC
GILL: DRAWINGS FROM LIFE

DATE OF PUBLICATION: 5 December 1940. MS. dated 5–16 July 1939.

PRICE: 7s. 6d.

REVIEWS: By A. M. A., *Liverpool Daily Post*, 15 January 1941. By the Rev.
Ivo Thomas, O.P., *Blackfriars*, February 1941.

49 AUTOBIOGRAPHY

TITLE-PAGE: Reproduced.

SIZE: $7\frac{7}{8} \times 5\frac{1}{4}$.　　COLLATION: [A]B–S⁸.

PAGINATION AND CONTENTS: Pp. ii + 286; [i] [ii] blank; [1] [2] half-title worded: AUTOBIOGRAPHY, verso list of books by the same author; [3] [4] title-page, verso: FIRST PUBLISHED 1940 | JONATHAN CAPE LTD. 30 BEDFORD SQUARE, LONDON | AND 91 WELLINGTON STREET WEST, TORONTO | and, at foot, printers' imprint worded: PRINTED IN GREAT BRITAIN IN THE CITY OF OXFORD | AT THE ALDEN PRESS | PAPER BY SPALDING & HODGE LTD. | BOUND BY A. W. BAIN & CO. LTD.; 5 Contents; 6 Illustrations; 7–9 Preface; [10] blank; [11] [12] dedication worded: TO | M.E.G. | AND | E.P.J. AND G., verso blank; [13] [14] half-title worded: AUTOBIOGRAPHY, verso blank; 15–283 text; [284]–[286] blank. Printed from 12 pt. *Perpetua*.

ILLUSTRATIONS: There are eight full-page illustrations, printed separately:
　Eric Gill, Self Portrait (1927). From a drawing, frontispiece.
　Mary Ethel Gill (1940). From a drawing, facing p. 90.
　Incised Alphabet (Hopton-wood stone) 1932. From a photograph, facing
　　p. 136.
　Elizabeth, Petra and Joanna Gill (1914) Gordian Gill (1920). From a
　　drawing, facing p. 172.
　The Engraver (1928). From a photograph by Howard Coster, facing p. 194.
　Father O'Connor (The Very Rev. Mgr. John O'Connor) 1929. From a
　　drawing, facing p. 208.
　The Deposition (Black Hopton-wood stone) 1925. From a photograph by
　　Howard Coster, facing p. 220.
　Bas Relief for the League of Nations Palace at Geneva (1938). From a
　　photograph by Howard Coster, facing p. 248.
There are, in addition, sketch-maps of Chichester and a part of Brighton, drawn by Denis Tegetmeier and printed on p. [80].

BINDING: Brick red cloth; lettered on spine in gilt: AUTO- | BIOGRAPHY [*line device*] | ERIC GILL | and, at foot the publishers' device blocked in gold. Top and fore-edges cut, the former coloured red to match the casing, bottom edges uncut.

BINDING VARIANT: The colour of the cloth varied considerably even in the first edition of this book as well as in subsequent impressions. GL copy is bound in coarse blue buckram.

DUST JACKET: Cream paper printed in red and black.

DATE OF PUBLICATION: 20 December 1940. MS. dated 28 February–1 June 1940.

PRICE: 12s. 6d.

REVIEWS: By Colin Summerford, *The Observer*, 29 December 1940. By

AUTOBIOGRAPHY
by
ERIC GILL

Quod ore sumpsimus . .

JONATHAN CAPE
THIRTY BEDFORD SQUARE
LONDON
1940

[49]

AUTOBIOGRAPHY
by
ERIC GILL

Quod ore sumpsimus . . .

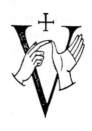

JONATHAN CAPE
THIRTY BEDFORD SQUARE
LONDON
1940

[49. Second impression]

Hugh Walpole, *Book Society News*, January 1941. By Edmund Seagrave, *Current Literature*, January 1941. *The Times Literary Supplement*, 4 January 1941. By Graham Greene, *The Spectator*, 10 January 1941 (Reprinted in *The Lost Childhood and Other Essays*, London: Eyre & Spottiswoode, 1951, pp. 132–4). By Eric Newton, *The Sunday Times*, 12 January 1941. By H. I'A. F[ausset], *The Manchester Guardian*, 17 January 1941. *The Times*, 18 January 1941. By 'Viator', *Blackfriars*, February 1941. By Clifford Bax, *John O'London's Weekly*, 7 February 1941. *The Church Times*, 14 February 1941. *Naval Warrant Officers' Journal*, March 1941. By Ralph Velarde, *The Beda Review*, March 1941. By Richard Church, *The New Statesman and Nation*, 22 March 1941. By Dom Alphege Shebbeare, *Downside Review*, April 1941. *The Sydney Morning Herald*, 5 April 1941. *The Guardian*, 18 April 1941: *Staples Digest*, December 1942 (cf. no. 581).

LATER IMPRESSIONS: Second impression, January 1941. Third impression, February 1941. Fourth impression, March 1941. Fifth impression, August 1941. Sixth impression, December 1941. Seventh impression, September 1942. Eighth impression, October 1943. Ninth impression, April 1944. Tenth impression, May 1944. Eleventh impression, September 1945. Twelfth impression, August 1947.

71

In the second and subsequent impressions the author's device: *S. Thomas'* *hands* (P889) was substituted for the publishers' device (see Illustration, Plate no. 49 Second Impression) the latter, in a smaller form, being transferred to p. [4] below the *Statement of Impressions*. A later dust jacket has excerpts from Hugh Walpole's review in *Book Society News* and a review in the *Nottingham Journal*.

An edition, in smaller format and without illustrations, was published by The Right Book Club, London, in 1944. Price 2s. 6d.

NOTE: Gill's remarks about Ananda Coomaraswamy appear on the verso of the cover of *Ananda Coomaraswamy – A New Planet in my Ken* by S. Durai Raja Singam, Kuala Lumpur: S. Lazar & Sons for S. Durai Raja Singam, [1963]. There is also a photo of Gill with the opening words of Gill's remarks, 'There was one person. . . .'

ADVANCE PROOF COPY: A small number of copies were issued. GL copy is in blue paper wrappers, lettered on front in gilt: AUTOBIOGRAPHY | ERIC GILL | Cape's publisher's device | and at the bottom: DUPLICATE PROOF FOR RETENTION | DOES NOT CONTAIN PROOF READER'S MARKS. The spine is printed in black with AUTOBIOGRAPHY reading upwards. On the lower back is THE ALDEN PRESS (OXFORD) LTD. | OXFORD lettered in gilt. Lacking are the blanks, the illustrations, the frontispiece, and the preface. No date on title-page. The contents page only lists dummy page numbers. Only one title, *Clothes*, is listed on the verso of the half-title. A half-title for an index follows the text.

VARIANTS: GL has an advance trial copy bound in shiny dark blue cloth crudely lettered in gold across the spine: AUTOBIO- | GRAPHY | ERIC GILL | CAPE Lacks blanks, half-title and frontispiece. The edges are uncoloured.

AMERICAN EDITION: An edition was published by The Devin-Adair Company, New York in 1941. ERIC GILL | AUTOBIOGRAPHY | QUOD ORE SUMPSIMUS . . . | [w-e. *S. Thomas' hands* (P889)] NEW YORK: THE DEVIN-ADAIR COMPANY: MCMXLI

SIZE: $8\frac{1}{2} \times 5\frac{1}{2}$.   COLLATION: [Unsigned: 1–20⁸, 21⁴, 22⁸.]

PAGINATION AND CONTENTS: Pp. xvi + 328; [i] [ii] half-title worded: ERIC GILL | AUTOBIOGRAPHY, verso list of books by the same author; [Frontispiece—printed separately]; [iii] [iv] title-page, verso publishers' imprint, at foot: COPYRIGHT, 1941, BY | THE DEVIN-ADAIR COMPANY | PRINTED IN THE UNITED STATES OF AMERICA; [v] [vi] Dedication worded: TO | M.E.G. | AND | E.P.J. AND G., verso blank; [vii] [viii] Contents, verso blank; ix–xii Introduction by Beatrice Warde; xiii–xv Author's Preface; [xvi] publishers' acknowledgements; [1] [2] half-title worded: ERIC GILL | AUTOBIOGRAPHY; 3–300 text; [301] [302] half-title to illustrations, verso blank; [303]–[327] illustrations; [328] statement by the publishers concerning the typography of this book.

ILLUSTRATIONS: There are thirty-four, mainly from wood-engravings, reproduced by the Sheetfed Intaglio Gravure process. The titles and numbers accorded to the wood and other engravings in the subjoined list are those accorded to them in the 'Cleverdon' chronological list. These, and other descriptive matter, are placed within square brackets. All the illustrations, with the exception of the tail-pieces on pp. [300] and [328], are printed separately on twenty-six unnumbered pages:

Self-Portrait [w-e. (P497)], frontispiece.

Palm Sunday [w-e. (P86) from *God and the Dragon*, S. Dominic's Press, 1917], p. [300]

Church at Gorleston designed by Gill [two photographs], p. [303]

Beatrice Warde's Panegyric showing Gill's Monotype Perpetua Capitals, p. [304]

Beatrice Warde [w-e. (P400) *Portrait: Beatrice Warde*], p. [305]

Madonna and Child [wood-cut on pearwood plank for a poster (P154)], p. [306]

Prior of Caldey [copper engraving (P369) *Portrait: The Prior of Caldey*], p. [307]

Autumn Midnight [w-e. (P231) from *Autumn Midnight* by Frances Cornford, The Poetry Bookshop, London, 1923], p. [308]

Joan of Arc [stone carving], p. [309]

Gordian Gill [zinc engraving (P280) *Portrait: Gordian G.*], p. [310]

Christmas Gifts: Daylight and Dawn [w-e.'s (P80 and 81) for a Christmas card and *The Game*, December 1916, respectively], p. [311]

Pencil Portrait, p. [312]

Vases: Steuben Glass [photograph], p. [313]

Resurrection [w-e. (P91) *The Resurrection*; published in *The Game*, Easter 1917], p. [314]

Crucifix [w-e. (P89)], p. [315]

Woman in Bath [w-e. (P194), *Girl in Bath*], p. [316]

Jesus condemned to death [w-e. (P93) *Jesus is condemned to death*; published in *The Way of the Cross*, S. Dominic's Press, 1917], p. [317]

Ascension [w-e. (P140); published in *The Game*, S. Dominic's Press, Ascension 1918], p. [318]

Head of the Redeemer [stone-carving], p. [319]

Clare [w-e. (P196)], p. [320]

Five Christmas Woodcuts [w-e.'s (P72) *Adeste Fideles*, (P73) *Three Kings*, (P76) *Madonna and Child with Chalice*, (P74) *The Manger*, (P75) *Cantet nunc Io*; published in *Adeste Fideles*, S. Dominic's Press, 1916], p. [321]

St. Christopher [w-e.'s (P220) *S. Christopher*, (P221) *A Rose-plant in Jericho*, (P222) *Wave*, (P224) *The Holy Ghost as Dove*, for *Daily Herald Order of Industrial Heroism*], p. [322]

Animals All [wood-cut on pearwood plank (P51)], p. [323]

Tobias and Sara [stone-carving], p. [324]

The Money Changers: War Memorial, Leeds [stone-carving; for Leeds University], p. [325]

Elizabeth, Petra and Joanna Gill (1914) Gordian Gill (1920) [pencil drawings], p. [326]

Mary Ethel Gill (1940) [pencil drawing], p. [327]

Adam and Eve [w-e. (P87); published in *God and the Dragon*, S. Dominic's Press, 1917], p. [328]

BINDING: Blue cloth, gold-blocked on front with facsimile of the author's signature—ERIC G, gold-lettered on spine: ERIC GILL | and, at foot: DEVIN-ADAIR All edges cut.

DATE OF PUBLICATION: 1941.

PRICE: $3.50.

REVIEWS: By Michael Williams, *The Commonweal*, 25 July and 1 August 1941. By K. W., *The New York Times Book Review*, 3 August 1941. By George N. Shuster, President of Hunter College, *New York Herald Tribune*, 3 August 1941. By Ade Bethune, *The Catholic Worker*, September 1941. By Jean Charlot, *The Commonweal*, 12 September 1941. *The New York Herald Tribune Weekly Book Review*, 23 July 1944. *The American Ecclesiastical Review*, December 1944.

NOTE: This book received the Catholic Literary Award (U.S.A.) for 1940.

SECONDARY ISSUES: CLC has a copy of the fifth impression dated 1942 on the title page.

SUBSEQUENT EDITIONS: In 1968 Biblo and Tannen of New York reissued the *Autobiography*.

1942

50 LAST ESSAYS

TITLE-PAGE: Reproduced. Shows w-e. *S. Thomas' hands* (P889)

SIZE: $7\frac{1}{8} \times 4\frac{1}{2}$.   COLLATION: [A]B–F⁸.

PAGINATION AND CONTENTS: Pp. 96; [1] half-title: LAST ESSAYS: ERIC GILL; [2] frontispiece; [3] title-page; [4] Statement of Editions: FIRST PUBLISHED 1942 | JONATHAN CAPE LTD. 30 BEDFORD SQUARE, LONDON | AND 91 WELLINGTON STREET WEST, TORONTO | [Device of the Publishers' Association and statement concerning War Economy Standard] | and, at foot: PRINTED IN GREAT BRITAIN IN THE CITY OF OXFORD | AT THE ALDEN PRESS | PAPER MADE BY JOHN DICKINSON & CO. LTD. | BOUND BY A. W. BAIN & CO. LTD.; 5 Contents: [I] *Art.* [II] *Work.* [III] *Private Property.* [IV] *Education for What?* [V] *Peace and Poverty.* [VI] *Art in Education.* [VII] *Five Hundred Years of Printing.* (Cf. no. 256) [VIII] *The*

LAST ESSAYS

by

Eric Gill

Introduction by
Mary Gill

Jonathan Cape
Thirty Bedford Square, London

[50]

Leisure State. [IX] *Secular and Sacred in Modern Industry*; [6] blank; 7 Introduction by Mary Gill, dated from Pigotts, Hughenden, 17 November 1941; [8] blank; 9–93 text; [94] wood-engraving; [95] [96] blank. Printed from 12 pt. *Perpetua*.

ILLUSTRATIONS: There are four wood-engravings:
Design for Christmas Card for the Peace Pledge Union (P980), Frontispiece.
Chalice and Host (P989), p. 53.
Book-plate for Austin St Barbe Harrison (P887), p. 72.
Design: Hart, for Broomfield Ordination Card (P988), p. [94]

BINDING: Dark blue cloth, the author's device, *S. Thomas' hands* (P889), stamped on front in silver. Lettered on spine, in silver, reading upwards: LAST ESSAYS [*two short rules placed diagonally*] ERIC GILL, and, at foot, publishers' device, an urn between the initials J and C. Top edges cut, others uncut.

DUST JACKET: Cream paper printed in red and black with *S. Thomas' hands* (P889) on front in red.

DATE OF PUBLICATION: October 1942.

PRICE: 5s.

REVIEWS: *The Times Literary Supplement*, 14 November 1942. By H. I'A. F[ausset], *The Manchester Guardian*, 20 November 1942. By Gerard Hopkins, *Sunday Times*, 6 December 1942. By Catherine Andrassy, *Time and Tide*, 5 December 1942. By the Rev. Albert Gille, D.D., Ph.D., *Pax Bulletin*, no. 34, July 1943.

ERRATA: p. 5 Contents. WORK: for '*Nov. 8th*' read '*Nov. 1st*'. ART IN EDUCATION: for '*Unpublished*' read '*Athene (March 1941)*', (where it appeared under its sub-title *Abolish Art and Teach Drawing*). SECULAR AND SACRED IN MODERN INDUSTRY: add '*(1940)*'.

p. 47 For '*Ananda Coomaraswamy*' read '*Thomas A Kempis*'.

p. 63 For 'sale ability' (five lines from the bottom) read 'saleability'.

p. 77 For 'have' (sixth line) read 'has'. For 'without' (seventh line) read 'with'.

AMERICAN EDITION: This volume, and the succeeding one, viz. *In A Strange Land*, were published together as one volume by The Devin-Adair Company, New York, in 1944 under the title *It All Goes Together* (no. 52).

SUBSEQUENT IMPRESSIONS AND EDITION: A second impression (of the English edition) was published in October 1942. Third impression, December 1942. Fourth impression, February 1943. In the latter, the volume has been repaginated, Mary Gill's Introduction transferred to the verso of the Contents list and below the Contents list is an acknowledgements note. This volume and the next succeeding one, viz. *In A Strange Land*, were re-set and published together in one volume as *Essays by Eric Gill* in 1947 (no. 53).

1944

51 IN A STRANGE LAND

TITLE-PAGE: Reproduced. Shows w-e. *S. Thomas' hands* (P889).

SIZE: $7\frac{1}{8} \times 4\frac{1}{2}$.   COLLATION: [A]B–K^8, L^4.

PAGINATION AND CONTENTS: Pp. 168; [3] half-title: IN A STRANGE LAND; [4] frontispiece; [5] title-page; [6] Statement of Editions: FIRST PUBLISHED IN 1944 | JONATHAN CAPE LTD. 30 BEDFORD SQUARE, LONDON | AND 91 WELLINGTON STREET WEST, TORONTO | and, at foot: PRINTED IN GREAT BRITAIN IN THE CITY OF OXFORD | AT THE ALDEN PRESS | PAPER BY SPALDING & HODGE LTD. | BOUND BY A. W. BAIN & CO. LTD.; [7] Contents: 1. *The Lord's Song*. 2. *The Factory System and Christianity*. 3. *A Diary in Ireland*. 4. *Idiocy or Ill-Will*. 5. *David Jones*. 6. *Clothing Without Cloth*. 7. *John Ruskin*. 8. *All Art Is Propaganda*. 9. *It All Goes Together*. 10. *Eating Your Cake*. 11. *Sculpture on Machine-Made Buildings*. 12. *Art in England Now*. 13. *Art and Business*. 14. *The Human Person and Society*; [8] frontispiece; 9–167 text; [168]–[170] blank. The last leaf is pasted down as an end-paper but forms an integral part of the book. Printed from 12 pt. *Perpetua*.

ILLUSTRATIONS: There are six wood-engravings:

Quia Amore Langueo (P916), frontispiece.

[*Easter Picture*] (P661), p. [8]

The Devil's Devices (P40), p. [18]

The Tyranny of Tailors (P719), p. [71]

All seeing and no believing (P919), p. [133]

[*Amorini*] (P394), p. 167.

BINDING: Dark blue cloth, the author's device, *S. Thomas' hands* (P889),

In a
Strange Land
Essays by
ERIC GILL

Jonathan Cape
Thirty Bedford Square, London

[51]

stamped on front in silver. Lettered on spine, in silver, reading upwards: I N A STRANGE LAND [*two short rules placed diagonally*] ERIC GILL, and, at foot, publishers' device, an urn between the initials J and C. Top and fore-edges cut, bottom edges uncut.

DUST JACKET: Cream paper printed in red and black with *S. Thomas' hands* (P889) on front in red.

DATE OF PUBLICATION: June 1944.

PRICE: 6*s*.

REVIEWS: By John Hayward, *Sunday Times*, July 1944. By John Betjeman, *Daily Herald*, 6 July 1944. By George Orwell, *The Observer*, 9 July 1944. *The Listener*, 13 July 1944. *Catholic Herald* (a leading article) 14 July 1944. By Edward Lane, *John O' London's Weekly*, 14 July 1944. By H. I'A. F[ausset], *The Manchester Guardian*, 19 July 1944. *The Times Literary Supplement*, 5 August 1944. By Janet Adam Smith, *Spectator*, 11 August 1944. By Richard Murry, *Adelphi*, January 1945. See also *Considerations on Eric Gill* by Walter Shewring, *The Dublin Review*, October 1944 (no. 595).

NOTES: After this book had been set up it was found that the Preface, written by Mary Gill for *Last Essays*, had been accidentally included. This was removed but the pagination remained unaltered. The book consists of 168 pages only (including the prelims) not 170 as the above pagination would appear to indicate.

AMERICAN EDITION: This volume, and the preceding one, viz. LAST ESSAYS, were published together as one volume by The Devin-Adair Company, New York, in 1944 under the title IT ALL GOES TOGETHER (no. 52).

SUBSEQUENT EDITION: The two volumes LAST ESSAYS and IN A STRANGE LAND, were re-set and published together as one volume by Jonathan Cape as *Essays by Eric Gill* in 1947 (no. 53).

77

52 IT ALL GOES TOGETHER

TITLE-PAGE: Reproduced. Shows w-e. *S. Thomas' hands* (P889).

SIZE: $8\frac{1}{4} \times 5\frac{1}{4}$.   COLLATION: [Unsigned: $1-4^{16}$, 5^{10}, $6-7^{16}$, 8^{14}.]

PAGINATION AND CONTENTS: Pp. xviii + 222; [i] [ii] half-title: IT ALL GOES TOGETHER, verso blank; [iii] [iv] title-page, verso publishers' statement concerning the typography and the illustrations which were made from reproductions, also their acknowledgements and, at foot, imprint: COPYRIGHT, 1944, BY | THE DEVIN-ADAIR COMPANY | PRINTED IN THE UNITED STATES OF AMERICA; v–xiv, Introduction by Ananda K. Coomaraswamy; [xv] Contents: 1. *Idiocy or Ill-Will.* 2. *The Lord's Song.* 3. *The Factory System and Christianity.* 4. *David Jones.* 5. *Clothing Without Cloth.* 6. *John Ruskin.* 7. *All Art Is Propaganda.* 8. *It All Goes Together.* 9. *Eating Your Cake.* 10. *Sculpture on Machine-Made Buildings.* 11. *Art in England Now.* 12. *Art and Business.* 13. *The Human Person and Society.* 14. *Art.* 15. *Work.* 16. *Private Property.* 17. *Education for What?* 18. *Peace and Poverty.* 19. *Art and Education.* 20. *Five Hundred Years of Printing.* 21. *The Leisure State.* 22. *Secular and Sacred in Modern Industry.* 23. *And Who Wants Peace? A list of books by Eric Gill. Illustrations*; [xvi] acknowledgements to publishers and others; xvii Preface by Mary Gill; [xviii] blank; [1] [2] half-title: IT ALL GOES TOGETHER, verso blank; 3–188 text; 189–92 list of books written by Eric Gill; [193] [194] half-title to illustrations, verso blank; [195]–[222] illustrations.

ILLUSTRATIONS: There are forty-five illustrations, mainly from wood-engravings by the author, printed on twenty-eight (unnumbered) pages of art paper:

Swineherd (P337), p. [195]

The Money Bag (P602), p. [196]

The Pardoner's Tale (P649), p. [197]

A Book Plate (P887), p. [198]

The Soul and the Bridegroom (P496), p. [199]

Initial Letters: Cut on Wood (P235), (P242), (P248), (P250), (P249), (P244), (P247), (P239), p. [200]

Initial Letters: Cut on Wood (P241), (P62), (P234), (P246), (P236), (P237), (P233), (P243), p. [201]

Chapter Opening: Golden Cockerel Press edition of The Four Gospels (P780), p. [202] *Chapter Opening: The same* (P795), p. [203]

Border Design and Initial Letters from Chaucer's 'Troilus and Criseyde': Golden Cockerel Press edition: body set in Caslon (P439), p. [204]

Title-page Design: Limited Editions Club (P838), p. [205]

Title-page: The First Use of Gill's Perpetua Type, p. [206]

Perpetua Roman: A Page from 'The Passion of Perpetua and Felicity', p. [207]

Perpetua Italic Type, p. [208]

Border decoration (P463), p. [209]

IT ALL GOES TOGETHER

Selected Essays by

ERIC GILL

NEW YORK : THE DEVIN-ADAIR COMPANY : MCMXLIV

[52]

Incised Alphabet on Hopton-Wood Stone, p. [210]
Rubbing of a Carved Gravestone Inscription, p. [211]
Dress 1920 (P186), p. [212]
Madonna and Child with Angel (P60), p. [213]
The Carrying of the Cross (P352), p. [214]
Wood Engraving (P988), p. [215]
Naked Girl on Grass (P284), p. [216]
The Last Judgment (P107) and *Ship* (P41), p. [217]
Jesus Falls the Third Time (P101), p. [218]
Mother and Child (P286), p. [219]
Spoil Bank Crucifix (P157), p. [220]
Gravestone with Angel (P61), *Chalice and Host* (P65), *Design for League of Nations Union Stamp* (P986), p. [221]
Carved Headboard of an Oak Bed, p. [222]

BINDING: Grey cloth, facsimile of author's signature 'ERIC G' blocked in gold on front. Lettered on spine, in gold, ERIC | GILL | [*stop*] | ESSAYS | and, at foot: DEVIN | ADAIR All edges cut.

DUST JACKET: Reproduced. Cream paper, blue printed background on front and spine with lettering in white. On the back are several excerpts from

79

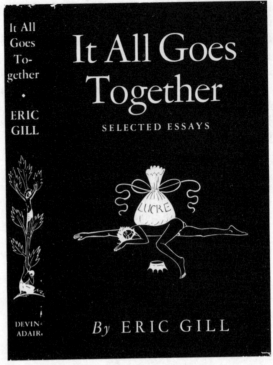

[52. Dust Jacket]

reviews of the *Autobiography* (no. 49) printed in blue. *The Money Bag* (P602) is printed on front, *Our Lord on Tree* (P463) is printed on spine.

DATE OF PUBLICATION: 1944.

PRICE: $3.50.

REVIEWS: *New York Herald Tribune, Weekly Book Review*, 23 July 1944. See also 'Considerations on Eric Gill' by Walter Shewring, *The Dublin Review*, October, 1944 (cf. no. 595) and *The Catholic Art Quarterly* (U.S.A.), Easter, 1945.

NOTE: This volume comprises the two volumes LAST ESSAYS and IN A STRANGE LAND except that *A Diary in Ireland* (from IN A STRANGE LAND) is omitted and *And Who Wants Peace?* (no. 36) is included.

ERRATA: P. [xv] Contents: 19. *Art and Education*. For 'and' read 'in' and for '(1940)' read '(1941)'.

    20. *Five Hundred Years of Printing*. For '(1940)' read '(1942)' (cf. no. 256).

    23. *And Who Wants Peace?* For '(1936)' read '(1938)'.

For 'A N D' in the title of the essay on p. 148 and throughout the running titles for that essay, read 'I N'.

For 'H I S T O R Y' in the title of the essay on p. 163 and throughout the running titles for that essay, read 'I N D U S T R Y'.

SUBSEQUENT EDITIONS: It was reprinted in 1971 by Books for Libraries Press of Freeport, N.Y. as one of their Essay Index Reprint Series. The firm's stock and titles were subsequently purchased by the Arno Press of New York. In 1983 both B F L and Arno were acquired by Ayer Co. Pubs. of Salem, New Hampshire.

ESSAYS

Last Essays and In a Strange Land

by

Eric Gill

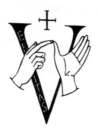

Introduction by
Mary Gill

Jonathan Cape
Thirty Bedford Square, London   [53]

1947

53 ESSAYS BY ERIC GILL

TITLE-PAGE: Reproduced. Shows w-e. *S. Thomas' hands* (P889).

SIZE: $7\frac{1}{2} \times 4\frac{3}{4}$.   COLLATION: $[A]^8$, $B-Q^8$.

PAGINATION AND CONTENTS: Pp. 256; [1] [2] half-title: ESSAYS BY ERIC GILL, verso frontispiece; [3] [4] title-page, verso Statement of Editions and Printers' Imprint: LAST ESSAYS | FIRST PUBLISHED OCTOBER 1942 | SECOND IMPRESSION OCTOBER 1942 | THIRD IMPRESSION DECEMBER

1942 | FOURTH IMPRESSION FEBRUARY 1943 | IN A STRANGE LAND |
FIRST PUBLISHED JUNE 1944 | PUBLISHED IN ONE VOLUME | AS |
ESSAYS BY ERIC GILL | 1947, and, at foot: PRINTED IN GREAT BRITAIN
IN THE CITY OF OXFORD | AT THE ALDEN PRESS | BOUND BY A. W.
BAIN & CO. LTD.; [5] [6] Contents: [as already described in the entries for the
two volumes of which the present volume is composed, cf. nos. 50 and 51],
verso, acknowledgement for leave to reprint these writings; [7] [8] preface by
Mary Gill, verso blank; 9–251 text; [252] illustration; [253]–[256] blank.
Printed from 12 pt. *Perpetua*.

ILLUSTRATIONS: The same ten wood-engravings as were used for the two
volumes referred to above were used to illustrate this volume, though two of
them, viz. nos. P887 and P916, are differently placed.

BINDING: Dark blue cloth, the author's device, *S. Thomas' hands* (P889),
stamped on front in silver. Lettered on spine, in silver: E S S A Y S | [*abstract
ornament*] | E R I C | G I L L | and, at foot, publishers' device, an urn between
the initials J and C. Top and fore-edges cut, bottom edges uncut.

DUST JACKET: White paper printed in red and black. *S. Thomas' hands*
(P889), reduced, printed in black on front.

DATE OF PUBLICATION: April 1947.

PRICE: 8*s*. 6*d*.

REVIEWS: By Charles Morgan, *Sunday Times*, 27 April 1947. *The Times
Literary Supplement* (Leading Article), 19 April 1947. By Richard Church,
New Statesman and Nation, 13 September 1947.

ERRATA: P. [5] Contents: *Five Hundred Years of Printing*, for '(*unpublished*)'
read '*1942*'. Add: '(*1940*)' after *Secular and Sacred in Modern Industry*.

54 LETTERS OF ERIC GILL

TITLE-PAGE: Reproduced. Shows w-e. *S. Thomas' hands* (P889).

SIZE: $8 \times 5\frac{1}{4}$.   COLLATION: [A]⁸, B–GG⁸.

PAGINATION AND CONTENTS: Pp. 480; [1] [2] half-title: LETTERS OF |
ERIC GILL and, at foot, publishers' device: J C and urn within a double
lined circle, verso blank; [3] [4] title-page verso printers' imprint: FIRST
PUBLISHED 1947 and, at foot: PRINTED IN GREAT BRITAIN IN THE
CITY OF OXFORD | AT THE ALDEN PRESS | BOUND BY A. W. BAIN & CO.
LTD., LONDON; 5 Contents and List of Illustrations; 6–7 Correspondents and
Journals addressed; 8–14 Preface; 15–474 text; 475–80 Index. Printed from
12 pt. *Perpetua*.

ILLUSTRATIONS: There are twelve illustrations, printed separately:

Letters to David Jones, frontispiece.
Letter to Gladys Gill, facing p. 17.
Eric Gill. Drawing by William Rothenstein, facing p. 82.

LETTERS OF
ERIC GILL
Edited by
WALTER SHEWRING

JONATHAN CAPE
THIRTY BEDFORD SQUARE
LONDON

[54]

Letter to Dr. Coomaraswamy, facing p. 101.
Eric Gill. Self-portrait (1925), facing p. 172.
Eric Gill. Drawing by Desmond Chute, facing p. 214.
Greek Alphabet: Postcard to Walter Shewring, facing p. 225.
Letter to Peter Gill, facing p. 264.
Postcard to Evan Gill, facing p. 269.
Father Desmond Chute. Drawing by E. G., facing p. 346.
Jerusalem. Drawing by E. G., facing p. 388.
Gorleston Church. Drawing by E. G., facing p. 420.

BINDING: Red cloth, the author's device, *S. Thomas' hands* (P889), blind-stamped on front. Lettered on spine: LETTERS | OF | ERIC | GILL and, at foot, publishers' device as on half-title. Top edges red to match the casing; all edges cut.

DUST JACKET: White paper printed in blue and black. *S. Thomas' hands* (P889), reduced, printed in black on front.

DATE OF PUBLICATION: 26 January 1948 not 1947 as stated on p. [4]

PRICE: 15s.

REVIEWS: By H. I'A. F[ausset], *The Manchester Guardian*, 10 February 1948. *Church Times*, 13 February 1948. By Iris Conlay, *Catholic Herald*, 13 February 1948. *Scotsman*, 19 February 1948. By Douglas Cleverdon, *Sunday Times*, 29 February 1948. *The Times Literary Supplement*, 13 March 1948. By David Jones, *Tablet*, 13 March 1948. By Vivian Ogilvie, *Britain To-Day*, May 1948. By the Rev. Conrad Pepler, O.P., *Blackfriars*, May 1948. By Dr Cecil Gill, *Pax*, Summer 1948. By Graham Greene, *New Statesman and Nation*, 13 March 1948.

83

ADDENDA AND CORRIGENDA:

Page	Letter	
[4]	—	Date of Publication. For '1947' read '1948 [Jan. 26]'.
[6]		Correspondents, etc. For 'Gill, Romney' read 'Gill, Kenneth'.
34	18	Add footnote relating to 'Masters & Servants': '1. "The Highway" Dec. 1910 & Jan. 1911'.
47	27	Insert stops after 'A' (twice) and 'C'.
90	64	Add footnote relating to *Slavery & Freedom*: '2. Reprinted in *Art-Nonsense and Other Essays* (1929)'.
103	69	For 'Romney' read 'Kenneth' and for 'R. C. G.' read 'K. C. G.'.
126	81	For 'write' read 'wrote'.
153	107	Add footnote relating to lecture printed in *The Game*: '1. Reprinted as *Quae ex Veritate et Bono* in *Art-Nonsense* (pp. 65–79) (1929)'.
187	132	Insert 'in' (or possibly 'last') before 'August'.
229	152	Wrong fount in 'well' (first line).
235	159	Insert 'not' between 'there is' and 'and cannot' sixth line from end.
245	169	For 'seem' read 'seems'.
249	175	Add footnote giving title of book reviewed, viz. '*Art-Nonsense and Other Essays* (1929)'.
251	178	For 'cards' read 'carols'.
254	180	Wrong fount in 'interval' (last line).
255	181	Wrong fount in 'very' (second line) and, add to footnote: 'A lime-stick or spatula'.
263	190	For 'Renà' read 'René'.
279	—	Add before Letter 201: 'Insert here Letter 240'.
302	216	Letter 't' of 'truth' inverted (fourth line from top of page).
321	224	Wrong fount 'f' in 'wilfully' (fourth line).
—	226	Add footnote giving title of book reviewed, viz. *Money & Morals*.
340	238	Add footnote giving title of article, viz. *The Necessity of Belief: West Africa and S. Ken.*
344	240	For '1935' read '1933'—transfer to place before Letter 201.
366	257	For 'CHARAADY' read 'CHARLADY'.
372	262	Insert figure '1' in the round brackets on line 2.
374	264	Footnote relating to this letter should be printed below E. G.'s footnote to Letter 265.
387	277	Add footnote: 'Reprinted as *Art in England Now* . . . in *In A Strange Land* (pp. 137–45) and *It All Goes Together*

(pp. 88–95).'

401   289   Substitute a mark of interrogation for a mark of exclamation after '. . . Social Programme.'

440   320   Add footnote relating to the pamphlet (cf. two lines from bottom of page): '1. *The Human Person & Society* (1940).'

475   *Index*   Add to Index: 'Books and writings by E. G.: *Art-Nonsense*, 249.'

478   *Index*   Add to page references to *Gill Sans*: '353.'

ADVANCE PROOF COPY: A small number of copies were issued. GL copy is in light brown wrappers printed in black. Printed on front: THE LETTERS | OF ERIC GILL | Cape's publishers' device | UNCORRECTED PROOF. On the spine, reading upwards: THE LETTERS OF ERIC GILL. On back: THE ALDEN PRESS (OXFORD) LTD | OXFORD. Lacks blanks, frontispiece, illustrations, contents and illustrations page and correspondents pages. Half-title and title-page are arranged differently and begin with THE. After title-page leaf are six blank leaves (12 pages). Preface starts on p. 17 and the index ends on p. 488.

AMERICAN EDITION: This volume was published by The Devin-Adair Company, New York in 1948. The following differences between the two editions may be noted:

TITLE-PAGE: For JONATHAN CAPE | THIRTY BEDFORD SQUARE | LONDON read: NEW YORK | THE DEVIN-ADAIR COMPANY | 1948

SIZE: $7\frac{5}{8} \times 5\frac{1}{4}$.

PAGINATION AND CONTENTS: The English publishers' device at foot of half-title is omitted. The publishers' imprint on verso of title-page reads: FIRST AMERICAN EDITION 1948 | ALL RIGHTS RESERVED. PERMISSION TO REPRINT | MATERIAL FROM THIS BOOK MUST BE OBTAINED | FROM THE DEVIN-ADAIR CO. and, at foot: PRINTED IN GREAT BRITAIN | SET IN GILL'S PERPETUA TYPE.

BINDING: The blind-stamped device *S. Thomas' hands* (P889) is displaced by the author's signature, reproduced in facsimile, in gilt, at foot and the lettering on spine reads: ERIC GILL | LETTERS with, at foot, DEVIN-ADAIR. All edges are uncoloured.

DUST JACKET: Tinted light grey paper printed in red and black. *S. Thomas' hands* (P889), reduced, printed in black on front.

DATE OF PUBLICATION: 1948.

PRICE: $5.00.

REVIEWS: By Ernestine Evans, *New York Herald Tribune, Weekly Book Review*, 28 November 1948. By James E. Walsh, under the title: *Eric Gill's Devotions* (cf. no. 625), *New York Times, Book Review*, 6 March 1949.

ADDENDA AND CORRIGENDA: As for the English edition.

FROM

THE JERUSALEM DIARY

OF

ERIC GILL

LONDON: MCMLIII   [54a]

1953

54a JERUSALEM DIARY

TITLE-PAGE: Reproduced.

SIZE: $5\frac{5}{8} \times 4\frac{1}{4}$.   COLLATION: [Unsigned: 1–7⁴, 8⁶.]

PAGINATION AND CONTENTS: Pp. viii + 60; [i] [ii] half-title: FROM THE
JERUSALEM DIARY | OF ERIC GILL, verso blank; [iii] [iv] title-page, verso
dedication worded: AFFECTIONATELY DEDICATED TO HIS FRIEND |
AUSTEN ST B. HARRISON and, at foot, imprint worded: PRINTED IN
GREAT BRITAIN; [v] note by Mary Gill 'signed' *M.E.G.*, [vi] blank; [vii] note
and list of the illustrations, [viii] blank; 1–59 text; [60] colophon worded: THE
TEXT OF THIS BOOK | IS COMPOSED IN THE 10-POINT SIZE OF |
PILGRIM | A LINOTYPE RECUTTING OF A TYPE FACE | DESIGNED BY
ERIC GILL. | 300 COPIES OF THE BOOK WERE PRODUCED | IN THE
PRINTING OFFICE OF | LINOTYPE & MACHINERY LIMITED LONDON |
THIS IS NO.

ILLUSTRATIONS: There are ten full-page reproductions, printed in collotype, of the carvings made by Eric Gill round the cloisters of the new Palestine
Archaeological Museum, Jerusalem. These are printed separately by Ganymed
Ltd., on Arnold & Foster hand-made paper. The illustrations are in conjugate
pairs folded round ff. 2–3 of each successive gathering beginning with the
third.

from the

Palestine Diary

of

Eric Gill

from the

Palestine Diary

of

Eric Gill

LONDON

THE HARVILL PRESS

1949

HIGH WYCOMBE

HAGUE GILL & DAVEY LTD

1942

BINDING: Ingres grey paper boards lettered on front, near the top: ERIC GILL: JERUSALEM DIARY, light brown cloth spine. All edges cut. Issued in a plain glassine protective wrapper.

DATE OF PUBLICATION: January 1953.

PRICE: n.p. Printed for private distribution by Linotype and Machinery Limited, 21 John Street, London, W.C.1.

PRINTING: 300 numbered copies.

NOTES: Eric Gill was commissioned to carve ten panels symbolizing the civilizations that have most affected the history of Palestine, together with the tympanum over the main entrance of the Palestine Archaeological Museum in Jerusalem (Architect: Austen St B. Harrison), cf. no. 512. These extracts, from the diary he kept from the time he left England until his return, cover the period 10 March to 13 May 1934. The *Pilgrim* type in which the text of this book is set is an adaptation of Eric Gill's *Bunyan* type.

EARLIER EDITION: In 1949 Hague & Gill printed a longer version of the diary excerpts for the Harvill Press. Title-page is reproduced. The text of this version is set in Joanna and Joanna italic and is printed on Arnold hand-made paper. There are 70 pages, the last one unnumbered. In addition to the longer text there are minor textual differences throughout. This edition was apparently never issued although the CLC has a copy bound in yellow buckram, the pages measuring $5\frac{3}{4} \times 4 \times \frac{1}{4}$. GL has a complete set of folded but unsewn sheets, the pages measuring $5\frac{3}{4} \times 4\frac{1}{2}$. Both the CLC and GL copies are without illustrations. G. F. Sims, on the inside of the back cover of his Catalogue 37, states that, 'It was originally planned that René Hague should publish this book at Pigotts, and indeed the type was completely set and some copies printed off on hand-made paper. Delays occurred and cancel title-pages were printed ... dated 1951 and 1952 [with the imprint "High Wycombe | Hague Gill & Davey Ltd" – reproduced]. The text is complete but there are no illustrations ... Unbound ...' Another copy was offered in his Catalogue 38 item 255. The 1952 cancel title measures $6 \times 4\frac{1}{2}$. G. F. Sims is also quoted in *British Modern Press Books A descriptive check list of unrecorded items* by William Ridler. London: Covent Garden Press, 1971: 'Due to a series of misadventures this book was never issued. We purchased the surviving sheets and had them bound by Sangorski in quarter black morocco and pre-war decorated boards. (Gilt & black on light blue.) Only a very small number of this aborted edition survived.'

REVIEW: *Liontype Matrix*, 16 June 1953, p. 6. Illustrations of 'Canaan', 'Egypt', 'Byzantium', 'Islam', 'The Crusaders', five of the carvings E. G. did in Jerusalem. Also illustrated are specimens of Pilgrim.

II

BOOKS, PERIODICALS, &c.
TO WHICH ERIC GILL
WAS A CONTRIBUTING AUTHOR

Numbers 55 – 257*c*

1900

55 CHICHESTER DOORWAYS. *The Building News*, Vol. LXXIX, no. 2399, 28 December 1900, p. 910 with double-spread of illustrations (pp. 920–1) from sketches with the caption 'National Prize Water-colour Sketches of Doorways'.

56 CHICHESTER MARKET CROSS. Two letters to 'The Chichester Observer' April 1901. These letters appear in *Letters of Eric Gill* (no. 54) under nos. 4 and 5.

1906

57 INSCRIPTIONS IN STONE. Appendix B, Chapter XVII of *Writing & Illuminating & Lettering*, by Edward Johnston. (*The Artistic Crafts Series of Technical Handbooks edited by W. R. Lethaby.*) London: John Hogg. 1906. Cf. Fig. 208, *From a Rubbing of a Stone at Oxford* and Plate XXIV, *Inscription cut in Stone* . . . with a note on pp. 486–7. Publication of this series of handbooks was later taken over by Sir Isaac Pitman & Sons, Ltd. MS. dated October 1906.
Note: A German edition was published with the title *Schreibschrift Zierschrift & Angewandte Schrift* translated by Anna Simons. Leipzig: Van Klinkhardt und Bierman, 1910.

1907

58 SOCIETY AND THE ARTS AND CRAFTS. *The Swallow* magazine. January and February 1907.

59 SOCIALISM AND THE ARTS AND CRAFTS. *Fabian News*, Vol. XVII, no. 8, July 1907, pp. 53–4. London: The Fabian Society. The substance of a lecture in continuance of a series on 'Socialism and the Middle Classes', by A. E. R. Gill delivered at Essex Hall, 31 May 1907.

1909

60 THE SOCIETY OF CALLIGRAPHERS. A Memorandum. October 1909.

61 THE FAILURE OF THE ARTS AND CRAFTS MOVEMENT. *The Socialist Review*, December 1909.

1910

62 INSCRIPTIONS. *The Burlington Magazine*, Vol. XVI, no. LXXXIV, March 1910, pp. 318–28. With eleven illustrations from photographs and two diagrams in the text. With an introduction by the editor.

63 A PREFACE TO AN UNWRITTEN BOOK. *The Highway. A Monthly Journal of Education for the People*. Vol. III, no. 25, October 1910, pp. 5–6. London: The Workers' Educational Association. Cf. issue of December 1910, p. 47, for letter from H. M. Goodman criticizing this article and Gill's reply in the issue of February 1911, p. 78. The latter was reprinted in *Letters of Eric Gill* (no. 54) under no. 20.

64 THE ARCHITECT: ECONOMICALLY A NECESSITY–ARTISTICALLY A FAILURE. *Architectural Association Journal*, Vol. XXV, no. 285, November 1910, pp. 316–18. London: The Architectural Association. The substance of a paper delivered to the Camera, Sketch, and Debate Club of the Association, 13 October 1910 with a report of the debate which followed. MS. dated 13 October 1910.

65 MASTERS AND SERVANTS. *The Highway*, Vol. III, no. 26, November 1910.

66 CHURCH AND STATE. *The Highway*, Vol. III, no. 27, December 1910 and no. 28, January 1911. Cf. issue of February 1911, *The Power of Religion* by William Temple (later Archbishop of Canterbury), commenting upon this article (cf. no. 397).

1914

67 VIŚVAKARMĀ. EXAMPLES OF INDIAN ARCHITECTURE, SCULPTURE, PAINTING, HANDICRAFT, CHOSEN BY ANANDA COOMARASWAMY, D.SC. First Series: One Hundred Examples of Indian Sculpture. Part VIII. With an Introduction by Eric Gill and twenty plates. London: Luzac & Co. June 1914.

$10\frac{7}{8} \times 8\frac{7}{8}$ green wrappers. Pp. 3–7. Gill's contribution is called the Preface on p. 3 but is referred to as the Introduction on the wrapper title and title-page. There are two sets of 71, 72 and 73. The first appeared in Part IV and the second in Part VII. The plates in the eight parts are not in order. A binder's note in the eighth part under Editorial Note, p. 31, mentions that 71–3 in Part VII are extra numbers, originally printed by oversight and that they should be bound immediately following Plate C, and that Plate I in Part VIII (Buddha with background) is to replace Plate I in Part I (Buddha without background).

1000 copies were printed, 500 in parts, 500 bound. G L has a bound set of the eight parts with the Introduction/Preface at the beginning and the photographic plates arranged in numerical order, with Plates 71–3 from Part VII following Plate 100. $\frac{1}{2}$ red linen, grey boards, title stamped on spine in gold $10\frac{7}{8} \times 8\frac{3}{4}$. Presentation copy from Gill to Pepler, Christmas 1916. Imprint is as found on Part VIII: Sold by Messrs. Luzac, 46 Great Russell Street, London, W.C.: Otto Harrasowitz, Querstrasse, Leipzig: and Messrs. Taraporevala, Meadows Street, Bombay. 1914.

1916

68 THE SHIP PAINTER'S HANDBOOK. WITH USEFUL IN-FORMATION FOR THE GENERAL PAINTER AND DECORATOR. By George S. Welch, Painter R.N. Third Edition, Revised. Gieve's, The Hard, Portsmouth. $6\frac{1}{2} \times 4$. Pp. xii + 146. Price 3s. Linen boards.

This edition was edited by Eric Gill above whose signature appears the following Note (p. vii) dated from Ditchling Common, Sussex, January 1916: 'In preparing the third edition the text has been revised and corrected throughout (with the exception of Chapter XVI) and many new receipts and directions added. In Chapter II the problems have been improved and made more immediately useful, and new figures have been drawn. Chapter XIII has been almost entirely rewritten. New diagrams have been made, and the subject of lettering, as it applies to sign-writing, has been more completely set out.'

The fifth edition (1936) reprinted in 1945 bears the imprint of Brown, Son & Ferguson, Ltd., Glasgow. Price 4s. 6d. This edition, the preface to which is 'signed' *G. S. W[elch]*, retains the many additions and alterations made for the third edition by Eric Gill, but nowhere mentions the latter's name.

1916–22

69 THE GAME. AN OCCASIONAL MAGAZINE PRINTED AND PUBLISHED AT S. DOMINIC'S PRESS, DITCHLING COMMON, SUSSEX.

'... a history of the Press would be incomplete without a reference to that lively magazine [*The Game*] which began during the first year [1916] of our existence. Edward Johnston, Eric Gill and myself decided to print our views about things in general which we regarded, as all men regard games, of supreme importance. In the strict sense of the word it was not with any idea of propaganda, it was more a corporate letter-writing to others who were willing to play with us. Our first Christmas number was a kind of joint Christmas card in which Johnston wrote by hand ... he did only a sufficient number for the exact needs of our subscribers.' From *The Hand Press*, by H. D. C. Pepler, Ditchling (1934) (no. 500).

THE GAME
AN OCCASIONAL MAGAZINE.

Surgant pueri et ludant I. Reg. 1. 12.

No. I   OCTOBER A.D. 1916   PRICE 6d.

PROLOGUE

IN PRINCIPIO ERAT VERBUM, ET VERBUM ERAT APUD DEUM, ET DEUS ERAT VERBUM. HOC ERAT IN PRINCIPIO APUD DEUM. OMNIA PER IPSUM FACTA SUNT : ET SINE IPSO FACTUM EST NIHIL QUOD FACTUM EST.
ET VERBUM CARO FACTUM EST, ET HABITAVIT IN NOBIS ; ET VIDIMUS GLORIAM EJUS, GLORIAM QUASI UNIGENITI A PATRE PLENUM GRATIÆ ET VERITATIS.

* * *

A man having seen the glory of God must thereafter work for the glory of God, the things which he makes he will make for *the glory of God*.

* * *

There are those who do not believe these things, who manitain that such beliefs are irrelevant to the modern problems of industrialism and social order, and that it is possible for Society to organise itself without agreement   [69]

Average size: $8\frac{1}{4} \times 5\frac{1}{2}$. The first six numbers, comprising Vols. I and II, were priced individually (the price ranged from 6d. to 2s. 6d.); afterwards the annual subscription was 5s. The complete run is from Vol. I, no. 1, October 1916 to Vol. VI, no. 34, January 1923. All edges trimmed. No. 1 was issued in light brown paper wrappers printed on front, in red: THE GAME | [w-e. *Angel with trumpet* (by Philip Hagreen)] | [*long rule*] | PRINTED AND PUBLISHED BY DOUGLAS PEPLER, DITCHLING, SUSSEX.

The following is a list of the written contributions made by Eric Gill (for a list of the wood-engravings he contributed, see no. 263):

(*a*)   THE CONTROL OF INDUSTRY. BEING AN ENQUIRY INTO THE PURPOSE AND ORGANIZATION OF MODERN INDUSTRY FROM A WORKMAN'S POINT OF VIEW.

   Vol. I, no. 1, October 1916, pp. 9–18.

(*b*)   THE DEVIL OF IT.

   Vol. I, no. 1, October 1916, pp. 19–20.

   Vol. II, no. 1, January 1918, pp. 25–6.

   Vol. III, no. 1, Corpus Christi 1919, p. 15.

   Vol. IV, no. 3, March 1921, p. 47 no. 4, April, 1921, pp. 63–4 [paginated '65' in error]; no. 6, June 1921, pp. 95–6.

   Vol. V, no. 26, May 1922, p. 60; no. 27, June 1922, p. 68.

(*c*) THE ENGRAVER. A verse (unsigned).
 Vol. I, no. 2, Christmas 1916, p. 31.

(*d*) SLAVERY & FREEDOM (unsigned).
 Vol. I, no. 3, Easter 1917, pp. 33–5.

(*e*) THE WAY OF IT.
 Vol. II, no. 1, January 1918, pp. 10–15.

(*f*) ESSENTIAL PERFECTION.
 Vol. II, no. 1, January 1918, pp. 21–3.

(*g*) Footnote to letter from Ananda Coomaraswamy.
 Vol. II, no. 1, January 1918, p. 24.

(*h*) Postscript in collaboration with D. P[epler].
 Vol. II, no. 1, January 1918, p. 26.

(*i*) THE FACTORY SYSTEM AND CHRISTIANITY (unsigned).
 Vol. II, no. 3, Advent 1918, pp. 47–54.

(*j*) RAILWAY CONVERSATIONS (unsigned).
 Vol. III, no. 1, Corpus Christi 1919, pp. 9–10.

(*k*) A GRAMMAR OF INDUSTRY. A LECTURE DELIVERED AT GLASGOW, 26 JAN. 1919.
 Vol. III, no. 1, Corpus Christi 1919, pp. 22–32.

(*l*) A DIARY IN IRELAND.
 Vol. III, no. 2, Advent 1919, pp. 33–40; no. 3, Easter 1920, pp. 65–87.

(*m*) A note in BREWING BEER from Cobbett's *Cottage Economy*.
 Vol. III, no. 2, Advent 1919, p. 51.

(*n*) ART AND INDUSTRY.
 Vol. III, no. 2, Advent 1919, pp. 55–8.

(*o*) THE SONG OF SOLOMON AND SUCH-LIKE SONGS (unsigned).
 Vol. IV, no. 2, February 1921, pp. 28–32; no. 3, March 1921, pp. 35–46; no. 5, May 1921, pp. 66–74; no. 7, July 1921, pp. 99–112; no. 8, August 1921, pp. 115–17.

(*p*) NOTE ON DIVORCE (unsigned).
 Vol. IV, no. 4, April 1921, pp. 58–60.

(*q*) A letter in reply to a correspondent.
 Vol. IV, no. 5, May 1921, pp. 74–5.

(*r*) ACTUS SEQUITUR ESSE (unsigned).
 Vol. IV, no. 9, September 1921, 124–8.

(*s*) OF THINGS NECESSARY & UNNECESSARY (unsigned).
 Vol. IV, no. 10, October 1921, pp. 131–66.

(*t*) CUSTARD. (A letter over the nom-de-plume *Philippa McDougall*.)
 Vol. IV, no. 11, November 1921, pp. 142–3.

(*u*) QUAE EX VERITATE BONOQUE (unsigned).
> Vol. V, no. 23, February 1922, pp. 11–20; no. 24, March 1922, pp. 23–32.

(*v*) CAELUM ET TERRA TRANSIBUNT (verses—unsigned).
> Vol. V, no. 24, March 1922, p. 32.

(*w*) IDIOCY OR ILL-WILL. A LECTURE DELIVERED TO THE CATHOLIC STUDENTS CLUB AT READING UNIVERSITY COLLEGE, NOV., 1922 (unsigned).
> Vol. V, no. 31, October 1922, pp. 92–8; no. 33, December 1922, pp. 109–16.

(*x*) IRELAND RE-VISITED (unsigned).
> Vol. V, no. 32, November 1922, pp. 100–6, no. 33, December 1922, pp. 117–18.

Ten of the above essays were subsequently reprinted as follows:

(*a*) *The Control of Industry*. In an abridged form in *The Architectural Review*, April 1926.

(*d*) *Slavery and Freedom*. As *Penny Tract, No. 1* (1917) (cf. no. 2), in *Loquela Mirabilis*, no. 1, The Latin Press (1936) and in *Art-Nonsense* (1929) (cf. no. 18).

(*f*) *Essential Perfection*. As a pamphlet (1918) (cf. no. 4) and in *Art-Nonsense* (1929) (cf. no. 18).

(*i*) *The Factory System and Christianity*. In *In A Strange Land* (1944) (cf. no. 51). American edition *It All Goes Together* (1944) (cf. no. 52).

(*k*) *A Grammar of Industry*. In *Blackfriars* (1926—Vol. VII, no. 70, pp. 31–8) and in *Art-Nonsense* (1929) (cf. no. 18).

(*l*) *A Diary in Ireland*. In *In A Strange Land* (1944) (cf. no. 51).

(*o*) *The Song of Solomon and Such-like Songs*. As a separate book under the title *Songs Without Clothes* (1921) (cf. no. 8) and in *Art-Nonsense* (1929) (cf. no. 18).

(*s*) *Of Things Necessary and Unnecessary*. In *Songs Without Clothes* (1921) (cf. no. 8) and in *Art-Nonsense* (1929) (cf. no. 18).

(*u*) *Quae ex Veritate Bonoque*. As a preface to *Sculpture* (1924) (cf. no. 10) under the title *Quae ex Veritate et Bono* and in *Art-Nonsense* (1929) (cf. no. 18).

(*w*) *Idiocy or Ill-will*. In *In A Strange Land* (1944) (cf. no. 51). American edition *It All Goes Together* (1944) (cf. no. 52). Monotype Corporation printed a broadside for Beatrice Warde using a quote from this essay. $17\frac{1}{2} \times 11$, n.d. 'ART | IS THAT WORK | AND THAT WAY OF WORKING | IN WHICH MAN USES | HIS FREE WILL...'

The Game is no. 11 of S. Dominic's Press publications.

1917

70 SCULPTURE. *The Highway.* June 1917. This essay was reprinted as a pamphlet published by S. Dominic's Press (1918) (no. 5) and, after extensive revision, in book form under the title *Stone-carving*, as the second part of *Sculpture* (1924) (no. 10). It was also reprinted under this title in *The Architectural Review*, April 1926. After further revision it was published in *Art-Nonsense* (1929) (no. 18) as *Stone-carving*. MS. of original essay dated October 1916.

1918

71 THE STATIONS OF THE CROSS. *Westminster Cathedral Chronicle*, Vol. XII, no. 3, March 1918, pp. 50–3. The article appears above the 'signature' E. *Rowton*. With two diagrams. With certain additions and amendments it was reprinted above his own name in *Blackfriars*, Vol. I, no. 5, August 1920, pp. 257–66, under the title: *The Stations of the Cross in Westminster Cathedral*. MS. of original article dated December 1917.

72 RELIGION AND ART. *The Burlington Magazine*, Vol. XXXIII, no. 187, October 1918, pp. 123–5. A review-article of *The Dance of Siva*, by Ananda Coomaraswamy. London: Luzac & Co.

1919

73 WAR GRAVES. *The Burlington Magazine*, Vol. XXXIV, no. cxciii, April 1919, pp. 158–60. Reprinted in *Letters of Eric Gill* (no. 54) under no. 84.

74 BREWING BEER to make 9 gallons of ale. A reprint of 8 pp. from Cobbett's *Cottage Economy*. Printed and published at S. Dominic's Press, Ditchling, 1919. There is a Note 'signed' E. G. *4–5–17* on p. 4 and tail-piece: w-e. *St George and the Dragon* (P90), on p. 7. This was reprinted in *The Game*, Vol. III, no. 2, Advent 1919, pp. 48–54 (no. 69). This is no. 8 of S. Dominic's Press publications.

74a AN APPEAL FOR ASSISTANCE IN THE ERECTION OF A CRUCIFIX AND ORATORY ON THE SPOIL BANK, DITCHLING COMMON, SUSSEX. [S. Dominic's Press, 1919] Proof of a broadside. G L copy $8\frac{7}{8} \times 8\frac{1}{8}$, C L C copy slightly smaller. An appeal for donations to The Spoil Bank Fund by Eric Gill and Hilary Pepler. Item no. 12 in Sewell Supplement, *Matrix* 4, p. 138. (Cf. Speaight, no. 636.46, p. 106.)

1920

75 POTBOILERS. *The New Witness*, January 1920. Review-article of a book by Clive Bell. MS. dated 4 January 1920.

76 WESTMINSTER CATHEDRAL. *Blackfriars*, Vol. 1, no. 3, June 1920, pp. 148–53. Review-article of *Westminster Cathedral and Its Architect*, by W. de L'Hopital. Two vols. London: Hutchinson & Co. £3. 3s. This article was revised and reprinted in *Art-Nonsense* (1929) (no. 18).

77 WOOD-ENGRAVING. By R. John Beedham. With an Introduction and Appendix by Eric Gill. Ditchling: S. Dominic's Press, on the feast of S. Bartholomew 1920. Price 5s. This is no. 33 of S. Dominic's Press publications. $8\frac{1}{4} \times 5\frac{1}{4}$, 40 pp., grey paper boards, cloth spine, cover title duplicates title page, printed black. There are five Eric Gill wood-engravings: *SDP and Cross* (P145) on the cover and title-page. *Woodcutter's Knife* (P168), Fig. 27, p. 36. *Tail-piece* (P169), p. 37. *Christ and the Money-changers* (P152), Fig. 29, p. 38. *Spoil Bank Crucifix* (P157), Fig. 31, p. 39. A second edition, entirely reset, was printed in 1925, $8\frac{5}{8} \times 5\frac{1}{2}$, [36 pp.], black paper boards, unbleached linen spine with the title Wood-Engraving printed in grey on the cover. The statement 'First printed 1921' on the verso of the title-page contradicts the printed date of 1920 on the title-page of the first edition. The 1925 second edition contains ten wood-engravings by Gill: *SDP and Cross* (P145) on the title-page. *Initial T with man and thistles* (P236), p. [1]. *Stalk* (P109), p. 10. *Spray of Leaves* (without initials) (P108), p. 17. *Initial T with a woman* (P246), p. 18. *Initial T with woman and child* (P234), p. 31. *Woodcutter's Knife* (P168), p. 32. *Tail-piece* (P169), p. 33. *Spoil Bank Crucifix* (P157), Fig. 32, p. [35] *Welsh Dragon* (P150), p. [36]. The introduction was revised and the book was enlarged and entirely reset and published as the fifth edition by Faber & Faber in 1938 at 3s. 6d. In this edition Gill's wood-engravings have been omitted. The introduction was revised and reprinted in *Art-Nonsense* (1929) (no. 18). The introduction was also printed separately in 1967 by The Library, University of British Columbia, Vancouver in an edition of 450 copies entitled *Foreword to a treatise upon the craft of wood engraving*.

78 ART AND RELIGION. *The Inter-University Magazine, A Journal for Catholic Students*. Vol. II, no. 1, October 1920, pp. 16–23. Extensively re-written and enlarged for *Pax, The Quarterly Review of the Benedictines of Caldey*, no. 72, Autumn 1924. The essay was continued in no. 73 (Winter 1924–5) with *Some Definitions* added to the title. These definitions were added to and reprinted in *Blackfriars*, Vol. VI, no. 67, October 1925 under the title: *Responsibility and the analogy between Slavery and Capitalism* under which title they appear in *Art-Nonsense* (1929) (no. 18).

79 DRESS. *Blackfriars*, Vol. 1, no. 9, December 1920, pp. 524–9. Reprinted in booklet form as *Welfare Handbook No. 7* by S. Dominic's Press (1921) (no. 7) and revised for inclusion in *Art-Nonsense* (1929) (no. 18).

80 THE SOCIETY OF WOOD ENGRAVERS. *Blackfriars*, Vol. 1, no. 9, December 1920, p. 555. An unsigned contribution concerning the formation of this Society. MS. dated November 1920.

81 T. J. COBDEN-SANDERSON. In *Twenty-four Portraits* by William Rothenstein. With critical appreciations by various hands. London: George Allen & Unwin, Ltd., 1920. Each drawing reproduced was faced by a 'critical appreciation'; that for Cobden-Sanderson being written by Eric Gill.

1921

82 AN ESSAY IN AID OF A GRAMMAR OF PRACTICAL AESTHETICS. *Blackfriars*, Vol. II, no. 1, April 1921, pp. 41–8. Revised and reprinted in a shortened form as an Appendix in *Christianity and Art* (1928) (no. 13), and again in *Art-Nonsense* (1929) (no. 18). MS. dated Autumn 1920.

1922

83 INDIAN SCULPTURE. *Blackfriars*, Vol. III, no. 25, April 1922, pp. 20–7. With four illustrations from Indian drawings. Reprinted in *Rupam. An Illustrated Quarterly Journal of Oriental Art. Chiefly Indian*. Ed. by Ordhendra C. Gangoly for The Indian Society of Oriental Art, Calcutta, no. 88, July 1922, pp. 74–6. The essay was revised and reprinted in a slightly condensed form in *Art-Nonsense* (1929) (no. 18).

84 SINGING BEADS. *Blackfriars*, Vol. III, no. 25, April 1922, pp. 58–9. A review-article of *Singing Beads: Woodcuts and Verses* by Dom Theodore Baily, O.S.B., Monk of Caldey. London: Heath Cranton.

1923

85 THE PHILOSOPHY OF ART. BEING 'ART ET SCHOLASTIQUE' BY JACQUES MARITAIN, TRANSLATED BY THE REV. JOHN O'CONNOR, S.T.P. WITH AN INTRODUCTION BY ERIC GILL, O.S.D. Ditchling: S. Dominic's Press. There are two wood-engravings by Eric Gill: *S. Michael and the Dragon* (P66), on title-page and *Animals All* (P50) tail-piece. The printing was of 400 copies. Price: paper wrappers, 10s. 6d. This is no. 39 of S.

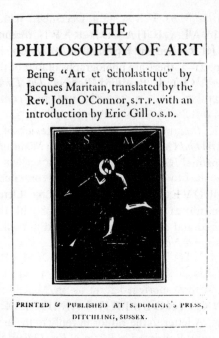

THE
PHILOSOPHY OF ART

Being "Art et Scholastique" by
Jacques Maritain, translated by the
Rev. John O'Connor, s.t.p. with an
introduction by Eric Gill o.s.d.

PRINTED & PUBLISHED AT S. DOMINIC's PRESS,
DITCHLING, SUSSEX.

[85]

Dominic's Press publications. MS. of Introduction dated 18 February 1923
(cf. no. 127).

86 LEONARDO DA VINCI, SCULPTOR. *Blackfriars*, Vol. IV, no. 42,
September 1923, pp. 1111–12. Review-article of book of this title by Sir
Theodore Andrea Cook (London: Humphreys, 10s. 6d.). The review appears
above the 'signature' *E. G.* MS. dated 21 August 1923.

87 IN PETRA. BEING A SEQUEL TO 'NISI DOMINUS', TOGETHER WITH
A PREFACE AND NOTES BY ERIC GILL AND HILARY PEPLER,
TT.O.S.D., Ditchling: S. Dominic's Press, 1923. Colophon is dated 25.x.23.
There are six wood-engravings by Eric Gill: *The Holy Ghost as Dove* (P224),
title-page. *Crucifix* (P259), p. [12] *Penny Pie* (P144), p. 17. *Initial G with vetch
and bee-hive* (P240), p. 19. *Initial C with bird-cage* (P245), p. 22. *Gravestone
with Angel* (P61), p. 23. This is no. 40 of S. Dominic's Press publications. G L
has a copy in decorated paper boards, $6\frac{5}{8} \times 4\frac{5}{8}$ with leather spine lettered 'In
Petra' in gold and a copy in blue cloth, $6\frac{1}{2} \times 5$ with a printed paper label on the
cover reading 'In Petra – being a sequel to Nisi Dominus by the author of
Concerning Dragons. Price, boards, Five Shillings'. Sewell (no. 636.76) gives
the measurements 5×7 and also mentions a binding of grey cloth.

100

1924

88 THE REVIVAL OF HANDICRAFT *Artwork*, Vol. 1, no. 1, July 1924, pp. 35–41. Revised and reprinted in *Art-Nonsense* (1929) (no. 18). In the same issue, pp. 21–2, there are photographs of four of the Stations of the Cross for St Cuthbert's Church, Bradford. Review: *The Times Literary Supplement*, 24 August 1924.

89 ARTWORK. *Pax*, no. 71, Summer 1924. Review of *Artwork, An Illustrated Quarterly of Arts and Crafts*, edited by Herbert Wauthier. The review appears above the 'signature' *E. R.*

90 ART AND LOVE. *Blackfriars*, Vol. v, no. 55, October 1924, pp. 420–35, also in *Rupam*, no. 21, January 1925, pp. 1–8 with three illustrations. This essay was revised and extended and published in book form in 1928 (no. 14) and reprinted in *Art-Nonsense* (1929) (no. 18).

1925

91 DESIGN AND INDUSTRIES ASSOCIATION. *Artwork*, no. 3, February 1925. A letter to the Editor in reply to the article 'Diabasis and Mr. Eric Gill' (no. 408). Reprinted in *Letters of Eric Gill* under no. 130.

92 WHAT'S IT ALL BLOOMIN' WELL FOR? *G.K.'s Weekly*, Vol. 1, no. 14, 20 June 1925, pp. 300–2.

93 ART APPRECIATION. *G.K.'s Weekly*, Vol. 1, no. 19, 25 July 1925, pp. 416–17. An unsigned contribution.

94*a* THE TOWN CHILD'S ALPHABET. *Pax*, no. 75, Summer 1925, p. 177. Review of book of verses by Eleanor Farjeon, designs by David Jones. (The Poetry Bookshop. Wrappers, 1*s*. 6*d*. Boards, 2*s*.)

94*b* THE COUNTRY CHILD'S ALPHABET. *Pax*, no. 75, Summer 1925, p. 177. Review of book of verses by Eleanor Farjeon, drawings by William M. Rothenstein. (The Poetry Bookshop. Wrappers, 1*s*. 6*d*. Boards, 2*s*.) These reviews appear above the 'signature' *G*.

95 THE PROBLEM OF PARISH CHURCH ARCHITECTURE. *Pax*, no. 76, Autumn 1925, pp. 216–29. Revised and reprinted, in considerably shortened form, in *Art-Nonsense* (1929) (no. 18). This essay gave rise to a leading article and considerable correspondence in *The Architects' Journal*, January and February 1926. See *The Superfluous Architect*, nos. 99 and 414.

96 THE STORY OF THE LITTLE FLOWER. *Pax*, no. 76, Autumn 1925, p. 273. An unsigned review of book with this title by David A. Lord, S.J. (New York: Benziger Bros.)

97 THE CONTROL OF MACHINERY. A letter in *G.K.'s Weekly*, 7 November 1925. Reprinted in *Letters of Eric Gill* under no. 134.

98 LITURGICAL ART: *A Proposed Confraternity. Pax*, no. 77, Winter 1925–6, pp. 293–6. An unsigned contribution. This must not be confused with an essay of the same title published in *Orate Fratres*, April 1927 (cf. no. 106).

1926

99 THE SUPERFLUOUS ARCHITECT. *The Architects' Journal*, Vol. 63, no. 1621, 27 January 1926, pp. 189–90 and no. 1624, 17 February, pp. 298–9. Letters to the editor in reply to the leading article in the issue of January 13 (cf. no. 414). These letters were reprinted in *Letters of Eric Gill* under nos. 136 and 137.

100 ENGLAND NEW AND NEWER. *Pax*, no. 78, Spring 1926, pp. 63–8. Review of *Mammonart*, by Upton Sinclair (Upton Sinclair, Pasadena, California, $2), and *Church Building*, by Ralph Adams Cram, Litt.D., LL.D., F.R.G.S. (Marshall Jones, Boston. n.p.)

101 THE CATHOLIC ART REVIEW. *Pax*, no. 78, Spring 1926, pp. 70–1. Review-article, above the initials *E. G.* of no. 1, November–December 1925 of this bi-monthly review.

102 THE CHURCH AND ART. *Blackfriars*, Vol. VII, no. 71, February 1926 (pp. 108–17), no. 72, March 1926 (pp. 178–84), no. 73, April 1926 (pp. 226–33) and no. 74, May 1926 (pp. 295–304). This was revised and reprinted, with an Appendix, as *Christianity and Art* (no. 13).

103 MILLES' WORK AT SALTSJÖBADEN. *The Architects' Journal*, Vol. 64, no. 1642, 7 July 1926, pp. 6–8. With six illustrations from photographs.

1927

104 WOOD-ENGRAVING. Foreword to catalogue of an Exhibition of Woodcuts by the Society of Wood-Engravers held at the Basnett Gallery, Liverpool, February 1–12, 1927. With w-e. *Tree and Burin* (P188), on front cover.

105 INTAGLIO PRINTING FROM WOOD BLOCKS. *The Woodcut,* no. 1. An Annual edited by Herbert Furst, 'The Fleuron' pp. 27–9. Gill's wood-engraving *The Carrying of the Cross* (P352) appears on p. 15 and *Madonna and Child, with Children* (P341) appears on p. 51. Ordinary edition 12*s.* 6*d.* *Edition de Luxe* (75 copies) containing an extra woodcut, £2. 2*s.* Published February 1927. Review: *The Times Literary Supplement,* 7 July 1927.

106 LITURGICAL ART. *Orate Fratres,* Vol. 1, no. 6, 17 April 1927, pp. 183–4. St Paul, Minn. U.S.A. A note on the distinction between liturgical and other arts.

107 DISTRIBUTISM AND PRODUCTION. *G.K.'s Weekly,* 30 April 1927, p. 372, and 7 May 1927, p. 380. Cf. issue of 4 June containing a letter from Eric Gill entitled *Father Vincent's Distributism,* a reply to this from T. M. Heron under the title *The Area of the Market* in the issue of 11 June and further letters from Eric Gill under the title *Father McNabb and Eric Gill,* in the issues of 27 August and 1 October.

108 CHURCH FURNITURE. *The Architectural Review,* Vol. LXII, July–December 1927, pp. 52–3.

109 AN ENEMY FOR FRIENDSHIP'S SAKE. *Pax,* no. 84, Autumn 1927, pp. 263–5. A review of *The Enemy.* Edited by Wyndham Lewis. Vol. 1, no. 1. (The Arthur Press. 2*s.* 6*d.*)

110 PRINTING AND BOOK CRAFTS FOR SCHOOLS. *Pax,* no. 84, Autumn 1927, pp. 275–6. A review-article above the initials *E. G.* of book by Frederick Goodyear. (Harrap. 10*s.* 6*d.*)

1928

111 THE ENORMITIES OF MODERN RELIGIOUS ART. *The Month,* January 1928, pp. 42–51. A lecture delivered to the Wiseman Society of London. Revised and reprinted in *Art-Nonsense* (1929) (no. 18).

112 SOME COMMENTS ON A PRIMER. *Pax,* no. 86, Spring 1928, pp. 76–8. Review-article of *Primer of the Principles of Social Science,* by the Very Rev. Michael Canon Cronin, M.A., D.D. (Gill, Dublin. 2*s.*)

113 THE FUTURE OF SCULPTURE. *Artwork*, Vol. IV, no. 13, Spring 1928, pp. 46–51. With three illustrations from photographs. A lecture delivered at the Victoria and Albert Museum, 1 December 1927. The three reproductions are of slides shown during the lecture. This lecture was reprinted in book form for private circulation in 1928 (no. 16), and revised and reprinted in *Art-Nonsense* (1929) (no. 18). In this issue of *Artwork* are photographs of the following carvings by Eric Gill: *Mankind* (p. 13), *Crucifix* and *Tobias & Sara* (p. 14), *Madonna* and *Adam & Eve* (p. 60), *Gravestone* and *Nude* (p. 61). This lecture was also reprinted in *The American Review*, Vol. 5, no. 3, Summer 1935, pp. 257–86, under the title *Sculpture in the Machine Age*.

114 REPOSITORY ART. *Order*, Vol. 1, no. 1, May 1928, pp. 14–16. An unsigned contribution. Reprinted in *Beauty Looks After Herself* (1933) (no. 24).

115 ART AND PRUDENCE. *The University Catholic Review*. Organ of the University Catholic Societies Federation of Great Britain. Vol. 1, no. 3, May 1928, pp. 94–101. With a note by the editor 'signed' *C. C. M[artindale]* This essay was revised and reprinted in book form in 1928 (no. 15). It was also reprinted in *Beauty Looks After Herself* (1933) (no. 24).

116 THE CRITERION IN ART. *The Dublin Review*, no. 366, July 1928, pp. 63–78. An abridgement of this essay was published in *The Studio*, Vol. 96, no. 427, October 1928, pp. 234–40, with seven illustrations and in *Creative Arts*, Vol. 3, no. 4, October 1928, pp. 234–40, with nine illustrations including one on p. 233. It was revised and reprinted in *Art-Nonsense* (1929) (no. 18).

117a TUPPENCE PLAIN, PENNY COLOURED. *Order*, Vol. 1, no. 2, August 1928, pp. 58–61. An unsigned contribution. Revised and reprinted in *Beauty Looks After Herself* (1933) (no. 24) as *Twopence Plain, Penny Coloured*.

117b DAVID JONES. A biographical note for catalogue of an exhibition at the Beaux Arts Gallery. MS. dated 7 August 1928.

118 ORDER. *Pax*, Autumn 1928. A review, 'signed' *X. Y. Z.* of *Order, An Occasional Catholic Review*, Vol. 1, nos. 1 and 2.

119 WHAT SHOULD ART MEAN? *The Evening News*, no. 14619, 1 November 1928, p. 8.

1929

120 STONECARVING. *The Encyclopaedia Britannica*, 14th edition, 1929. Vol. 21, pp. 437–8. With eight illustrations from photographs.

121 RIGHT LETTERING. *Advertising Display*, Vol. 7, no. 3, September 1929, pp. 134–6. A review-article of *Lettering, A Series of 240 plates illustrating modes of writing in Western Europe from Antiquity to the end of the 18th Century*, with an Introduction by Hermann Degering of the Prussian State Library. (London: Ernest Benn, Ltd. 50s.)

122 ARCHITECTURE AS SCULPTURE. *Journal of the Royal Institute of British Architects*, Vol. XXXVI, no. 20, Third Series, 19 October 1929, pp. [779]–783. Notes of a Lecture delivered to the Liverpool Architectural Society, 21 November 1928. Cf. comments by A. Trystan Edwards, pp. 783–4 (no. 438). This lecture was printed in *Beauty Looks After Herself* (1933) (no. 24).

123 THE RIGHT-MINDEDNESS OF MODERN ART. *Order*, Vol. 1, no. 4, November 1929, pp. 116–19. Revised and reprinted under the title *Art and Sanctification* in *Beauty Looks After Herself* (1933) (no. 24).

124 PYLONS ON THE DOWNS. *The Times*, 6 November 1929. This letter was reprinted in *Letters of Eric Gill*, under no. 170.

124a THE SANCTUARY. Caldy Notes, Vol. X, no. 2, February 1929, pp. 17–18. Notice of a book about the Benedictine sanctuary signed *E. G.* Published by the Benedictines of New Caldy Abbey.

1930

125 STYLE IN SCULPTURE. *The Builder*, Vol. CXXXVIII, no. 4547, 28 March 1930, p. 612. The substance of a lecture delivered to The Arundel Society of Manchester, 17 January 1930 and to the Architectural Association, 24 March 1930. This lecture is also printed in substance in the *Reprint of Minutes of Activities during Session* 1929–1930 (circulated September 1930) of The Arundel Society, pp. 30–6. A reference to the occasion of this lecture is made on pp. 50–1 of the same publication. The lecture was originally delivered 20 June 1929 in the Faculty of Arts Hall. It was corrected and extended for The Arundel Society and still further added to for the meeting of the Architectural Association.

126 PAINTINGS AND CRITICISM. *Architectural Review*, Vol. 67, March 1930, pp. 111–12. Revised and reprinted in *Beauty Looks After Herself* (1933) (cf. no. 24).

127 THE PHILOSOPHY OF ART. *G.K.'s Weekly*, Vol. XI, no. 264, 5 April 1930, p. 58. Review-article of *Art and Scholasticism with Other Essays*, by Jacques Maritain, translated by J. F. Scanlan. (Sheed & Ward. 7s. 6d.). (Cf. no. 85).

128 WHAT IS TRUTH? *G.K.'s Weekly*, Vol. XI, no. 268, 3 May 1930, p. 122. Review-article of *An Introduction to Philosophy*, by Jacques Maritain. (Sheed & Ward. 8s. 6d.). Cf. issue of May 10 for a letter from Gill correcting a point in this review. MS. dated 20 April 1930.

129 THE LIVERPOOL FIRST EDITION CLUB. Foreword to Catalogue of the *First Exhibition by Members of Finely Printed Books from Modern Presses*, held at the Basnett Gallery, Liverpool, 12–24 May 1930. Price 1s. Fifty copies of this Catalogue, signed by Eric Gill, were sold at 5s. Cf. notice in *The Bookman*, June 1930, and by Iolo A. Williams, *The London Mercury*, August 1930. MS. dated April 1930.

130 DAVID JONES. *Artwork*, Vol. VI, no. 23, Autumn 1930, pp. 171–7. With eight reproductions of David Jones's work. Revised and reprinted in *In A Strange Land* (1944) (no. 51) and in American edition, *It All Goes Together* (1944) (no. 52).

131 MODERN ARCHITECTURAL SCULPTURE. JOURNAL OF THE ROYAL SOCIETY OF ARTS, Vol. LXXVIII, no. 4061, 19 September 1930, Supplement of two pages. Review-article of book by W. Aumonier. (London: The Architectural Press. Three guineas.) Cf. issues of 10 and 24 October and 7 November for letters from Eric Newton, J. W. M. Harvey and Stanley Casson respectively, commenting upon this review. MS. dated September 1930.

131*a* CHRISTIANITY AND SEX AND COMMENTS ON BIRTH CONTROL. *The Dublin Review*, no. 374, July, August, September 1930, pp. 174–6. A review-article of *Christianity and Sex* by Christopher Dawson and *Comments on Birth Control* by Naomi Mitchison, two pamphlets of the *Criterion Miscellany* (Faber and Faber, 2s. each).

1931

132 CASSELL'S CATHOLIC ENCYCLOPAEDIC DICTIONARY. London: Cassell & Co. Ltd. 25s. (o.p.). Published in U.S.A. by The Macmillan Co. $4. Contains definitions under the following heads by Eric Gill: *Aesthetics, Art, Beauty, Beuron School, Capitalism, Distributism, Fabianism,*

Image, Industrialism, Money, Plainchant, Social Reform and *Wealth*. MS. dated December 1928.

133 A PROPOS OF LADY CHATTERLEY'S LOVER. *The Dublin Review*, no. 376, January 1931, pp. 161–2. Review-article above the 'signature' *E.G.* of book by D. H. Lawrence. (London: Mandrake Press. 1931. 3*s.* 6*d.*) Cf. *Apropos Lady Chatterley* by G. M. Turnell, *Colosseum*, September 1935 in which the writer quotes Eric Gill's review with approval.

134 ARCHITECTURE VERSUS ENGINEERING II: ENGINEERS AND AESTHETICS. *The Architects' Journal*, Vol. 73, 4 March 1931, p. 350. A letter to the Editor commenting upon an article by A. J. Penty in the issue of 18 February (pp. 279–80). This letter was reprinted in *Letters of Eric Gill* under no. 184 with the title *Engineers and Aesthetics*.

134*a* W. E. CAMPBELL'S UTOPIA: HIS SOCIAL TEACHING. *The Dublin Review*, April 1931. Review.

1932

135 BEAUTY AND THE INDIAN WORKMAN. *The India Review*, Vol. IV, no. 4, 27 February 1932, pp. 4–5. MS. dated 20–30 January 1932.

136 ARCHITECTURE AND INDUSTRIALISM. *Blackfriars*, Vol. 13, no. 145, April 1932, pp. 199–211. A lecture delivered to the Cambridge Architectural Society, 9 February 1932. Reprinted in *The Catholic World*, Vol. 135, June 1932, pp. 352–4. Revised and reprinted in *Beauty Looks After Herself* (1933) (no. 24), under the title *Architecture and Machines*. MS. dated 9 February 1932.

137 ART AND THE PEOPLE. *Journal of the Royal Institute of British Architects*, Vol. 39, no. 17, Third Series, 9 July 1932, pp. 685–92. A Symposium by H. S. Goodhart-Rendel, Eric Gill and Thomas D. Barlow. Lectures delivered at the R.I.B.A. Conference, Manchester, 16 June 1932. E. G.'s lecture (pp. 688–90) was revised and reprinted in *Beauty Looks After Herself* (1933) (no. 24). MS. dated 16 June 1932. Cf. *Plain Architecture* (no. 138 below).

138 PLAIN ARCHITECTURE. *Architectural Design & Construction*, Vol. II, no. 10, August 1932, pp. 446–8. A reply to a communication from A. Trystan Edwards arising out of Gill's address to the R.I.B.A. Conference, cf. no. 137 above. With six architectural sketches. Cf. no. 470 for reply by

A. Trystan Edwards. This address, together with the sketches, was reprinted in *Beauty Looks After Herself* (1933) (no. 24).

138a BEAUTY AND THE BEASTY LAND FOR THE PEOPLE Vol. I, no. 10, April 1932, pp. 16–17. Organ of the Catholic Land Assn. of Gt. Britain.

139 INDUSTRIAL ART: THE BEST FOR THE PURPOSE. *The Times*, 30 September 1932. A letter commenting upon the terminology in the leading article in the issue of 27 September on the subject of 'An Industrial Art Exhibition'. Cf. reply by the Chairman, Executive Committee, of the Exhibition of British Industrial Art, in the issue of 7 October.

140 'THE TIMES' COAT OF ARMS. *New Statesman and Nation*, 8 October 1932. A letter to the Editor commenting upon a reference to him in the issue of 1 October. This was reprinted in *Letters of Eric Gill* under no. 195.

1933

141 ON THE FLYING SCOTSMAN. *London & North Eastern Railway Magazine*, Vol. 23, no. 1, January 1933, pp. 3–5. A description of a ride on the foot-plate of the 'Flying Scotsman'. With photograph of Gill executing one of his sculptures on Broadcasting House (p. 4) and reproduction of a drawing by him, at the age of fifteen, of *North Eastern Railway Engine No. 1870* (*built 1897*) (p. 6). MS. dated 9–12 December 1932. Reprinted in *Letters of Eric Gill* under no. 197.

142 WHAT IS LETTERING? *Architectural Review*, Vol. LXXIII, no. 434, January 1933, pp. 26–8. With a full-page illustration of stamped metal letters designed by Eric Munday and three diagrams in the text. Cf. the *Architectural Review* of February 1933 (no. 476) containing letters from Percy J. Smith and Graily Hewitt (pp. 97–8) severely criticizing this article.

143 PAINTING AND THE PUBLIC. *Blackfriars*, Vol. XIV, no. 155, February 1933, pp. 118–26. A speech at the opening of a picture exhibition at a restaurant, 17 November 1932. Revised and reprinted in *Beauty Looks After Herself* (1933) (no. 24). MS. dated 17 November 1932.

144 A SIGN AND A SYMBOL. *The Listener*, 15 March 1933, p. 397. With four photographs of the stone-carving *Prospero and Ariel* for Broadcasting House. MS. dated 5 March 1933. Cf. article by Christian Barman, *Eric Gill 'Furnishes' Broadcasting House*, (no. 478).

145 MODELLING AND CARVING. *Architectural Design & Construction*, Vol. III, no. 6, April 1933, pp. 212–15. With six illustrations from photographs. A lecture, here printed after revision, to the Art Workers Guild, 3 March 1933.

146 ART AND BOOKS. *The Book-Collector's Quarterly*, no. X, April 1933, pp. 1–8. An Address to the Members of the First Edition Club at the opening of an exhibition of his work in Typography and Book Decoration, 8 February 1933.

147 THE TECHNIQUE OF EARLY GREEK SCULPTURE. *Architectural Design & Construction*, Vol. III, no. 7, May 1933, p. 275. An unsigned review-article of book by Stanley Casson (Oxford Univ. Press. 25s.). (Cf. nos. 475 and 483.)

148 ART AND REALITY. An Introductory Essay to *The Hindu View of Art*, by Mulk Raj Anand, Ph.D. (London), pp. 9–28. With a drawing by Eric Gill (p. 193). (London: George Allen & Unwin. 1933. 8s. 6d.) MS. dated November 1931, revised and added to December 1932.

149 THE 'PRIVATE PRESS'. *The Monotype Recorder*, Vol. XXXII, no. 3, Autumn 1933, p. 32. A letter in which E. G. takes exception to the use of the term 'Private Press' as applied to the firm of 'Hague and Gill Printers'. Cf. Special Type Faces Number of *The Monotype Recorder*, Spring 1933, p. 30 (no. 481). There is also a portrait opposite p. [16] entitled: 'Francis Meynell, Chief Director of the Nonesuch Press: From a pencil drawing by Eric Gill'.

150 MACHINE-MADE MANCHESTER. *The Manchester Evening Chronicle*, 18 September 1933. MS. dated 14 September 1933.

150a MACHINES – DESTROYERS OF BEAUTY – THE CLASH OF ART AND INDUSTRIALISM. Adapted from an address to the Central School of Arts and Crafts. *Marketing and Design* supplement Dec. 14, 1933.

150b PRINTED LETTERING IN THE BRAVE NEW WORLD. *The Three Ridings Journal*, Vol. 5, no. 1, n.d. [1933] pp. 8–12. E. G.'s address to the Yorkshire Young Master Printers. The entire issue is devoted to the conference and Gill's talk is referred to by many of the contributors to the 'issue' (cf. no. 495a).

1934

151 THE SEVEN DEADLY VIRTUES. DRAWN BY DENIS TEGET-
MEIER, WITH A FOREWORD BY ERIC GILL. London: Lovat Dickson,
Limited. n.d. [1934] Published in a Limited Edition of 250 copies, signed by
Denis Tegetmeier and Eric Gill. 21*s*. MS. dated 24 July 1933.

152 JOHN RUSKIN. TO THE MEMORY OF JOHN RUSKIN. Edited by
J. Howard Whitehouse. Cambridge: Printed at the University Press for the
Ruskin Society. 1934. 3*s*. An address (pp. 12–15) given at a dinner held at the
English Speaking Union, 8 February 1934, to commemorate the birth of John
Ruskin. This is the third of eight addresses given on this occasion and here
printed. Other speakers included Sir William Rothenstein and J. Howard
Whitehouse, both of whom made reference to Eric Gill and his work. This
address was reprinted in *In a Strange Land* (1944) (no. 51). American edition
It All Goes Together (1944) (no. 52). Cf. *Pax Bulletin*, no. 19, Christmas 1940
(no. 555). MS. dated 8 February 1934.

153 THE POLITICS OF INDUSTRIALISM. *Blackfriars*, Vol. xv, no.
167, February 1934, pp. 128–37. This was reprinted in *Money and Morals*
(1934) (no. 28). See issue of *Blackfriars*, April 1934 for letter from E. G. and
letters in the following issue from H. Robbins and P. D. Foster. See footnote
(p. 330) in *Blackfriars*, May 1937. MS. dated 4 January 1934.

154 WHAT IS SCULPTURE? *The Highway*, March 1934. A lecture
delivered in Edinburgh.

155 MORALS AND MONEY. A PROTEST BY ERIC GILL. *The Colosseum*,
no. 2, June 1934, pp. 19–24. Cf. *Catholic Herald*, 16 June 1934 wherein this
article is reviewed at length by Michael de la Bedoyere, also the issues of
23 and 30 June (no. 498) where, under the caption *The World at Large:
A Correction* the Rev. John Baptist Reeves, O.P., writes a lengthy criticism of
both article and review.

156 THE ROYAL PORCH AT CHARTRES. *The Listener*, Vol. xii,
no. 289, 25 July 1934, pp. 144–6. A contribution to the series *What I Like in
Art*. With two photographs of Chartres Cathedral.

156a MAN WITHOUT AESTHETICS. *The New English Weekly*, 22
November 1934, pp. 129–32. Review-article of Herbert Read's review of
Upton Sinclair's *Mammonart* which appeared in N.E.W., 1 November 1934.

157 BEAUTY DOES NOT LOOK AFTER HERSELF. *The Criterion,* Vol. XIV, no. liv, October 1934, pp. 114–20. A letter to the Editor dated from Jerusalem [10] May 1934. This is reprinted in *Letters of Eric Gill* under no. 216.

158 PROLETARIAN ART. *Catholic Herald,* 3 November 1934 and 19 January 1935. These letters to the editor were reprinted in *Letters of Eric Gill* under nos. 217 and 223 respectively.

159 A. R. ORAGE. *The New English Weekly,* Vol. VI, no. 5, 15 November 1934, p. 116. A letter for the special Memorial Number. This was reprinted in *Letters of Eric Gill* under no. 219.

160 ART AS PROPAGANDA. *Catholic Herald,* 24 November 1934. A letter to the editor. This was reprinted in *Letters of Eric Gill* under no. 220.

161 ART AND AUTHORITY. *Universe,* 7 December 1934. A letter to the editor. This was reprinted in *Letters of Eric Gill* under no. 222.

162 THE NEW TESTAMENT IN NEW DRESS. *The Bookmark,* Vol. X, no. 37, Winter 1934, pp. 10–11. Concerns the *New Testament,* edited by M. R. James, O.M., assisted by Delia Lyttelton, S.Th., hand-set by Hague & Gill at Pigotts, with a reproduction of E. G.'s w-e. for the wrapper: *Bartimeus* (P868). (Cf. no. 292.) MS. dated 16 October 1934.

163 IN HONOUR OF WILLIAM SHAKESPEARE. *The Bookmark,* Vol. X, no. 37, Winter 1934, p. 24. Summary of a speech by E. G. proposing the health of the chairman at a dinner celebrating the 40th anniversary of the *Temple Shakespeare.* With a reproduction of one of his w-e.'s for the *New Temple Shakespeare: Romance* (P860) and a photograph of the gathering at the Savoy Hotel. (Cf. no. 290.)

163a ART IN THE MODERN WORLD. *The New University,* No. 1. New Series, May 1934, p. 16. An interview with E.G.

1935
164 BRITISH ART IN INDUSTRY. *Catholic Herald,* 26 January 1935. A review of the Exhibition of Industrial Art at Burlington House.

165 ON CLOTHES AND MAN NAKED. *The Sun Bathing Review,* Quarterly Journal of the Sun Societies, Vol. II, no. 8, January, February,

March 1935, pp. 116–18 and 136. 'Eric Gill, Mason-Sculptor, gives his views on Clothes and Man Naked.' With a photograph of the author and his 'Prospero and Ariel' on Broadcasting House. Cf. pp. 46–7 of the Summer number (Vol. III, no. 10) for Eric Gill's reply to criticisms of this article by Prof. C. E. M. Joad and Prof. J. C. Flugel reprinted in *Letters of Eric Gill* under no. 239.

166 ST. ANDREW. St Andrew's Church, Croydon. A description of E.G.'s carving at St Andrew's Church Hall sent to the parish magazine (February 1935). Reprinted in *Letters of Eric Gill* under no. 228.

167 ART AND PROPAGANDA. *The Colosseum*, Vol. II, no. 5, March 1935, pp. 8–12. This essay was reprinted in a bowdlerized and revised form and with cross-headings added in *The Grail Magazine*, Vol. II, no. 8, June 1935, pp. 4–7. This version, considerably condensed and revised, was printed in 5 *On Revolutionary Art* (London: Wishart, 1935; 1s.) under the title *All Art is Propaganda*. In this form it was published in *In A Strange Land* (1944) (no. 51). American edition *It All Goes Together* (1944) (no. 52).

168 ARCHITECTS AND BUILDERS: ENGINEERS IN STONE. *Catholic Herald*, 6 April 1935, p. 7. An article on the development of medieval building, with two line-drawings by Denis Tegetmeier. Reprinted in *Work and Property* (1937) (no. 33). MS. dated 17 March 1935.

168a ART: THE TRUTH WILL OUT: FITNESS FOR PURPOSE NOW THE ONLY PRINCIPLE. *Catholic Herald*, 27 April 1935. Reviews of M. D. Anderson's *The Medieval Carver* and Noel Carrington's *Design and a Changing Civilization*.

169 SOCIAL CREDIT AND DEMECHANISATION. *The Engineer*, 3 May 1935. Reprinted in *Letters of Eric Gill* under no. 232.

170 ERIC GILL ON ART AND PROPAGANDA. *The Left Review*, Vol. I, no. 9, June 1935, pp. 341–2. Two letters to the *Catholic Herald* here reprinted with editorial comments quoting an article in that journal of 27 October 1934 which was inspired by the first Artists' International Exhibition. Cf. *A Reply to Eric Gill* (no. 511) and *Artist and Craftsman* (no. 511) in the issues of *The Left Review* for July and November 1935 respectively, which reply to these two letters.

171 ARCHITECTURE AND SCULPTURE. A DESTROYED UNITY. *Manchester Guardian*, 4 June 1935. A letter to the Editor commenting upon the

leading article in the issue of 25 May. For replies to this by Eric Newton and Prof. C. H. Reilly, cf. no. 510.

172 THE NECESSITY OF BELIEF: WEST AFRICA AND SOUTH KEN. *Catholic Herald*, 3 August 1935. Review-article of *Arts of West Africa (excluding Music)*, edited by Michael E. Sadler, with an Introduction by Sir William Rothenstein. (London: Humphrey Milford for the International Institute of African Languages and Cultures. 1935. 5s.) Reprinted in *Letters of Eric Gill* under no. 238.

173 SCULPTURE. *The Colosseum*, Vol. II, no. 7, September 1935, pp. 207–8. A contribution to a series of articles under the general heading *Art Annexe*.

174 THE VALUE OF THE CREATIVE FACULTY IN MAN. *Blackfriars*, Vol. XIV, no. 186, September 1935, pp. 658–66. The substance of a lecture given to the Leicester Aquinas Society, 17 June 1935. It was reprinted in *The American Review* (U.S.A.), Vol. VI, November 1935, pp. 41–51, and in *Work and Property* (1937) (no. 33). MS. dated 17 June 1935.

175 PLAIN CHANT & THE PLAIN MAN. *Music and Liturgy*, Vol. V, no. 2, October 1935, pp. 45–7. MS. dated 20 June 1935.

176 MAN AND THE MACHINE. *Catholic Herald*, 25 October 1935. Review-article of book of this title edited by Hubert Williams. (Preface by J. B. Priestley. London: George Routledge & Sons, Ltd. 1935. 6s.) '. . . an extremely valuable compendium of essays on the relations between man and the machine. E. G.' MS. dated 5 October 1935.

177 THE MEDIÆVAL SCULPTOR. *The Listener*, 30 October 1935. With four illustrations from photographs. MS. dated 5 October 1935.

178 WHEN BODY HOLDS ITS NOISE. *The New English Weekly*, Vol. VIII, no. 6, 21 November 1935, pp. 111–13.

179 THE FUNCTION OF NEWS TYPE. *The British Press Review*, Vol. I, no. 1, December 1935, pp. 24–5, over the initials *E. G.*

180 THE CHINESE EXHIBITION. *Catholic Herald*, 20 December 1935. Reprinted in *Letters of Eric Gill* under no. 244.

1936

181 ART IN RELATION TO INDUSTRIALISM. *Blackfriars*, Vol. XV, no. 190, January 1936, pp. 6–23. The substance of a lecture to London County Council school teachers, 18 November 1935. Reprinted in *The American Review*, Vol. VI, January 1936, pp. 305–30. Revised and reprinted in *Work and Property* (1937) (cf. no. 33). MS. dated 26 October 1935. Review by Geoffrey Grigson, *Catholic Herald*, 7 February 1936.

182 WHY I DESIGNED 'JUBILEE'. *Printing*, Vol. IV, no. 40, March 1936, p. 17. See also a notice of this type-design by B. H. Newdigate under 'Book-Production Notes', *London Mercury*, October 1935, pp. 583–4. With specimens in both caps and lower-case.

183 SCULPTURE. *The Journal of the R.I.B.A.* Vol. XLIII, Third Series, 7 March 1936, pp. 462–4. Report of E. G.'s speech seconding the vote of thanks to Mr Frank Dobson for a Paper entitled *Sculpture* read before the Institute, Monday 24 February 1936. References to this speech in the subsequent discussion appear on pp. 464–6.

183a MAN AND THE MODERN WORLD: SOME PROPO-SITIONS. *Catholic Herald*, 27 March 1936.

184 SCULPTURE ON MACHINE-MADE BUILDINGS. *Industrial Arts*, Summer 1936, pp. 95–100. With illustrations from photographs. This must not be confused with lecture of the same title delivered to the Birmingham and Five Counties Architectural Association, November 1936 (no. 34).

185 WORK AND LEISURE. *The Burlington Magazine*, Vol. LXVIII, June 1936, p. 299. A letter to the Editor concerning review by F. D. Klingender of his book of Essays of this title (cf. no. 31) published in the issue of April 1936.

185a ART, PURE AND MIXED. *Left Review*, Vol. 2, no. 9, June 1936, pp. 420–3. Gill's wood-engraving *The Leisure State* (P850) is shown on p. 421. Title on cover is given as ERIC GILL ON ART.

186 JEWS AND ARABS IN PALESTINE. *Tablet*, 13 June and 11 July 1936. Reprinted in *Letters of Eric Gill* under nos. 251 and 254 respectively.

187 AN ANALYSIS OF THE RIGHT TO PRIVATE PROPERTY. *Catholic Herald*, 3 July 1936. Reprinted in *Pax Bulletin*, no. 19, Christmas 1940, pp. 8–9, and in *Letters of Eric Gill* under no. 253. (Cf. no. 557.) Gill

responded to criticism of the article, especially that of Bernard Killy and Noel Purgold, in the 7 August 1936 issue of *Catholic Herald*.

188 ART AND PROPERTY. *G.K.'s Weekly*, Vol. XXIII, no. 592, 16 July 1936, pp. 288–90 and 23 July, pp. 304–6. (Cf. letter from Gerald Flanagan in issue of 13 August.) Originally delivered as a lecture at Downside School, 4 July 1936. Extracts from this were reprinted in *The Highway*, December 1936, pp. 40–2 under the title *Work and Property*, under which title, after revision, it was reprinted as no. 7 in the volume of essays *Work and Property* (no. 33).

189 COTSWOLD ART & CRAFTSMANSHIP. Foreword to Catalogue of an Exhibition at Campden, Gloucestershire, 1–31 August 1936, pp. 3–6. Reprinted in *G.K.'s Weekly*, Vol. XXIII, no. 597, 20 August 1936, p. 368, under the title *For An Arts and Crafts Exhibition*. MS. dated 6 July 1936.

189a PARTNERSHIP & STATE OWNERSHIP. *G.K.'s Weekly*, 6 August 1936.

190 EYELESS IN GAZA. *G.K.'s Weekly*, Vol. XXIII, no. 596, 13 August 1936, p. 356. A review of book of this title by Aldous Huxley. (London: Chatto & Windus.)

191 NEW POSTAGE STAMPS OF KING EDWARD VIII. Letters to *The Times*, 22, 28 September and 5 October, also to *Manchester Guardian*, 29 September and 10 October 1936. The first and last of these were reprinted in *Letters of Eric Gill* under nos. 256 and 258 respectively. Cf. no. 519 of this compilation, for reference to the leading articles and correspondence which these letters provoked in both journals.

192 PROPERTY, CAPITALIST AND HUMAN. *Blackfriars*, Vol. XVII, no. 199, October 1936, pp. 739–44. A review-article of *De la Propriété Capitaliste à la Propriété Humaine*, par Emmanuel Mounier. (Paris: Desclée et Brouwer. 8 frs.) An excerpt from this review was reprinted in *The Catholic World* (U.S.A.), Vol. 144, November 1936, pp. 232–4, under the title *Question of Property*. MS. dated 9 September 1936.

193 BALANCING THE BOOKS. *The New English Weekly*, 8 October 1936. A letter to the Editor over the pen-name *The Charlady Next Door*. Reprinted in *Letters of Eric Gill* under no. 257. Cf. issues of 29 October and 12 November where E. G. followed the subject up under his own name.

194 PROPERTY AND CATHOLIC MORALS. *The American Review*, Vol. VIII, no. 1, November 1936, pp. 71–85. (New York: The Bookman Publishing Co., Inc.)

195 PATRON AND ARTIST. *Blackfriars*, Vol. XVII, no. 200, November 1936, pp. 842–6. A review-article of *Patron and Artist: Pre-Renaissance and Modern*, by A. K. Coomaraswamy and A. Graham Carey. (Norton, Mass: Wheaton College Press. $1.) MS. dated 14 September 1936.

196 PROSPERO OR ABRAHAM? *The Listener*, 2 December 1936. A letter to the Editor. This was reprinted in *Letters of Eric Gill* under no. 260.

197 PAX. *The New English Weekly*, 26 November and 3 December 1936. A speech delivered at Kingsway Hall, 11 November 1936. Cf. letter from A. Romney Green in the issue of 24 December 1936. This speech was reprinted in *Reconciliation*, THE JOURNAL OF THE FELLOWSHIP OF RECONCILI-ATION, London, Vol. XIV, no. 12, December 1936, pp. 315–17. MS. dated 17 October 1936.

198 IT ALL GOES TOGETHER. *The Cross and The Plough*, Vol. III, no. 2, Christmas 1936, pp. 8–10. Reprinted in *In A Strange Land* (1944) (no. 51). American edition *It All Goes Together* (1944) (no. 52). MS. dated 4 November 1936.

199 ENGLISH ART. *The New English Weekly*, 31 December 1936. A review of *Creative Art in England from the Earliest Times to the Present* by William Johnstone. (London: Stanley Nott, 1936. 21*s*.)

1937

200 EATING YOUR CAKE. *The Penrose Annual*, Vol. XXXIX, pp. 17–20. (London: Lund, Humphries, 1937.) This essay was set in 14 pt. *Bunyan* type (a type designed by E. G.) specially for this Annual. Review: *The Times Literary Supplement*, 8 May 1937. Reprinted in *In A Strange Land* (1944) (no. 51). American edition *It All Goes Together* (1944) (no. 52). MS. dated 26 August 1936. This issue of *The Penrose Annual* also contains no. 524 and no. 525.

201 THE WORLD OF HUMAN WORK AND THE WORLD OF INDUSTRIALISM. D.I. [Designer for Industry to the Royal Society of Arts] *Art and Industry*, Vol. XXII, no. 127, January 1937, p. 30. With one illustration from a photograph. A speech delivered on the occasion of his receiving the 'D.I.'.

201*a* THE COMPLETE PACIFIST. By Ronald Duncan. London: Boriswood, January 1937. 32 pp. Wrappers. Gill is one of seven who contribute Introductions i.e. endorsements. Gill's is the fourth contribution, on p. 3: 'I think this is a very good statement, and I strongly support the author's contentions and proposals.'

202 WAR AND PEACE. *The Colosseum*, Vol. III, no. 13, March 1937, pp. 18–19. A contribution to a symposium.

203 THE MACHINE PROBLEM. *The Catholic Worker* (U.S.A.), 4 March 1937. Reprinted in *Letters of Eric Gill* under no. 272.

204 AUTOBIOGRAPHY. *The Dublin Review*, no. 401, April 1937, pp. 361–4. A review-article of G. K. Chesterton's *Autobiography*. MS. dated 15 December 1936.

205 FUNCTIONALISM. *G.K.'s Weekly*, Vol. XXV, no. 631, 15 April 1937, p. 86. A letter prompted by a review of *The Majority Report on Art* by A. Graham Carey.

206*a* MONETARY REFORM. *Ireland To-Day*, May 1937. (Dublin: Ireland To-Day. 1*s*.)

206*b* OWNERSHIP AND INDUSTRIALISM: ERIC GILL SPEAKS HIS MIND. A letter in *Catholic Herald*, 14 May 1937. There is an editorial comment on p. 8 of the same issue. This provoked much correspondence in subsequent issues, cf. no. 531 *Christian Social Ideals and Communism*, also letter to *Catholic Herald*, 21 July 1937 reprinted in *Letters of Eric Gill* under no. 278.

207 OWNERSHIP AND INDUSTRIALISM. *Ireland To-Day*, Part One, June 1937, Part Two, July 1937. Cf. *Irish Times*, 3 July 1937 and a letter from the Rev. Victor White, O.P., under the heading *Catholic Social Principles* in *Ireland To-Day* for August and Gill's reply in the issue for September. Revised and reprinted in *Sacred and Secular* (1940) (no. 45). MS. dated June–July 1937.

208 TRADITION AND MODERNISM IN POLITICS. *Blackfriars*, Vol. XVIII, no. 208, July 1937, pp. 550–1. A review of book of this title by A. J. Penty. (London: Sheed & Ward. 5*s*.) MS. dated 16 May 1937.

209 THE STATIONS OF THE CROSS. *Blackfriars*, Vol. XVIII, no. 209, August 1937, pp. 580–91. Reprinted in book form under the title *Social Justice and The Stations of the Cross* (1939) (no. 40). Reprinted in *The Catholic Worker*, Vol. VIII, March 1941, pp. 2–3. MS. dated 18–22 March 1937.

210 WHAT'S THE USE OF ART ANYWAY? *Blackfriars*, Vol. XVIII, no. 210, September 1937, pp. 715–16. A review of book by this title by A. K. Coomaraswamy and others. (Newport, Rhode Island: John Stevens; 50 c.) MS. dated July 1937.

211 ART IN ENGLAND NOW. *The Cross and The Plough*, Vol. IV, no. 1, Michaelmas 1937, pp. 5–7. The substance of a broadcast talk given at Jerusalem, 15 June 1937. Revised and reprinted in *In A Strange Land* (1944) (no. 51). American edition *It All Goes Together* (1944) (no. 52). Also reprinted in *The Sower*, Vol. 1, no. 1, Winter 1938. (Berkeley Heights, N.J., U.S.A. The Sower Press.)

1938

212 CRAFTSMANSHIP. A contribution to *The Encyclopaedia Britannica Year Book—1937*, pp. 181–2. (London: The Encyclopaedia Britannica Co., Ltd. 1938. 45s.) MS. dated 30 December 1937.

213 SCULPTURE. A contribution to *The Encyclopaedia Britannica Year Book—1937*, p. 571. (London: The Encyclopaedia Britannica Co., Ltd. 1938. 45s.) MS. dated 30 December 1937. Reviews: *The Scotsman*, 5 May 1938. *Truth*, 11 May 1938.

214 IS THERE A PAPAL SOCIAL PROGRAMME? *Ireland To-Day*, Vol. III, no. 3, March 1938, pp. 195–200. Reviews: *The Irish Press*, 8 March 1938. *Blackfriars*, April 1938. MS. dated 13 January 1938 *et seq*.

215 THE WORK OF DENIS TEGETMEIER. *Typography*, no. 5, Spring 1938, pp. 1–7. (London: *Typography*, Edited by Robert Harling. Published by James Shand at the Shenval Press, 1938. 2s.) MS. dated 1 December 1937.

216 COLLECTIVISM AND WORKERS' OWNERSHIP. *Blackfriars*, Vol. XIX, no. 218, May 1938. A letter in reply to an article under this title contributed to *Ireland To-Day*, March 1938, by Prof. James Hogan. Reprinted in *Letters of Eric Gill* under no. 289.

216a GREETING ON MAY DAY. *Left Review*, Vol. III, no. 16, May 1938, p. 962. Six contributors from various fields send their greetings. Gill's appears under *Art*.

217 WORK AND CULTURE. *Journal of the Royal Society of Arts*, Vol. LXXXVI, no. 4465, 17 June 1938, pp. 744–58. a lecture delivered to the Society, 27 April 1938, with report of the discussion which followed (pp. 759–62). This lecture was awarded the Silver Medal of the Society. MS. dated 27 April 1938. It was first reprinted in substance, in *Public Opinion*, 22 July 1938, under the title *Union of Work and Culture*. It was published (1938) in the Second Series of *John Stevens Pamphlets* (cf. no. 39). See no. 39 also for correspondence in *The Examiner*. The lecture was reprinted in *Sacred and Secular* (1940) (no. 45).

218 MASS FOR THE MASSES: WITH SPECIAL REFERENCE TO CHURCHES IN ENGLAND. *The Cross and The Plough*, Vol. IV, no. 4, SS. Peter & Paul, 1938. Reprinted in *Orate Fratres* (U.S.A.), Vol. XII, no. 9, 24 July 1938, pp. 385–92. (Cf. no. 231.) This essay was revised and reprinted in *Sacred and Secular* (1940) (no. 45). MS dated 28 February 1938.

219 CHRIST AND THE WORKERS. *The Dublin Review*, no. 407, October 1938, pp. 366–70. Review of book by Stanley B. James. (London: Sands. 5s.)

220 COMMUNISM AND MAN. *The Dublin Review*, no. 407, October 1938, pp. 366–70. Review of book by F. J. Sheed. (London: Sheed & Ward. 5s.)

221 A PHILOSOPHY OF WORK. *The Dublin Review*, no. 407, October 1938, pp. 366–70. Review of book by Étienne Borne and François Henry, trans. by Francis Jackson. (London: Sheed & Ward. 6s.)

222 FOOLS AND BEASTS. *Pax Bulletin*, no. 6, October 1938, pp. 4–6. An address given at a Public Meeting convened at Friends' House, London, by the Council of Christian Pacifist Groups, 26 September 1938. (London: Pax Society, 1938. Stencilled foolscap sheets.) Reprinted in *Social Problems. A Magazine Devoted to the Critical Examination of the Ills of Contemporary Society*, Vol. II, no. 1, January 1939, pp. 2–3. (Philadelphia: The Sociology Department of the College of Chestnut Hill.) MS. dated 26 September 1938.

223 BEAUTY. *Art Notes*, Vol. 2, no. 2, November–December 1938, p. 19. (London: *Art Notes*, 40 Eccleston Square. 1s.) E.G.'s wood-engraving *The Martyrdom* (P973) is shown.

224 PAX. *Reconciliation* Vol. XVI, no. 11, November 1938, pp. 331–2. Special Armistice number. (London: The Fellowship of Reconciliation, 17 Red Lion Square. 3*d*.) MS. dated 30 September–2 October 1938.

225 ST TERESA OF LISIEUX. *The Cross and The Plough*, Vol. V, no. 2, Christmas 1938, pp. 13–17. Reprinted in *Christian Social Arts Quarterly*, Vol. II, no. 2, Spring 1939, p. 19. Revised and reprinted in *Sacred and Secular* (1940) (no. 45). MS. dated 22–8 December 1937.

225*a* NINETEENTH CENTURY ORNAMENTED TYPES AND TITLE PAGES. *Journal of the Royal Society of Arts*, Vol. LXXXVII, no. 44, 30 December 1938, pp. 200–1. A review-article of the book by Mrs Nicolete Gray. MS. dated 26 October 1938.

1939

226 THE GALLERY. Published monthly for the Proprietors by H. Toms, Pigotts, High Wycombe. This publication, the first four issues of which consisted of stencilled sheets, first appeared in December 1938. It ceased publication with the issue of April 1939. Subscription 5*s*. p.a. E. G. made the following contributions: *Neutrality*, no. 2, January 1939, p. 3 (over the signature 'E. Rowton'). *Letter or Spirit?* no. 3, February 1939, p. 5 (over the signature 'E. Rowton'). *Layman to Priest*, no. 4, March 1939, pp. 2–4 (unsigned). *Pagan Grandeurs*, no. 5, April 1939, pp. 6–7 (over the initials *E. R.*). No. 5 was printed by Hague & Gill as an 8 pp. stapled pamphlet.

227 WORK IS HOLY: INDUSTRIALISM IS NOT. *Glasgow Observer and Scottish Herald*, 3 and 10 March 1939. Verbatim extracts from lecture *Sacred and Secular in Modern Industry* delivered to Edinburgh University, 28 February 1939. Cf. lecture to The Royal Institution of Great Britain, 4 February 1939, published in volume of essays *Sacred and Secular* (1940) (no. 45).

228 RELIGION IS POLITICS: POLITICS IS BROTHERHOOD: BROTHERHOOD IS POVERTY. TOWARDS THE COMING ORDER. *The Plough*, Vol. II, no. 1, Spring 1939, pp. 10–12. (Ashton Keynes, Wilts.: The Plough Publishing House. 1*s*. 6*d*.)

229 SUN OF JUSTICE. AN ESSAY ON THE SOCIAL TEACHING OF THE CATHOLIC CHURCH. *The Dublin Review*, no. 409, April 1939. Review of book of this title by Harold Robbins. (London: Heath Cranton, 1938. 3*s*. 6*d*.)

230 SECULAR AND SACRED IN MODERN INDUSTRY. *The Students' Distributist Review*, Easter Term, 1939, pp. 19–21. London: The Distributist League. Price 4*d*. MS. dated 29 December 1938.

230*a* WAR AND ECONOMICS. *The Christian Pacifist*, A New Series of Reconciliation. Vol. I, no. 7, July 1939, pp. 182–3. Part of a supplement to *The Christian Pacifist* entitled *Pax Bulletin* edited by E.G. and Gerald Vann.

231 THE CHURCH OF ST PETER THE APOSTLE AT GORLESTON-ON-THE-SEA, NORFOLK, ENGLAND. *The Christian Social Art Quarterly*, Vol. II, no. 4, Fall 1939, pp. 8–14. Some notes *What is a Church?* by Eric Gill prefaced by a brief editorial introduction entitled *Eric Gill Designs a Church*. This is followed (pp. 11–14) by a description of the problem, planning and construction, etc., of the church above the joint signatures of the architects and builders. With four illustrations from photographs and four drawings in the text. For other notices concerning this church see: *Universe*, 23 June 1939, *Architectural Review*, October 1939 and *Architect & Building News*, 8 December 1939. Cf. *Mass for the Masses* under no. 218.

232 WE ARE PERSONS. *The Catholic Worker*, New York, Vol. VII, p. 2, November 1939. From an Address given at a public meeting convened at Friends' House, London, by the Council of Christian Pacifist Groups, 26 November 1938.

233 WORK AND WAR. *The Catholic Worker*, New York, Vol. VII, p. 6, December 1939. From an Address given at a public meeting convened at Friends' House, London, by the Council of Christian Pacifist Groups, 26 September 1938.

1940

234 ST JOHN CHRYSOSTOM. *The Dublin Review*, No. 412, January 1940. Review of book of this title by Donald Attwater. (Milwaukee, U.S.A.: Bruce Publishing Co. 1939. $3.50.)

235 PEACE AND POVERTY. *The Christian Pacifist*, January 1940. London: The Fellowship of Reconciliation. Price 6*d*. A lecture given at Farnham, 17 November 1939. Reprinted in *Last Essays* (1942) (no. 50). American edition *It All Goes Together* (1944) (no. 52). MS. dated 12 November 1939. An off-print of 4 pp. of this lecture was distributed by the 'Pax' Society for 1*d*.

236 OLD POVERTY. *The New English Weekly*, 18 January 1940. Cf. letter in the issue of this journal for 1 February, 15 February and other critical letters and Eric Gill's reply, 28 March 1940.

237 THE EVOLUTION OF PEACE. By G. C. [the Rev. Albert Gille, D.D., Ph.D.] With a Foreword by Eric Gill. High Wycombe: Stormont Murray. Price 6d. Printed by Hague, Gill & Davey. The Foreword appears on the inside of the front and back covers. This Foreword was also published in leaflet form. It was reprinted in a slightly shortened form in *A Catholic Approach to the Problem of War* (cf. no. 593) under the title *A Note on Christian Unity*. It was also reprinted in *The Catholic Worker* (New York), February 1941. MS. dated 8 April 1940.

238 WAR, CONSCIENCE & THE RULE OF CHRIST. COMPILED FROM THE ENCYCLICALS OF LEO XIII, BENEDICT XV, PIUS XI & PIUS XII BY MARK FITZROY WITH A FOREWORD BY ERIC GILL, T.O.S.D. Published by the Pax Society (of which Eric Gill was at that time Chairman). High Wycombe: Stormont Murray. Price 6d. Printed by Hague, Gill & Davey.

239 THE LEISURE STATE. *The Clergy Review*, Vol. XVIII, no. 2, New Series, February 1940, pp. 123–9. Reprinted in *Last Essays* (1942) (no. 50). American edition *It All Goes Together* (1944) (no. 52). MS. dated 16–27 May 1939.

240 WORK AND POVERTY. *The New English Weekly*, Vol. XVI, no. 19, 29 February 1940, p. 287, and 29 March 1940. Two letters to the Editor, the second of which was reprinted in *Letters of Eric Gill* under no. 323.

241 THE FIRST STEP TO PEACE: STOP FALSE THINKING. *Peace News*, no. 198, 29 March 1940, pp. 1 and 8. London: Peace News, Ltd. for The Peace Pledge Union. Price 2d. MS. dated 23 March 1940.

242 ART AND BUSINESS. Bristol: P. E. Gane, Ltd. A catalogue of an Exhibition of Handicrafts, Spring 1940, with a Foreword covering 4 pp. by E. G. Reviewed in *Bristol Evening Post*, 12 April 1940 and *The Cabinet Maker*, 20 April 1940. The Foreword was reprinted in *In A Strange Land* (no. 51). American edition *It All Goes Together* (no. 52).

242a SIMPLICITY IN CHURCHES. *Liturgical Arts*, Vol. 8, no. 3, April 1940. Letter from E. G. commenting on the above topic.

243 THE POSTAGE STAMP. London: *Journal of the Royal Society of Arts*, Vol. LXXXVIII, no. 4562, 31 May 1940, pp. 650–62. A paper read before the Society, 8 May 1940, by B. Guy Harrison. A Communication on the subject from E. G., who was prevented by illness from attending the meeting, is printed at pp. 661–2.

244 EDUCATION FOR WHAT? *The Schoolmaster & Woman Teacher's Chronicle*, Vol. CXXXVII, no. 1614, New Series, 16 May 1940, pp. 533, 536 and 538, with a photograph of the author. London: The Schoolmaster Publishing Co. Cf. issues of 8 August and 19 September for correspondence arising out of this article. The article was reprinted in *Last Essays* (no. 50). American edition *It All Goes Together* (no. 52).

244a CATHEDRAL DECORATION. CHAPEL OF ST GEORGE AND THE ENGLISH MARTYRS. *Westminster Cathedral Chronicle*, Vol. XXXIV, no. 7, July 1940, p. 167. Notes provided by Gill about his sculpture of the altarpiece for the chapel, prefaced by an editorial note about Mrs John Boland for whom the altarpiece was a memorial. Page 148 features a full-page photo of Gill at work on the altarpiece in his studio. A postcard is known, produced by Valentine's, H6528, of a black-and-white photograph showing the altarpiece in place.

245 THE TRUE PHILOSOPHY OF ART. *The New English Weekly*, Vol. XVII, no. 14, 25 July and no. 18, 22 August 1940. Two letters to the Editor. These were reprinted in *Letters of Eric Gill* under nos. 330 and 337 respectively.

246 TWO WORLDS: THERE ARE TWO WORLDS—ONE RULED BY FEAR AND THE OTHER BY CHARITY (CARITAS, SUPERNATURAL LOVE). *Peace News*, no. 216, 2 August 1940, p. 2.

247 WORK. TOWARDS A CHRISTIAN SOCIAL ORDER: POINT III. *Catholic Herald*, no. 2853, 1 November 1940, p. 3. One of a series of articles contributed by various writers. Reprinted in *Last Essays* (no. 50). American edition *It All Goes Together* (no. 52). MS. dated 27 September 1940. This article was reprinted, in part, in *The Catholic Worker* (New York) January 1941, under the title *A Philosophy of Work*. It must not be confused with review-article under the same title in *Dublin Review*, October 1938 (cf. no. 221).

248 PROPERTY. TOWARDS A CHRISTIAN SOCIAL ORDER: POINT VI. *Catholic Herald*, no. 2855, 15 November 1940, p. 3 (cf. no. 247 *supra*).

Reprinted under the title *Private Property* in *Last Essays* (no. 50). American edition, *It All Goes Together* (no. 52). MS. dated 4 October 1940.

249 ART. *Blackfriars*, Vol. XXI, no. 249, December 1940, pp. 680–9. Reprinted in *Last Essays* (no. 50). American edition *It All Goes Together* (no. 52). MS. dated 9–17 October 1940. This was the last article E. G. wrote for publication; he died 17 November 1940. Excerpts from this article appeared in *Catholic World* (U.S.A.), Vol. 152, February 1941, pp. 614–15, under the title *Art Versus Science*.

1941

250 ABOLISH ART AND TEACH DRAWING. *Athene*, Vol. I, no. 5, March 1941, pp. 21–3. London: The Society for Education in Art. Price 2s. Reprinted in *Last Essays* (1942) (no. 50), as *Art in Education* and in American edition, *It All Goes Together* (1944) (no. 52), as *Art and Education*. MS. dated 14 January 1940.

251 WAR IS NOT ROMANCE. *Unity, Freedom, Fellowship and Character in Religion*. Vol. CXXVII, no. 2, April 1941, pp. 26–8. Chicago: The Abraham Lincoln Centre. The larger part of a lecture to the Reading (England) branch of the Peace Pledge Union, 23 February 1940. The MS. dated February 1940 was entitled *The Shame of the Neighbours* under which title excerpts from it were reprinted in *Pax Bulletin*, Christmas 1945 (no. 257). An excerpt from the same lecture was reprinted in *The Catholic Worker* (New York), Vol. VIII, no. 10, September 1941.

252 OWNERSHIP OF THE MEANS OF PRODUCTION. *Christendom: A Journal of Christian Sociology*. Vol. XI, no. 44, December 1941, pp. 211–20. (Oxford: Basil Blackwell. Price 2s. In America: 50 cents.)

1943

253 FOR RECONCILIATION. *Pax Bulletin*, no. 34, July 1943, pp. 2–3. (High Wycombe: Pax Society. n.p.) MS. dated 30 September 1938.

254 SECULAR AND SACRED IN HUMAN LABOUR. *Pax Bulletin*, no. 36, Christmas 1943, pp. 3–5. (High Wycombe: Pax Society. n.p.)

1944

255 NOT BY SUCH MEANS. *A Catholic Approach to the Problem of War. A Symposium edited by Hubert Grant Scarfe.* (High Wycombe: Pax Society [Autumn 1944], pp. 13–15. Price 1s.) A paper read to the Society, 20 September 1938. Reprinted under the title *The Horrible Fatuity* in *Pax Bulletin*, no. 49, Michaelmas 1946. (Cf. nos. 237 and 593.)

256 FIVE HUNDRED YEARS OF PRINTING. *Printing Review*, Vol. X, no. 36, 1942–3, pp. 25–6. MS. dated 11–12 April 1940. Written specifically for this journal; publication of the essay was delayed until 1944. In the meantime it was published in *Last Essays* (1942) (no. 50). American edition *It All Goes Together* (1944) (no. 52). There is a brief reference to Eric Gill in the Editorial Notes on p. 3. The essay was reprinted for the Northern Group of the Printing Historical Society in 1982 in a limited edition of 200 copies.

1945

257 THE SHAME OF THE NEIGHBOURS. *Pax Bulletin*, no. 45 [sic], Christmas 1945, pp. 2–3. This is a portion of the lecture already recorded under the title *War is not Romance* (cf. no. 251 above). As here printed there is a good deal of preliminary matter and there are certain passages which did not appear in the 'Unity' printing. (Note: this number of *Pax Bulletin* should have been given the serial no. 46.)

1958

257a A NOTE ON GREEK SCULPTURE. By Eric Gill, in *Making and Thinking* Essays by Walter H. Shewring, pp. 83–4. Buffalo, NY: Catholic Art Association. 1958. London: Hollis and Carter. 1959.

1982

257b THE ARTIST & BOOK PRODUCTION. *Fine Print*: A Review for the Arts of the Book, Vol. VIII, no. 3, July 1982, pp. 96 ff. The text of Gill's Double Crown Club lecture on 8 April 1926, printed in full for the first time. In a foreword to the article John Bidwell of the Clark Library states that 'Gill scavenged a few of the themes from his lecture for his article *Art and Books*' (no. 146), 1933.

257c LETTER BY ERIC GILL. Published in the *Hawkesyard Review*, Vol. 2, no. 1, in 1918, on virtues of Caslon Old Face. *Matrix* 2, Winter 1982.

III

BOOKS AND OTHER PUBLICATIONS
ILLUSTRATED BY ERIC GILL

Numbers 258 – 396*e*

SECTION III(*a*)

1915

258 THE TAKING OF TOLL

TITLE-PAGE: THE TAKING OF TOLL [*in red*] | BEING THE
DĀNA LĪLĀ OF RĀJENDRA | TRANSLATED INTO
ENGLISH BY ANANDA | COOMARASWAMY WITH AN
INTRODUCTION | AND NOTES AND A WOODCUT BY
ERIC GILL | THE OLD BOURNE PRESS | LONDON |
1915

SIZE: 10⅜ × 8¾.   COLLATION: Two unsigned gatherings of four leaves.
PAGINATION AND CONTENTS: Pp. viii + 8; [i] [ii] title-page, verso four
lines of verse; iii–[vi] Introduction; [vii] [viii].half-title: THE TAKING OF
TOLL., verso Frontispiece: *The Taking of Toll* (P33); 1–[6] text; [7] [8]
Elucidations. The marginal notes in the text are rubricated.
ILLUSTRATIONS: In addition to the frontispiece, which is after a damaged
Indian drawing of the later eighteenth century, there is a reproduction from an
Indian drawing on p. [8].
BINDING: Buff paper wrappers, stapled. Printed on front (in red throughout)
exactly as on title-page.

259 THE DEVIL'S DEVICES

TITLE-PAGE: Reproduced. Shows w-e. *Dumb-Driven Cattle* (P36).
SIZE: 7½ × 5.   COLLATION: [A]⁴, B–I⁸.
PAGINATION AND CONTENTS: Pp. viii + 128; [i] [ii] half-title: THE
DEVIL'S DEVICES, verso list of books by the same author; [iii] [iv] blank,
verso illustration depicting a sword inscribed: *It is not given* ...; [v] [vi]
title-page, verso blank; vii–viii The Emblems; 1–9 An Apology; 10–122 text;
123 illustration; [124] blank; [125] tail-piece; [126] blank; [127] page of
advertisements; [128] imprint worded: PRINTED BY THE WESTMINSTER
PRESS | 411a HARROW ROAD, LONDON, W. Top edges cut, others uncut.
ILLUSTRATIONS: There are twelve illustrations or devices all of which, with
the exception of that on p. [iv], are from wood-engravings by Eric Gill. These
are placed:

> *Dumb-Driven Cattle* (P36), title-page.
> *No. 27* (P37), p. 3.
> *The Money-Bag and the Whip* (P38), p. 31.
> *Triangular Device: Five stalks of leaves* (P39), p. 46.
> *The Purchaser* (P40), p. 54.

THE DEVIL'S DEVICES
OR
CONTROL *versus* SERVICE

BY DOUGLAS PEPLER

WITH WOODCUTS BY ERIC GILL

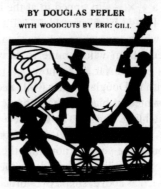

Published at
THE HAMPSHIRE HOUSE WORKSHOPS, HAMP-
SHIRE HOG LANE, HAMMERSMITH, LONDON
1915   [259]

Triangular Device: Ship: On Sail, PRO- | GRE- | SS (P41), p. 79.
The Happy Labourer (P42), p. 82.
Triangular Device: Devil's Tails (P43), p. 107.
Triangular Device: Calvary (P44), p. 122.
The Symbol of Christ Crucified (P46), p. 123.
Triangular Device: H.D.C.P. | E. G. | 1915 (P47), p. [125]

BINDING: Red paper boards, ¼ smooth canvas. Printed on front from an electrotype of the w-e. on the title-page but with the price, viz. *Price 2s. 6d. net*, added immediately below it. This is omitted from the 'proof' copies. Lettered on spine, reading upwards: THE DEVIL'S DEVICES. DOUGLAS PEPLER. I have seen copies ¼ bound in rough canvas and without this lettering. GL has a copy ¼-bound in black cloth without lettering. A number of copies were issued in brown paper wrappers. In these the same w-e. was printed on front cover but the words: THE | DEVIL'S | DEVICES only were printed above it and, printed beneath it: PRICE ONE SHILLING. The whole printed throughout in red.

DATE OF PUBLICATION: 1915.

PRICE: In boards: 2s. 6d. In wrappers: 1s. The first 200 copies, described as 'proof' copies, which were numbered and signed by author and illustrator, were sold at 3s. 6d.

PRINTING: 1500 copies.

NOTES: In the 'proof' copies a Statement of Editions was substituted for the half-title. This is worded: THE FIRST TWO HUNDRED COPIES OF THIS

130

EDITION | ARE 'PROOF' COPIES WHICH ARE NUMBERED | AND | SIGNED | NO. . . . . This is no. 1 of S. Dominic's Press publications. The G L's 'proof' copy has a $3\frac{1}{4} \times 4\frac{3}{4}$ slip tipped in at the limitation page with this notice printed in red: 'I have been grieved to learn that some have imagined the "advertisement" which appears on page 105, to refer to a real Reverend Jones. The advertisement, from which mine is derived, was actually issued by a religious body – but, so far as I know, no one of the name of Jones had anything to do with it. Douglas Pepler.' G L also has a copy of a separate $7\frac{1}{2} \times 5$ announcement printed in black on hand-made paper with the following text: 'High Street, Ditchling, Sussex. To the Reverend Jones Dear Sir Should a copy of my book, "The Devil's Devices, or Control Versus Service" appear in your parish I would like you to know that the notice below is now sent with each copy. Yours faithfully' (followed by the text beginning 'I have been grieved to learn . . .', as above, slightly reworded).

REVIEW: *Land and Water*, 20 January 1916.

REISSUE: This book was reissued in 1934 in full red linen, no printing on front but lettered on spine: THE DEVIL'S DEVICES. PEPLER. Price 5s.

EMBLEMS ENGRAVED
ON WOOD BY ERIC GILL

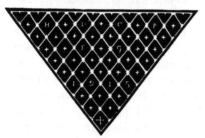

[260]

260 EMBLEMS

EMBLEMS | ENGRAVED ON WOOD BY | ERIC GILL [front cover—see reproduction]

SIZE: $12\frac{7}{8} \times 10\frac{3}{8}$.

COLLATION AND CONTENTS: This consists of eight leaves (unpaginated) of Japanese tissue, being seven of the wood-engravings for *The Devil's Devices* with explanatory text. These were printed on one side of the leaf only and in the following order:

p. [1]   *Triangular Device: H.D.C.P.* | *E. G.* | *1915* (P47).

p. [3]   *Dumb-Driven Cattle* (P36).

p. [5]   *No. 27* (P37).

p. [7]   *The Money-Bag and the Whip* (P38).

p. [9]   *The Purchaser* (P40).

p. [11]   *The Happy Labourer* (P42).

p. [13]   *The Symbol of Christ Crucified* (P46).

p. [15]   [blank]

BINDING: Stout blue paper wrappers, sewn. All edges trimmed. Printed on front as described above for 'title' and on back: THESE EMBLEMS WERE ENGRAVED FOR THE | DEVIL'S DEVICES OR CONTROL VERSUS SERVICE | A BOOK WRITTEN BY DOUGLAS PEPLER AND | PUBLISHED AT THE HAMPSHIRE HOUSE | WORKSHOPS, HAMMERSMITH, LONDON | ON SAINT THOMAS'S DAY, 1915 [w-e. *Triangular Device: Devil's Tails* (P43)] | and, in red: FIFTEEN COPIES OF THIS EDITION PRINTED IN DITCH- | LING BY DOUGLAS PEPLER AND ERIC GILL ON THE | FEAST OF THE PURIFICATION 1916

DATE OF PUBLICATION: 1916 [February].

PRICE: $1\frac{1}{2}$ guineas.

PRINTING: Fifteen signed and numbered copies. (Signed by Eric Gill.)

SUBSEQUENT EDITIONS: A second edition was published in the same month (February 1916). This was issued in brown paper wrappers ($9\frac{1}{8} \times 6$) printed in all respects as described above save for the Statement of Limitation on the back cover which reads: THIRTY-THREE COPIES OF THIS SECOND EDITION | HAVE BEEN PRINTED AT DITCHLING SUSSEX BY THE | AUTHOR AND THE ENGRAVER NAMELY DOUGLAS | PEPLER AND ERIC GILL FEBRUARY A.D. 1916 This edition was also numbered and signed. Price: fifteen shillings. In G. F. Sims (Rare Books) Catalogue 70 (1968?), item no. 109 is Gill's own copy, no. 1, measuring $11 \times 9\frac{1}{4}$.

261 CANADIAN FIELD ARTILLERY—CONCERT PRO- GRAMMES AND MENU

COVER-TITLE: Reproduced. Shows w-e. *Union Jack* (P49).

SIZE: $10 \times 7\frac{3}{4}$.   COLLATION: A single, unnumbered, conjugate pair.

PAGINATION AND CONTENTS: Pp. 4 (unnumbered); [1]–[4] text of concert programmes. Printed from *Caslon O.F.* on hand-made paper, watermarked 'Aldwych'. Edges untrimmed.

ILLUSTRATIONS: In addition to the w-e. on the cover-title, which was engraved specially for this Programme, the printer utilized the w-e. *Dumb-Driven Cattle* (P36) as described under 'Binding'.

BINDING: Stout blue paper wrappers, sewn, printed as shown in the

CHRISTMAS
A.D.1915

CANADIAN FIELD
BATTERY
1914—1915
THE FIRST BATTERY IS THE BEST
THAT EVER CAME OVER TO
FIGHT GERMANY.
Officer Commanding
M^{AJR.}GOODEVE
[261] Printed at Ditchling, Sussex, by Order or General Proclamation,
February, 1916, by Douglas Pepler.

AN ELEGY UPON OLD

FREEMAN

Us'd hardly by the *Committee*, for lying
in the *Cathedral*, and in *Church
Porches*, praying the Common-
prayer by heart, &c.

BY MATTHEW STEVENSON

*First printed in 1665 ; since overlooked by the
Anthologists.*

PUBLISHED BY MR. EVERARD
MEYNELL, AT 46 MUSEUM ST. W.C.
A.D. 1916. PRICE 6D.

[262]

---

reproduction. The menu was printed on the inner side of the front cover. The
w-e. *Dumb-Driven Cattle* (P36) was printed on the inner side of the back cover
on the outside of which there is the printer's device: *Hog in Triangle: HHW*
(P58).

DATE OF PUBLICATION: February 1916.

PRICE: n.p. Printed for private distribution.

NOTE: Only a few copies of this Programme were printed at my request for the
1st Battery Canadian Field Artillery at that time serving in Flanders.

262 AN ELEGY UPON OLD FREEMAN

TITLE-PAGE: Reproduced.

SIZE: $7\frac{3}{4} \times 5\frac{1}{8}$.

COLLATION: A quarter-sheet folded as two leaves, unsigned.

PAGINATION AND CONTENTS: Pp. 4 (unnumbered); [1] title-page; [2]–[4]
text. Printed from *Caslon O.F.* on Batchelor hand-made paper.

ILLUSTRATIONS: None save that described under 'Binding'.

BINDING: White paper wrappers, sewn, lettered on front: AN ELEGY
UPON OLD | FREEMAN [*in red*] | BY | MATTHEW
STEVENSON | Cover device: *Gravestone with Angel: OLD | FREE- |
MAN* (P61). On back, in centre: *Imprint: D P and Cross* (P64) and, at foot:
[*long rule*] PRINTED BY DOUGLAS PEPLER, DITCHLING, SUSSEX. Edges
untrimmed.

DATE OF PUBLICATION: 1916.

PRICE: 6d.

NOTES: This is not listed in S. Dominic's Press Book List (1930).

133

1916

263 THE GAME

TITLE-PAGE and p. 1, Vol. 1, reproduced (p. 94). For a detailed description of this publication see no. 69.

THE GAME contains the following wood-engravings by Eric Gill:

(a) *Triangular Device: Devil's Tails* (P43), Vol. 1, no. 1, October 1916, p. 20.

(b) *Imprint: D P and Cross* (P64), Vol. 1, no. 2, December 1916, p. [25]; Vol. II, no. 1, January 1918, p. 28; Vol. II, no. 2, The Ascension, p. [40]

(c) *Christmas Gifts: Dawn* (P81), Vol. 1, no. 2, December 1916, p. 28.

(d) *Circular Device* (P78), Vol. 1, no. 2, December 1916, p. 31.

(e) *The Resurrection* (P91), Vol. 1, no. 3, Easter 1917, p. [37].

(f) *Paschal Lamb* (P92), Vol. 1, no. 3, Easter 1917, p. 40.

(g) *Cross* (P112), Vol. II, no. 1, January 1918, p. [1]

(h) *Device: Axe and Block* (P135), Vol. II, no. 1, January 1918, p. 9; Vol. III, no. 2, Advent 1919, p. 62.

(i) *Device: Hangman's Rope* (P136), Vol. II, no. 1, January 1918, p. 15.

(j) *Device: Gravestone with Angel* (P61), Vol. II, no. 1, January 1918, p. [27].

(k) *Ascension* (P140), Vol. II, no. 2, The Ascension 1918, p. [31].

(l) *Madonna and Child: with gallows* (P82), Vol. II, no. 3, Advent 1918, p. [41].

(m) *Imprint: S D P and Cross* (P145), Vol. III, no. 1, Corpus Christi 1919 [cover].

(n) *Welsh Dragon* (P150), Vol. III, no. 1, Corpus Christi 1919, p. 13.

(o) *Christ and the Money-Changers* (P153), Vol. III, no. 1, Corpus Christi 1919, p. [17].

(p) *Madonna and Child: with base* (P155), Vol. III, no. 2, Advent 1919, p. 41.

(q) *Triangular Device: Calvary* (P44), Vol. III, no. 2, Advent 1919, p. 47.

(r) *St George & the Dragon* (P90), Vol. III, no. 2, Advent 1919, p. 54.

(s) *The Holy Childhood* (P180), Vol. IV, no. 1, January 1921, p. [1]

(t) *The Blessed Trinity with the Blessed Virgin* (P181), Vol. IV, no. 2, February 1921, p. [17].

(u) *S. Joseph* (P182), Vol. IV, no. 3, March 1921, p. [33].

(v) *The Holy Ghost* (P183), Vol. IV, no. 4, April 1921, p. [49].

(w) *The Nuptials of God* (P184), Vol. VI, no. 34, January 1923, p. 3.

CONCERNING DRAGONS

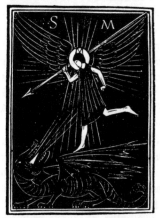

A RHYME BY H.D.C.P.
ENGRAVINGS BY A.E.R.G.
ANNO DOMNI MCMXXI   [264]

264 CONCERNING DRAGONS
COVER-TITLE: Reproduced. Shows w-e. *S. Michael and the Dragon* (P66) in red.
SIZE: $5\frac{3}{4} \times 4\frac{1}{2}$.
COLLATION: A quarter-sheet folded as four leaves, unsigned.
PAGINATION AND CONTENTS: Pp. 8 (unnumbered); [1] cover-title; [2]–[6] text; [7] blank; [8] Imprint: *D P and Cross* (P64) and, at foot: [*long rule*] PRINTED AND PUBLISHED BY DOUGLAS PEPLER, DITCHLING, SUSSEX. Printed throughout in black and red from *Caslon O.F.* on Batchelor hand-made paper. Sewn. Edges untrimmed.
ILLUSTRATIONS: In addition to the w-e. on cover-title there are four others, placed:

> *Child and Nurse* (P67), p. [3]
> *Child and Ghost* (P69), p. [4]
> *Child in Bed* (P68), p. [5]
> *Child and Spectre* (P70), p. [6]

DATE OF PUBLICATION: 1916.
PRICE: n.p. The 1918 S. Dominic's Press catalogue lists the price of the then o.p. first edition as 1s.
NOTE: This is no. 9 of S. Dominic's Press publications.
SUBSEQUENT EDITIONS: A number of editions were printed of this title. These later editions are printed only in black and were sold at 6d. each. The 1919 fourth edition lists three previous editions, 1916, 1917, 1918. Dated editions are known for 1920 and 1921, presumably the fifth and sixth editions.

135

A seventh edition was offered in the 1922 S. Dominic's Press catalogue. Other dated editions are known for 1923, 1926, 1928, 1929 and 1930. The 1919 and 1920 editions have an additional w-e., *Dragon* (P88) on p. [3] followed by the usual four w-e's on pp. [4–7]. In the 1920 and subsequent editions the *D P and Cross* (P64) is replaced with the *S D P and Cross* (P145). The editions are all similar in size except the 1921 edition which measures $4\frac{3}{4} \times 3$ and has sixteen pages, with the text and illustrations printed on one side only. The 1921 edition also has a sixth w-e., the *Welsh Dragon* (P150) on p. [3]. From 1923 on the editions follow the format of the 1919 and 1920 editions except that from the 1926 edition on the *Welsh Dragon* replaces the earlier *Dragon* on p. [3]. In 1929 the S. Dominic's catalogue lists this title in two versions, as a broadsheet, red and black at 1s. as well as a booklet at 6d. Variant wording of the cover title: Copies of the 1916 first edition at CLC and GL use the word Emblems instead of With Engravings, and the w-e. is slightly more orange than red. From 1919 (perhaps earlier) the word Engravings is used for several years, at least until 1923. From 1928 on (perhaps earlier) the word Emblems is used. The rhyme was reprinted in *God and the Dragon*, 1917 (no. 267).

265 ADESTE FIDELES

COVER-TITLE: Reproduced. Shows w-e. *Madonna and Child with Chalice* (P76) in red.

SIZE: $7\frac{1}{2} \times 5$. GL copy measures $7\frac{1}{2} \times 4\frac{5}{8}$.

COLLATION: A half-sheet folded as four leaves, unsigned.

PAGINATION AND CONTENTS: Pp. 8 (unnumbered); [1] [2] cover-title, verso blank; [3]–[6] text; [7] [8] blank, verso printer's imprint: PRINTED BY DOUGLAS PEPLER, DITCHLING, SUSSEX, | WITH WOOD ENGRAVINGS BY ERIC GILL. | A. MCMXVI D. | [*Imprint: D P and Cross* (P64)] Printed from *Caslon O.F.* on Batchelor hand-made paper. Sewn. Top and fore-edges trimmed, bottom edges untrimmed.

ILLUSTRATIONS: In addition to the w-e. on cover-title there are four wood-engravings, placed:

Adeste Fideles (P72), p. [3]	*The Manager* (P74), p. [5]
Three Kings (P73), p. [4]	*Cantet nunc lo* (P75), p. [6]

DATE OF PUBLICATION: 1916.

PRICE: n.p. [2s. 6d.]

NOTE: This is no. 12 of S. Dominic's Press publications.

SUBSEQUENT EDITIONS: A second edition was issued in 1919, $7\frac{1}{2} \times 4\frac{1}{2}$, printed in black only. Printer's imprint, p. [8] is reworded. Ransom lists a reprint with two additional engravings, n.d.

A D E S T E

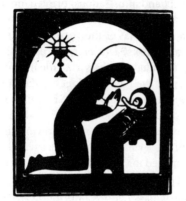

F I D E L E S

A CHRISTMAS HYMN

Ex libris
Desmonde Bernardine-Mane Chuli
AD 1913

266 CHRISTMAS

TITLE-PAGE: There is neither title-page nor cover-title.

SIZE: 8 × 5.

COLLATION: A quarter-sheet folded as two leaves, unsigned.

PAGINATION AND CONTENTS: Pp. [4]; [1] blank; [2] [3] text; [4] blank. Printed from *Caslon O.F.* on Batchelor hand-made paper. All edges trimmed.

ILLUSTRATION: There is one wood-engraving: *Christmas Gifts: Daylight* (P80) on p. [2].

NOTES: This leaflet, which bears no imprint, date or price, was printed and published at S. Dominic's Press towards the end of 1916. It must not be confused with the booklet of verses *Christmas Gifts*, published by the same Press in 1923 (no. 387). It is not listed in S. Dominic's Press List Book (1930). The poem *Christmas* was reprinted in *God and the Dragon* (1917) (no. 267) as *Christmas Gifts*.

1917

267 GOD AND THE DRAGON

TITLE-PAGE: Reproduced. Shows imprint: *D P and Cross* (P64) and the word 'GOD' in red.

SIZE: $5\frac{3}{8} \times 3\frac{7}{8}$.   COLLATION: [Unsigned: [1]⁴, [2] [3]⁸, [4] [5]⁴.]

PAGINATION AND CONTENTS: Pp. viii + 48; [i] [ii] blank, which leaf is pasted down as the front end-paper but forms an integral part of the book; [iii] [iv] half-title: GOD AND THE DRAGON, verso blank; [v] [vi] title-page, verso blank; [vii] [viii] Contents; 1–44 text; 45 tail-piece: *Paschal Lamb* (P92) | [*long rule*] | imprint worded: PRINTED BY DOUGLAS PEPLER | AT DITCHLING SUSSEX. A.D. 1917; 46–7 list of books published by Douglas Pepler; [48] blank and pasted down as back end-paper. Printed from *Caslon O.F.* on Batchelor hand-made paper.

ILLUSTRATIONS: In addition to the tail-piece on p. 45, *Paschal Lamb* (P92), there are fifteen wood-engravings, placed:

> *Epiphany* (P84), p. 1.
> *Device: Spray of leaves* (variant of P108), p. 2.
> *Christmas Gifts* (P83), p. 3.
> *Palm Sunday* (P86), p. 6.
> *Lion* (engraved by John Beedham), p. 9.
> *St George and the Dragon* (P90), p. 14.[1]
> *S. Michael and the Dragon* (P66), p. 18.
> *Dragon* (P88), p. 19.

[1] This was engraved partly by John Beedham from a drawing on wood by Eric Gill. The white lines on the man, horse and dragon were engraved by Eric Gill.

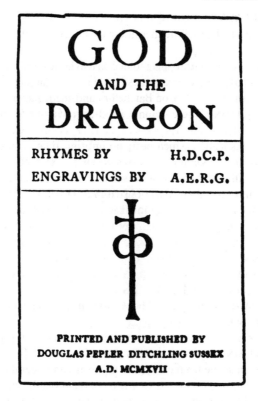

GOD

AND THE

DRAGON

RHYMES BY   H.D.C.P.

ENGRAVINGS BY   A.E.R.G.

PRINTED AND PUBLISHED BY
DOUGLAS PEPLER DITCHLING SUSSEX
A.D. MCMXVII

[267]

Child and Nurse (P67), p. 20.
Child and Ghost (P69), p. 21.
Child in Bed (P68), p. 22.
Child and Spectre (P70), p. 23.
Parlers (P85), p. 27.
Device: Gravestone with Angel (P60), p. 36.
Adam and Eve (P87), p. 40.

BINDING: Cream paper boards, sewn, printed on front: GOD AND THE DRAGON | A BOOK OF RHYMES BY | H. D. C. P. | TWO SHILLINGS NET All edges cut.
DATE OF PUBLICATION: 1917.
PRICE: 2*s*.
PRINTING: 200 copies.
NOTES: This is no. 15 of S. Dominic's Press publications. Tipped in on the inner side of the front cover there should be found a slip (printed in red) concerning the engravings on pp. 9 and 14.

139

268 THE WAY OF THE CROSS

TITLE-PAGE: Reproduced. Shows: w-e. *Imprint: D P and Cross* (P64) the word 'CROSS' in red.

SIZE: $7\frac{3}{4} \times 4\frac{3}{4}$.   COLLATION: [Unsigned: [1]–[3]⁴, [4]².]

PAGINATION AND CONTENTS: Pp. 28 (no pagination); [1] [2] blank, which leaf is pasted down as the front end-paper but forms an integral part of the book; [3] [4] title-page, verso imprimatur; [5]–[7] the *Stabat Mater*; [8] blank; [9]–[22] text; [23] publisher's note: THE WAY OF THE CROSS | PRINTED FROM ENGRAVINGS ON WOOD AFTER THE | DESIGNS FOR THE STATIONS OF THE CROSS NOW BEING | SET UP IN WESTMINSTER CATHEDRAL.; [24] tailpiece: *Paschal Lamb* (P92) and, at foot [*long rule*], printer's imprint: PRINTED AND PUBLISHED BY | DOUGLAS PEPLER, DITCHLING, SUSSEX.; [25] [26] blank; [27] [28] blank and pasted down as the back end-paper and though not forming an integral part of the book is of the same paper as the text and may be treated as such. Printed in black and red from *Caslon O.F.* on Batchelor hand-made paper.

ILLUSTRATIONS: There are fifteen wood-engravings (excluding the imprint and tail-piece described above), placed:

> *Device: Chalice and Host with Candles* (P53), p. [7]
> *Jesus is condemned to death* (P93), p. [9]
> *Jesus receives His Cross* (P94), p. [10]
> *Jesus falls the first time* (P95), p. [11]
> *Jesus meets His Mother* (P96), p. [12]
> *Simon of Cyrene helps Jesus to carry the Cross* (P97), p. [13]
> *Jesus meets Veronica* (P98), p. [14]
> *Jesus falls the second time* (P99), p. [15]
> *Jesus speaks to the women of Jerusalem* (P100), p. [16]
> *Jesus falls the third time* (P101), p. [17]
> *Jesus is stripped* (P102), p. [18]
> *Jesus is nailed to the Cross* (P103), p. [19]
> *Jesus dies upon the Cross* (P104), p. [20]
> *The Body of Jesus is taken down from the Cross* (P105), p. [21]
> *The Body of Jesus is laid in the tomb* (P106), p. [22]

BINDING: Stiff black paper wrappers, sewn, printed on front with device: *D P and Cross* (P112) in gilt and lettered, in gilt: THE WAY OF THE CROSS Top and fore-edges trimmed, bottom edges untrimmed. GL copy is in grey paper covered boards, linen spine, unprinted.

DATE OF PUBLICATION: 1917.

PRICE: n.p. [2s. 6d.]

NOTE: This is no. 17 of S. Dominic's Press publications.

SUBSEQUENT EDITIONS: A second edition ($4\frac{3}{4} \times 3\frac{1}{2}$) was published in 1918, a third (5×4), 33 pp., reset in a different format, in stiff brown paper

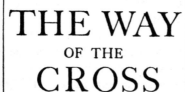

THE WAY
OF THE
CROSS

Being devotions on the progress of
Our Lord Jesus Christ from the Judgment Hall to Calvary as traditionally
venerated by the Catholic Church.

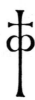

PUBLISHED BY DOUGLAS PEPLER

AT DITCHLING SUSSEX

A.D. MCMXVII

[268]

wrappers, in 1920, a fourth in 1923 and a fifth ($6\frac{1}{2} \times 3\frac{3}{4}$), [24] pp., in blue paper wrappers, in 1926. According to Sewell the fourth edition and onwards have a devotional commentary in verse (anonymous but actually by H. D. C. Pepler). The C L C copy of the 1926 fifth edition is bound in black paper boards, unbleached linen spine, printed in silver on front: The Way of the Cross, with a red dust-jacket lettered in black.

AMERICAN EDITION: An American edition ($7\frac{1}{2} \times 5$), [40] pp., in blue paper wrappers over boards, was published in 1927, printed by Doubleday, Page & Company at the Country Life Press, Garden City, N.Y., in an edition of 350 copies. In this edition the *D P and Cross* is replaced with the *Paschal Lamb* (P92) which is printed in gold on the cover and in black on the title-page.

1918
269 WOODWORK
TITLE-PAGE: Reproduced.
SIZE: $7\frac{3}{4} \times 4\frac{3}{4}$.
COLLATION: [A]^8, B–D^8, E–H^4, [I]–[M]^4. It will be noted that the last four gatherings are unsigned.
PAGINATION AND CONTENTS: Pp. xvi + 112; [i] [ii] title-page, verso blank; [iii] [iv] half-title: *Principles and Practice | of Woodwork* and list of contents, verso *Errata*; v–xvi Introduction; [1]–110 text; [111] [112] blank. Imprint at foot of p. 110 worded: PRINTED AT THE DITCHLING PRESS BY DOUGLAS PEPLER. Printed from *Caslon O.F.* on Batchelor hand-made paper water-marked hammer and anvil.
ILLUSTRATIONS: There are thirty-one wood-engravings in the text. Of these twenty-one are diagrams of carpentry tools engraved by E. G. (The remaining ten were engraved by R. John Beedham.) These are placed:

Fig. 1.	*The bench* (P114), p. 3.	12.	*Sawing block* (P130), p. 20.
2.	*Sawing stool* (P116), p. 6.	13.	*Plough* (P127), p. 21.
3.	*Carpenter's square* (P117), p. 7.	14.	*Gluepot* (P118), p. 24.
4.	*Saw* (P119), p. 7.	15.	*Bevel* (P126), p. 24.
5.	*Plane* (P120), p. 10.	16.	*Striking knife* (P131), p. 25.
6.	*Carpenter's gauge* (P115), p. 11.	17.	*Old woman's tooth* (P122), p. 32.
7.	*Shooting board* (P129), p. 14.	18.	*Shoulder plane* (P128), p. 36.
8.	*Dovetail saw* (P121), p. 14.	19.	*Paring chisel* (P132), p. 39.
9.	*Handscrew* (P123), p. 17.	25.	*A table* (P133), p. 91.
10.	*G cramp* (P124), p. 17.	28.	*Bench-hook* (P134), p. 97.
11.	*Brace* (P125), p. 17.		

The ten wood-engravings by R. John Beedham are placed as follows: figs. 20–2, p. 68; fig. 23, p. 74; fig. 24, p. 75; fig. 26, p. 94; fig. 27, p. 95; fig. 29, p. 105; fig. 30, p. 107; fig. 31, p. 109.
BINDING: Brown paper wrappers, lettered on front: WOODWORK | BY | A. ROMNEY GREEN | VOL. I | [*long rule*] | PRINTED AND PUBLISHED BY DOUGLAS PEPLER, DITCHLING, SUSSEX, | A.D. MCMXVIII. All edges trimmed.
BINDING VARIANT: Copies of this book were at some later date issued in orange paper boards with canvas spine with paper name and title label pasted on front worded: WOODWORK | A. ROMNEY GREEN the whole within a frame of plain rules. CLC and GL both have a copy in marbled paper-covered boards with paper label as above.
DATE OF PUBLICATION: 1918.
PRICE: 8s.
PRINTING: 240 copies.
NOTES: This is no. 26 of S. Dominic's Press publications. Though it is

WOODWORK

IN PRINCIPLE AND PRACTICE

BY

A. ROMNEY GREEN

VOL. I

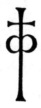

PRINTED AND PUBLISHED BY DOUGLAS PEPLER, DITCHLING, SUSSEX
A.D. MCMXVIII

[269]

entitled Volume I, no later volume was published.

ERRATA: In addition to the errata printed on p. [iv] the following should be noted:

    p. [iv] For 'page 68' read 'page 69'.

    p. 14 For 'Sawing block' [fig. 7] read 'Shooting board'.

    p. 73 For 'figs. 19 and 20' read 'figs. 20 and 21'.

    p. 76 For 'fig. 21' read 'fig. 20'.

    p. 77 For 'fig. 23' read 'fig. 24'.

    p. 84 Insert chapter heading, viz. 'CHAPTER IV'.

Touching the error in description of fig. 7 on p. 14, I have seen a copy of the book wherein the words 'Sawing block' were ruled out and 'Shooting board' printed underneath. In the copy in my possession this correction, curiously enough, has been made on the wrong page, viz. on p. 10! C L C and G L copies in marbled paper-covered boards have the caption 'Sawing block' ruled out on p. 14.

RICHES

Being extracts from **The New Testa-
ment** of **Our Lord** and Saviour *Jesus
Christ*, as translated from the Latin
Vulgate by the English College at
Rheims, A. D. 1582

PRINTED AND PUBLISHED AT S. DOMINIC'S PRESS,
DITCHLING, SUSSEX. A.D. MCMXIX.   [270]

1919
270 RICHES
TITLE-PAGE: Reproduced.
SIZE: $5\frac{3}{4} \times 4\frac{1}{4}$.
COLLATION: Three unsigned gatherings of 2, 8 and 4 leaves respectively.
PAGINATION AND CONTENTS: Pp. iv + 24; [i] [ii] title-page, verso blank;
[iii] [iv] illustration and quotation from the Gospel of St Matthew, verso blank;
[I]–24 text. Printed from *Caslon O.F.* on Batchelor hand-made paper.
ILLUSTRATION: There is one wood-engraving: *Christ and the Money-
Changers* (P152), p. [iii].
BINDING: Stout, light grey, paper wrappers, sewn, lettered on front exactly
as on title-page but with *Price 1s.* added at foot. Top and fore-edges trimmed,
bottom edges untrimmed. C L C copy has brown wrappers.
DATE OF PUBLICATION: 1919.
PRICE: 1s.
NOTE: This is no. 28 (3) of S. Dominic's Press publications.

THREE POEMS

BY

ANANDA COOMARASWAMY

with a woodcut by

ERIC GILL

PRINTED AT S. DOMINIC'S PRESS, DITCHLING, SUSSEX.
A.D. MCMXX.   [271]

1920
271 THREE POEMS
(Coomaraswamy)
COVER-TITLE: Reproduced. Shows w-e. *Welsh Dragon* (P150) in red.
SIZE: 10 × 7, but numerous variations are known. Gill's own copy, at the G L,
is untrimmed, and measures $10\frac{1}{2} \times 7\frac{1}{2}$.
COLLATION: A half-sheet folded as four leaves, unsigned.
PAGINATION AND CONTENTS: Pp. 8; [1] Cover-title; 2 illustration; 3–6
text; [7] [8] tailpiece, verso blank. Printed in red and black from *Caslon O.F.*
on Batchelor hand-made paper. Sewn. All edges cut.
ILLUSTRATIONS: In addition to the device on cover there are two other
wood-engravings, placed: *New England Woods* (P163), p. 2 and: *Tail-piece:
Invitation* (P164), p. [7].
NOTES: These poems were printed for private distribution.

PROPRIUM MISSARUM

DIOECESIS WESTMONASTERIENSIS
A Sacra Rituum Congregatione di. 5 Jan. 1914 approbatum

DIE XXIX NOVEMBRIS
B. CUTHBERTI MAINE
MARTYRIS

Introitus   Psalmus 20

IN virtúte tua, Dómine, laetábitur justus: et super salutáre tuum exúltábit veheménter: desidérium ánimae ejus tribuísti ei. Ps *Ibid.* Quóniam praevenísti eum in benedictiónibus dulcédinis: posuísti in cápite ejus corónam de lápide pretióso. ℣ Glória Patri.

Oratio

DEUS, qui beáto Cuthbérto ante céteros Seminariórum alúmnos cruciátuum iter pro salúte animárum cúrrere dedísti: concéde nobis propítius; ut eódem animárum zelo accénsi, vitam nostram pro áliis impéndere non dubitémus. Per Dóminum.

In Adventu fit com. Feriae. Deinde: pro com. Vig. S. Andreae Apostoli.

Oratio

QUAESUMUS, omnípotens Deus: ut beátus Andréas Apóstolus, cujus praevenímus festivitátem, tuum pro nobis implóret auxílium; ut a nostris reátibus absolúti, a cunctis étiam perículis eruámur.

Pro Com. S. Saturnini Martyris
Oratio

DEUS, qui nos beáti Saturníni Mártyris tui concédis natalítio pérfrui: ejus nos tríbue méritis adjuvári. Per Dóminum.

Léctio Epístolae beáti Jacóbi Apóstoli
cap. 1

CARISSIMI: Omne gaúdium existimáte, cum in tentatiónes várias incidéritis: sciéntes quod probátio fidei vestrae patiéntiam operátur. Patiéntia autem opus perféctum habet: ut sitis perfécti, et íntegri in nullo deficiéntes. Si quis autem vestrum índiget sapiéntia, póstulet a Deo, qui dat ómnibus afflúenter, et non impróperat: et dábitur ei. Póstulet autem in fide nihil haésitans: qui enim haésitat, símilis est flúctui maris, qui a vento movétur, et circumfértur. Non ergo aéstimet homo ille, quod accípiat áliquid a Dómino. Vir duplex ánimo incónstans est in ómnibus viis suis. Gloriétur autem frater húmilis in exaltatióne sua: dives autem in humilitáte sua, quóniam sicut flos foeni transíbit: exórtus est enim sol cum ardóre, et arefécit foenum, et flos ejus décidit, et decor vultus ejus depériit: ita et dives in itinéribus suis marcéscet. Beátus vir, qui

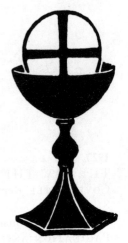

[271a. P65 Chalice and Host]

[271a]

1922
271a PROPRIUM MISSARUM DIOECESIS WESTMONASTE-
RIENSIS.
FIRST PAGE: Reproduced. There is no title-page as such. Shows unrecorded Gill w-e. of *Chalice and Host* similar to (P65).
SIZE: 15 × 10.
COLLATION: Six unsigned gatherings of 6, 4, 4, 4, 5, and 6 leaves respectively.
PAGINATION AND CONTENTS: xii + 34 + xii. [i]–[xii] blank; [1]–33 text; [34] Index Alphabeticus and colophon: TYPOGRAPHIA SANCTI DOMINICI DITCHLING SUSSEX IN ANGLIA, ANNO DOMINI MCMXXII; [i]–[xii] blank.
ILLUSTRATIONS: In addition to the unrecorded *Chalice and Host*, the *Paschal Lamb* (P92) is used as a tailpiece at the end of the text on p. 33.
BINDING: Dark grey paper covered boards, grey linen spine. Lettered in gilt on spine, reading upwards: PROPRIUM MISSARUM DIOECESIS WESTMONASTERIENSIS — S. DOMINIC'S PRESS All edges trimmed.
DATE OF PUBLICATION: 1927.
NOTE: Not recorded in Sewell.

146

THE LAW THE
LAWYERS

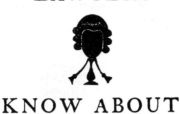

KNOW ABOUT

1923

272 THE LAW THE LAWYERS KNOW ABOUT

COVER-TITLE: Reproduced. Shows w-e. *Lawyer's wig* (P230).

SIZE: 5 × 3¾.

COLLATION: A quarter-sheet folded as four leaves, unsigned.

PAGINATION AND CONTENTS: Pp. 8 (unnumbered); [1] [2] cover-title, verso imprint: PRINTED AT S. DOMINIC'S PRESS | DITCHLING, SUSSEX. | A.D. 1923; [3]–[8] text, p. [4] blank. Printed from *Caslon O.F.* on Batchelor hand-made paper. Sewn. All edges trimmed.

ILLUSTRATIONS: In addition to the w-e. on cover-title there are three wood-engravings, placed:

  Witanbel Watloo (by David Jones, not E. G.), p. [5]

  Initial C with bird-cage (P245), p. [7]

  Gravestone with Angel: OLD | FREE- | MAN (P61), p. [8]

DATE OF PUBLICATION: 1923.

PRICE: n.p. [6d.]

NOTE: This is no. 9 [a] of S. Dominic's Press publications.

SUBSEQUENT EDITIONS: I have a copy which was differently imposed and bears the date '1929' on the cover-title. There is a w-e. (not by E. G.) of a bewigged lawyer on p. [2], the initial letter C is transferred to p. [6], the text ends on p. [7] and the imprint is printed on the back cover: PRINTED AT | ST DOMINIC'S PRESS | DITCHLING | SUSSEX. C L C and G L have copies of an undated edition in which p. [2] is blank, there is an additional caption under *Witanbel Watloo* reading 'Telegraphic address of the L.C.C.' on p. [5], the text ends on p. [8], and the imprint at the bottom of p. [8] is printed in one line under a long rule. These verses originally appeared in *God and the Dragon* (1917) (no. 267).

AUTUMN MIDNIGHT

BY

FRANCES CORNFORD

LONDON
THE POETRY BOOKSHOP
35 DEVONSHIRE STREET, THEOBALDS ROAD, W.C.
1923

[273]

273 AUTUMN MIDNIGHT

TITLE-PAGE: Reproduced. Shows w-e. *Device: To J. & G. R.* | *from* | *F. C.* *& E. G.* (P232). The dedication is to Jacques and Gwen Raverat.

SIZE: $8\frac{3}{4} \times 5\frac{3}{4}$.   COLLATION: [Unsigned: [1]–[3]^4.]

PAGINATION AND CONTENTS: Pp. 24; [1] [2] blank, verso frontispiece; [3] [4] title-page, verso Contents; 5–23 text; [24] author's and publisher's notes, *Imprint: S D P and Cross* (P145) and, at foot: PRINTED AT S. DOMINIC'S PRESS, DITCHLING, SUSSEX. | 31. vii. 1923 Printed from *Caslon O.F.* on Batchelor hand-made paper.

ILLUSTRATIONS: There are twenty-two wood-engravings, chiefly decorated initial letters, placed:

> *Autumn Midnight* (P231), frontispiece, p. [2]
> *Initial W with mirror and chest of drawers* (P233), p. 5.
> *Initial T with woman and child* (P234), p. 6.
> *Initial A with woman and child* (P235), p. 7.
> *Initial T with man and thistles* (P236), p. 7.
> *Initial W with woman and child* (P237), p. 8.
> *Child on foot-rule* (P238), p. 8.
> *Initial M with bedroom* (P239), p. 9.
> *Initial G with vetch and beehive* (P240), p. 10.
> *Initial O with house* (P241), p. 11.
> *Initial A with princess and gypsy* (P242), p. 12.
> *Initial Y with Susan and Diana* (P243), p. 15.

148

Initial I with old nurse (P244), p. 16.
S. Cuthbert's Cross (P159), p. 17.
Initial C with bird-cage (P245), p. 18.
Initial T with woman (P246), p. 19.
S. Joan of Arc (P206), p. 19.
Initial L with woman (P247), p. 20.
Initial B with column (P248), p. 21.
Welsh Dragon (P150), p. 21.
Initial I with trumpeter and drummer (P249), p. 22.
Initial I with witch (P250), p. [24]

BINDING: Pink stiff paper wrappers, sewn. Lettered on front: AUTUMN | MIDNIGHT | BY FRANCES CORNFORD | [*long rule*] | [Device: *Spray of leaves (variant of* P108)] | [*long rule*] | THE POETRY BOOK-SHOP | PRICE TWO SHILLINGS & SXIPENCE | NET [Note the transposition of the letters 'IX' of SIXPENCE] The whole set within a frame of plain rules. *Note:* The initial letter 'A' of 'AUTUMN' is the w-e. *Initial A with woman and child* (P235). Top edges cut, others trimmed.
DATE OF PUBLICATION: [September] 1923.
PRICE: 2s. 6d.
NOTES: I have a copy which is a half an inch shorter than the one described above. In this the cover was differently imposed, the name of the author being enclosed within rules. In other respects the copies are identical even to the misspelling of the word SIXPENCE. GL's copy of this variant has no hyphen in MIDNIGHT on cover. GL has another variant $8\frac{7}{8} \times 5\frac{7}{8}$, in green stiff paper wrappers with a hyphen in MID-NIGHT on cover and SIXPENCE spelled correctly.

1925
274 SONNETS AND VERSES
TITLE-PAGE: Reproduced. Shows w-e. *Youth and Love* (P283).
SIZE: $9 \times 5\frac{1}{4}$.   COLLATION: [a]⁸, b–c⁸, d⁴.
PAGINATION AND CONTENTS: Pp. xiv + 42; [i]–[vi] blank; [vii] [viii] recto blank, verso imprint: PRINTED AND MADE IN GREAT BRITAIN; [ix] [x] title-page, verso blank; [xi] [xii] Contents, verso author's acknowledgments; [xiii] [xiv] Dedication: TO EDITH OLIVE APPLIN, verso blank; 1–35 text; [36] blank; [37] [38] colophon: THIS BOOK OF POEMS BY ENID CLAY, WITH WOOD- | ENGRAVINGS BY ERIC GILL, WAS PRINTED AT THE | GOLDEN COCKEREL PRESS, AT WALTHAM ST. LAWRENCE, | IN BERK-SHIRE, AND COMPLETED ON THE 14TH DAY OF | MARCH, 1925. COMPOSITORS: A. H. GIBBS AND | F. YOUNG. PRESSMEN: A. C. COOPER AND | W. R. MILLS. THE EDITION IS LIMITED | TO 450

SONNETS
AND VERSES
BY ENID CLAY

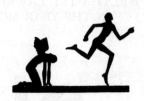

THE GOLDEN COCKEREL PRESS
MCMXXV.

[274]

COPIES, OF WHICH THIS IS | NUMBER [number filled in by hand] | and, at foot, printer's device: *Cockerel* (Chute) in gold, verso blank; [39]–[42] blank. Printed from 14 pt. *Caslon O.F.* on Batchelor hand-made paper watermarked hammer and anvil.

ILLUSTRATIONS: In addition to the engraving on title-page, there are seven wood-engravings, placed:

    Lovers on a Bank (P288), p. 3.
    Child picking Flowers (P287), p. 6.
    Death and the Lady (full-page) (P285), p. [10]
    Naked Girl with Cloak (P282), p. 16.
    Naked Girl on Grass (P284), p. 17.
    Mother and Child (full-page) (P286), p. [24]
    Flower-piece (full-page) (P281), p. [32]

BINDING: Quarter linen, blue boards. Paste-on label on spine printed, reading upwards: SONNETS & VERSES | BY ENID CLAY Top edges cut, others uncut.

DATE OF PUBLICATION: April 1925.

PRICE: 15s.

PRINTING: 450 copies.

NOTE: This book, which is no. 25 of the Golden Cockerel Press publications, was crowned by the Double-Crown Club as being the best-produced book of its price published during 1925.

REVIEWS: *The Observer*, 31 May 1925. *The Times Literary Supplement*, 27 August 1925.

150

THE
SONG OF SONGS

CALLED BY MANY THE CANTICLE OF CANTICLES
PRINTED AND PUBLISHED AT THE GOLDEN COCKEREL
PRESS AT WALTHAM ST. LAWRENCE IN BERKSHIRE
IN THE YEAR MCMXXV

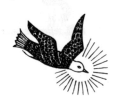

[275]

275 THE SONG OF SONGS

TITLE-PAGE: Reproduced. Shows w-e. *Holy Ghost as dove* (P224) in red.
SIZE: $10\frac{1}{2} \times 7\frac{1}{2}$.
COLLATION: [a]⁴, b–f⁴.
PAGINATION AND CONTENTS: Pp. 48; [1] [2] blank, which leaf is pasted
down as the front end-paper but forms an integral part of the book; [3] [4]
blank; [5] [6] recto blank, verso imprint, at foot: PRINTED AND MADE IN
GREAT BRITAIN [7] [8] title-page, verso blank; 9–42 text; [43] [44] tail-piece,
verso blank; [45] [46] colophon: THIS BOOK WAS PRINTED BY ROBERT
GIBBINGS AT | THE GOLDEN COCKEREL PRESS AND COMPLETED ON |
THE XVII. DAY OF OCTOBER MCMXXV. THE ILLUS- | TRATIONS HAVE
BEEN DESIGNED AND ENGRAVED | ON WOOD BY ERIC GILL. COMPOSI-
TORS: F. YOUNG | AND A. H. GIBBS. PRESSMAN: A. C. COOPER. THE |
EDITION IS LIMITED TO SEVEN HUNDRED & FIFTY | NUMBERED
COPIES, OF WHICH THIS IS NO. ... | [signed: *Robert Gibbings* | *Eric Gill*
O.S.D.] and, at foot, printer's device: *Cockerel* (Chute) in black, verso blank;
[47] [48] blank. The back fly-leaf and end-paper though of Batchelor paper are
of a different texture and cannot be treated as an integral part of the book.
Printed in black and red from 18 pt. *Caslon O.F.* on Batchelor hand-made
paper.
ILLUSTRATIONS: In addition to the engraving on the title-page there are
eighteen illustrations from wood-engravings, placed:

> *The Harem* (P316), p. [12]
> *Inter Ubera Mea* (P320), p. 15.
> *His left hand beneath my Head* (P318), p. 17.

151

Skipping upon the Mountains (P319), p. 18.
On my Bed by Night (P317), p. 20.
Wake not my Beloved (P321), p. 21.
The Serenade (P322), p. 24.
The Kiss (P323), p. 26.
A Garden enclosed (P324), p. 27.
The voice of my Beloved (P325), p. 28.
The Watchmen (P326), p. 30.
My Love among the Lilies (P327), p. 32.
The Dancer (P338), p. 36.
The Lust of Solomon (P329), p. 37.
Let us fare forth into the fields (P330), p. 38.
Ibi Dabo Tibi (P331), p. 39.
The Juice of my Pomegranates (P332), p. 40.
Young Fawn (P333), p. [43]

Thirty copies were hand-coloured.

An engraving: *Stay me with apples* (P305), not used in the book, was published in the prospectus of *The Song of Songs*.

BINDING: Bound in white buckram, lettered in gilt on spine, reading upwards THE SONG OF SONGS. The thirty hand-coloured copies have the *Holy Ghost as Dove* (P224) design stamped in gold on front cover. T.e.g., other edges uncut.

DATE OF PUBLICATION: October 1925.

PRICE: 21*s*. The thirty copies hand-coloured and signed by Eric Gill: five guineas.

PRINTING: 750 numbered copies which include the thirty hand-coloured and signed copies.

NOTE: This is no. 31 of the Golden Cockerel Press publications.

1926

276 PASSIO DOMINI (THE PASSION)

TITLE-PAGE: Reproduced. Shows w-e. *Mary Magdalen* (P349). The words 'PASSIO DOMINI' in red.

SIZE: $10\frac{1}{2} \times 7\frac{1}{2}$.   COLLATION: [Unsigned: [1]–[4]⁴.]

PAGINATION AND CONTENTS: Pp. viii + 24; [i]–[vi] blank, of which the first leaf is pasted down as the front end-paper but forms an integral part of the book; [vii] [viii] recto blank, verso imprint: PRINTED AND MADE IN GREAT BRITAIN; [1] title-page; 2–15 text; [16] blank; [17] [18] colophon: THIS BOOK WAS PRINTED BY ROBERT GIBBINGS AT | THE GOLDEN COCKEREL PRESS, AND COMPLETED | ON THE XX DAY OF FEBRUARY, MCMXXVI. | THE TEXT IS THAT OF THE VULGATE ACCORDING | TO

PASSIO DOMINI
NOSTRI JESU CHRISTI
BEING THE 26TH AND 27TH CHAPTERS OF SAINT
MATTHEW'S GOSPEL FROM THE LATIN TEXT

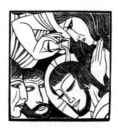

WALTHAM SAINT LAWRENCE IN ENGLAND
AT THE GOLDEN COCKEREL PRESS
MCMXXVI   [276]

THE EDITION OF ALOYSIUS FILLION (PARIS, LE- | TOUZY ET ANE,
MCMXXI). THE ILLUSTRATIONS ARE | DESIGNED AND ENGRAVED ON
WOOD BY ERIC GILL. | COMPOSITORS: A. H. GIBBS AND F. YOUNG.
PRESS- | MAN: A. C. COOPER. THE EDITION IS LIMITED TO | CCL
COPIES, OF WHICH THIS IS NUMBER ... and, at foot, printer's device:
Cockerel (Chute) in black, verso blank; [19]–[22] blank; [23] [24] blank and
pasted down as end-paper forming an integral part of the book. Printed from
18 pt. *Caslon O.F.* (with initial letters in red) on Batchelor hand-made paper
watermarked bible and crown.

ILLUSTRATIONS: In addition to the w-e. on title-page there are five, placed:

> *The Agony in the Garden* [full-page] (P350), p. [4]
> *The Kiss of Judas* (P351), p. 7.
> *The Carrying of the Cross* (P352), p. 9.
> *The Crucifixion* [full-page] [P353], p. [12]
> *The Deposition* (P354), p. 15.

BINDING: Full bound in white buckram, lettered on spine, in gilt, reading
upwards THE PASSION Top edges cut, others uncut. White dust jacket
with title etc. printed in black, with *Mary Magdalen* (P349).

DATE OF PUBLICATION: March 1926.

PRICE: 25s.

PRINTING: 250 numbered copies.

REVIEW: *The Times Literary Supplement*, 29 July 1926.

NOTES: This is no. 35 of the Golden Cockerel Press publications. It was
shown at the *Exhibition of Books Illustrating British and Foreign Printing,*

153

1919–1929, organized by the British Museum and figures as no. 52 in the Great Britain section of the catalogue faced by a specimen page of the book, p. [19] (cf. no. 642).

277 PROCREANT HYMN

TITLE-PAGE: PROCREANT | HYMN | BY | E. POWYS MATHERS | and, at foot: THE GOLDEN COCKEREL PRESS
SIZE: 10 × 6.   COLLATION: [a]⁴, b–d⁴.
PAGINATION AND CONTENTS: Pp. viii + 24; [i] [ii] blank, which leaf is pasted down as the front end-paper but forms an integral part of the book; [iii]–[vi] blank; [vii] [viii] recto blank, verso imprint: PRINTED AND MADE IN GREAT BRITAIN; [1] [2] title-page, verso blank; [3] [4] dedication: FOR | VIRET AND ROBERT, verso blank; 5–20 text; [21] [22] recto blank, verso colophon: THIS BOOK WAS PRINTED BY ROBERT GIBBINGS AT WALTHAM | SAINT LAWRENCE IN BERKSHIRE, AND COMPLETED ON THE 6TH | DAY OF FEBRUARY, 1926. | THE ENGRAVINGS ARE BY ERIC GILL. | COMPOSITORS: F. YOUNG AND A. H. GIBBS. PRESSMAN: | A. C. COOPER. THE EDITION IS LIMITED TO 175 NUMBERED | COPIES FOR SALE & 25 FOR PRESENTATION. THIS IS NO. [. . .], and, at foot, printer's device: *Cockerel* (Chute) in black; [23] [24] blank. Printed from 14 pt. *Caslon O.F. Italic* on Batchelor hand-made paper watermarked hammer and anvil.
ILLUSTRATIONS: There are five full-page line-engravings on copper, printed separately and placed:

> *God Sending* (P359), frontispiece.
> *Earth Waiting* (P360), facing p. 8.
> *Earth Inviting* (P361), facing p. 10.
> *Dalliance* (P362), facing p. 15.
> *Earth Receiving* (P363), facing p. 19.

BINDING: Full bound in white buckram, lettered in gilt on spine, reading upwards: PROCREANT HYMN. MATHERS T.e.g., other edges uncut. Buff dust jacket, printed in black, wording as per the title-page, with the addition of the date MCMXXVI.
DATE OF PUBLICATION: June 1926.
PRICE: Two guineas.
PRINTING: 200 numbered copies, 175 of which were for sale.
NOTES: This is no. 37 of the Golden Cockerel Press publications. Three alternative designs (nos. P364, P365, and P366) were engraved for this book. They were limited to twenty-five sets, signed by the artist, of which twenty were for sale at two guineas the set.

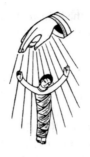

GLORIA IN PROFUNDIS

By G. K. CHESTERTON

WOOD ENGRAVINGS BY ERIC GILL   [278]

1927

278 GLORIA IN PROFUNDIS

COVER-TITLE: Reproduced. Shows w-e. *Bambino* (P478).

SIZE: $7\frac{1}{4} \times 4\frac{3}{4}$.

COLLATION: A half-sheet folded as four leaves, unsigned.

PAGINATION AND CONTENTS: Pp. 4 [unpaged]; [1] illustration; [2] [3] text headed: GLORIA IN PROFUNDIS | (*Chorus from an Unfinished Play*); [4] list of *The Ariel Poems*.

ILLUSTRATIONS: In addition to the w-e. on cover-title there is one full-page w-e. *Nativity* (P479) on p. [1]

BINDING: Bright yellow paper wrappers with overlaps, sewn; printed on front in black as reproduced and on back: THIS IS NUMBER 5 OF | THE ARIEL POEMS | PUBLISHED BY FABER & GWYER LIMITED | AT 24 RUSSELL SQUARE, LONDON, W.C. I | PRINTED AT THE CURWEN PRESS, PLAISTOW All edges trimmed.

DATE OF PUBLICATION: [August] 1927.

PRICE: 1s.

NOTE: This booklet was issued in a buff coloured envelope ready for posting.

DE LUXE EDITION: There was also an edition limited to 350 copies printed on Zanders' hand-made paper and signed by Eric Gill. It consists of eight unnumbered pages preceded and followed by one blank leaf. Bound in yellow paper boards, printed on front (only) as for the 'ordinary' edition. Price: 5s. The poem and w-e. were reproduced in the *Catholic Art Quarterly*, Vol. XVII, no. I, Christmas 1953, on p. 4.

279 TROILUS AND CRISEYDE

TITLE-PAGE: Reproduced. Shows w-e. TROILUS | AND | CRISEYDE | BY | GEOF- | FREY | CHAUCER (P474). SIZE: 12 × 7¼. COLLATION: [A]⁸, B⁸–X⁸. PAGINATION AND CONTENTS: Pp. xvi + 320; [four blank pages]; [i] [ii] half-title: TROILUS AND CRISEYDE BY GEOFFREY | CHAUCER [w-e. *line-filling* (P392)] EDITED BY ARUNDELL | DEL RE WITH WOOD ENGRAVINGS BY | ERIC GILL PRINTED AND PUBLISHED | AT THE GOLDEN COCKEREL PRESS AT | WALTHAM SAINT LAWRENCE IN | BERKSHIRE ENGLAND | A.D. MCMXXVII, verso imprint: PRINTED AND MADE IN GREAT BRITAIN; [iii] [iv] title-page, verso blank; v–xi Introduction and Notes; [xii] blank; [1] title-page to *Book I*. [*II., III., IV., V.*] (in red or blue) enclosed within w-e. *Circular Border* (P432); 2–[310] text; [311] [312] blank [313] [314] colophon: THIS BOOK WAS PRINTED BY ROBERT GIBBINGS | AT THE GOLDEN COCKEREL PRESS, WALTHAM | SAINT LAWRENCE IN BERKSHIRE. BEGINNING | ON THE 20TH DAY OF SEPTEMBER, 1926, IT WAS | COMPLETED ON JULY 22ND, 1927. COMPOSITORS: F. YOUNG AND A. H. GIBBS. PRESSMAN: A. C. | COOPER. THE EDITION IS LIMITED TO 225 | COPIES, OF WHICH NOS. 1–6 ARE ON | VELLUM. THIS IS NUMBER . . . [Printer's device: *Cockerel* (David Jones) in black], verso blank; [316]–[320] blank. Printed in red, black and blue from 18 pt. *Caslon O.F.* on vellum (nos. 1–6) and on Kelmscott hand-made paper watermarked hammer and anvil, also oak leaves (nos. 7–225).

ILLUSTRATIONS: In addition to the engraved title-page and circular border described above, there are five full-page illustrations, four tail-pieces and sixty decorative borders from wood-engravings, placed:

Border: *Chaucer and Cupid* (P443), pp. 2, 106, [176], 234.

„ *Cupid running, Ape and Satyr in Tree* (P440), pp. 3, 25, 111, 197, 229, 265, 291.

Full-page illustration: *Meeting of Troilus and Criseyde* (P433), p. [4]

Border: *Man climbing to Girl* (P410), pp. 5, 13, 90, 139, 277.

„ *Girl and Cupid* (P403), pp. 6, 27, 72, 96, 146, 172, 292.

„ *Girl with knee raised, and Cupid* (P404), pp. 7, 147, 293.

„ *Cupid, with Bow on arm* (P405), pp. 8, 30, 58, 88, 148, 208, 238.

„ *Girl, and Man with Sword* (P406), pp. 9, 31, 55, 83, 119, 149, 209, 294.

„ *Cupid holding Bow* (P407), pp. 10, 54, 118, 164, 300.

„ *Lovers* (P408), pp. 11, 107, 165, 219, 301.

„ *Girl standing* (P409), p. 12.

„ *Girl praying, Man on Tree* (P419), pp. 14, 53, 77, 114, 166, 200, 260.

„ *Man reading, Girl on Tree* (P420), pp. 15, 71, 115, 167, 201, [239],

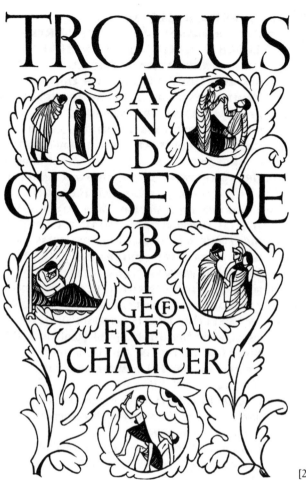

[279]

157

Border: *Man on Tree, and Naked Girl below* (P426), pp. 23, [45], 225, 259.
  „ *Man with Raised Sword* (P439), pp. 24, 52, 188, 210, 228, 264, 298.
  „ *Acanthus Leaves* (P435), pp. 26, 82, 252, 288.
  „ *Naked Youth* (P423), pp. 28, 56, 92, 122, 150, 280.
  „ *Naked Girl looking back* (P424), pp. 29, 49, 123, 151, 192, 281.
  „ *Man piping* (P429), pp. 32, 48, 70, 94, 116, 154, 244.
  „ *Woman with two Children* (P430), pp. 33, 73, 169, 245.
  „ *Branch with fourteen leaves* (P468), pp. 35, 100, 144, 162, 198, 270.
  „ *Man and Girl in four groups on way to Church* (P427), pp. 36, 93, 152, 222.
  „ *Man and Girl in four groups on way from Church* (P428), pp. 37, 117, 153, 223.
  „ *Nine Leaves* (P436), pp. 126, 189, 249.
  „ *Ten Leaves with Flower at side* (P438), pp. 38, 57, 86, 104, 160, 199.
  „ *Naked Girl holding Branch* (P445), pp. 40, 206, 248.
  „ *Cupid; Bow on Tree* (P446), pp. 41, 50, 135, 207.
  „ *Man looking up* (P389), p. 44.
Tail-piece: *Spray of Leaves* (P391), p. [45]
Full-page illustration: *Criseyde visits Troilus* (P455), p. [46]
Border: *Two men with Spears* (P450), pp. 51, 67, 97, 181, 233, 279, 297.
  „ *Girl repulsing Man* (P442), pp. 59, 79, 91, 185, 217, 247, 273, 299.
  „ *Eleven Leaves* (P437), pp. 60, 218, 268.
  „ *Lovers in Tree* (P454), pp. 61, 87, 213.
  „ *Harpy facing right* (P451), pp. 62, 142, 194, 274.
  „ *Harpy facing left* (P452), pp. 63, 143, 195, 275.
  „ *Man shading his Eyes with his Hand* (P441), pp. 64, 89, 184, 216, 246, 272, 290, 306.
  „ *Man throwing Spear* (P449), pp. 68, 180, 232, 278, 296.
  „ *Lovers facing left* (P448), pp. 69, 127, 171, 211, 263, 307.
  „ *Man trying Sword* (P447), pp. 80, 170, 196, 262.
  „ *Girl turning into Tree: facing left* (P456), pp. 98, 130, 190, 254, 287.
  „ *Girl turning into Tree: facing right* (P457), pp. 99, 131, 155, 191, 255, 286.
  „ *Girl lying at bottom of branch, Child above* (P469), pp. 101, 145, 269.
  „ *Faun piping* (P458), pp. 102, 134, 168, 214, 282.
  „ *Naked girl facing right* (P460), pp. 103, 124, 136, 156, 202, 284.
  „ *Venus Instructrix Artis Amoris* (P453), pp. 110, 212.
  „ *Naked girl with back turned* (P459), pp. 125, 161, 215, 283.
Tail-piece: *Man with Sword, kneeling* (P471), pp. [111], [239]
Full-page illustration: *Approaching Dawn* (P470), p. [112]
Border: *Prickly Leaves* (P464), pp. 113, 138, 175, 237, 276.
  „ *Girl in Skirt facing right* (P466), pp. 120, 132, 186, 226, 256, 302.

Border: *Girl in Skirt, full-face* (P467), pp. 133, 187, 227, 257, 303.

„ *Naked girl facing left* (P461), pp. 137, 157, 203, 235, 285.

„ *Virgin and Child on Tree* (P462), pp. 174, 236, 308.

Tail-piece: *Lovers* (P475), p. [176]

Full-page illustration: *The Parting* (P472), p. [178]

Border: *Chaucer writing* (P444 second state), pp. 179, 243, [310]

„ *Leaves with Flower at top* (P465), pp. 224, 258, 289.

Full-page illustration: *The Death of Troilus* (P473), p. [242]

Border: *Our Lord on Tree* (P463), p. 309.

Tail-piece: *Child with letter T as Crucifix* (P487), p. [310]

There are also twenty-two initial letters, engraved on wood, represented in *Engravings, 1928–1933* (Faber & Faber) by no. 120 [P402] (for the letter C) and no. 194 [P477] (for the remainder) printed in either red or blue.

BINDING: $\frac{1}{4}$ red niger morocco, patterned boards, panelled spine lettered in gilt: T R O I L U S | A N D | C R I S E Y D E T.e.g. other edges uncut. Vellum edition, full niger morocco.

DATE OF PUBLICATION: September 1927.

PRICE: Paper edition: ten guineas. Vellum edition: forty guineas.

PRINTING: 225 numbered copies: Nos. 1–6 on vellum. Nos. 7–225 on Kelmscott hand-made paper.

REVIEW: John Rothenstein, *The Bibliophile's Almanack*, 1928, pp. 75–9.

NOTE: This is no. 50 of the Golden Cockerel Press publications.

AMERICAN EDITION: TROILUS AND CRESSIDA. A LOVE | POEM IN FIVE BOOKS. ENGLISHED ANEW | BY GEORGE PHILIP KNAPP WITH WOOD | ENGRAVINGS BY ERIC GILL. PUBLISHED | BY RANDOM HOUSE IN NEW YORK | A.D. MCMXXXII

Size: $9\frac{1}{4} \times 6\frac{1}{2}$. *Illustrations:* The illustrations are those which were engraved for the Golden Cockerel Press edition but are slightly reduced in size. *Binding:* Full canvas, lettered on front in gilt: T R O I L U S | A N D | C R E S S I D A | G E O F F R E Y C H A U C E R | [*device*] | on a dark brown panel placed between reproductions of two of the border decorations (in red). Lettered on spine, in gilt, reading downwards: G E O F F R E Y | C H A U C E R | T R O I L U S A N D C R E S S I D A | R A N D O M | H O U S E Top-edges cut and coloured brown to match the binding, other edges uncut. G L copy has cover panel in red, lettering on spine: (in red) device of three leaves, reading across spine, GEOFFREY/CHAUCER reading downwards (in gilt) T R O I L U S A N D C R E S S I D A, reading across spine (in red) R A N D O M | H O U S E | device of three leaves. Printed red and brown dust jacket, with lettering and decorations in white. *Date of publication:* 1932. *Price:* $3.50. The Literary Guild of New York also issued the book in 1932 in blue cloth covered boards, vegetable parchment spine.

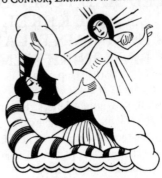

THE SONG OF THE SOUL
By SAINT JOHN-OF-THE-CROSS, *Barefooted Carmelite; Doctor of the Church.* TRANSLATED *by* JOHN O'CONNOR, *Licentiate in Sacred Theology*

FRANCIS WALTERSON
CAPEL-Y-FFIN
ABERGAVENNY
1927

[280]

280 THE SONG OF THE SOUL

TITLE-PAGE: Reproduced. Shows w-e. *The Flight* (P493).

SIZE: $8\frac{1}{2}\times 7$.   COLLATION: $[A]^4$, B–C^4.

PAGINATION AND CONTENTS: Pp. 24; [1] [2] title-page, verso blank; 3–6 Introduction by John O'Connor; 7–21 text; [22] blank; [23] [24] colophon: PRINTED BY THE CHISWICK PRESS | IN LONDON FOR FRANCIS WALTERSON | AT CAPEL-Y-FFIN IN WALES. THIS | EDITION OF THE SONG OF THE SOUL | WITH WOOD-ENGRAVINGS BY ERIC | GILL IS LIMITED TO 150 COPIES, OF | WHICH THIS IS NO. ... | [Signed: *Eric Gill*], verso blank. Hand-printed on Batchelor hand-made paper.

ILLUSTRATIONS: In addition to the w-e. on title-page there are three, placed:

> *No Wild Beast shall dismay me* (P494), p. 7.
> *Our Bed is all of Flowers* (P495), p. 14.
> *The Soul and the Bridegroom* (P496), p. 21.

BINDING: $\frac{1}{4}$ bound red buckram, green and blue mottled batik boards, lettered in gilt on spine, reading downwards: THE SONG OF THE SOUL All edges untrimmed.

DATE OF PUBLICATION: 1927.

PRICE: 25*s*.

PRINTING: 150 signed and numbered copies.

160

THE CANTERBURY TALES
BY GEOFFREY CHAUCER ⚜ WITH
WOOD ENGRAVINGS BY ERIC GILL
PRINTED AND PUBLISHED AT THE
GOLDEN COCKEREL PRESS AT
WALTHAM SAINT LAWRENCE IN
BERKSHIRE MCMXXIX

VOLUME I [281]

1929
281 THE CANTERBURY TALES
TITLE-PAGE: Reproduced. Shows w-e. *Line filling* (P392).
SIZE: $12\frac{1}{2} \times 7\frac{1}{2}$.   Four volumes.
COLLATION: Vol. I. [A]^4, [B]^8, C–K^8, L^6. Vol. II. [A]^4, B–N^8. Vol. III. [A]^4, B–N^8, O^6. Vol. IV. [A]^4, [B]^8, C–O^8, [P]^8.
PAGINATION AND CONTENTS: Vol. I. Pp. viii + 156; [i]–[iv] blank; [v] [vi] title-page, verso Imprint: PRINTED AND MADE IN GREAT BRITAIN; [vii] [viii] dedication: DEDICATED | TO | HUBERT PIKE [enclosed within *Circular Border* (P432)], verso blank; [1]–[151] text; [152] Contents of Vol. I; [153]–[156] blank.
Vol. II. Pp. viii + 192; [i]–[iv] blank; [v] [vi] blank, verso Imprint: PRINTED AND MADE IN GREAT BRITAIN; [vii] [viii] title-page, verso blank; [1]–[189] text; [190] Contents of Vol. II; [191] [192] blank.
Vol. III. Pp. viii + 204; [i]–[iv] blank; [v] [vi] blank, verso Imprint: PRINTED AND MADE IN GREAT BRITAIN; [vii] [viii] title-page, verso blank; [1]–[197] text; [198] Contents of Vol. III; [199]–[204] blank.
Vol. IV. Pp. viii + 224; [i]–[iv] blank; [v] [vi] blank, verso Imprint: PRINTED AND MADE IN GREAT BRITAIN; [vii] [viii] title-page, verso blank; [1]–[219] text; [220] Contents of Vol. IV; [221] [222] colophon: THIS EDITION OF THE CANTERBURY TALES, IN FOUR VOLUMES, WAS | PRINTED BY ROBERT & MOIRA GIBBINGS AT THE GOLDEN COCKEREL | PRESS, WALTHAM SAINT LAWRENCE, BERKSHIRE. BY PERMISSION | OF THE OXFORD UNIVERSITY PRESS THE TEXT FOLLOWS THEIR EDITION | EDITED BY

161

Books illustrated by Gill

THE REV. WALTER W. SKEAT, M.A. THE FIRST PAGES | OF VOLUME I
WERE SET ON THE 6TH OF JUNE, 1928, AND THE LAST | PAGES OF
VOLUME IV PRINTED ON THE 29TH OF JANUARY, 1931. | COM-
POSITORS: F. YOUNG AND A. H. GIBBS. PRESSMAN: | A. C. COOPER.
15 COPIES ON VELLUM AND 485 | ON PAPER HAVE BEEN PRINTED, OF
| WHICH THIS IS NO. [. . .] [*The number filled in by hand*] Printer's device:
Cockerel (David Jones) in black, at foot, verso blank; [223] [224] blank.
Printed from 18 pt. *Caslon O.F.* (some of the initial letters in red or blue) on
vellum (nos. 1–15) and on Batchelor hand-made paper (nos. 16–500) with
Cockerel watermark.

ILLUSTRATIONS:

VOLUME I. In addition to the *Circular Border* for the Dedication, p. [vii],
there are one full-page and five half-page illustrations and forty-five decorated
borders, tail-pieces and line-fillings, engraved on wood, placed:

Opening page: *Venus with the Golden Cockerel* (P535) and *line-filling, two
   leaves* (P536), p. [1]

Opening page for Prologue: *St Thomas' Martyrdom* (P537), p. 2.

Border: *Spray of twelve triple-lobed leaves* (P539), pp. 3, 77.

„ *Spray of eight leaves and four flowers* (P538), pp. 4, 30, 62, 96, 128.
„ *Two jesters* (P508), pp. 5, 36, 64, 93, 139.
„ *Spray of seven leaves and flower bud* (P509), pp. 6, 58, 92.
„ *Girl and bird* (P507), pp. 7, 37, 59, 87, 105, 145.
„ *Nun blowing kiss* (P533), pp. 8, 40, 102, 126.
„ *Cherub on branch* (P534), pp. 9, 41, 63, 95.
„ *Child pointing* (P525), pp. 10, 53, 80, [106]
„ *Chaucer writing at foot of spray* (P526), pp. 11, 52, 81.
„ *Spray of eight leaves* (P521), pp. 12, 72, 144.
„ *Branch with fifteen leaves* (variant of P468), pp. 13, 136, 146.
„ *Woman beseeching* (P523), pp. 14, 44, 90, 120, 142.
„ *Man in love* (P524), pp. 15, 46, 91, 121, 143.
„ *King Solomon* (P498), pp. 16, 60, 88.
„ *The Wife of Bath* (P499), pp. 17, 61, 89, 135.
„ *Child peeping* (P546), pp. 18, 65, 101, 149.
„ *Clergyman shocked* (P527), pp. 19, 86, 118, 141.
„ *Eleven leaves with flower at side* (variant of P438), pp. 20, 94.
„ *Smith with poker* (P528), pp. 21, 129.
„ *Man dead drunk* (P515), pp. 22, 82, 108, 124.
„ *Woman and ape* (P511), pp. 23, 32, 78, 98.
„ *St. Thomas of Canterbury* (P519), pp. 24, 76, 104, 134.
„ *Crucifix on tree* (P520), pp. 25, 47, 97.
„ *Man waving eight-leaved spray* (P529), pp. 26, 54, 70, 122.
„ *Man waving ten-leaved spray* (P530), pp. 27, 55, 71, 123.

162

Border: *Faun piping* (variant of P458), pp. 28, 50, 112.

„ *Naked girl with back turned* (variant of P459), pp. 29, 51, 113.

Half-page illustration: *The Knight's Tale* (P540), p. 31.

Border: *Naked men fighting* (P512), pp. 33, 57, 83, 99.

„ *Tree woman (leaves for hands)* (P517), pp. 34, 66, 100, 140.

„ *Spray of fifteen leaves* (P518), pp. 35, 88.

„ *Youth blowing kiss* (P531), pp. 38, 68, 110, 138, 150.

„ *Girl all agog* (P532), pp. 39, 69, 103, 147.

„ *Man climbing* (P513), pp. 42, 56, 74, 114, 130, [152]

„ *Man & girl drinking* (P516), pp. 43, 79, 109, 125.

„ *Naughty boy climbing* (P522), pp. 45, 73, 127, [151]

„ *Man piping* (variant of P429), pp. 48, 116.

„ *Girl lying at bottom of branch, Child above* (variant of P469), pp. 49, 137.

„ *Child crawling at foot of spray* (P544), pp. 67, 117, 133.

„ *Man dead* (P514), pp. 75, 115, 131.

„ *Thirteen leaves* (variant of P437), pp. 84, 119.

Tail-piece for *The Knight's Tale: Spray with nine pointed leaves* (P541), p. [106]

Half-page illustration: *The Miller's Tale* (P542), p. 107.

Border: *Woman climbing floreated phallus* (P510), p. 111.

Half-page illustration: *The Reeve's Tale* (P543), p. 132.

„ „ *The Cook's Tale* (P545), p. 148.

Tail-piece for *The Cook's Tale: the inadequate fig leaf* (P547), p. [151]

Tail-piece for the Index of Vol. I: *Spray with five pointed leaves* (P548), p. [152]

There are also eleven initial letters, engraved on wood (represented in *Engravings 1928–1933 by Eric Gill* (Faber & Faber, 1934), by nos. 265–7 [P549–51]) printed in either black, red or blue.

VOLUME II

There are eight half-page illustrations, sixty-seven decorated borders and tail-pieces and a line-filling, engraved on wood and placed:

Opening page: *Venus modestly holding spray, Cupid playing football with the world* (P582) and *line-filling, one double leaf* (P583), p. [1]

Border: *Man in love* (P524), pp. 2, 35, 52.

„ *Spray of ten leaves and one leaf bud* (P587), pp. 3, 45, 187.

„ *Spray of seven rounded leaves* (P584), p. 4.

Half-page illustration: *The Lawyer's Tale* (P585), p. 5.

Border: *Tree woman (leaves for hands)* (P517), pp. 6, 176.

„ *Spray of thirteen leaves* (P595), pp. 7, 79, 150.

„ *Child pointing* (P525), pp. 8, 40, 164.

„ *Chaucer writing at foot of spray* (P526), pp. 9, 41, [165]

Border: *Branch with fifteen leaves* (variant of P468), pp. 10, 170.
„   *Girl lying at bottom of branch, Child above* (variant of P469), pp. 11, 171.
„   *Spray of seven leaves and four curls* (P565), pp. 12, 46, 172.
„   *Man holding curl of spray* (P566), pp. 13, 47, 173.
„   *Girl with lace-edged drawers* (P567), p. 14.
„   *Man beseeching* (P568), p. 15.
„   *Man waving eight-leaved spray* (P529), pp. 16, 76, 142, 184.
„   *Man waving ten-leaved spray* (P530), pp. 17, 65, 77, 185.
„   *Spray of eight leaves and four flowers* (P538), pp. 18, 62, 182.
„   *Crucifix on tree* (P520), pp. 19, 63, 159.
„   *Youth blowing kiss* (P531), pp. 20, 38, 72, 188.
„   *Girl all agog* (P532), pp. 21, 39, 73.
„   *Naked man dead* (P569), pp. 22, 36, 154, 186.
„   *Woman weeping for dead man* (P570), pp. 23, 37, 155.
„   *Clergyman shocked* (P527), pp. 24, 50, 137, 148, [189]
„   *Thirteen leaves* (variant of P437), pp. 25, 157, 174.
„   *Bird with spray in his beak* (P578), pp. 26, 68, 178.
„   *Spray of one rounded and nineteen pointed leaves* (P579), pp. 27, [69], 179.
„   *Man with wine cup spilling* (P563), p. 28.
„   *Man drunk and man drinking* (P564), p. 29.
„   *Man climbing* (P513), pp. 30, 153.
„   *Woman and ape* (P511), pp. 31, 64, 160, [190]
„   *King Solomon* (P498), pp. 32, 146.
„   *Spray of seven leaves and flower bud* (P509), pp. 33, 58, 149.
„   *Woman beseeching* (P523), pp. 34, 56, 158.
„   *Spray of ten rounded leaves* (P580), pp. 42, 140, 177.
„   *Woman climbing, Cupid above* (P581), p. [43]
Tail-piece: *Spray of five rounded leaves* (P596), pp. [43], [189]
Half-page illustration: *The Shipman's Tale* (P586), p. 44.
Border: *Child peeping* (P546), pp. 48, 66, 141.
„   *Child crawling at foot of spray* (P544), pp. 49, 67, 183.
„   *Eleven leaves with flower at side* (second variant of P438), pp. 51, 156, 175.
„   *Naughty boy climbing* (P522), p. 53.
„   *Man climbing to girl on spray* (P571), p. 54.
„   *Cuckold asleep, lovers above* (P572), p. 55.
„   *Spray of eight leaves* (P521), p. 57.
„   *Woman climbing floreated phallus* (P510), p. 59.
Half-page illustration: *The Prioress's Tale* (P588), p. 60.
Border: *Spray of leaves without stalks* (P589), p. 61.

Tail-piece *(The Prioress's Tale): Christchild* (P597), p. [69]
Half-page illustration: *The Tale of Sir Topas* (P590), p. 70.
Border: *Spray of ten pointed leaves with curl* (P591), p. 70.
    „   *Three sprays, each of six pointed leaves* (P592), p. 71.
    „   *Man dead drunk* (P515), pp. 74, 144.
    „   *Naked men fighting* (P512), pp. 75, 143, 161.
Half-page illustration: *The Tale of Melibeus* (P593), p. 78.
Border: *Spray of six leaves and one leaf bud* (P594), p. 78.
Initial A with flourish (P562), p. 80.
Tail-piece: *Crucifix with man kneeling* (P599), p. [133]
Half-page illustration: *The Monk's Tale* (P600), p. 134.
Border: *Delilah* (P601), pp. 135, 151.
    „   *Girl and bird* (P507), pp. 136, 162.
    „   *Faun piping* (variant of P458), p. 138.
    „   *Naked girl with back turned* (variant of P459), p. 139.
    „   *Man & girl drinking* (P516), p. 145.
    „   *The Wife of Bath* (P499), p. 147.
    „   *Man dead* (P514), p. 152.
    „   *Two jesters* (P508), p. 163.
Tail-piece: *The money bag* (P602), p. [165]
Half-page illustration: *The Nun's Priest's Tale* (P603), p. 166.
Border: *Spray of twelve rounded leaves* (P604), p. 167.
    „   *Nun blowing kiss* (P533), p. 168.
    „   *Spray of fifteen leaves* (P518), p. 169.
    „   *Fox on hind legs* (P573), p. 180.
    „   *Cock and hen with three chicks* (P574), p. 181.
Tail-piece: *Spray with five pointed leaves* (P548), p. [190]
There are also twenty-one initial letters, engraved on wood (represented in *Engravings 1928–1933 by Eric Gill* (Faber & Faber, 1934) by nos. 265–7 [P549–51]) printed in either black, red or blue.
VOLUME III
There are eight half-page illustrations and eighty-two decorated borders, tail-pieces or line-fillings, engraved on wood and placed:
Half-page illustration: *The Doctor's Tale* (P646) and line-filling: *One double leaf* (P583), p. [1]
Border: *Naked girl in spray, head thrown back to left, four leaves* (P646), pp. 2, 120, 165.
    „   *Naked girl in spray, head thrown back to right* (P639), pp. 3, 39, 81, 143, 189.
    „   *Blind old man at foot of tree* (P644), pp. 4, 56, 122, 172.
    „   *Woman climbing, Cupid above* (P581), pp. 5, 71, 133.
    „   *Snake in spray* (P634), pp. 6, 36, 74, 102, 186.

Border: *Girl in spray naked and frightened* (P635), pp. 7, 37, 75.

    „   *Death at foot of tree* (P632), pp. 8, 26.

    „   *Young wife looking up to lover in tree* (P645), pp. 9, 57, 67, 127, 173.

    „   *Spray of nine rounded leaves* (P630), pp. 10, 50, 62, 118, 188.

Half-page illustration: *The Pardoner's Tale* (P649), p. 11.

Border: *Naked man dead* (P569), pp. 12, 76, 97, 135, 160.

    „   *Crucifix on tree* (P520), pp. 13, 87.

    „   *Child pointing* (P525), pp. 14, 60, 104, [198]

    „   *Chaucer writing at foot of spray* (P526), pp. 15, 61, 105.

    „   *Man dead drunk* (P515), p. 16.

    „   *Man & girl drinking* (P516), pp. 17, 59, 177.

    „   *Man waving eight-leaved spray* (P529), pp. 18, 162.

    „   *Man waving ten-leaved spray* (P530), pp. 19, 163.

    „   *Man with wine cup spilling* (P563), pp. 20, 99, 174.

    „   *Branch with fifteen leaves* (variant of P468), pp. 21, 98.

    „   *Girl with lace-edged drawers* (P567), pp. 22, 44, 108, 124, 152.

    „   *Man drunk & man drinking* (P564), pp. 23, 175.

    „   *Young man in spray, black petticoat* (P641), pp. 24, 52, 78, 106, 158, 182.

    „   *Man in spray with toe turned up* (P637), pp. 25, 49, 107, 183.

    „   *Three men hanged* (P633), p. 27.

    „   *Two jesters* (P508), pp. 28, 65, 86, 103.

    „   *Naughty boy climbing* (P522), pp. 29, 55, 115, 149.

    „   *Man climbing* (P513), pp. 30, 110, 190.

    „   *Naked men fighting* (P512), pp. 31, 89.

    „   *Fox on hind legs* (P573), pp. 32, 58, 130.

    „   *Bird with spray in his beak* (P578), pp. 33, 111, 154, 191.

Half-page illustration: *The Wife of Bath's Tale (Prologue)* (P650), p. 34.

Border: *Snake with phallic head* (P651), pp. 35, 187.

    „   *Naked girl in spray, head thrown to left, six leaves* (P638), pp. 38, 142, 164.

    „   *Naked young man sitting on lopped branch* (P642), pp. 40, 134, 166.

    „   *Naked young woman sitting on branch without holding on* (P643), pp. 41, 123, 167.

    „   *Man climbing to girl on spray* (P571), pp. 42, 72, 98, 117, 146.

    „   *Cuckold asleep, lovers above* (P572), pp. 43, 73, 139, 161.

    „   *Man beseeching* (P568), pp. 45, 153.

    „   *King Solomon* (P498), p. 46.

    „   *The Wife of Bath* (P499), p. 47.

    „   *Woman holding mask* (P636), pp. 48, 66, 178.

    „   *Naked woman holding spray* (P631), pp. 51, 121.

    „   *Girl in spray, black petticoat* (P640), pp. 53, 79, 159.

Border: *Spray of eight leaves* (P521), pp. 54, 138, 196.
Half-page illustration: *The Wife of Bath's Tale* (P652), p. 63.
Border: *Girl and bird* (P507), p. 64.
„ *Naked girl in spray, head thrown back to left, four leaves* (P646), p. 68.
„ *Naked girl in spray, head upright, hands over head* (P647), pp. 69, 181.
„ *Spray of ten rounded leaves* (P580), pp. 70, 128, 145.
Half-page illustration: *The Friar's Tale* (P653), p. 77.
Border: *St Thomas of Canterbury* (P519), p. 80.
„ *Tree woman (leaves for hands)* (P517), pp. 82, 144.
„ *Spray of fifteen leaves* (P518), p. 83.
„ *Thirteen leaves* (variant of P437), p. 84.
„ *Eleven leaves with flower at side* (variant of P438), pp. 85, 140.
„ *Woman and ape* (P511), pp. 88, 131, 170.
„ *Clergyman shocked* (P527), p. 90.
Half-page illustration: *The Summoner's Tale* (P654), p. 91.
Border: *Spray of eight leaves and four flowers* (P538), pp. 92, 116, 168.
„ *Child crawling at foot of spray* (P544), p. 93.
„ *Faun piping* (variant of P458), pp. 94, 184.
„ *Naked girl with back turned* (variant of P459), p. 95.
„ *Spray of seven leaves and four curls* (P565), p. 100.
„ *Man holding curl of spray* (P566), pp. 101, 125, 185.
„ *Boy about to climb tree* (P658), pp. 109, 157.
Tail-piece: ('*The Windy Beggar*') (P655), p. [112]
Half-page illustration: *The Clerk's Tale* (P656), p. 113.
Border: *Woman beseeching* (P523), pp. 114, 148, 192.
„ *Spray of seven leaves and flower bud* (P509), p. 119.
„ *Nun blowing kiss* (P533), p. 126.
„ *Ten leaves with flower at side* (second variant of P438), p. 129.
„ *Youth blowing kiss* (P531), pp. 132, 150.
„ *Child pointing* (P524), p. 136.
„ *Woman weeping for dead man* (P570), pp. 137, 147, 193.
„ *Delilah* (P601), p. 141.
„ *Girl all agog* (P532), p. 151.
„ *Spray of one rounded and nineteen pointed leaves* (P579), p. 155.
Half-page illustration: *The Merchant's Tale* (P657), p. 156.
Border: *Cherub on branch* (P534), p. 169.
„ *Cock and hen with three chicks* (P574), p. 171.
„ *Man dead* (P514), p. 176.
„ *Spray of seven rounded leaves* (P584), p. 179.
„ *Child peeping* (P546), p. 180.
„ *Spray of twelve rounded leaves* (P604), p. 194.

Border: *Spray of twelve triple-lobed leaves* (P539), p. 195.
Tail-piece: *(The unsuspecting cuckold)* (P659), p. [197]
„   *(Chaucer writing)* (P660), p. [198]
There are also thirteen initial letters, engraved on wood (represented in *Engravings, 1928–1933 by Eric Gill* (Faber & Faber, 1934) by nos. 265–7 [P549–51]) printed in either black, red or blue.

VOLUME IV
There are eight half-page illustrations and seventy-three decorated borders and tail-pieces, engraved on wood and placed:
Half-page illustration: *The Squire's Tale* (P701), p. [1]
Border: *King Solomon* (P498), pp. 2, 88.
„   *Girl lying at bottom of branch, Child above* (variant of P469), p. 3.
„   *Jockey* (P679), pp. 4, 78.
„   *Horse prancing* (P680), pp. 5, 79.
„   *Thirteen leaves* (variant of P437), p. 6.
„   *Spray of eight rounded leaves and one branch lopped off* (P689), p. 7.
„   *Woman growing out of a tree holding apple in closed left hand* (P693), pp. 8, 49.
„   *Woman growing out of a tree, holding apple in open right hand* (P694), pp. 9, 81.
„   *Boy in black 'tights', white kilt* (P697), pp. 10, 43, 56.
„   *Devil on dead branch* (P698), pp. 11, 77, 89.
„   *Spray of eleven rounded leaves: seven large on right, four small on left* (P681), pp. 12, 67.
„   *Girl holding wounded bird* (P682), p. 13.
„   *Spray with four birds* (P695), pp. 14, 44, 118.
„   *Girl with magic ring on right thumb* (P696), pp. 15, 45, 69, 119.
„   *Man waving eight-leaved spray* (P529), pp. 16, 106.
„   *Man waving ten-leaved spray* (P530), pp. 17, [107]
„   *Child pointing* (P525), p. 18.
„   *Chaucer writing at foot of spray* (P526), p. 19.
„   *Naked pygmy looking up to naked girl* (P691), pp. 20, 40, 110.
„   *Naked boy looking to hermaphrodite* (P692), pp. 21, 41.
„   *Spray of eight leaves* (P521), p. 22.
„   *Cupid with black wings cheering* (P700), pp. 23, 37, 121.
Tail-piece: *Pegasus* (P703), p. [24]
Half-page illustration: *The Franklyn's Tale* (P704), p. 405.
Border: *Young man in black tunic bowing to angel* (P685), pp. 26, 36, 62, 112.
„   *Woman in black frightened* (P684), p. 27.
„   *Man climbing to girl on spray* (P571), p. 28.
„   *Cuckold asleep, lovers above* (P572), pp. 29, 115.
„   *Woman holding mask* (P636), pp. 30, 84.

Border: *Naughty boy climbing* (P522), pp. 31, 93.
„   *Girl with lace-edged drawers* (P567), pp. 32, 96.
„   *Man beseeching* (P568), pp. 33, 97, 113.
„   *Bird on bough with parson's hat on* (P687), pp. 34, 64, 92.
„   *The Wife of Bath* (P499), p. 35.
„   *Naked man making outcry* (P683), pp. 38, 52.
„   *Naked woman holding spray* (P631), p. 39.
„   *Blind old man at foot of tree* (P644), pp. 42, 68.
„   *Bird with spray in his beak* (P578), pp. 46, 72.
„   *Three sprays, each of six pointed leaves* (P592), pp. 47, 111.
„   *Tree woman (leaves for hands)* (P517), p. 48.
„   *Youth blowing kiss* (P531), pp. 50, 82.
„   *Two jesters* (P508), pp. 51, 87.
„   *Crucifix on tree* (variant of P520), p. 53.
„   *Naked young man sitting on lopped branch* (P642), pp. 54, 66.
„   *Naked young woman sitting on branch without holding on* (P643), p. 55.
Half-page illustration: *The Second Nun's Tale* (P705), p. 57.
Border: *Naked man dead* (P569), p. 58.
„   *Woman weeping for dead man* (P570), p. 59.
„   *Man dead* (P514), p. 60.
„   *Woman climbing floreated phallus* (P511), pp. 61, 122.
Tail-piece: *Spray of nine pointed leaves and three curls* (P726), p. 61.
Border: *Angel* (P686), p. 63.
„   *Woman climbing, Cupid above* (P581), pp. 65, 75.
„   *St Thomas of Canterbury* (P519), p. 70.
„   *Man on branch with boy holding his toe* (P690), p. 71.
„   *Cock and hen with three chicks* (P574), p. 73.
„   *Death at foot of tree* (P632), pp. 74, 116.
Half-page illustration: *The Yeoman's Tale* (P706), p. 76.
Border: *Naked girl in spray, head upright, hands over head* (P647), p. 80.
„   *Young wife looking up to lover in tree* (P645), p. 83.
„   *Frightened young man with what he wanted in a cage* (P688), pp. 85, 117.
„   *Man piping* (variant of P429), p. 86.
„   *Snake in spray* (P634), pp. 90, 114.
„   *Man in spray with toe turned up* (P637), p. 91.
„   *Young man in spray, black petticoat* (P641), p. 94.
„   *Man holding curl of spray* (P566), p. 95.
„   *Spray of nine rounded leaves* (P630), p. 98.
„   *Spray of seven leaves and four curls* (P565), p. 99.
„   *Spray of ten rounded leaves* (P580), p. 100.

Border: *Snake with phallic head* (P651), p. 101.
„ *Branch with fifteen leaves* (variant of P648), p. 102.
„ *Clergyman shocked* (P527), p. 103.
„ *Man climbing* (P513), p. 104.
„ *Fox on hind legs* (P573), p. 105.
Tail-piece: *Crucible and smoke* (P678), p. [107]
Half-page illustration: *The Manciple's Tale* (P707), p. 108.
Border: *Man shooting arrow, bird with parson's hat* (P699), p. 109.
Half-page illustration: *Prologue. The Parson's Tale* (P708), p. 120.
„ „ *The Parson's Tale* (P677), p. 123.
Tail-piece: *(The Prioress's Tale). Christchild* (P597), p. [220]
There are also sixteen initial letters, engraved on wood (represented in *Engravings 1928–1933 by Eric Gill* (Faber & Faber, 1934), by no. 403a [P702] for the letters *S, H with ring* and by nos. 265–7 [P549–51] for the remainder) printed in black, red or blue.

BINDING: (*a*) Vellum edition: full-bound red niger morocco, g.e., by Sangorski & Sutcliffe. A different design for each volume gold-stamped on front, viz. Vol. I, *Sword and Mitre on spray of leaves*. Vol. II, *Man on Horseback*. Vol. III, *The Wife of Bath*. Vol. IV, *Cupid in spray of leaves*. Panelled spine lettered in gilt: THE | CANTER- | BURY TALES BY | GEOFFREY | CHAUCER | VOLUME I [II, III, IV]. Decorated endpapers. Metal clasps. Each volume was supplied in a red cloth box lined, lettered on spine as for the volume.

(*b*) Paper edition: ¼ red niger morocco, patterned boards, by Sangorski & Sutcliffe; t.e.g. other edges trimmed. Panelled spine lettered as for the vellum edition.

DATE OF PUBLICATION: Vol. I, February 1929. Vol. II, November 1929. Vol. III, August 1930. Vol. IV, March 1931.

PRICE: Vellum edition: £30. 5s. Hand-made paper edition: six guineas.

PRINTING: 500 copies: nos. 1–15 on vellum, numbered and signed by Eric Gill; nos. 16–500 on hand-made paper, numbered. The above numbers include all copies printed, whether for sale or presentation.

REVIEWS: *The Times Literary Supplement*, 18 April 1929. *The Observer*, 13 July 1929. *Liverpool Daily Post*, 2 October 1929, 1 January, 10 September 1930 and 15 April 1931. *The Studio*, Vol. 100, no. 452, November 1930, Vol. 102, no. 461, August 1931.

NOTES: This is no. 63 of the Golden Cockerel Press publications. It was shown at the *Exhibition of Books Illustrating British and Foreign Printing, 1919–1929*, organized by the British Museum, and figures as no. 53 in the Great Britain section of the catalogue (cf. no. 642).

170

LEDA

By ALDOUS HUXLEY

With Engravings by

ERIC GILL

Garden City, N.Y.

Doubleday, Doran & Company, Inc.

1929   [282]

282 LEDA
    TITLE-PAGE: Reproduced. Shows w-e. *Fig leaf* (P615).
    SIZE: $9\frac{1}{2} \times 6\frac{1}{4}$.   COLLATION: [Unsigned: [2] + [1]–[6]⁴.]
    PAGINATION AND CONTENTS: Pp. 2 + 48; of which the first leaf forms a
fly-leaf and though not an integral part of the book is of the same substance as
the text and is folded round the first gathering; [1] [2] half-title: LEDA, verso
blank; [3] [4] recto blank, verso frontispiece; [5] [6] title-page, verso printer's
imprint and publisher's note: COPYRIGHT 1929, DOUBLEDAY, DORAN &
COMPANY, INC. | PUBLISHER'S NOTE: THIS BOOK HAS BEEN ILLUS-
TRATED BY MR. ERIC GILL BY SPECIAL ARRANGEMENT | WITH THE

171

GOLDEN COCKEREL PRESS | and, at foot: ALL RIGHTS RESERVED; [7] [8] half-title: LEDA, verso blank; [9]–44 text; [45] [46] recto blank, verso colophon: THIS BOOK IS SET IN BODONI MONOTYPE AND PRINTED | ON UTOPIA WHITE LAID BY THE MARCHBANKS PRESS; | PUBLISHED IN AN EDITION OF 361 COPIES, OF WHICH THIS IS | NO. ... [Signed: *Aldous Huxley*.]; [47] [48] blank.

ILLUSTRATIONS: In addition to the engraving on the title-page, reproduced, there are two wood-engravings, placed:

Leda loved (P617, second state), frontispiece.

Leda waiting (P616), p. [9]

BINDING: Full bound in white cloth, black leather label on spine, lettered in gilt, reading downwards: L E D A Top edges cut, others uncut.

DATE OF PUBLICATION: 1929.

PRICE: $7.50.

PRINTING: 361 signed and numbered copies.

1930

283 THE STORY OF AMNON

TITLE-PAGE: There is no title-page as such. THE STORY OF HOW AMNON RAVISHED | HIS SISTER THAMAR FOR WHICH ABSA- | LOM KILLED HIM AS IT IS WRITTEN IN | THE SECOND BOOK OF KINGS.

SIZE: $5 \times 3\frac{3}{4}$.

COLLATION: A single, unsigned, gathering of four leaves.

PAGINATION AND CONTENTS: Pp. 8 (unpaged); [1] [2] recto blank, verso frontispiece; [3]–[7] text with imprint at foot of p. [7]: PRINTED BY | RENÉ HAGUE & ERIC GILL | AT PIGOTTS, NEAR SPEEN, BUCKINGHAMSHIRE | 1930 | 1.9.30. (225) I; [8] blank. Printed from 8 pt. *Baskerville* on hand-made paper specially made for Hague & Gill by J. Batchelor & Sons and watermarked with the device: *ER*—the letter 'E' reversed (after w-e. P723).

ILLUSTRATIONS: There is one illustration from a wood-engraving, placed:

Amnon (P709), frontispiece.

BINDING: Blue paper wrappers, sewn. All edges uncut.

DATE OF PUBLICATION: This little booklet was never published. A few copies were distributed privately. It was printed in September 1930.

PRICE: n.p.

PRINTING: 225 copies.

NOTES: As stated, this book was never put on sale. It was the first to be printed on the hand-press at Eric Gill's home, Pigotts, Buckinghamshire, as is signified by the numeral 'I' in the imprint quoted above.

1931
284 CANTICUM CANTICORUM
TITLE-PAGE: CANTICUM CANTICORUM | SALOMONIS |
QUOD HEBRAICE DICITUR | SIR HASIRIM
SIZE: $10\frac{1}{4} \times 5\frac{1}{4}$.   COLLATION: [Unsigned: [1]–[6]^4.]
PAGINATION AND CONTENTS: Pp. vi + 42; [i]–[vi] blank, of which the first
leaf is pasted down as the front end-paper but forms an integral part of the
book; [1] [2] blank; [3]–4 title-page, verso frontispiece; 5–31 text; [32] blank;
[33] [34] colophon: HAEC CANTICI CANTICORUM EDITIO EA LIBRI
DIVINI | VULGATA NITITUR EDITIONE, QUAM OCTAVAM CURAVIT
ALO- | ISIUS CLAUDIUS FILLON (PARISIIS, SUMPTIBUS LETOUZEY |
ET ANE EDITORUM). | HARRY GRAF KESSLER HUNC LIBELLUM
IN- | STITUIT ET REDEGIT; FIGURAS PRIMASQUE LITTERAS IN
LIG- | NUM INCIDIT ERIC GILL. LITTERARUM FORMA JENSON |
QUAE VOCATUR ANTIQUA EST, AB E. PRINCE IN USUM PRELI |
CRANACHENSIS INCISA. | CHARTA EDITIONIS VULGARIS E CUPA |
HAUSTA EST, QUAE ORIGINEM DUCIT A MAILLOL-KESSLER. |
LIBELLUS TRIBUS COLORIBUS TINCTUS VERE INEUNTE ANNI |
MCMXXXI MODERANTIBUS HARRY GRAF KESSLER | ET MAX
GOERTZ PRELO MANUARIO CRANACHENSI SUB- | JECTUS EST.
LITTERAS COMPOSUERUNT WALTER TANZ ET | H. SCHULZE,
TYPIS EXPRESSIT LIBELLUM H. GAGE-COLE. | TYPIS EXSCRIBENDA
CURANTUR HUIUSCE LIBELLI VIII EX- | EMPLARIA MEMBRANEA
AUROQUE POLITA. NOTIS A–H | SIGNANTUR, EX-EMPLARIA NOTIS
G ET H SIGNATA NON DI- | VENDUNTUR. LX EXEMPLARIA, EX
QUIBUS V NON VENEUNT, | CHARTAE JAPONICAE, CC EXEMPLARIA,
EX QUIBUS X NON | PRODEUNT, CHARTAE ILLI E CUPA HAUSTAE
IMPRIMUNTUR. | ACCEDIT ET GERMANICA ET GALLICA EDITIO. |
HIC LIBELLUS [...] EST., verso blank; [36]–[42] blank, of which the last
leaf is pasted down as the back end-paper but forms an integral part of the
book. Printed from Jenson's *Antiqua*, cut for the Cranach Press by E. P.
Prince, on Maillol-Kessler hand-made paper.
ILLUSTRATIONS: There are eleven illustrations, all wood-engravings, and
placed:

> '*Nigra sum sed formosa*' (P618), *frontispiece*, p. 4.
> *Inter ubera mea* (P662), p. 7.
> *Transiliens colles* (P666), p. 9.
> *Qui pascitur inter lilia* (P664), p. 11.
> *Vadam ad montem* (P757), p. 14.
> *Hortus conclusus* (P667), p. 17.
> *Dilecti mei pulsantis* (P668), p. 19.
> *Invenerunt me custodes* (P665), p. 21.

Ibi dabo tibi (P669), p. 26.

In domum matris meae (P670), p. 29.

Fuge, dilecte mi (P663), p. 31.

There are also eighteen initial letters, all sixteen of (P674) plus a *Q* (P752) and an *F* (P755). The eighteen initial letters are represented in *Engravings, 1928–1933, by Eric Gill* (no. 27) at numbers 377 and 452.

BINDING, PRICE AND PRINTING:

CANTICUM CANTICORUM SALOMONIS. The Latin edition was limited to 268 copies:

(*a*) 200 numbered copies on hand-made Maillol-Kessler paper with the watermark of the Cranach Presse, bound in quarter vellum, buff coloured boards, lettered in gilt on spine, reading upwards: CANTICUM CANTICORUM SALOMONIS. $3\frac{1}{2}$ guineas.

(*b*) Sixty numbered copies on imperial Japanese paper, bound in levant morocco. Seven guineas.

(*c*) Eight numbered copies on vellum with hand-gilded initial letters, bound in levant morocco. Thirty guineas. An extra set of the engravings, printed under Eric Gill's supervision and signed by him, was included with each copy of this edition.

DAS HOHE LIED SOLOMO. The German edition was limited to 158 copies: 100 numbered copies on Maillol-Kessler hand-made paper, 50 copies on Japanese paper and 8 on vellum. Contains: the eleven w-e.'s as above plus thirteen initial letters from (P674) and from (P735–756).

CANTIQUE DES CANTIQUES DE SALOMON. The French edition was limited to 164 copies: 100 on Maillol-Kessler hand-made paper, 50 copies on Japanese paper and 14 on vellum. Contains: the eleven w-e.'s as above and initial letters from (P674) and from (P735–756).

DATE OF PUBLICATION: October 1931.

REVIEWS: *The Times Literary Supplement*, 10 March 1932. Mention is also made in 'Notes on Books', *The Book-Collector's Quarterly*, no. 1, December 1930–February 1931.

NOTES: Cf. *Imprimatur, 1931* (nos. 452–3)[1] for reference to this book and the work of the Cranach Press, with inset of a specimen page of the edition with the text in German. German edition is R M K 55, Latin edition is R M K 56 and French edition is R M K 57.

---

[1] Rudolf Alexander Schröder, *Die Cranach-Presse in Weimar*, pp. 92 ff. and Harry Graf Kessler, *Verzeichnis der Drucke der Cranach-Presse in Weimar. Gegründet 1913*, p. 112.

THE
FOUR GOSPELS OF THE LORD JESUS CHRIST
ACCORDING TO THE AUTHORIZED
VERSION OF KING JAMES I
WITH DECORATIONS BY ERIC GILL
PRINTED AND PUBLISHED AT THE
GOLDEN COCKEREL PRESS
MCMXXXI

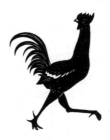

[285]

285 THE FOUR GOSPELS
TITLE-PAGE: Reproduced. Shows w-e. *Cockerel* (Robert Gibbings).
SIZE: $13\frac{1}{2} \times 9$.   COLLATION: [A]², [B]⁸, C–S⁸.
PAGINATION AND CONTENTS: Pp. iv + 272; [i] [ii] blank; [iii] [iv] recto
blank, verso imprint: PRINTED AND MADE IN GREAT BRITAIN; [1] [2]
title-page, verso blank; [3] [4] *Headpiece for St Matthew*, verso blank; [5]–[269]
text; [270] blank; [271] [272] colophon: THIS BOOK WAS PRINTED BY
ROBERT | AND MOIRA GIBBINGS AT THE GOLDEN | COCKEREL PRESS
AT WALTHAM SAINT | LAWRENCE IN BERKSHIRE, BEGUN ON | THE
20TH OF FEBRUARY, 1931, IT WAS | COMPLETED ON THE 28TH OF
OCTOBER | IN THE SAME YEAR. COMPOSITORS: F. | YOUNG AND
A. H. GIBBS. PRESSMAN: | A. C. COOPER. 500 COPIES HAVE BEEN |
PRINTED, OF WHICH NUMBERS | 1–12 ARE ON VELLUM. | THIS IS NO.
[. . .], verso blank. Printed from 18 pt. *Golden Cockerel* (designed for the Press
by Eric Gill) on Batchelor hand-made paper, special watermark of a dove and
the initials G. C. P. (copies nos. 13–500) and on Roman vellum (nos. 1–12).
ILLUSTRATIONS: There are sixty-four illustrations and initial letters (counting the initial 'N' and the lettering which goes with it (p. 8) as one
'illustration'—though they are actually from two separate blocks) from
wood-engravings, placed:

175

Headpiece for St Matthew: The Angel of St Matthew (P761), p. [3]

Initial T, Vesica (P765), p. [5]

Initial N: The Epiphany (P626) and lettering to go with it: O W W H E N
JESUS (P627), p. 8.

Initial T, Devil's serpent (P766), p. 11.

AND, Christ and the Leper (P769), p. 20.

T, The Sower (P770), p. 33.

AT, John the Baptist's beheading (P771), p. 37.

A, The Transfiguration (P768), p. 44.

AND, Palm Sunday (P772), p. 52.

AND, Mary Magdalen (P773), p. 66.

A, with Chalice (P774), p. [68]

THEN, Gethsemane (P775), p. 69.

WHEN, Peter and Cock (P776), p. 72.

A, with Whip (P777), p. 73.

THEN, The Crucifixion (P778), p. [74]

IN, Mary at the Tomb (P779), p. 77.

Headpiece for St Mark: The Lion of St Mark (P762), p. [79]

THE, The Baptism of Jesus (P780), p. [81]

AND, with Devil (P781), p. 82.

Initial A, with left-hand limb flourished (P767), p. 88.

A, with floreated left-hand limb (P782), p. 90.

AND, Herod's feast (P783), p. 95.

IN, The Feeding of the multitude (P784), p. 100.

AND, The Money Changers (P785), p. 110.

AND, The Last Supper (P786), p. 119.

A, with Cock (P787), p. 122.

AND, The Deposition (P788), p. [125]

Initial, GO YE (P789), p. 127.

Headpiece for St Luke: The Bull calf of St Luke (P763), p. [129]

Initial F, with pointed leaves (P790), p. 131.

THERE, The Visitation (P791), p. 131.

AND, The Annunciation (P792), p. 133.

M, for the Magnificat, with lily (P793), p. 134.

B, The Benedictus, flourished (P794), p. 136.

AND, The Nativity (P795), p. 137.

L, for the Nunc Dimittis, with flourish (P796), p. 139.

AND, The Temptation (P797), p. 145.

N, with Fish (P798), p. 148.

NOW, The Widow's son of Nain (P800), p. 155.

N, with Ship (P801), p. 159.

AND, Christ with child (P802), p. 165.

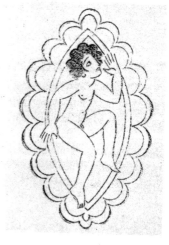

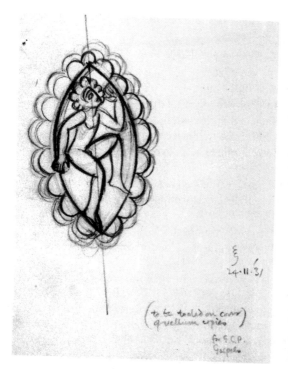

[285]

Left. E.G.'s original drawing of the design for the covers of the vellum copies.

Above. The design as used, stamped in gilt. Both reduced.

O, for Our Father (P803), p. 169.
AND, The Prodigal Son (P804), p. 182.
A, flourished, with leaves (P805), p. 188.
T, The Pharisee and the Publican (P806), p. 189.
B, flourished, with leaves (P807), p. 198.
A, The Roman Eagle (P808), p. 203.
AND, The Burial of Christ (P809), p. [206]
AND, Emmaus (P810), p. 208.
Headpiece for St John: The Eagle of St John (P764), p. [211]
IN, The Creation (P811), p. [213]
THERE, John the Baptist preaching (P812), p. 214.
J, flourished, with leaves (P813), p. 215.
A, Cana of Galilee (P814), p. 217.
THEN, The Woman of Samaria (P815), p. 221.
AND, The Woman taken in adultery (P816), p. 234.
A, with leaves (P817), p. 237.
AND, The raising of Lazarus (P818), p. 244.
Jesus, washing Peter's feet (P819), p. 249.

I, with crosses (P820), p. 253.
THEN, Peter and Malchus (P821), p. 259.
JESUS, Christ crowned (P822), p. [263]
A, St Thomas's doubt (P823), p. 267.

BINDING: (*a*) Vellum edition: full-bound white pigskin, g.e., by Sangorski & Sutcliffe. Gold-stamped on front with design drawn by E. G. of a *Child in Vesica*, as shown below. Panelled spine lettered in gilt: T H E | F O U R | G O S P E L S and, at foot, the *Cockerel* device (Chute). The volume is fitted with two metal clasps and was supplied in a boxed case, lined, and lettered on spine as above.

(*b*) Paper edition: half-bound white pigskin, maize buckram boards, by Sangorski & Sutcliffe, t.e.g., other edges trimmed. Panelled spine lettered as for vellum edition.

DATE OF PUBLICATION: 1931 [November]

PRICE: Vellum edition: eighty guineas. Hand-made paper edition: eight guineas.

PRINTING: 500 copies: nos. I–12 on vellum, numbered and signed. Nos. 13–500 on hand-made paper, numbered.

REVIEWS: *The Times Literary Supplement*, 18 February 1932. By R. E[llis] R[oberts], *New Statesman and Nation*, 7 May 1932. By B. H. Newdigate, *The London Mercury*, June–July 1932.

NOTES: This is no. 78 of the Golden Cockerel Press publications. It was the first book printed from the 18-point size of the new Golden Cockerel type designed by E. G. (Cf. no. 636.137.)

SUBSEQUENT EDITION: A reproduction edition of 600 copies was issued by Christopher Skelton at The September Press in 1988. 13 × 10. 290 pp. – 276 pp. of the Gospels followed by publisher's notes and Robert Gibbings' 'Memories of Eric Gill' (see no. 636.9). Nos. I to 120 were printed on T. H. Saunders mould-made 150 g/m, all rag paper. Nos. 121 to 600 were printed on St Cuthbert's mould-made 140 g/m half rag paper (this is for the reproduction pages). Nos. I–80 bound in full leather with laced-in boards, with gilt top, blocked on spine and blind stamped on front cover, with a slip case. Nos. 81–100 bound by Clare Skelton. Nos. 100–120 sold unbound in folded sheets. 480 unnumbered copies case-bound in full Archive Buckram, with gilt top, blocked label on spine, with a slip case.

[286]

1932
286 THE PASSION OF PERPETUA AND FELICITY
TITLE-PAGE: Reproduced. Shows w-e. *Device: Chalice and Host with Candles*
(P53). The words 'PERPETUA AND | FELICITY' printed in red.
SIZE: 11 × 8½.   COLLATION: [Unsigned: [1]–[4]⁴.]
PAGINATION AND CONTENTS: Pp. 32; [1] [2] half-titles: S S | PERPETUA |
& FELICITY | M M within the arms of a cross (the cross in red), verso blank;
[3] [4] title-page, verso blank; [5] [6] Note concerning the *Perpetua* type,
'signed' E. G., verso blank; 7–10 Introduction 'signed' W. H. S.; 11–[29] text;
[30] blank; [31] [32] specimen alphabets from *Perpetua* type in lower-case and
titling capitals, signed at foot: *Eric G.* and numbered by him, e.g. *1–30*, verso
blank. Printed from 13 pt. *Perpetua* on pure Japanese vellum.
ILLUSTRATIONS: In addition to the device on the title-page, there are three
illustrations and a device from wood-engravings, placed:
   Chapter heading: *Device: Paschal Lamb* (P92), p. 11.
   The flight of St Perpetua (P554), p. 15.
   The triumph of St Perpetua (P555) and *four pairs of apples and halo* (burnished
   in gold) (P555), p. 20.
   The Martyrdom of St Saturus (P559), p. [29] (The blood for robe, printed in
   red.)
BINDING: ¼ vellum, black paper boards, lettered on spine in gilt, reading
downwards: SS. PERPETUA AND FELICITY T.e.g. other edges
cut.

179

DATE OF PUBLICATION: In its present form, as a separate publication, 1932. See note below.

PRICE: £1. 11s. 6d.

PRINTING: Thirty signed and numbered copies.

NOTES: This was originally printed 1929 for Stanley Morison as an inset for no. VII of *The Fleuron* (1930) (no. 346a) being the first specimen of the *Perpetua* type (cf. E. G's note on p. [5]). It was distributed in its present form by Douglas Cleverdon, Bristol in 1932. The four pairs of apples and the halo (p. 20) were printed in red in *The Fleuron*.

1933

287 HAMLET

TITLE-PAGE: Reproduced. Shows w-e. *Title-page: 'HAMLET PRINCE OF DENMARK'* (P838).

SIZE: 8 × 5.

COLLATION: [a]⁴, b⁴, a–t⁴. The signatures on pp. [i] and vii are printed in italics. Those for the remaining gatherings are in roman letters.

PAGINATION AND CONTENTS: Pp. 2 + xiv + 152; [1] [2] half-title: THE TRAGEDY OF | HAMLET, PRINCE OF DENMARK | BY WILLIAM SHAKESPEARE | WITH ENGRAVINGS BY ERIC GILL | & AN INTRO-DUCTION BY GILBERT MURRAY, verso imprint: PRINTED IN GREAT BRITAIN; [i]–[ix] Introduction; [x] blank; [xi] [xii] Note upon the text, verso blank; [xiii] [xiv] title-page, verso Dramatis Personae; [1]–149 text; [150] blank; [151] [152] colophon: THIS EDITION OF HAMLET IS DESIGNED & ILLUSTRATED BY ERIC | GILL. FIFTEEN HUNDRED COPIES HAVE BEEN PRINTED FROM THE | JOANNA TYPES ON BARCHAM GREEN PAPER, BY HAGUE AND | GILL, HIGH WYCOMBE, FOR THE MEMBERS OF THE LIMITED | EDITIONS CLUB, 1933. | THIS COPY IS NUMBER [...] | AND IS SIGNED BY [*Eric G*] [Press mark: *Tree and dog, white line with flames in tree* (P759)], verso blank.

ILLUSTRATIONS: In addition to the title-page there are five half-page illustrations and twenty initial letters from wood-engravings, placed:

> *Hamlet and the Ghost* (P833), p. [1]
> *Hamlet and Polonius* (P844), p. 34.
> *The play scene* (P845), p. 61.
> *'I am set naked on your kingdom'* (P846), p. 96.
> *The Death of the King* (P847), p. 123.

The initial letters are represented in *Engravings 1928–1933* (Faber & Faber, 1934) by no. 533 [P840–43] as four distinct engravings only. In point of fact there are fifteen different engravings (counting the I S (p. 123) as one engraving) four of which were used more than once.

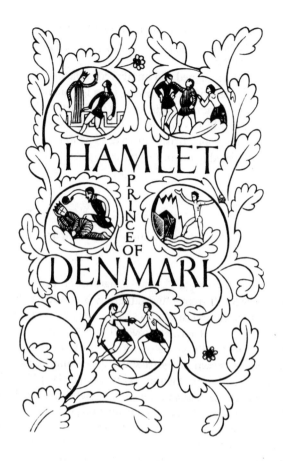

[287]

BINDING: Full-bound light brown pigskin, blind-stamped on front with a device representing the Ghost. Lettered on spine: H | A | M | L | E | T Blind-stamped on back with design after the Press mark of Hague & Gill: *Tree and Dog* (P759). Top edges trimmed, others uncut. Issued in a grey laid paper-covered slipcase, lettered in brown on spine H | A | M | L | E | T
DATE OF PUBLICATION: 1933.
PRICE: (Offered to members of the Limited Editions Club, New York, only, at $10.)
PRINTING: 1500 numbered and signed copies.
NOTES: Cf. *The Limited Editions Club. A New Influence in American Printing.* By Paul Standard. *Penrose's Annual*, London, Vol. XXXVII, 1935, pp. 44–9. This is no. 44, Fourth Series—1932–1933, of the books published by the Limited Editions Club, New York.

The S O N N E T S of

WILLIAM SHAKESPEARE

edited by

Margaret Flower

CASSELL & COMPANY LTD

London, Toronto, Melbourne, & Sydney

MCMXXXIII

288 THE SONNETS OF WILLIAM SHAKESPEARE
TITLE-PAGE: Reproduced.
SIZE: $6\frac{1}{2} \times 4$.   COLLATION: $[\ ]^6$, a–1^8.
PAGINATION AND CONTENTS: Pp. xii + 176; [i]–[iv] blank, the first leaf of
which is pasted down as the front end-paper but forms an integral part of the
book; [vii] [viii] recto blank, verso frontispiece; [ix] [x] title-page, verso
imprint: PRINTED & MADE IN GREAT BRITAIN: [xi] [xii] Dedication, verso
blank; 1–154 text; [155] [156] blank; [157] editor's note: [158]–[162]
TEXTUAL NOTES; [163] WORDS ITALICIZED IN 1609 QUARTO; [164]–
[171] INDEX OF FIRST LINES; [172] colophon: THIS EDITION CONSISTS
OF 500 COPIES | PRINTED BY HAGUE & GILL, HIGH WYCOMBE | WITH
AN ENGRAVING BY ERIC GILL | MCMXXXIII; [173]–[176] blank. Printed
from 12 pt. *Joanna* on Basingwerk Parchment paper.
ILLUSTRATION: There is one illustration from a wood-engraving, placed:
            Man and Woman in garden (P852), frontispiece.
BINDING: Dark green cloth, gold-stamped on front with the letters W. S
within a two-ringed circle. Lettered in gilt on spine, reading upwards:
SHAKESPEARE'S SONNETS T.e.g. other edges cut. Buff dust
jacket, cover lettered in green: THE SONNETS | OF WILLIAM
SHAKESPEARE | Edited by | MARGARET | FLOWER; WITH
| An engraving | by ERIC GILL | CASSELL and the spine, reading
downwards, THE SONNETS OF WILLIAM SHAKESPEARE
DATE OF PUBLICATION: 1933.
PRICE: 10s. 6d.
PRINTING: 500 copies.

182

THE LOST CHILD

and other stories by

MULK RAJ ANAND

with an engraving by Eric Gill   [289]

1934

289 THE LOST CHILD

COVER-TITLE: Reproduced. There is no title-page as such.

SIZE: $6\frac{3}{4} \times 4\frac{1}{4}$.

COLLATION: A single unsigned gathering of twelve leaves.

PAGINATION AND CONTENTS: Pp. iv + 20; [i] [ii] half-title: THE LOST CHILD | AND OTHER STORIES, BY | MULK RAJ ANAND, verso blank; [iii] [iv] Dedication: FOR | FRANCES, verso frontispiece; [1]–[20] text. Printed from 12 pt. *Joanna*.

ILLUSTRATION: There is one illustration from a wood-engraving, placed:
The Lost Child (P855), frontispiece.

BINDING: Bright yellow paper wrappers with overlaps, sewn, printed on front in red and black as reproduced (the first and third lines printed in red) and on back: PRINTED BY | HAGUE & GILL, HIGH WYCOMBE | PUBLISHED BY J. A. ALLEN & CO. | 16, GRENVILLE STREET, LONDON, WC 1 | 1934. A Statement of Editions is printed on the inside flap of the wrapper: THIS EDITION IS LIMITED TO 200 COPIES | OF WHICH THIS IS NUMBER [. . .] [Signed: *Mulk Raj Anand | Eric G*]

DATE OF PUBLICATION: 1934 [April]

PRICE: 5s.

PRINTING: 200 signed and numbered copies.

1934

290 THE NEW TEMPLE SHAKESPEARE

Edited, with an Introduction, Notes and Glossary to each volume, by M. R. Ridley, M.A. (Fellow, and Tutor in English Literature, of Balliol College, Oxford). With title-pages, half-titles, binding and jacket designs by Eric Gill. Printed from *Monotype Garamond*. Title-page of first vol., viz. HAMLET, reproduced. 40 Volumes. *Size:* $5\frac{1}{8} \times 4$.

ILLUSTRATIONS: There is a general half-title design and a title-page design for each volume embodying the idea of Comedy, Tragedy, History or Romance as the case may be with special designs for the last volume, viz. the INTRODUCTORY VOLUME: WILLIAM SHAKESPEARE: A COMMENTARY by M. R. Ridley, M.A. The illustrations, from wood-engravings, are as follows:

General half-title page, *Puck Juggling* (P857).
Title-page: *Comedy; Man trying to fly* (P858).
    „   *History; Man just going on walking* (P859).
    „   *Romance; Man seizing unreality* (P860).
    „   *Tragedy; Man trying to escape* (P861).
    „   *Coat of Arms* (P911).
Frontispiece: *William Shakespeare. After the Durnford portrait* (P910).

Here follows a list of the volumes in the order of publication together with a note of the engraving in each:

1934	September	HAMLET (P861).
		TITUS ANDRONICUS (P861).
		A MIDSUMMER NIGHT'S DREAM (P858).
		TIMON OF ATHENS (P861).
		AS YOU LIKE IT (P858).
		THE COMEDY OF ERRORS (P858).
	October	CORIOLANUS (P861).
		THE SONNETS (P860).
	November	THE TAMING OF THE SHREW (P858).
		LOVE'S LABOUR'S LOST (P858).
	December	KING HENRY IV. PARTS I & II (P859).
1935	January	JULIUS CAESAR (P861).
		KING RICHARD III (P859).
	February	THE LIFE OF KING HENRY VIII (P859).
		THE MERCHANT OF VENICE (P858).
	March	KING LEAR (P861).
		ANTONY AND CLEOPATRA (P861).
	April	THE MERRY WIVES OF WINDSOR (P858).
		THE LIFE OF KING HENRY V (P859).
	May	MACBETH (P861).

HAMLET

by William Shakespeare

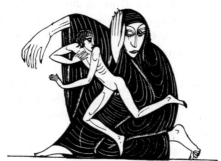

London: J. M. DENT & SONS LTD.
New York: E. P. DUTTON & CO. INC.   [290]

1935	May	MEASURE FOR MEASURE (P858).
	June	OTHELLO (P861).
		TROILUS AND CRESSIDA (P861).
	July	ROMEO AND JULIET (P861).
		ALL'S WELL THAT END'S WELL (P858).
	August	TWELFTH NIGHT (P858).
		PERICLES (P860).
	September	THE WINTER'S TALE (P860).
		THE LIFE AND DEATH OF KING JOHN (P859).
	October	MUCH ADO ABOUT NOTHING (P858).
		CYMBELINE (P860).
	November	THE TEMPEST (P860).
		VENUS & ADONIS. THE RAPE OF LUCRECE. THE PHOENIX & TURTLE (P860).
	December	KING RICHARD II (P859).
		THE TWO GENTLEMEN OF VERONA (P858).
1936	February	KING HENRY VI. PARTS I, II & III (P859).
	July	WILLIAM SHAKESPEARE. A COMMENTARY. By M. R. Ridley, M.A. (P911) and (P910).

BINDING: (a) Bright red cloth, gold-stamped on front with a device representing the globe, on which is imposed a jester's cap surmounted by a crown with sword and headsman's axe crossed and, below, a mask. Lettered in gilt on spine, the letters reading downwards. T.e.g., other edges cut. Buff dust jacket, printed in black and red.

(b) Full black leather with device as above picked out in red and gold.

185

Lettered as above. T.e.g., other edges cut.
DATE OF PUBLICATION: (See above.)
PRICE: (*a*) Cloth edition: 2*s*. per volume. (*b*) Leather edition: 3*s*. per volume.
SUBSEQUENT EDITIONS: Many of these volumes have been reprinted on successive dates. In most cases the top edge of later editions is yellow not gold.
REVIEWS: *The Times*, 28 September 1934. *Liverpool Daily Post*, 12 December 1934. Extracts from numerous reviews appear on the inside flap of the paper jackets of all except the first two volumes.
NOTE: A Souvenir issue of *As You Like It* is known with a preliminary leaf commemorating the inauguration of *The New Temple Shakespeare* at the Savoy Hotel on 27 November 1934, signed and dated by E. G. (Ian McKelvie, 1985, Catalogue 60, item no. 92).

See *The Bookmark*, Vol. X, no. 37, Winter 1934, p. 24 (cf. no. 163 in this compilation) for a report of gathering celebrating the fortieth anniversary of the *Temple Shakespeare*.

291 THE PASSION OF OUR LORD

TITLE-PAGE: THE PASSION | OF OUR LORD JESUS CHRIST, ACCORDING TO | THE FOUR EVANGELISTS
SIZE: 7 × 4.
COLLATION: [Unsigned: [1]–[9]⁴, leaves 1 and 4 of the first gathering being front board-paper and its conjugate leaf.]
PAGINATION AND CONTENTS: Pp. viii + 64; [i] [ii] which leaf is pasted down as the front end-paper (see collation); [iii] [iv] blank; [v] [vi] title-page, verso Imprint: PRINTED BY | HAGUE & GILL, HIGH WYCOMBE | WITH ENGRAVINGS BY ERIC GILL | AND PUBLISHED BY | FABER & FABER, LTD | 24 RUSSELL SQUARE, LONDON | MCMXXXIV; [vii] [viii] blank (see collation); [1] illustration; 2–[57] text (printed in Latin and English on alternate pages), [58] blank save for three small asterisks at foot; [59] [60] illustration, verso blank; [61]–[64] blank. Printed from 8 pt. *Joanna* on Barcham Green hand-made paper watermarked: *J. B. Green*, the initials *E.R.* and *1932*.
ILLUSTRATIONS: There are five full-page illustrations from wood-engravings, placed:

> *St Matthew* (P862), p. [1]
> *St Mark* (P863), p. [19]
> *St Luke* (P864), p. [33]
> *St John* (P865), p. [47]
> *Resurrexit* (P886), p. [59]

BINDING: Blue cloth, lettered in gilt on spine, reading downwards: THE PASSION Top edges trimmed, others uncut. Cream dust jacket printed in

blue on front and spine.
DATE OF PUBLICATION: 1934 [October]
PRICE: 8s. 6d.
PRINTING: 300 copies.
NOTES: This book contains the Passions according to Saints Matthew, Mark, Luke, and John, as read in the Roman Missal during Holy Week. The Latin text is faced by the English translation, taken from the Rheims version.

292 THE ALDINE BIBLE
TITLE-PAGE: THE NEW TESTAMENT | EDITED WITH AN INTRODUCTION BY M. R. JAMES | O.M., Litt.D., Hon. D.C.L. | ASSISTED BY DELIA LYTTELTON, S.TH. | ENGRAVINGS BY ERIC GILL | [here follow the volume number and title] | LONDON | J. M. DENT AND SONS LIMITED
4 Volumes.
Vol. I. SIZE: $7\frac{3}{4} \times 4\frac{7}{8}$. COLLATION: [A]⁸, B–L⁸.
PAGINATION AND CONTENTS: Pp. x + 166; [i] [ii] blank, verso list of contents of the four volumes of the series; [iii] [iv] title-page, verso imprint: All rights reserved | PRINTED IN GREAT BRITAIN | BY THE TEMPLE PRESS LETCHWORTH | FROM THE JOANNA TYPES SET BY | HAGUE & GILL, HIGH WYCOMBE | FOR | J. M. DENT & SONS LTD. | ALDINE HOUSE BEDFORD ST. LONDON | TORONTO–VANCOUVER | MELBOURNE– WELLINGTON | FIRST PUBLISHED IN THIS EDITION 1934; v–viii Introduction 'signed' *M. R. J. Eton College 1934*; [ix] Contents and list of Illustrations; [x] Editorial Note, 'signed' *D. L.*; [1] [2] half-title: ST. MATTHEW; verso note concerning the date of St Matthew's Gospel; [3] [4] blank, verso illustration; 5–142 text of the Gospels according to St Matthew and St Mark; [143] blank, save for the word: NOTES: [144]–165 Notes concerning the two Gospels; [166] blank. Printed from 12 pt. *Joanna* hand-set.
ILLUSTRATIONS: There are two full-page illustrations from wood-engravings, placed:

St Matthew (P869), p. [4]

St Mark (P870), p. [90]

BINDING: Dark red Sundour cloth, lettered in gilt on front: THE NEW TESTAMENT and, on spine: THE | NEW | TESTA- | MENT | I | MAT- | THEW | MARK | and, at foot: DENT. The volumes were also published in a red leather binding. End-paper map of Palestine at both back and front of this volume. On the wrapper, which is general to the series, there is a wood-engraving: *Bartimeus* (P868).
DATE OF PUBLICATION: November 1934.
PRICE: Cloth edition: 5s. Leather edition: 7s. 6d. (In U.S.A. $2.)

187

REVIEWS: *The Times Literary Supplement*, 25 January and 10 October 1936. *Methodist Recorder*, 5 March 1936. Extracts from other reviews will be found on the wrappers of the succeeding volumes of the series.

VOLUMES II–IV: The other three volumes are in precisely the same format, etc., as that described above. It will suffice, therefore, if description is confined to contents, illustrations, etc.:

Vol. II. THE GOSPEL ACCORDING TO ST. LUKE and THE ACTS OF THE APOSTLES. Pp. vi + 204. Illustrations: *St Luke* (P879), p. [4] and *The Acts of the Apostles* (P880), p. [96] On recto of back end-paper a map of Palestine and on back end-paper a double-front map: *The Journeys of St Paul*. Date of publication: July 1935.

Vol. III. THE PAULINE AND PASTORAL EPISTLES. Pp. vi + 218. Illustrations: *St Paul* (P894), p. [6] and *Woman with Ship* (P893), p. [116] Maps as for Vol. II. Date of publication: January 1936.

Vol. IV. THE GOSPEL ACCORDING TO ST JOHN. THE CATHOLIC EPISTLES (JOHN, HEBREWS, JAMES, PETER, JUDE). THE REVELATION OF ST. JOHN THE DIVINE. Pp. vi + 216. Illustrations: *St John* (P908), p. [4] and *Apocalypse* (P909), p. [138] Maps as for Vol. II save that the end-paper one is titled: *The Eastern Mediterranean*. Date of publication: Spring 1936.

NOTE: Cf. *The New Testament in New Dress* (no. 162) also *The Function of the Book Jacket* (no. 522).

293 THE CONSTANT MISTRESS

TITLE-PAGE: Reproduced. Shows w-e. *The Constant Mistress* (P867).
SIZE: $8\frac{1}{2} \times 6$.   COLLATION: [A]^8, B–C^8.
PAGINATION AND CONTENTS: Pp. 44; [1] [2] blank; [3] [4] title-page, verso, at foot: PRINTED AND MADE IN GREAT BRITAIN; [5] [6] dedication: TO | MARGARET, verso blank; [7] [8] Contents, verso frontispiece; 9–40 text; [41] [42] colophon: UNIFORM WITH ENID CLAY'S SONNETS & VERSES, ALSO | ILLUSTRATED BY ERIC GILL, AND PUBLISHED BY THIS | PRESS IN MARCH, 1925, THIS BOOK HAS BEEN | PRINTED AT THE GOLDEN COCKEREL PRESS, 10 STAPLE | INN, LONDON, & COMPLETED ON THE TWENTIETH DAY | OF NOVEMBER, 1934. COMPOSITORS: A. H. GIBBS | AND E. J. WARD. PRESSMAN: H. BARKER. THE | EDITION IS LIMITED TO 300 COPIES, OF | WHICH THIS IS NUMBER . . . | [Signed *Enid Clay*. | *Eric G*], [Printer's device: *Cockerel* (Chute) in gold, at foot]; [43] [44] blank. Printed from *Caslon O.F.* on Batchelor hand-made paper watermarked

THE CONSTANT MISTRESS
by
ENID CLAY
with Engravings
by
ERIC GILL

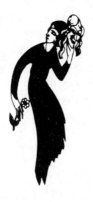

THE GOLDEN COCKEREL PRESS
1934

[293]

hammer and anvil.

ILLUSTRATIONS: In addition to the engraving on the title-page there are five illustrations from wood-engravings, placed:

The Spring Cleaner (P873), p. [8]
Marionette (P872), p. [15]
Babe on Bough (P874), p. [26]
The Single Bed ('Thanks') (P875), p. [34]
The Empty Bed (P876), p. [38]

BINDING: (a) 250 copies ¼ bound in canvas with green paper boards, with printed label on spine, the wording reading upwards: THE CONSTANT MISTRESS | BY ENID CLAY Top edges trimmed, others uncut.

(b) Fifty copies bound in full red morocco lettered on spine in gilt, reading upwards: THE CONSTANT MISTRESS T.e.g. other edges uncut.

DATE OF PUBLICATION: 1934 [December]

PRICE: De Luxe edition, with an extra set of the engravings: two guineas. Ordinary edition: 15s.

PRINTING: De Luxe edition: fifty numbered copies. Ordinary edition: 250 numbered copies. Both editions were signed by author and artist.

NOTE: This is no. 101 of the Golden Cockerel Press publications.

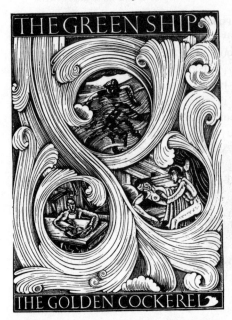 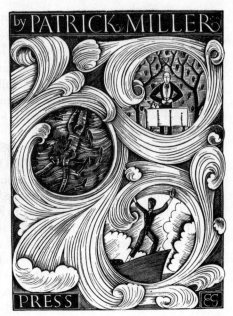

[294 Verso]   [294 Recto]

1936

294 THE GREEN SHIP

TITLE-PAGE: Reproduced. A double-fronted title-page showing w-e.'s *The Green Ship* (P898 and P899).

SIZE: $10 \times 7\frac{1}{2}$.   COLLATION: [A]⁴, B–M⁸.

PAGINATION AND CONTENTS: Pp. 184; [1] blank; [2] [3] title-pages; [4] colophon: PRINTED AND PUBLISHED IN GREAT BRITAIN BY CHRISTOPHER SANDFORD, FRANCIS J. NEWBERY AND OWEN RUTTER AT THE GOLDEN COCKEREL PRESS, WITH EIGHT WOOD-ENGRAVINGS BY ERIC GILL, AND COMPLETED ON MAY DAY 1936. THIS EDITION IS LIMITED TO 200 COPIES: 1 TO 4 ON VELLUM, 5 TO 200 ON BRITISH MOULD-MADE PAPER (5–66 BEING SIGNED, FULL-BOUND, AND ACCOMPANIED BY AN EXTRA SET OF THE PLATES). NUMBER ...; [5] [6] dedication: FOR | G. H. CRICHTON; verso blank; 7–8 (paginated 5–6) Foreword by Edward Garnett; 9–184 (paginated 7–[182]) text. Printed from 13 pt. *Perpetua*, copies 1–4 on vellum and copies 5–200 on Portals paper watermarked 'Laverstoke'.

ILLUSTRATIONS: In addition to the wood-engraved title-page there are six chapter-headings from wood-engravings, placed:

> *Man swimming* (P900), p. 7.
> *Woman asleep* (P901), p. 15.

190

Mr Scribner (P902), p. 42.
Woman diving (P903), p. 74.
Mr Brown (P904), p. 118.
The dying patriot (P905), p. 163.
BINDING: (*a*) Vellum edition: full-bound green levant morocco, g.e., by
Zaehnsdorf. Panelled spine lettered in gilt: THE | GREEN | SHIP |
PATRICK | MILLER and, at foot, *Cockerel* device (Chute).
(*b*) Paper edition: (i) full-bound green levant morocco and marbled
paper-covered boards, by Sangorski & Sutcliffe, t.e.g. other edges trimmed.
Panelled spine lettered in gilt: THE | GREEN | SHIP and, at foot, the
Cockerel device (Chute). (ii) ¼ bound green levant morocco by Sangorski &
Sutcliffe. T.e.g. other edges trimmed. Panelled spine lettered as above.
DATE OF PUBLICATION: May 1936.
PRICE: Vellum edition: fifty guineas. Full-bound paper edition: five guineas.
¼ bound paper edition: two guineas.
PRINTING: 200 copies: nos. 1–4 on vellum, with an extra set of the plates,
numbered and signed by author and artist. Nos. 5–66 on Portals paper, with
an extra set of the plates, numbered and signed by author and artist. Nos.
67–200 on Portals paper, numbered only.
NOTES: This is no. 111 of the Golden Cockerel Press publications. According
to G. F. Sims (Rare Books) Catalogue 86 (1974?), item no. 59, copy no. 6 is
unique in that instead of having an extra set of plates on japon there is an
additional set of proofs on hand-made paper, bound in (matching) quarter
morocco. This copy originally came from the library of Owen Rutter, one of
the Press's partners, who preferred the effect of the engravings on hand-made
paper to the japon impressions.

1936
295 MORALS AND MARRIAGE
TITLE-PAGE: MORALS AND MARRIAGE | THE CATHOLIC
BACKGROUND TO SEX | BY T. G. WAYNE | [*Quotation from
St Thomas Aquinas*] | LONGMANS, GREEN AND CO. |
LONDON + NEW YORK + TORONTO
SIZE: 7½ × 5. COLLATION: [A]⁸, B–F⁸.
PAGINATION AND CONTENTS: Pp. xii + 84; [i] [ii] blank; [iii] [iv] half-title:
MORALS AND MARRIAGE, verso blank; [v] [vi] title-page, verso printers'
imprint and imprimatur dated 27 June 1936; [vii] [viii] dedication: TO |
W.A.E. | FOR MORE THAN HALF, verso blank; [ix] [x] Contents, verso
blank; xi–xii (paginated ix–x) Preface; 1–81 Introduction and text; [82]–[84]
blank. The first leaf, though not included in the pagination, is a part of the first
gathering and must, therefore, be treated as an integral part of the book.

Similarly with the last leaf.

ILLUSTRATION: There is one illustration from a wood-engraving, printed separately, and placed: *Divine Lovers* (P915), frontispiece. (This is a copy of an earlier engraving of the same title (P194).)

BINDING: Blue cloth, lettered on spine in gilt: MORALS | AND | MARRIAGE | [*short rule*] | T. G. | WAYNE | and, at foot: LONGMANS Blue dust-jacket printed in purple and red on front and spine.

DATE OF PUBLICATION: 1936. Reprinted in 1937 and 1941.

PRICE: 3s. 6d. Reprints: 4s.

REVIEW: *Catholic Times*, 8 January 1937.

QUIA AMORE LANGUEO

edited by H. S. Bennett, M. A.

Emmanuel College, Cambridge

University Lecturer in English

with engravings by Eric Gill

Faber & Faber, Ltd / 1937   [296]

1937

296 QUIA AMORE LANGUEO

TITLE-PAGE: Reproduced.

SIZE: $5\frac{3}{4} \times 4\frac{1}{2}$.   COLLATION: $[a]^4$, b–e^4.

PAGINATION AND CONTENTS: Pp. ii + 38; [i] [ii] title-page, verso printers' imprint: PRINTED BY HAGUE & GILL LTD, HIGH WYCOMBE | AND PUBLISHED BY FABER & FABER LTD | 24 RUSSELL SQUARE, LONDON WC | MCMXXXVII and, at foot, PRINTED AND MADE IN GREAT BRITAIN; 1–[2] Note; [3] [4] half-title for Part 1, verso illustration; 5–38 text and illustrations. Printed from 12 pt. *Joanna* on Bareham Green hand-made paper.

ILLUSTRATIONS: There are four full-page illustrations from wood-engravings, placed:

Mother & Stars & Moon (P916), p. [4]

Mother and Child (P917), p. [12]

Christ seated (P918), p. [20]

Girl with Mirror (P919), p. [30]

BINDING: Green cloth, lettered on spine in gilt, reading downwards: QUIA

192

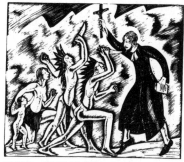

THE TRAVELS
OF FATHER JEAN
AMONG THE HURONS
CRIBED BY HIMSELF
ED FROM THE FRENCH

THE GOLDEN COCKEREL

[297 Verso]

& SUFFERINGS
DE BRÉBEUF ✠
OF CANADA AS DES-
EDITED & TRANSLAT-
AND LATIN BY THEO-
DORE BESTERMAN

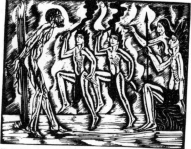

PRESS MCMXXXVIII

[297 Recto]

AMORE LANGUEO edited by H. S. BENNETT—FABER T.e.g. other edges uncut. Blue dust jacket printed in black and red.
DATE OF PUBLICATION: October 1937.
PRICE: 10s. 6d.
PRINTING: 420 copies of which 400 were for sale.
REVIEWS: By Iris Conlay, *Catholic Herald*, 10 December 1937. *The Times Literary Supplement*, 4 September, 11 December 1937. *The Tablet*, 25 December 1937.

1938
297 TRAVELS AND SUFFERINGS OF BRÉBEUF
TITLE-PAGE: Reproduced. This is a double-fronted title-page showing w-e.'s *The Attack* (P972) and *The Martyrdom* (P973). Six distinct blocks go to the making of this title-page, three for the verso which in his file of engravings E. G. lettered A, B and C and three for the recto lettered D, E and F. They are: A, the four lines of lettering; B, the w-e. *The Attack*; C, one line of lettering; D, the four lines of lettering; E, the w-e. *The Martyrdom*; F, one line of lettering.
SIZE: $12\frac{1}{2} \times 7\frac{1}{2}$. COLLATION: $[A]^8$, $B–M^8$, N^4.
PAGINATION AND CONTENTS: Pp. 200; [1] blank; [2] [3] title-page; [4]

imprint: PRINTED AND MADE IN GREAT BRITAIN | COPR: 1938—THE GOLDEN COCKEREL PRESS; 5–20 INTRODUCTION 'signed' *Th. B.*; 21–193 text; 194–5 Notes; 196–[197] BIOGRAPHICAL NOTE; [198] blank; [199] colophon: THIS BOOK HAS BEEN PRINTED AND PUBLISHED BY CHRISTOPHER | SANDFORD & OWEN RUTTER AT THE GOLDEN COCKEREL PRESS, 7 ROLLS | PASSAGE, LONDON, E.C.4, IN BEMBO TYPE ON ARNOLD'S MOULD- | MADE PAPER AND COMPLETED THE 19TH DAY OF AUGUST, 1938. THE | TWO ILLUSTRATIONS AND THE ENGRAVED TITLING ON THE TITLE PAGE ARE | THE WORK OF ERIC GILL. THE EDITION IS LIMITED TO 300 NUMBERED | COPIES. NO. ...; [200] blank. Printed from 16 pt. *Bembo* on Arnold's mould-made paper.
ILLUSTRATIONS: None save the engraved title-page as described above.
BINDING: $\frac{1}{4}$ bound in red canvas and black cloth boards. Black morocco label on spine lettered in gilt: TRAVELS & | SUFFERINGS | OF BRÉBEUF and, at foot, the printer's device: *Cockerel* (Chute) in gilt. The end-papers, both back and front, are a Map of The Huron Country. Top edges cut, others uncut.
DATE OF PUBLICATION: August 1938.
PRICE: Three guineas.
PRINTING: 300 numbered copies.
REVIEW: By Peter F. Anson, *Catholic Herald*, 10 March 1939. Cf. *English Prayer Books* by Stanley Morison, pp. 96 and 102 of 1943 ed. (Cf. no. 586.)
NOTE: This is no. 136 of the Golden Cockerel Press publications.

298 THE HOLY SONNETS
TITLE-PAGE: Reproduced.
SIZE: $9\frac{1}{4} \times 5\frac{1}{2}$.
COLLATION: [a]⁴, b–[e]⁴. The first leaf of the last gathering is not signed; the signature 'e 2' appears on the second leaf of that gathering.
PAGINATION AND CONTENTS: Pp. xiv + 26. (The pages of the illustrations and text are not paginated.) [i] [ii] title-page, verso imprint: PRINTED & MADE IN GREAT BRITAIN BY | HAGUE & GILL LTD, HIGH WYCOMBE | AND PUBLISHED FOR THEM BY | J. M. DENT & SONS LTD, ALDINE HOUSE | BEDFORD STREET, LONDON, W.C. 2 | 1938; [iii] [iv] ACKNOW-LEDGEMENT, verso blank; [v] [vi] half-title: INTRODUCTION, verso illustra-tion; vii–xiv Introduction; [1] half-title: THE HOLY SONNETS; [2] illustration; [3]–[25] text and illustrations; [26] colophon: [*device: Three-leaved clover* (P897)] 550 COPIES OF THE HOLY SONNETS | (OF WHICH 500 ARE FOR SALE) | WERE PRINTED IN OCTOBER | MCMXXXVIII | AND SIGNED BY | [Signed: *Eric G*] Reproduced. Printed from 14 pt. *Bunyan* on Barcham Green hand-made paper.

Introduction by Hugh I'A. Fausset
Engravings by Eric Gill

THE HOLY SONNETS
OF JOHN DONNE

London : J. M. Dent & Sons Ltd
for Hague & Gill Ltd

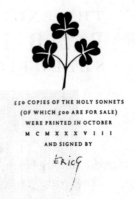

550 COPIES OF THE HOLY SONNETS
(OF WHICH 500 ARE FOR SALE)
WERE PRINTED IN OCTOBER
M C M X X X V I I I
AND SIGNED BY

ЄRicÇ

[298]

ILLUSTRATIONS: There are four full-page illustrations from wood-engravings, thus underlined and placed:

V.   *I am a little world* (P976), p. [vi]
I.   *Thou hast made me* (P975), p. [2]
VII.   *At the round earths imagin'd corners* (P977), p. [10]
X.   *Death be not proud* (P978), p. [19]

Eric Gill left the following notes concerning three of these engravings:

'"Matter and Spirit" [p. vi] God fingering creation broadcast—matter and spirit (the sprite in the spirit, the other things are matter—elements and elemental life). The same hand of God, but now it is Christ's hand, recalls all creation to Himself. "I am a little world made cunningly . . .".

"Repentance" [p. 2] Man turns to Christ and flings away power and riches and luxury. His alter egos are seen; the male with sword and machines (power), the female with motor steering wheel and money bag (luxury).

"Death of Death" [p. 19] Disintegration and decay. The sword—power, force. The cup of poison—cunning. "Death be not proud, though some . . .".'

BINDING: Black cloth lettered in gilt on front: THE HOLY SONNETS | [device: *Three-leaved clover* (after w-e. P897 as used for colophon)] | OF JOHN DONNE and, on spine, reading downwards: THE HOLY SONNETS OF JOHN DONNE Top edges cut, others uncut.

DATE OF PUBLICATION: 3 November 1938.

PRICE: 10s. 6d.

PRINTING: 550 signed copies of which 500 were for sale.

REVIEWS: By Humbert Wolfe, *The Observer*, 4 December 1938. By E. H. Blakeney, *Record*, 9 December 1938. *Time and Tide*, 10 December 1938. *The Times Literary Supplement*, 24 December 1938. *The Times*, 24 December 1938.

NOTE: This was the first book to be published in England printed from Gill's *Bunyan* type.

THE ENGLISH
B I B L E
SELECTIONS

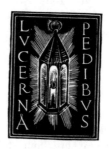

EDITED BY ARTHUR MAYHEW
WITH ENGRAVINGS BY ERIC GILL

GINN AND COMPANY LTD
QUEEN SQUARE, LONDON, W.C. 1   [299]

299 THE ENGLISH BIBLE—SELECTIONS
TITLE-PAGE: Reproduced. Shows w-e. *A Lantern—Lucerna Pedibus* (P981).
SIZE: $6\frac{1}{2} \times 4\frac{1}{2}$.   COLLATION: [A]⁶, B–S⁸, T¹⁰.
PAGINATION AND CONTENTS: Pp. xii + 292; [i] [ii] half-title: SELECTED
ENGLISH CLASSICS | GENERAL EDITOR: A. H. R. BALL, M.A. | THE
ENGLISH BIBLE | SELECTIONS, verso blank; [iii] [iv] title-page, verso
imprint: GINN AND COMPANY LTD. | ALL RIGHTS RESERVED | 053902 |
and, at foot: PRINTED IN GREAT BRITAIN | AT THE UNIVERSITY PRESS,
OXFORD | BY JOHN JOHNSON, PRINTER TO THE UNIVERSITY; [v]–viii
Preface, 'signed' ARTHUR MAYHEW. SECOND SUNDAY IN ADVENT,
1938.; [ix] [x] NOTES AND GLOSSARY and A NOTE ON REFERENCE
BOOKS, verso blank; [xi] [xii] CONTENTS, verso blank; [1]–254 text; [255]
[256] half-title: NOTES, verso blank; [257]–281 NOTES; [282] blank; [283]–
284 GLOSSARY; [285]–286 SOME IMPORTANT DATES; [287]–291 INDEX;
[292] blank.
ILLUSTRATIONS: In addition to the device on title-page, as described above,
there are three wood-engravings used as headings for the three groups of
Selections, viz. *Story and Song*, *The Law and the Prophets* and *Wit and Wisdom*,
respectively. These are placed:
> *David and Goliath* (P982), p. [49]
> *Moneychangers* (P983), p. [191]
> *Jesus and the Doctors* (P984), p. [225]

197

BINDING: Green cloth, limp boards, lettered on front in gilt: THE ENGLISH BIBLE | SELECTIONS | [ornament] and on spine, reading downwards: THE ENGLISH BIBLE SELECTIONS MAYHEW and, at foot, (reading across) GINN There are two double-fronted end-paper maps, viz. front: *The Middle East in Old Testament Times* and, back: *The Promised Land*. All edges cut.
DATE OF PUBLICATION: n.d. [1938]
PRICE: 2s. 9d.

1939

300 HENRY THE EIGHTH
TITLE-PAGE: HENRY THE EIGHTH | THE TEXT OF THE FIRST FOLIO | EDITED AND AMENDED WHERE OBSCURE BY | HERBERT FARJEON | ILLUSTRATED WITH WOOD ENGRAVINGS BY | ERIC GILL
SIZE: $13 \times 8\frac{3}{4}$.
PAGINATION AND CONTENTS: Pp. x + 120; [i] [ii] blank; [iii] [iv] half-title to series: THE PLAYS OF | WILLIAM SHAKESPEARE | IN THIRTY-SEVEN VOLUMES, verso blank; [v] [vi] title-page to series: THE COMEDIES | HISTORIES | & TRAGEDIES | OF | WILLIAM SHAKESPEARE | [*heraldic device*] | NEW YORK | THE LIMITED EDITIONS CLUB | 1939, verso blank; [vii] [viii] blank, verso frontispiece; [ix] [x] title-page for this volume, verso imprint: THE ENTIRE CONTENTS OF THIS VOLUME ARE COPYRIGHT 1939 BY | THE LIMITED EDITIONS CLUB, INC. | PRINTED IN THE UNITED STATES OF AMERICA.; [1]–116 text; [117] [118] blank, verso printer's device and colophon: THIS EDITION OF THE LIFE OF KING HENRY THE EIGHTH | IS ONE OF THE THIRTY-SEVEN VOLUMES OF THE PLAYS OF | WILLIAM SHAKESPEARE PUBLISHED FOR SUBSCRIBERS BY THE | LIMITED EDITIONS CLUB OF NEW YORK. | IT WAS DESIGNED BY BRUCE ROGERS AND PRINTED AT THE PRESS | OF A. COLISH, NEW YORK. | THE ILLUSTRATIONS ARE WOOD ENGRAVINGS BY ERIC GILL | OF ENGLAND. | THE EDITION CONSISTS OF NINETEEN HUNDRED AND FIFTY COPIES, | OF WHICH THIS IS NUMBER [. . .]; [119] [120] blank. Printed from 18 pt. *Monotype Jenson* on paper specially made by The Worthy Paper Company. t.e.g. other edges uncut.
ILLUSTRATIONS: There are six full-page wood-engravings, printed separately and placed:

> *The History of King Henry VIII* (P925), frontispiece.
> Act I   *The King enamoured of Anne* (P926), facing p. 26.
>   II   *Henry's doubts* (P927), facing p. 54.
>   III *The fall of Wolsey* (P928), facing p. 76.

IV   The coronation of Anne (P929), facing p. 88.

V   The baptism of Elizabeth (P930), facing p. 112.

BINDING: ¼ linen, decorative paper boards lettered on front and back: THE PLAYS OF W. SHAKESPEARE, and in gilt, on spine, reading upwards: HENRY THE EIGHTH. The paper printed in four colours from a pattern redrawn by Bruce Rogers after a wall-painting in the house at Oxford occupied by John Davenant from 1592 to 1614, where Shakespeare is known to have visited.

DATE OF PUBLICATION: 1939.

PRICE: n.p. Privately printed for members of the Limited Editions Club, New York.

PRINTING: 1950 numbered copies, and 15 copies marked with a circular embossed stamp at the bottom of the colophon: 'THIS IS ONE OF 15 PRESENTATION COPIES OUT OF SERIES'. CLC copy is lettered in ink E.G., following; 1 of which this is number [...]

NOTE: The typography was planned and the production supervised by Bruce Rogers.

1941

301 GLUE AND LACQUER

TITLE-PAGE: Reproduced.

SIZE: $9\frac{7}{8} \times 7\frac{1}{4}$.   COLLATION: [A]⁸, B–I⁸.

PAGINATION AND CONTENTS: Pp. 144; [1] [2] blank, verso frontispiece; [3] [4] title-page, verso note 'signed' H. A. concerning the title chosen for these tales and, at foot: PRINTED IN ENGLAND; [5] [6] dedication: TO | BERYL DE ZOETE, verso blank; [7] [8] CONTENTS, verso blank; 9–12 PREFACE 'signed' ARTHUR WALEY; [13] [14] half-title: GLUE AND LACQUER, verso illustration; 15–129 text; 130–8 NOTES; 139 colophon: PRINTED IN LONDON BY CHRISTOPHER SANDFORD AND OWEN RUTTER AT THE GOLDEN | COCKEREL PRESS DURING THE BATTLE OF LONDON. COMPOSITOR, E. W. TREVIS. | PRESSMAN, W. H. SOLLY. THE EDI-TION, COMPLETED ON THE 28TH DAY OF APRIL, | 1941, IS LIMITED TO 350 COPIES. THE 'SPECIALS' (NOS. 1–30) ARE PRINTED ON HAND- | MADE PAPER, BOUND IN FULL MOROCCO, AND ACCOMPANIED BY COLLOTYPE REPRO- | DUCTIONS OF ERIC GILL'S DRAWINGS. THE 'ORDINARIES' (NOS. 31–350) ARE PRINTED | ON MOULD-MADE PAPER AND BOUND IN ¼ MOROCCO. COPY NUMBER: [...] | and, in middle of page: NOTE ON THE ILLUSTRATIONS | ERIC GILL HAD ARRANGED TO ILLUSTRATE THESE STORIES WITH ENGRAVINGS. DURING THE | LAST WEEK OF HIS LIFE, WHILE IN HOSPITAL, HE COMPLETED THE DRAWINGS, WHICH AFTER | HIS DEATH WERE

GLUE AND LACQUER

FOUR CAUTIONARY TALES
TRANSLATED FROM THE CHINESE BY
HAROLD ACTON & LEE YI-HSIEH

PREFACE BY
ARTHUR WALEY

With Illustrations from Drawings by
ERIC GILL
interpreted on copper by
Denis Tegetmeier

THE GOLDEN COCKEREL PRESS [301]

INTERPRETED ON COPPER BY HIS SON-IN-LAW, DENIS TEGETMEIER.; [140]–[144] blank.[1] Printed from 14 pt. *Perpetua* on hand-made paper (the 'Specials') and Arnold's mould-made paper (the 'Ordinaries').

ILLUSTRATIONS: There are five full-page copper-plate engravings by Denis Tegetmeier from drawings made by Eric Gill, placed:

> *Glue and Lacquer*, frontispiece.
> *The Mandarin-Duck Girdle*, p. [14]
> *Brother or Bride?*, p. [52]
> *The Predestined Couple*, p. [78]
> *Love in a Junk*, p. [102]

BINDING: (*a*) The 'Specials'. Full-bound blue morocco, gold-stamped on front with four Chinese characters. Panelled spine, lettered in gilt: GLUE | AND | LACQUER and, at foot, in gilt, printer's device: *Cockerel* (Chute). Edges (of binding) gilt-tooled. T.e.g., other edges uncut.

(*b*) The 'Ordinaries'. $\frac{1}{4}$ blue morocco, chinese yellow boards stamped and lettered on spine as above. t.e.g., other edges uncut. Both bindings are by Sangorski and Sutcliffe.

DATE OF PUBLICATION: April 1941.

PRICE: The 'Specials': ten guineas. The 'Ordinaries': two guineas.

PRINTING: The 'Specials': thirty numbered copies. The 'Ordinaries': 320 numbered copies.

REVIEW: *The Times Literary Supplement*, 16 August 1941.

NOTE: This is no. 149 of the Golden Cockerel Press publications.

[1] In the special edition p. [144] is followed by a leaf on the recto of which is printed: FACSIMILE REPRODUCTIONS OF | ERIC GILL'S DRAWINGS, this is followed by the five collotype reproductions.

SECTION III(*b*)
1905-21

1905

302 GROSSHERZOG WILHELM ERNST EDITION OF THE
GERMAN CLASSICS. This edition comprises the following thirty-four
volumes:

SCHILLER. *Dramatische Dichtungen*, Bd. I and II, 1905–6.
    Bd. III. *Gedichte und Erzaehlungen*, 1906.
    Bd. IV. *Philosophische Schriften*, 1906.
    Bd. V. *Historische Schriften*, 1906.
    Bd. VI. *Übersetzungen*, 1906.

SCHOPENHAUER. *Sämmtliche Werke in fünf Bänden:*
    Bd. I & II. *Die Welt als Wille und Vorstellung*, 1905.
    Bd. III. *Kleinere Schriften herausgegeben von Max Brahn*, 1908.
    Bd. IV & V. *Parerga und Paralipomena. Erster Theil, herausgegeben von
    Hans Henning*, 1909–10.

KOERNER. *Werke*, 1906.

GOETHE.   Bd. I & II. *Romane und Novellen.*
              Bd. III–V. *Autobiographische Schriften.*
              Bd. VI–VIII. *Dramatische Dichtungen.*
              Bd. IX & X. *Kunstschriften.*
              Bd. XI. *Ubersetzungen und Bearbeitungen fremder dichtungen.*
              Bd. XII & XIII. *Aufsatze zur Kultur-theater- und literatur-
              geschichte, Maximen, Reflexionen.*
              Bd. XIV & XV. *Lyrische und Epische Dichtungen.*
              Bd. XVI. *Naturwissenschaftliche Schriften in auswahl.*

KANT.   Bd. I. *Vermische Schriften.*
              Bd. II. *Naturwissenschaftliche Schriften.*
              Bd. III. *Kritik der reiner Vernuft.*
              Bd. IV. *Kleinere philosophische Schriften.*
              Bd. V. *Moralische Schriften.*
              Bd. VI. *Asthetiche und Religionsphilosophische Schriften.*

The volumes were uniformly bound in red limp leather, lettered in gilt on
front and spine. $6\frac{1}{2} \times 3\frac{3}{4}$. t.e.g. Leipzig: Insel Verlag. 1905–11. The book titles
and headings Eric Gill did for this edition (in 1904–5) were his earliest
typographic work. Emery Walker was responsible for the format of the series.

GOETHES
ROMANE UND
NOVELLEN
BAND I

.

MCMV
LEIPZIG
IM INSELVERLAG   [302]

Bernhard Suphan was responsible for the text and Harry Graf Kessler supervised the decorations. The half-titles were designed by Edward Johnston and Douglas Cockerell was responsible for the binding. The series was printed by Poeschel and Trepte.

NOTE: See *Four Centuries of Fine Printing* (no. 411) and *Eric Gill: Sculptor of Letters* (no. 449). RMK 10.

302a AUSSTELLUNG VON WERKEN DER MODERNEN DRUCK UND SCHREIB. Grossherzogliches Museum für Kunst und Kunstgewerbe. Karlsplatz Weimar. Catalogue of an Exhibition April–May 1905. Contains title-page probably done by Eric Gill. Title-page reproduced. See illustration RMK 7.

1906

302b PAUL GAUGUIN. 1848–1903. By Jean de Rotonchamp. $10\frac{1}{4} \times 7\frac{5}{8}$. 300 copies, 250 for sale. Paris: Edouard Druet. 1906. Printed at Weimar, 'par les soins du Comte de Kessler'. Contains title-page lettering by Eric Gill. Title-page reproduced. RMK 16.

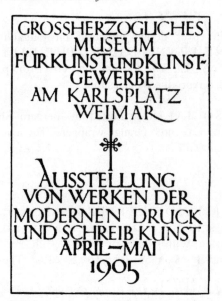

GROSSHERZOGLICHES
MUSEUM
FÜR KUNST und KUNST-
GEWERBE
AM KARLSPLATZ
WEIMAR

AUSSTELLUNG
VON WERKEN DER
MODERNEN DRUCK
UND SCHREIB KUNST
APRIL—MAI
1905

[302*a*]

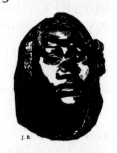

PAUL GAUGUIN
1848-1903
PAR JEAN DE ROTONCHAMP

J. B.

IMPRIME A WEIMAR
PAR LES SOINS DU COMTE
D KESSLER.ET SE TROUVE A
PARIS chez EDOUARD DRUET
EDITEUR.RUE du FAUBOURG
ST.HONORE NO.114.
MDCCCCVI

[302*b*]

303 UTOPIA. Sir Thomas More's UTOPIA. Reprinted from the text of the second edition of Ralphe Robynson's translation of 1556. The Ashendene Press. 1906. Initials designed by Eric Gill. $11\frac{1}{4} \times 7\frac{3}{4}$, black and red. 100 paper, boards, 31*s*. 6*d*.; 20 vellum, green vellum, ten guineas.

1907

303*a* KLEINE DRAMEN. By Hugo von Hoffmannsthal. 2 vols. $8\frac{1}{4} \times 5\frac{5}{8}$. Leipzig: Insel-Verlag. 1907. Printed by W. Drugulin, Leipzig. $\frac{1}{4}$ vellum, silvered paper covered boards. Contains title-page lettering by Eric Gill, as stated in the colophon, Vol. I, opposite p. 128.

1908–9

304 MENSCHLICHE KOMÖDIE. Balzac's MENSCHLICHE KOMÖDIE in four volumes with title-pages and half-title pages drawn by Eric Gill. $7\frac{1}{4} \times 4\frac{1}{4}$. Red cloth, t.e.g. Leipzig: Insel Verlag. 1908–9.
The volumes comprise:

    I   Ein Junggesellenheim, 1908.

    II   Erzählungen aus der Napoleonischen Sphäre, 1908.

    III   Eugenie Grandet der Ehevertrag, 1908.

    IV   Verlorene Illusionen. I Teil, 1909.

NOTE: See *Eric Gill: Sculptor of Letters* (no. 449).

1908

305 FABIAN TRACTS. With cover design engraved on four blocks:
FABIAN TRACTS | ONE PENNY EACH | THE FABIAN
SOCIETY | LONDON (D2). Cf. *The Fleuron*, no. VII, 1930, p. 32
(no. 449) wherein this engraving is reproduced in facsimile.

305*a* FABIAN ESSAYS IN SOCIALISM. Edited by Bernard Shaw.
London: Walter Scott Publishing Co. 1908. Orange wrappers. The lettering
for the cover and spine was done by Gill.

1909

306 MANUSCRIPT & INSCRIPTION LETTERS. MANUSCRIPT &
INSCRIPTION LETTERS FOR SCHOOLS & CLASSES & FOR THE USE OF
CRAFTSMEN, by Edward Johnston. With 5 Plates by A. E. R. Gill. (Portfolio
No. 2, 'School Copies & Examples'.) London: John Hogg. 3*s.* 6*d.* The five
plates ($10 \times 12\frac{1}{2}$) by Gill are:

Plate 12. *Alphabet from the Inscription on the Trajan Column, Rome, circa
114 A.D. Drawn from a photograph.*

Plate 13. *Roman Capital letters, incised with 'V' section, in Hopton Wood
Stone.*

Plate 14. *'Lower-Case', Italics & Numerals incised with 'V' section in Hopton
Wood Stone.*

Plate 15. *'Raised' Letters—Capitals & Numerals–carved in Hopton Wood
Stone.*

Plate 16. *Roman Capitals, 'Lower-case' & Italics and Arabic Numerals suitable
for ordinary sign-writing, written (with brush).*

This portfolio was first published in September 1909. Second impression,
revised, 1911. Third impression, a reprint of second impression, 1916.
Reprinted, by Sir Isaac Pitman & Sons, Ltd., 1920, 1922, 1930, 1938 and
1946.

GERMAN EDITION: CLC has a German edition entitled HAND:
INSCHRIFT ALPHABETE, LEIPZIG: KLINKHARDT
& BIERMANN, 1912. The captions were translated by Anna Simons.
The five plates by Gill are nos. 12–16. GL has a 1922 German edition as above.

307 SHAKESPEARE'S SONNETS. TERCENTENARY EDITION. From
the first edition, 1609. Hammersmith: The Doves Press. November 1909.
With capitals designed by Edward Johnston and engraved on wood by Eric
Gill and Noel Rooke. These are: Sonnet 1, whole-page 'F' (G24). Sonnet 127,
half-page 'I' (G26). Sonnet 151, whole-page 'L' (G25). Sonnet 153, five-line 'C'
(G27). Black and Red. 250 paper, 30*s.*; 15 vellum, £7. 10*s.*

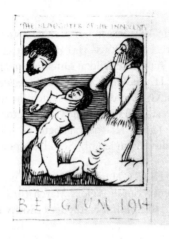

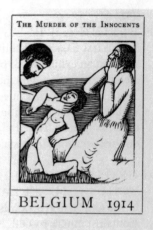

[309]

Catalogue
PRICE 2ᴰ

1910

308 DIE ODYSSEE. NEU INS DEUTSCHE ÜBERTRAGEN VON RUDOLF
ALEXANDER SCHRÖDER. THE ODYSSEY. NEWLY TRANSLATED INTO
THE GERMAN BY RUDOLF ALEXANDER SCHRÖDER. 2 vols. ($11\frac{1}{4} \times 8\frac{1}{2}$).
Vol. I, Books I–XII, pp. 179. Vol. II, Books XIII–XXIV, pp. 170. Printed from
Caslon Antiqua under the supervision of Harry Graf Kessler. 425 copies, of
which 350 were for sale. Weimar: Cranach Press, 1910. Contains w-e. title
pages for Vol. I (G1–4) and Vol. II (G1,2,5); an initial letter N for Book I, Vol. I
(G11) and an initial letter A for Book XIII, Vol. II (G12); initials for the other
books in both volumes (G14); headings (G16), shoulder titles (G17) and roman
numbers (G18); initials E and F (G19) on Contents page, Vol. I and initial word
DRIEZEHNTER (G20) on Contents page, Vol. II, and a colophon
monogram H K (G21) for both volumes.
NOTE: See *Four Centuries of Fine Printing* (no. 411), *Eric Gill: Sculptor of
Letters* (no. 449), *Die Cranach-Presse in Weimar* (no. 452) and *Verzeichnis der
Drucke der Cranach-Presse in Weimar* (no. 453). R M K 17.

206

1914

309 BELGIAN REFUGEES. THE MURDER OF THE INNOCENTS
BELGIUM 1914. Ditchling, January, 1914. 7×4½. [4] pp. Price 2*d*. Catalogue of an exhibition of painting and sculpture held at Ditchling in aid of the Belgian Refugees. On the cover, p. [1], is Gill's w-e. *The Slaughter of the Innocents* (P18). This title was used in Gill's preliminary sketch for the cover and even for a trial printing of the cover, both now at the GL. But the caption was changed to *The Murder of the Innocents* for the catalogue as issued, the shorter word making the title a more convenient length. See illus. opposite.

309*a* GROSSHERZOGLICH-SÄCHSISCHE KUNSTGEWERBE-SCHULE ZU WEIMAR. By Henry van de Velde. March 1914. Printed at the Cranach Press, Weimar. 9×6½. 10 unnumbered pages. Stiff wrappers. Contains: initials by Gill. RMK 19.

1915

310 ORDO ADMINISTRANDI SACRAMENTA, ET ALIA
QUAEDAM OFFICIA ECCLESIASTICA RITE PERAGENDI IN MISSIONE
ANGLICANA. London: Burns & Oates. 1915. Contains a half-title device:
Three Martlets (in red): the Arms of St Thomas of Canterbury, with the petition: NOS NE CESSES THOMA TUERI (P28). The full reading is: E LIBRIS LITVRGICIS | CVRA SOCIETIS LIBRARIAE | BURNS ET OATES | NVNCVPATAE PRELO DATIS | NOS NE CESSES | THOMA TUERI. N.B. While the above is correct Latin, the actual inscription reads SOCIETAS AND DATUS. GL owns a label version of the half-title device with no border inscription, only the petition, with a single white line rule around the three birds, not mentioned in Physick. Cf. *English Prayer Books* (Third ed. 1949) by Stanley Morison (no. 586).

1916

311 COPY SHEETS. Single sheets of hand-made paper (11¼×8¾) were published by Douglas Pepler at Hammersmith for the use of Edward Johnston's students. (See illustration.) The main part of each sheet was occupied by a piece of formal writing by Johnston himself (in black); above and below this there was printed matter in red, of which the lower portion embodied a wood-block of lettering by Eric Gill (*Lettering with nib* (P71)). The latter must not be confused with similar lettering in the book *A Carol and Other Rhymes*, by Edward Johnston (Douglas Pepler, *Hampshire House Workshops*, 1915, p. 29), erroneously described as being the same engraving in A LIST OF

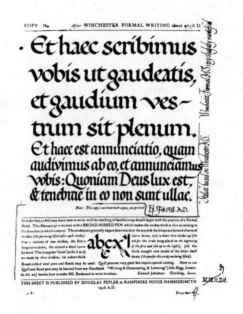

[311]

BOOKS WITH LETTERING OR ILLUSTRATIONS ENGRAVED BY ERIC GILL printed in *The Fleuron*, No. VII (1930) at p. 52 (no. 449).

312 THE PARABLES OF JESUS. Published by Burns & Oates for whom Eric Gill engraved the device: *Paschal Lamb* (P20). (Not seen by the compiler.)

313 COTTAGE ECONOMY. By William Cobbett. With an introduction by G. K. Chesterton. $7\frac{1}{4} \times 4\frac{3}{4}$. 250 copies. Douglas Pepler, The Hampshire House Workshops, Hammersmith, 1916. 2s. 6d. Contains w-e. *Diagram for Ice-House* (P57) at p. 165. Reprinted from the 17th edition. This is no. 3 of S. Dominic's Press publications.

314 A BOOK ON VEGETABLE DYES. By Ethel M. Mairet. $11\frac{1}{4} \times 7\frac{5}{8}$. [4] pp., grey wrappers. Printed by Douglas Pepler at Ditchling, Sussex, and published by him at The Hampshire House Workshops, Hammersmith, 24 June 1916. Black paper wrappers printed in silver. 5s. Device on title-page and front cover: *Hog in Triangle* (P58). This was the first book to be printed at what, shortly afterwards, came to be S. Dominic's Press. It is no. 4 of S. Dominic's Press publications. A second edition was issued in 1917 in brown paper wrappers printed in red. A fourth edition, revised and enlarged, was issued in 1924 and a fifth edition is known.

208

315*a* THE HAMPSHIRE HOUSE WORKSHOPS LTD. A STATE-
MENT OF AIM ISSUED BY THE FOUNDERS. Ditchling Press: Douglas and
David Pepler. November 1916. 3*d.* Contains two w-e.'s, *Hog in Triangle:
H H W* (P58), on front cover and *Hog and Wheatsheaf* (P31), on inner side of
back cover. This is no. 8 of S. Dominic's Press publications. Note: The
activities of the Workshops comprised Dressmaking, 6 Upper Mall, Wood
Work Shop, 7 Upper Mall, The Doves Bakery, 10 Upper Mall, Hammer-
smith, and Printing and Publishing, 2 Upper Mall, Hammersmith and
Ditchling, Sussex.

315*b* MARY SAT A-WORKING. [By H. D. C. Pepler.] A Rhyme-Sheet
printed in black and red and published at S. Dominic's Press, Ditchling. 1916.
Contains w-e. *Madonna and Child with Angel: Madonna knitting* (P60). This
engraving was subsequently used for *Song of the Dressmaker* (1923) (see no.
386) which, in turn, was later published as *The Dressmaker and Milkmaid*
(1926). This is recorded in S. Dominic's Press 'Book List' (1930 under no. 67
(16) as *Dressmaker.*

1917
316 THE LAST JUDGMENT. A broadsheet printed and published at
S. Dominic's Press (5⅝ × 4¼) containing w-e. of the same title (P107). [n.p.]

317 IN MEMORIAM OLOF ALICE JOHNSTON VERONICA MARY. A funeral
'card' printed by Douglas Pepler, Ditchling, Sussex. Contains the following
w-e.'s *Chalice and Host* (P65), *Device: Spray of leaves: M.V.O.J.* (P108),
Device: Stalk with leaves (P109), and *Initial O with speedwell* (P110). Note: The
last three were subsequently used for other purposes by S. Dominic's Press,
the letters M V O J having been cut away from w-e. P108. This item is similar
to item no. 5 in Sewell, *Matrix* 4, depending on the implication of the use of
the word 'card' above. Certainly Sewell is describing a pamphlet since he is
describing a version of no. 361. As neither item is described in any detail it is
possible that no. 317 and Sewell's item are the same. G L has a variant of these,
apparently, which is 5 × 3¾, has 20 pages and is a sewn pamphlet. It contains
the *Chalice and Host* (P65) on the cover (p. [1]), *Spray of leaves: MVOJ* (P108)
on p. [19] and *D P and Cross* (P64) on the back (p. [20]). The G L copy
contains a reset version of the English text only of the Order of the Burial of the
Dead (cf. no. 361) and does not contain the text of the Note by a Friend nor the
two w-e.'s associated with it, *Stalk with leaves* (P109) and *Initial Letter O with
speedwell* (P110). Item no. 6 in Sewell, *Matrix* 4, describes a broadside version
in which, 'The text is longer than the booklet version but the Order of Service
is omitted.' G L has a version of this broadside measuring 20 × 7½ but which

lacks the title In Memorian Olof Alice Johnston and simply begins: Note by A Friend. The broadside uses (PI10) and the *Stalk with leaves* (PI09) is printed at the foot of the text.

1918

318 SPIRIT AND FLESH. By A. K. Coomaraswamy. A poem, printed at S. Dominic's Press, for private distribution. Contains w-e. *Spirit and Flesh* (PI37).

319 SAINT GEORGE AND THE DRAGON AND OTHER STORIES. $10\frac{1}{4} \times 7\frac{1}{2}$. Eighty-five copies. Printed and published by Douglas Pepler, Ditchling, Sussex. 1918. Brown paper wrappers. 5s. Contains, among several illustrations, three w-e.'s by Gill: Device for title-page: *St George & the Dragon* (P90), *Entire Dragon* (PI41), p. [45] and *Imprint: D P and Cross* (P64), p. [50]. This is no. 5 of S. Dominic's Press publications. GL has a variant copy $11\frac{1}{4} \times 7\frac{3}{4}$. Pp. 24, n.d. Brown paper wrappers. 1s. Children's Series Vol. I, no. I. None of the illustrations are by Gill. There is also a publisher's note tipped onto the inside front wrapper concerning the Children's Series.

1919

320 CHANGE. THE BEGINNING OF A CHAPTER. IN TWELVE VOLUMES. Edited by John Hilton & Joseph Thorp. $6\frac{3}{8} \times 3\frac{7}{8}$. London: The Decoy Press, Plaistow. Brown paper boards, cloth spine. Only two volumes of this little magazine appeared. Each contains the w-e. *Imprint: Decoy Duck* (P35) in Vol. I at p. [107] and Vol. II at p. [101] In addition there is, in Vol. I, at p. 55, a photograph of a tablet of lettering carved by E. G. This accompanies a contribution [unsigned] 'An Inscription'. The tablet reads as follows: HEREABOUTS DIED A VERY GALLANT GENTLEMAN | J. G. NEIGHBOUR. AGED 37: DECEMBER 28TH. 1908 These little volumes were exhibited at the National Book League Exhibition of Wood-Engraving in Modern English Books (1949). Cf. catalogue of the Exhibition, item 7 and reference in the Introduction by Thomas Balston at p. 12 (no. 626), also *Image: 5* (1950), p. 10 (no. 626).

1920

321 HOW TO SING PLAIN CHANT. CHIEFLY FOR THE USE OF DOMINICAN CHOIRS. By Fr. James Harrison, O.P. $7 \times 4\frac{1}{2}$. 450 copies. S. Dominic's Press, Ditchling. 1920. 5s. Contains title-page device (also printed on front cover): *Dominican Shield: on scroll: VERITAS* (PI49a). This is no. 32 of S. Dominic's Press publications.

1925

322 PICTOR IGNOTUS, FRA LIPPO LIPPI, ANDREA DEL SARTO. By Robert Browning. $10\frac{1}{2} \times 7\frac{1}{2}$. 360 numbered copies, printed in black and red from 18 pt. *Caslon O.F.* on unbleached Arnold paper. $\frac{1}{4}$ bound parchment, blue boards. Golden Cockerel Press, May 1925. 17s. 6d. Contains two initial letters (printed in red) by Eric Gill, an initial letter 'I' on pp. 9 and 13 and an initial letter 'B' on p. 29. The 'B' is also stamped in gold on the cover. This is no. 26 of the Golden Cockerel Press publications.

323 AN APOLOGY FOR THE LIFE OF COLLEY CIBBER. By Himself. Two vols. 10×6. 450 numbered copies, printed in black and blue from 14 pt. *Caslon O.F.* on Antique de luxe paper. $\frac{1}{4}$ bound white buckram, buff boards. Golden Cockerel Press, August 1925. 36s. Contains thirteen decorated initial letters (printed in blue) by Eric Gill, from (P309). This is no. 29 of the Golden Cockerel Press publications.

324 GULLIVER'S TRAVELS. By Jonathan Swift, D.D. Two vols., $10 \times 7\frac{1}{2}$. 450 copies, printed from 14 pt. *Caslon O.F.* $\frac{1}{2}$ bound white buckram, black boards, three guineas. There was also an edition of thirty copies on English hand-made paper, signed by the Artist, full-bound white buckram, six guineas. Golden Cockerel Press, December 1925. With forty wood-engravings by David Jones and fifteen initial letters by Eric Gill. This is no. 33 of the Golden Cockerel Press publications. Note: The initial letters for this and the two preceding entries are numbered 37a in Eric Gill's private file. (Cf. note in *Engravings by Eric Gill* (Cleverdon, Bristol, 1929), p. 39.) The initial letter 'I' on p. 11 of Vol. 1 is the same as that on p. 102 but inverted.

325 IN MEMORIAM WALTHER RATHENAU 22 JUNI 1922. By Hugo F. Simon, Georg Bernhard, Harry Graf Kessler. Cranach Press, Weimar. December 1925. A Memorial booklet of twenty-three pages with title-page engraved by Eric Gill (P312) as well as an initial letter 'M' on p. 3 from the (P314) series. The 'M' was then gilt by hand by Aristide Maillol. Printed from *Jenson Antiqua* under the direction of Harry Graf Kessler. Printing: fifty copies. $\frac{1}{4}$ vellum. See *Die Cranach-Presse in Weimar* (no. 452) and *Verzeichnis der Drucke der Cranach-Presse in Weimar* (no. 453). RMK 39.

326 PAUL VALÉRY: GEDICHTE. TRANSLATED BY RAINER MARIA RILKE. Cranach Press, Weimar. 1925. For Insel Verlag, Leipzig. $\frac{1}{4}$ vellum, blue paste paper boards. Contains: title-page device, a sailing-ship, a decorated initial letter V, on front cover, letter G on p. 7 and a colophon, all from wood-engravings by Eric Gill, (P310) and (P311). Cf. note after no. 9, p. 39 of

Engravings By Eric Gill (Bristol, 1929). These engravings were numbered 37 b in Gill's private file. Printed from *Caslon-Antiqua* under the direction of Harry Graf Kessler and Georg Alexander Mathéy. Printing: 450 copies. See *Die Cranach-Presse in Weimar* (no. 452) and *Verzeichnis der Drucke der Cranach-Presse in Weimar* (no. 453). R M K 38.

326a THE BALANCE WHICH PAYS BEST? *The Labour Woman*, Vol. XIII, no. 3, 1 March 1925. $6\frac{1}{2} \times 7\frac{1}{2}$ drawing on cover, paragraph of description of the drawing on verso, p. 34, written by Gill.

1926
327 THE ARCHITECTS' JOURNAL. London: The Architectural Press; 9 Queen Anne's Gate, Westminster. Contains cover device: *Inigo Jones: I J* (P339) and title-page device: *Boy with drawing board* (P346). Both devices first appeared in the issue of the journal for 6 January 1926 (Vol. 63, no. 1618). The letters I J in no. 62 were subsequently removed. This variant of the engraving first appeared with the issue of 5 January 1927.

328 DIE ECLOGEN VERGILS. In the original Latin, revised by Thomas Achelis and Alfred Koerte, German translation by Rudolph Alexander Schroeder. Leipzig: Insel-Verlag. 1926. Contains: lettering for title-page D I E ECLOGEN VERGILS (P399a) and initial letters. Cf. the note following no. 9, p. 39, in *Engravings by Eric Gill* (no. 17). The boxes, bindings and preliminary pages of the vellum, leather-bound and Japanese paper editions also use the additional lettering: P. | VERGILI MARONIS | ECLOGAE & GEORGICA | LATINE ET GERMANICE | VOLUMEN PRIUS | ECLOGAE | ORNAVIT | ARISTIDE MAILLOL (P399). All of the above are by Eric Gill.* Printed from *Jenson-Antiqua* at the Cranach Presse, Weimar, under the supervision of Harry Graf Kessler. This edition comprised: 294 copies, eight on vellum, thirty-six on Japanese paper and 250 on special hand-made Maillol-Kessler paper. There are forty-three woodcuts by Aristide Maillol. Printing was begun in 1914 and interrupted by World War I. Work on the book was resumed in 1925 and finished in April 1926. In addition to the German translation there appeared a French and an English edition. Cf. (no. 449), (no. 452), (no. 453) German edition is R M K 40, French edition is R M K 41 and English edition is R M K 43.
LATIN AND FRENCH EDITION, 1926: LES ECLOGUES DE

* In addition Gill did the lettering for the circular Cranach Press mark (P313) on the verso of the colophon.

VIRGILE. In the original Latin, with a French translation by Marc Lafargue. Contains: lettering for title-page LES ECLOGUES DE VIRGILE (P399a) and initial letters. The boxes, bindings and preliminary pages also use the additional lettering as above for the German special copies, except the third line reads: Latine et Gallice (P399). This edition comprised: 292 copies, six on vellum, thirty-six on special Maillol-Kessler Japan vellum and 250 copies on special Maillol-Kessler hand-made paper.
LATIN AND ENGLISH EDITION, 1927: THE ECLOGUES OF VIRGIL. In the original Latin with an English prose translation by J. H. Mason. Contains: lettering for title-page THE ECLOGUES OF VIRGIL (P488) and initial letters. The preliminary pages of the Japanese paper copies use the additional lettering: THE ECLOGUES AND | GEORGICS OF VERGIL | VOLUME I | ANGLICE (P488). The boxes, bindings and preliminary pages also use the additional lettering as above for the German special copies, except the third line reads: Latine et Anglice. This edition comprised: 264 copies, six on vellum, thirty-three on imperial Japanese paper and 225 copies on special hand-made Maillol-Kessler paper with the watermark of the Cranach Presse.

329 IN MEMORIAM PAUL CASSIRER 7. JANUAR 1926. GEDÄCHT-NISREDEN VON MAX LIEBERMANN HARRY GRAF KESSLER BEI DER TOTENFEIER UND EIN NACHRUF VON RENÉ SCHICKELE. Weimar: Cranach-Presse, 1926. Contains lettering: IN MEMORIAM | PAUL CASSIRER | 7 JANUAR 1926 (P357) and, on title-page, *Imprint: Woman:* CRANACH PRESSE WEIMAR (P358) the latter after a design by Aristide Maillol. A memorial booklet of fifteen pages printed from *Jenson-Antiqua*. See *Verzeichnis der Drucke der Cranach-Presse in Weimar* (no. 453). RMK 42.

330 THE GOLDEN COCKEREL PRESS—AUTUMN 1926. Autumn announcement of books just published or in preparation, with list of those printed and published from March 1923 to July 1926. Contains, on front cover: Border: *Leaves* (P384) printed in green.

331 THE GOLDEN COCKEREL PRESS—WINTER 1926. Winter announcement similar to the above with Device: *Cockerel and Printing Press* (P393) on front cover. The same device was used on the announcements for Spring and Autumn 1927.

332 THE FLEURON. A JOURNAL OF TYPOGRAPHY. Edited by Stanley Morison. No. V, December 1926. Cambridge: The University Press. 1926 [December] Ordinary edition: 21*s*. Edition de Luxe: 63*s*. The edition de luxe contains a device: w-e. *Two Amorini* (P394) used on the title-page of an insert, *Eulogy of Pierre Simon Fournier le Jeune*.

332*a* THE PSALTER OR PSALMS OF DAVID TAKEN FROM THE BOOK OF COMMON PRAYER. The Golden Cockerel Press, 1927. Red initial 'P' on title page, all red 4-line initials by E. G. See letter from E. G. to Gibbings 10 June 1928, and *Alphabet & Image* No. 3, p. 64.

1928

333 JESUS BEFORE PILATE. Print of a woodcut on pearwood plank (P190) cut in 1921. Published in an edition of sixty signed and numbered copies, mounted on *Arches* paper and enclosed in folio wrappers (20 × 16 in.). Bristol: Douglas Cleverdon, 1928. Ten copies were for presentation and fifty (of which twenty-five were reserved for U.S.A.) were sold at three guineas each. Printed by the Fanfare Press.

334 LAMIA, AND OTHER POEMS. By John Keats. $12\frac{1}{2} \times 7\frac{1}{2}$. 485 numbered copies, printed from 18 pt. *Caslon O.F.* on Batchelor hand-made paper, $\frac{1}{4}$ bound sharkskin with buff buckram boards, three guineas. There was also an edition of fourteen copies on vellum, full-bound in sharkskin, thirty-six guineas. Golden Cockerel Press, November 1928. With seventeen wood-engravings by Robert Gibbings. The initials 'IT' engraved by E. G. (w-e. P401) for *Troilus and Criseyde* but not used are used here on p. 18 together with fifteen floreated initial letters printed in red and blue. This is no. 62 of the Golden Cockerel Press publications.

1929

335 INITIAL LETTERS ETC., ENGRAVED BY ERIC GILL. Printed for *The Fleuron* at the Golden Cockerel Press, 1929. The initial letters, borders, etc., were selected from engravings done by Eric Gill for the Golden Cockerel Press. This booklet of 8 pp. ($11\frac{5}{8} \times 8\frac{5}{8}$) was printed in an edition of twelve copies for presentation. It appeared subsequently as an inset in *The Fleuron*, No. VII (following p. 40), (no. 346).

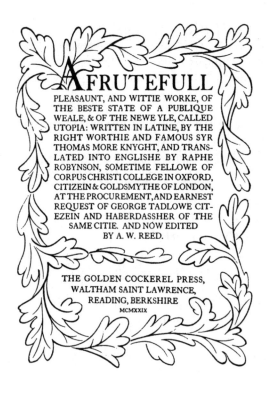

[336]

336 UTOPIA. By Sir Thomas More. $10 \times 7\frac{1}{2}$. 500 numbered copies, printed (in black and blue) from 12 pt. *Caslon O.F.* on English hand-made paper. Full-bound blue-green buckram. 36*s*. Golden Cockerel Press, April 1929. Christopher Skelton has shown in *The Engravings of Eric Gill*, no. 636.113, that the decorated title-page and the ten floriated initials in the text, were engravings cut by Ralph Beedham (1879–1975) to Gill's drawings. These are listed by Skelton as G/B1 and G/B4–G/B11. Gill is credited with the *Circular Border* (P432) on p. [1] and *More's Utopian Alphabet* (P560) on p. [138] This is no. 65 of the Golden Cockerel Press publications.

337 TRISTRAM SHANDY. By Laurence Sterne. In three vols., $9 \times 5\frac{1}{2}$. 500 copies, printed from 14 pt. *Caslon O.F.* on English hand-made paper. Full-bound buckram. Golden Cockerel Press, November 1929 and April 1930. With five engravings on copper by J. E. Laboureur and the following w-e.'s by Gill: Vol. I, p. 249 *Marbling* (P561). Vol. II, p. 256 *Diagram—one line* (P619) and *Diagram—four lines* (P620). Vol. III, p. 149 *Diagram—curly line* (P635). This is no. 66 of the Golden Cockerel Press publications.

338 THE LEGION BOOK. Edited by Captain H. Cotton Minchin. London: The Curwen Press. 1929 [October] The *édition de luxe*, limited to 600 copies of which only 500 were for sale, contains the first engraving of *La Belle Sauvage—Girl sitting in leaves* (P558), p. 205.

339 ZWEI NOVELLEN. By Max Goertz. $10\frac{1}{4} \times 6\frac{7}{8}$. Sixty numbered copies, printed from *Caslon Antiqua* on Maillol-Kessler hand-made paper under the direction of Harry Graf Kessler and Max Kopp. Two guineas. Weimar: Cranach Press. 1929. Contains lettering for binding and title-page, i.e. MAX GOERTZ | ZWEI NOVELLEN in two sizes (G44) designed and engraved by Gill and three initials from (P314). This book was judged to be one of the fifty finest books of 1929 by the German Society for the promotion of book-craft at the Deutschen Bücherei. See *Verzeichnis der Drucke der Cranach-Presse in Weimar* (no. 453). RMK 47.

340 THE TESTAMENT OF BEAUTY. By Robert Bridges. Oxford: Clarendon Press. 1929. Deluxe edition of 250 copies. Contains w-e. *To The King* (P621) Reproduced. Colophon: OCTOBER 24, 1929 | TWO HUNDRED & FIFTY COPIES OF THIS EDITION | HAVE BEEN PRINTED IN GREAT BRITAIN BY | JOHN JOHNSON AT THE UNIVERSITY PRESS | OXFORD, AND THE TYPE DISTRIBUTED. | No. [...] October 24, 1929, was the day after Bridges' 85th birthday. The book was designed by Stanley Morison.

340*a* DIE TRAGISCHE GESCHICHTE VON HAMLET, PRINZEN VON DANEMARK. By William Shakespeare. German translations of the English text of Hamlet, the Latin text of Saxo Grammaticus and the French text of Francoise de Belleforest by Gerhart Hauptmann. Printed at the Cranach Press, Weimar, for Insel-Verlag in Leipzig and S. Fischer-Verlag in Berlin, 1929. $14 \times 9\frac{1}{2}$. Printed in black and red. Edition limited to 255 numbered copies (*a*) 230 on Maillol-Kessler hand-made paper, bound in leather or half-vellum; (*b*) seventeen on Imperial Japanese paper with two extra sets of loose proofs of the wood-engravings signed by the artist printed on two different Japanese papers, bound in full leather or half-vellum; and (*c*) eight copies on English vellum with three sets of loose proofs signed by the artist, one on vellum and two on different Japanese papers laid in two vellum portfolios, bound in full red morocco with the portfolios of prints in a leather slipcase. Contains Gill's wood-engraved half-title lettering for HAMLET (P607) and 74 wood-engravings by Edward Gordon Craig. RMK 48.

216

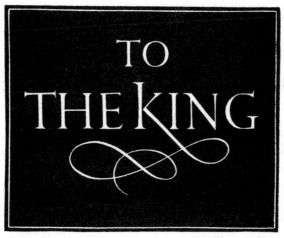

[340. Wood-engraving]

1930
341 THE TRAGEDIE OF HAMLET, PRINCE OF DENMARK.
By William Shakespeare. Edited from the Text of the Second Quarto by
J. Dover Wilson, Litt.D. Contains, also, the original Hamlet stories from Saxo
Grammaticus and Belleforest and the English translations therefrom. Contains: HAMLET lettering for half-title (P607) and THE TRAGEDY OF
HAMLET PRINCE OF DENMARK on the title-page (P608). There
are eighty wood-engravings by Edward Gordon Craig, six more than for the
German edition. The edition was limited to 325 copies: (*a*) 300 numbered
copies on Maillol-Kessler hand-made paper. 14 × 9½. Bound in ¼ vellum £14,
bound in levant morocco £20. 100 copies were reserved for America, distributed
by Random House, 50 in ¼ vellum for $95 and 50 in full levant morocco for
$125. (*b*) seventeen numbered copies on Japanese paper, containing a set of
loose proofs signed by the artist. Bound in vellum, forty guineas, bound in
levant morocco, with portfolio for the proofs fifty guineas. (*c*) eight numbered
copies on vellum, containing three extra sets of loose proofs signed by the
artist. Bound in levant morocco, with portfolio 105 guineas. Printed, in black
and red, from hand-set black-letter type designed by Edward Johnston.
Weimar: Cranach Press. 1930. Published in England by Emery Walker, Ltd.,
16 Clifford's Inn, London. In a pocket inside the back cover of the vellum and
Japanese paper copies, and the copies bound in full morocco, printed on the
appropriate material of the volume it accompanies, is a 35-page sewn pamphlet
in stiff plain wrappers, 13¾ × 9, entitled *Notes of the Tragedie of Hamlet Prince
of Denmark* by J. Dover Wilson, 'for the convenience of readers who may
desire to lay them open beside the text of the play'. Cf. no. 453. RMK 50, but

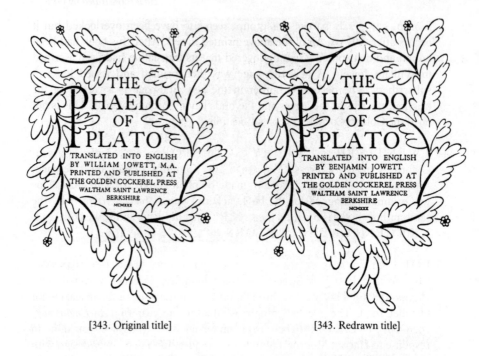

[343. Original title]   [343. Redrawn title]

reference to Gill's half-title wood-engraved lettering is omitted, although it is mentioned in the entry for the German edition, R M K 48 (no. 340a).

342 GESAMMELTE GEDICHTE. By Rainer Maria Rilke. Four vols. $10\frac{1}{2} \times 6\frac{3}{8}$. Leipzig: Insel-Verlag. 1930–1934. Printed at the Cranach Press from *Jenson Antiqua* under the direction of Harry Graf Kessler and Max Goertz. Of 225 copies, five were printed on vellum and bound in parchment, lettered A–E; twenty on Japan vellum, numbered I–XX; and 200 on Maillol-Kessler hand-made paper, numbered 1–200. Contains w-e. title-page lettering and other lettering (P609) and initials by Gill ornamented by Maillol. R M K 52.

343 THE PHAEDO OF PLATO. Translated into English by Benjamin Jowett. $10\frac{1}{2} \times 7\frac{1}{2}$. 500 numbered copies, printed in black and red from 12 pt. *Caslon O.F.* Lining type on Arnold unbleached hand-made paper. Full-bound blue-green buckram with cover-design by Eric Gill. 36s. Golden Cockerel Press. April 1930. Contains title-page *Border of Leaves and Initial Letter P* (P623a). Christopher Skelton has shown in *The Engravings of Eric Gill*, no. 636.113, that the floriated border on p. [3] and the eleven floriated initial letters used in the text were engravings cut by Ralph Beedham to Gill's drawings. These are listed by Skelton as G/B 12 and G/B 13–21. The floriated initial letter

S on p. 53, clearly part of this group, seems to have been overlooked but it occurs after G/B 19. All of the above printed in red. After this book had been bound and distributed it was discovered that its translation had been ascribed to William Jowett. A new title-page was then printed and issued loose to subscribers. The decorated border in the new title-page is a variant of the original, the ribs of the leaves and the buds having been lightened. This is no. 69 of the Golden Cockerel Press publications.

344 TWENTIETH CENTURY SCULPTORS. By Stanley Casson. Oxford: University Press. May 1930. 9s. Contains design for title-page: *Sculpture, No. 1* a reduced version, made by photography, of w-e. P628. This was originally designed for the book-jacket of *Some Modern Sculptors* by the same author, but was not used there. N.B.: The title-page and spine both read: XXth CENTURY SCULPTORS

345 POETRY. A MAGAZINE OF VERSE EDITED BY HARRIET MONROE. Chicago: 232 East Erie Street. Published monthly. 25 cents. Cover design: *Pegasus* (P826). This was first brought into use in the issue of the magazine for October 1930. The w-e. is wrongly ascribed to the year 1931 in *Engravings, 1928–1933 by Eric Gill* (Faber, 1934) under no. 522. Gill's w-e. was done in response to Harriet Monroe's March 1930 request for a new cover design with 'a gay, highly stylized Pegasus . . . which will carry us all off on his wings!' In October 1931, moved by Gill's offer to change the design if it displeased, Monroe wrote to him. Although she thought the lettering 'perfect', the Pegasus seemed 'a little too violent in his action . . . and in certain details, notably the ears and the tail, he doesn't seem . . . quite a proper horse. Some critics have . . . said he was a gelding instead of a stallion.' In May of 1932, Gill presented a new Pegasus (P824) which was, he hoped, 'generally a better bird'. (Cf. no. 664.28)

346a THE FLEURON. A JOURNAL OF TYPOGRAPHY. No. VII. Edited by Stanley Morison. 11 × 8¼. Cambridge: The University Press. Garden City, N.Y.: Doubleday Doran & Co. November 1930. This, the final number, contains tail-piece: *Explicit, Fleuron VII, S. M.* (P673) on p. [253] In the *édition de luxe* there is a reproduction by photogravure of Gill's sculpture *Madonna and Child*, facing p. 27 and on the cover of the dust jacket. (Cf. nos. 335 and 449.)

346b TWENTY-THREE CAROLS WITH AN ENGRAVING BY JOANNA GILL. Printed by René Hague and Eric Gill at Pigotts, near Hughenden, Bucks. MCMXXX. 6½ × 3½. 32 pp. (Unsigned and unpaginated.) Printed from 8 pt. *Baskerville* on Batchelor hand-made paper. Printing: fifty copies. On p. 25

is printed the w-e. *Letters; E. R.* [Eric and René] (P723) above: *3.22.12.30. 50* which figures denote the third book printed by René Hague & Eric Gill, printed 22 December 1930 in an edition of fifty copies. The wood-engraving mentioned was used here as a printer's mark and was very rarely used.

346c FLEURON BOOKS 1930 (Catalogue—pamphlet) p. 398 Curwen Press mark. Printed at the Curwen Press.

1931

347 THE DUINESE ELEGIES. By Rainer Maria Rilke. In the original German with an English verse translation by E. and V. Sackville-West. $9\frac{7}{8} \times 5\frac{7}{8}$. The colophon states that the edition consisted of: 238 numbered copies (*a*) 230 copies on Maillol-Kessler hand-made paper and (*b*) eight copies on vellum with the initial letters gilt. Note: according to Kessler's records, however, the edition was as follows: (*a*) 240 numbered copies on Maillol-Kessler hand-made paper, of which forty were not for sale. Bound in $\frac{1}{4}$ vellum. Three guineas. (*b*) ten numbered copies, on vellum, of which three were not for sale. Bound in levant morocco. Twenty-five guineas. Printed from an italic type newly designed by Edward Johnston and cut by E. Prince and G. T. Friend, at the Cranach Press, Weimar, 1931, under the direction of Harry Graf Kessler and Max Goertz. Published in England by the Hogarth Press, 52 Tavistock Square, London, and in Germany by Insel-Verlag, Leipzig. Contains twenty initial letters designed and cut in wood by Eric Gill which were hand-gilded for the vellum copies. Reviews: *The Times Literary Supplement*, 1 October 1931 and *The Book-Collector's Quarterly*, Vol. II, no. 1, December 1930–February 1931, p. 113. See *Verzeichnis der Drucke der Cranach-Presse in Weimar* (no. 453). RMK54.

347a ELOGE DE LA TYPOGRAPHIE. By Pierre de Margerie. Allocution prononcée à l'ouverture de l'exposition 'Le Salon des Bibliophiles' à Berlin le xii Oct. MCMXXIX. *Eloge de la Typoraphie* prononce par S.E. Monsieur Pierre de Margerie. Printed by the Cranach Press for Editions de Cluny, Paris, 1931. 11×7. Edition limited to 185 numbered copies, 170 on Maillol-Kessler hand-made paper and fifteen on vellum, or 129 numbered copies, 115 on Maillol-Kessler hand-made paper and fourteen on vellum; different copies contain conflicting information. Contains an initial letter C (G47) ornamented by Aristide Maillol and gilded by Max Goertz. RMK53.

348 R.I.B.A. JOURNAL. Cover device 'ROYAL INSTITUTE OF BRITISH ARCHITECTS 1834 VSVI CIVIUM DECORI VRBIVM' (in scroll) (w-e. P824). This was used for the first time in the issue for 7 November 1931

(Vol. 39, Third Series, no. 1) when the whole format of the journal was changed. Reference is made to it in the editorial notes (p. 4). See also issues of 14 and 21 November and 5 December 1931 for correspondence under the general heading 'The Journal changes', criticizing this amongst other changes. In 1946 the journal cover was redesigned, replacing Gill's. Within the journal, however, the cover design device, (P824), continued to be used until 1960. The device was also discussed and reproduced in a pamphlet printed at the Vine Press, Hemingford Grey, England, n.d. [1963], in brown paste paper wrappers made by Margaret Forster, in an edition of 50 copies.

349 GOETHE CENTENARY PRINTING EXHIBITION. A booklet (?) printed by the University Press, Cambridge, 1932 for the Cambridge University Press commemorating the Goethe Centenary Printing Exhibition, Leipzig, 1932. Contains initial letter G and tail-piece of three leaves (w-e. P829) by Eric Gill. Not seen by the compiler.

1933

350 FRANCIS MEYNELL. *The Monotype Recorder*, XXXII, 3, Autumn 1933, facing p. [16] London: The Monotype Corporation Limited. A pencil portrait of Francis Meynell, Chief Director of the Nonesuch Press, specially drawn for this number.

351 THE EUROPEAN MEDITERRANEAN ACADEMY, Cavalière, Cap Nègre, Le Lavandou (Var), France. Société Anonyme: Académie Européenne 'Méditerrranée'. Registered Office: 10 rue des Marronniers, Paris, XVI. Secretary for England, A. E. M. 173 Oxford Street, London W 1. A prospectus of four pages, printed by Hague and Gill, High Wycombe, with w-e. *Map of Europe* (P851), printed in blue on front page. 'The A. E. M. was formed on the 27th June 1933 in Paris as a limited liability company whose purpose is the creation of an Academy of Arts on the Mediterranean coast. The Academy will concern itself with Architecture, Painting, Sculpture, Ceramics, Textiles, Typography, the Theatre, Music and Dancing, Photography and Films.' [Quoted from the prospectus.] Eric Gill's name as an engraver appears in the list of those who 'have been engaged to direct the Academy'. The academy came to naught.

1934

351a CONDITION OF INDIA. By Monica Whatley et al. London: Essential News, [1934]. Green paper wrappers, 534 pp. On p. iv is the note: The cover design is by Eric Gill. The text itself is set in Gill Sans.

1935

352 PETERSFIELD MUSICAL FESTIVAL. Programme for evening concert on the third day of the Festival, 26 April 1935, with cover design: w-e. *Cherub 'In Victory & Defeat alike is Harmony'* (P882) printed in brown.

353 CAPEL-Y-FFIN SCHOOL, LLANTHONY. Boarding School for Girls. Prospectus of four pages with a drawing of the school by Eric Gill (p. [1]) and a map of the locality, drawn by Denis Tegetmeier, on inside of back wrapper. The school was established in 1935. GL has an $8\frac{3}{4} \times 5\frac{5}{8}$ 4-page french-fold prospectus for 1937. The Gill drawing is on p. [1] as above, but as the 1937 prospectus does not have wrappers, the Tegetmeier map is on p. [4].

354 RELIGION AND THE MODERN STATE. By Christopher Dawson. London: Sheed & Ward, first published June 1935, second impression August 1935. 6s. With Frontispiece by Eric Gill thus underlined: *Mulier, quam vidisti, est civitas magna, quae habet regnum super reges terrae.* The book was reprinted 1938, 3s. 6d. Review: *The Times Literary Supplement,* 19 February 1938.

1936

355 COLLINS' ILLUSTRATED POCKET CLASSICS. London: William Collins Sons & Co. Ltd. In the Autumn of 1936 Messrs Collins began to publish this series in an entirely new format. Bound in three alternative colours—red, blue and green with the new *Fontana* device, designed and cut by Eric Gill, blocked blind on the front. The end-papers with Eric Gill's w-e. *Naiad and Triton* (P890-1) reproduced in white line on pearl grey paper. Cf. *Collins' Illustrated Pocket Classics Re-styled* by Beatrice L. Warde in *The Bookseller* 25 November 1936.

355a THE GAZETTE, ST. GEORGE'S HOSPITAL. Vol. 30, no. 1, December 1936. E. G. did the cover device, St George & the Dragon.

356 COLLINS' FONTANA. Specimens of a new type face for books designed by Hans Mardersteig for the exclusive use of the House of Collins. London: Collins Publishers, 48 Pall Mall. 1936. Shows colophon: *Fountain* (P892) on title-page and w-e. *Naiad* (P891) on front cover. Cf. 'An Advance in Book Production' *The Times,* 31 March 1936 and 'Guard the Children's Eyes', *Education,* 2 July 1937.

356a RELIGIONS. The Journal of Transactions of the Society for Promoting the Study of Religions. No. 14, January 1936. Cover design by Gill shows a procession of workers with a madonna in their midst and an angel in one corner. Gill is mentioned on p. 2.

357 ULYSSES. By James Joyce. London: John Lane The Bodley Head. October 1936. With cover-device, a bow, on front designed by Gill. Published in an edition limited to 1000 copies, viz. 100 signed copies at six guineas and 900 unsigned at three guineas. The first English publication of this book.

1937

358*a* BRITISH MEDICAL ASSOCIATION JOURNAL. London: British Medical Association, Tavistock Square, W.C. 1. The Journal of the Association published weekly. Cover-device, the usual attribute of Aesculapius, a club-like staff with a serpent coiled round it, set within a scroll: THE BRITISH MEDICAL ASSOCIATION MDCCC | XXXII (P913). First used on the cover of the journal in the issue of 2 January 1937.

358*b* SCULPTURED MEMORIALS AND HEADSTONES. London: Sculpture and Memorials. With cover-device—the letter 'S' above an 'M' (P965). This was first used on the front cover of the second edition of the handbook published by 'Sculpture and Memorials' (Jan. 1937, cf. no. 499). In the third edition (1938) it appears on the title-page.

1938

359 SAINT BARTHOLOMEW'S HOSPITAL JOURNAL. London: St Bartholomew's Hospital, E.C. 1. With cover-device: *Rahere* (P964). This device was first used on the cover of this Journal in the issue of February 1938 (Vol. XLV, no. 5) but discontinued after the following issue (March 1938). (Cf. no. 636.36.)

360 POEMS. By Helen Foley. London: J. M. Dent & Sons, Ltd. Printed by Hague & Gill, Ltd., High Wycombe from *Perpetua*. With design (by E. G.), bird on hand and initials H F set within a circle, on title-page and (in gilt) front cover.

SECTION III(*c*)

1916

360*a* HAMPSHIRE HOUSE WORKSHOPS. Catalogue of books & prints published by Douglas Pepler. September 1916. No. 2. $5\frac{3}{4} \times 4\frac{1}{2}$. [8] pp. Contains *Animals All* (P50) on p. [6] and *Hog in Triangle* (P58) on p. [8].

1917

361 THE ORDER OF THE BURIAL OF THE DEAD. Ditchling, Sussex: Douglas Pepler. 1917. $5\frac{1}{4} \times 3\frac{3}{4}$. 240 copies, printed from *Caslon O.F.*, $\frac{1}{4}$ linen, green paper boards, sewn. G L copy is in $\frac{1}{4}$ linen, brown paper boards. 1*s.* 6*d.* Contains: title-page device: *Chalice and Host* (P65), tail-piece: *Chalice and Host with Candles* (P53), p. 45 and *Imprint: DP and Cross* (P64), p. 47. This is no. 13 of S. Dominic's Press publications.

362 POOR MAN'S PENCE. A Book of Verses by Faith Ashford. Ditchling: Douglas Pepler. 1917. 5×4. Printed from *Caslon O.F.* Brown paper wrappers, sewn. G L copy is printed in black on front POOR | MAN'S | PENCE. 3*s.* 6*d.* Contains w-e.'s *Imprint: S D P and Cross* (P145) on title-page (G L copy has a w-e. of an angel on a horse, instead), *Spray of leaves* (a variant of P108), p. 25, *Stalk* (P109), p. 31 and *Imprint: D P and Cross* (P64), p. [86]. This is no. 16 of S. Dominic's Press publications.

1918

363 CHRIST. Verses by F. A[shford] Ditchling: Douglas Pepler. 1918. $7\frac{5}{8} \times 4\frac{5}{8}$. Printed from *Caslon O.F.* White paper wrappers, sewn. 6*d.* Contains w-e. *Paschal Lamb* (P92), p. 7. This is no. 18 of S. Dominic's Press publications.

364 ALPINE CLUB GALLERY. A Catalogue of Drawings & Engravings by Eric Gill. Alpine Club Gallery, 5th to 14th May A.D. 1918. Ditchling: Douglas Pepler. 1918. With a Foreword by D. P[epler] $6\frac{1}{4} \times 4\frac{3}{4}$. [16] pp. Printed from *Caslon O.F.* White paper wrappers, sewn. 6*d.* Contains w-e.'s *Spray of leaves* (a variant of P108), front cover, *Axe and Block* (P135), p. 8, *Gravestone with Angel* (P61), p. 10, *Paschal Lamb* (P92), p. [12], *Madonna and Child: with Crucifix* (P113), p. [13] and *Imprint: D P and Cross* (P64) on back cover.

224

365 THE SEVEN AGES OF MAN. Anon. Ditchling: S. Dominic's Press. [1918] A single sheet, $7\frac{1}{2}\times 5$. Printed from *Caslon O.F.* 1*d*. Contains w-e. *Gravestone with Angel* (P61). This is one of the *Penny Tracts*. Not listed in S. Dominic's Press list (1930). Though numbered '1' it appears as no. 4 of the Tracts in the advertisement of the Press' books in *The Mistress of Vision* (1918) where no. 1 is accorded to *Slavery and Freedom* (cf. no. 2). Reprinted from *The Game*, Vol. II, no. 1, January 1918 (no. 69). GL has a variant copy numbered '4', dated 20 xi 17, with a w-e. of a rampant winged demon instead of (P61), and printed in red and black.

366 THE MISTRESS OF VISION. By Francis Thompson. With a Commentary by the Rev. John O'Connor, S.T.P. and with a Preface by Father Vincent McNabb, O.P. Ditchling: Douglas Pepler. 1918. $10\frac{1}{4}\times 8$. $\frac{1}{4}$ linen, grey paper boards, brown dust jacket printed in black THE MISTRESS | OF VISION with the w-e. *Madonna and Child* (P215) below the title, 5*s*. Contains w-e.'s *Imprint: D P and Cross* (P64) on title-page (in red), *Paschal Lamb* (P92), p. 3 and *Spray of leaves* (variant of P108), p. 23. This is no. 24 of S. Dominic's Press publications. This was also published in black paper wrappers lettered on front in gilt. According to Sewell (*The Private Library*, Vol. 3, no. 3, July 1960) this publication was printed 'on the last sheets of an exceptionally pleasing thin handmade paper made by Batchelor for William Morris'.

367 [THREE POEMS]. By H.D.C.P[epler] Ditchling: Douglas Pepler. 1918 (17.xii.18). $7\times 4\frac{1}{2}$. Printed from *Caslon O.F.* White paper wrappers, sewn. [8] pp. There is no title as such. The titles of the three poems are: 'Transeamus Usque Bethlehem', 'Nisi Dominus' and 'A Penny Pie'. Contains w-e.'s *Madonna and Child in vesica* (P143) on front wrapper, tail-piece *Penny Pie* (P144), p. [5] and *Imprint: D P and Cross* (P64) on back wrapper. Not listed in S. Dominic's Press list (1930).

1919

368 A CHRISTMAS BOOK. By E., P. and J. Gill, D., S. and M. Pepler. Ditchling: S. Dominic's Press. 1919. $7\frac{1}{4}\times 4\frac{1}{2}$. Printed from *Caslon O.F.* Stiff black paper wrappers, sewn. [n.p.] Contains drawing by Elizabeth Gill *Ave Jesu Parvule* engraved on wood by Eric Gill (P48). This is no. 22 of S. Dominic's Press publications.

369 THE DITCHLING WAR MEMORIAL. Ditchling: S. Dominic's Press. [1919] $7\times 4\frac{1}{2}$. GL copy is $8\times 5\frac{1}{4}$. Printed from *Caslon O.F.* [n.p.] This leaflet of 4 pp. outlines the projected memorial 'to the men of Ditchling who

gave their lives in the Great War' with a list of names of the fallen. Contains w-e. *View of Ditchling* (P138).

370 HEALTH. WELFARE HANDBOOK NO. 1. By the Author of The Devil's Devices. Ditchling: S. Dominic's Press. 1919. $5\frac{1}{4} \times 4$. Printed from *Caslon O.F.* Brown paper wrappers, sewn. 1s. Contains w-e.'s *Hangman's rope* (P136), p. 13, *Gravestone with Angel* (P61), p. 17, *Axe and Block* (P135), p. 27 and tail-piece: *Entire Dragon* (P141), p. [32] This is no. 28 (1) of S. Dominic's Press publications. Note: this is one of the few uses to which the engraving *Entire Dragon* was put.

371 WOES. WELFARE HANDBOOK NO. 4. BEING EXTRACTS FROM THE NEW TESTAMENT OF OUR LORD AND SAVIOUR JESUS CHRIST, AS TRANSLATED FROM THE LATIN VULGATE BY THE ENGLISH COLLEGE AT RHEIMS A.D. 1582. Ditchling: S. Dominic's Press. [1919] $5\frac{3}{4} \times 4\frac{1}{2}$. Printed from *Caslon O.F.* Brown paper wrappers, sewn. 1s. Contains w-e. *The Last Judgment* (P107), p. [7] This is no. 28 (4) of S. Dominic's Press publications.

372 NISI DOMINUS. Rimes by H. D. C. P[epler] Engravings by E. P. J. G[ill] Ditchling: S. Dominic's Press. 1919. $7\frac{1}{2} \times 4\frac{3}{4}$. Printed from *Caslon O.F.* on Batchelor hand-made paper. Brown paper wrappers, sewn, with the Welsh Dragon (P150) on the front. GL has a similar copy in grey wrappers and another in black wrappers printed in gold. 500 copies. 3s. Contains w-e.'s *Imprint: S D P and Cross* (P145) on title-page (in red), *Madonna and Child in vesica* (P143), p. [4] *Christmas Gifts: Dawn* (P81), p. 6. *View of Ditchling* (P138), p. 9. *Epiphany* (P84), p. 10. *Palm Sunday* (P86), p. 11. *Crucifix: En Ego* (P148), p. [14] *S. George and the Dragon* (P90), p. 22. *S. Michael and the Dragon* (P66), p. 25. *Child and Nurse* (P67), p. 26. *Child and Ghost* (P69), p. 27. *Child in Bed* (P68), p. 28. *Child and Spectre* (P70), p. 29. *Parlers* (P85), p. 33. *Triangular device: Ship* (P41), p. 39. *Dumb-driven Cattle* (P36), p. [40] *The Slaughter of the Innocents* (P18), p. 42. *Device: Gravestone with Angel* (P61), p. 51. *Adam and Eve* (P87), p. 55. *Tail-piece: Paschal Lamb* (P92), p. [57] This is no. 29 of S. Dominic's Press publications. Later printings of this book, in grey stiff paper wrappers, were sold at 3s. 6d. There was also an edition, bound in brown paper boards, at 5s.

373 RITUS SERVANDUS IN BENEDICTIONE. Ditchling: S. Dominic's Press. 1919. $11\frac{1}{4} \times 8$. Printed in black and red from *Caslon O.F.* on Batchelor hand-made paper. Contains w-e.'s *Crucifix, Chalice and Host* (P45) on front cover. *Chalice and Host* (P65), p. [3] *Mother and Child: with gallows* (P82), p. [4] *The Holy Face* (P111), p. [8] *Chalice and Host with Candles* (P53),

p. [12] The engraving *Crucifix, Chalice and Host* (P45) was not used elsewhere. It was originally engraved for *The Devil's Devices* but discarded. Not listed in S. Dominic's Press list (1930).

373*a* A MAY FESTIVAL. PROGRAMME [OF] A MAY FESTIVAL AND OLD COUNTRY FAIR ON STAPLEFIELD GREEN, 22 May 1919. Ditchling: S. Dominic's Press. $8\frac{1}{4} \times 5\frac{1}{4}$. Single-fold, [4] pp. Contains w-e.'s *View of Ditchling* (P138) and *Welsh Dragon* (P150) on p. [1]. Not listed in S. Dominic's Press list (1930).

1920

374 A MAY FESTIVAL. PROGRAMME OF A MAY FESTIVAL AND OLD COUNTRY FAIR ON STAPLEFIELD GREEN, 20 May 1920. Ditchling: S. Dominic's Press. 1920. $8\frac{1}{4} \times 5\frac{1}{4}$. Printed from *Caslon O.F.* on Batchelor hand-made paper. 3*d.* Contains w-e.'s *Welsh Dragon* (P150), p. 5 and *Device: Spray of leaves* (variant of P108), p. [8] Not listed in S. Dominic's Press list (1930).

375 A CAROL—'LULLAY! LULLAY!' reprinted from *Corn from olde fields* (London: John Lane). Ditchling: S. Dominic's Press. 1920. $10\frac{7}{8} \times 5\frac{3}{4}$. Printed from *Caslon O.F.* on hand-made paper. Contains w-e. *Madonna and Child: with gallows* (P82), coloured black, red and yellow (C L C copy is uncoloured). This is S. Dominic's Press 'Broadsheet No. 2'.

376 SONGS TO OUR LADY OF SILENCE. A BOOK OF VERSE. (Anon.) Ditchling: S. Dominic's Press. 1920. $7\frac{3}{4} \times 5$. 71 numbered pages. Printed from *Caslon O.F.* on Batchelor hand-made paper. $\frac{1}{4}$ linen, grey paper boards, sewn, with *DP and Cross* (P64) on the front. 5*s.* Contains w-e.'s *Emblem: Flower* (P139), pp. 25 and 51. *Chalice and Host with Candles* (P53), p. 30. *S. Cuthbert's Cross* (P159), p. 49 and *SDP and Cross* (P145) on p. [72] This is no. 31 of S. Dominic's Press publications. A second edition was published in 1922 at 7*s.* 6*d.* and Burns and Oates reprinted the text in 1950. S. Dominic's Press also issued this title in 1921 with w-e.'s by Desmond Chute in a different format, $8\frac{3}{4} \times 6$, $\frac{1}{4}$ linen spine with plain brown paper boards with a printed paper spine label, with 55 numbered pages. The only Gill w-e. is the *S D P and Cross* (P145) on the title-page.

1921

377 MANUALE TERTII ORDINIS SANCTI DOMINICI. Auctore Fabiano Dix, O.P. Ex Typographia S. Dominici Ditchling in Anglia. 1921.

$4\frac{3}{8} \times 3\frac{7}{8}$. Black leather boards. Contains w-e.'s *Dominican Shield* (PI49a), title-page. *Chalice and Host with Candles* (P53), p. 17. *S. Cuthbert's Cross* (PI59), p. [102] *Paschal Lamb* (P92), p. [157] Type set but not printed at this Press. This is no. 50 of S. Dominic's Press publications. There is also an English edition *The Dominican Tertiary's Daily Manual* [n.d.] which contains the first three only of the above engravings.

378 CALENDAR FOR 1922. Ditchling: S. Dominic's Press. [n.d.] $9 \times 6\frac{1}{4}$. A single card with w-e. *Christmas Gifts* (P83). [n.p.]

379 SAINT DOMINIC'S CALENDAR A.D. 1922. Ditchling: S. Dominic's Press. 1921. $7 \times 4\frac{1}{4}$. A sheet calendar of twelve leaves with a half-page w-e. for each month. Contains: w-e.'s *Dominican Shield* (PI49a) on front. *The Holy Childhood* (PI80), January. *The Blessed Trinity with the Blessed Virgin* (PI81), February. *S. Joseph* (PI82), March. *The Holy Ghost* (PI83), April.

1922

380 MISSIONS OR SHEEPFOLDS & SHAMBLES BY A. SHEEP [H. D. C. Pepler] (Reprinted from the *Catholic Gazette*.) WELFARE HANDBOOK NO. 9. Ditchling: S. Dominic's Press. 1922. $6\frac{1}{4} \times 4\frac{3}{4}$. Printed from *Caslon O.F.* hand-made paper. Brown paper wrappers, sewn. [n.p.] [1s.] Contains w-e.'s *Paschal Lamb* (P92), on cover. *Gravestone with Angel* (P61), p. 6. *Chalice and Host with Candles* (P53), p. 10. *Initial O with speedwell* (PI10), p. 16. *Paschal Lamb* (P92), p. [22] *Imprint: S D P and Cross* (P145), on back cover. This is no. 28 (9) of S. Dominic's Press publications.

381 A PLAIN PLANTAIN: COUNTRY WINES, DISHES, AND HERBAL CURES, FROM A SEVENTEENTH-CENTURY HOUSEHOLD MS. RECEIPT BOOK; ARRANGED, WITH VARIOUS DETAILS, BY RUSSELL GEORGE ALEXANDER. Ditchling: S. Dominic's Press. 1922. $6\frac{1}{4} \times 4$. Printed from *Caslon O.F.* 400 copies. $\frac{1}{4}$ linen, brown paper boards all edges trimmed. Printed paper label on front. Paper wrappers, 5s., boards, 7s. 6d. Contains w-e.'s *Spray of leaves* (variant of PI08), p. 12. *Penny Pie* (PI44), p. 18. *Emblem: Flower* (PI39), p. 62. Also published in green paper wrappers, $7\frac{1}{4} \times 4\frac{1}{2}$. This is no. 36 of S. Dominic's Press publications.

382 CALENDAR for 1923. Ditchling: S. Dominic's Press. [n.d.] $9 \times 6\frac{1}{4}$. A single card with w-e. *Epiphany* (P84). [n.p.]

383 SAINT DOMINIC'S CALENDAR A.D. 1923. Ditchling: S. Dominic's Press. 1922. 16×16. Two sheets of hand-made paper, six months to a

sheet, with various wood-engravings among which are: *The Holy childhood* (P180). *The Blessed Trinity with the Blessed Virgin* (P181). *S. Joseph* (P182). *The Holy Ghost* (P183).

1923

384 HORAE BEATAE VIRGINIS MARIAE JUXTA RITUM SACRI ORDINIS PRAEDICATORUM JUSSU EDITAE. Ditchling: S. Dominic's Press. 1923. 11¼ × 8¾. 220 copies. Printed, in red and black, from *Caslon O.F.* on Batchelor hand-made paper. Full-bound white linen. Brown paper dust jacket printed H O R A E | w-e. *Mother and Child* (not by Gill) | B.V.M. in red and black (reproduced). 25s. Contains w-e.'s *Dominican Shield* (P149a), title-page (reproduced). *Cantet nunc lo* (P75), p. 1. *Adeste Fideles* (P72), p. 10. *Three Kings* (P73), p. 19. *The Manger* (P74), p. 27. *Palm Sunday* (P86), p. 35. *Madonna and Child in vesica* (P143), p. 42 [misnumbered 24] *Madonna and Child with Chalice* (P76), p. 56. *Paschal Lamb* (P92), p. 58. *The Resurrection* (P91), p. 59. *Epiphany* (P84), p. 61. This is no. 37 of S. Dominic's Press publications. A reference to this finely printed edition of the Dominican Rite will be found in *English Prayer Books* by Stanley Morison (Cambridge: University Press, 1943). (See no. 586.)

385 CHILD MEDIUMS. BEING AN EXPOSURE OF AN EVIL WHICH IS WORKING THE RUIN OF THE BODIES AND SOULS OF OUR CHILDREN, BY IRENE HERNAMAN WITH AN INTRODUCTION BY G. K. CHESTERTON. Ditchling: S. Dominic's Press. 1923. 8 × 5⅛. Printed from *Caslon O.F.* Light brown paper wrappers. 1s. Contains w-e. *S. George and the Dragon* (P90) on front cover.

386 SONG OF THE DRESSMAKER. [By H. D. C. Pepler.] Ditchling: S. Dominic's Press. 1923. 5 × 3¾. Printed from *Caslon O.F.* on hand-made paper. Contains w-e.'s *Madonna and Child with Angel: Madonna knitting* (P60), cover-title. *Initial O with speedwell* (P110), p. [1] This is no. 67 (16) of S. Dominic's Press publications. There were at least two reprints in which the title was altered to read *The Dressmaker and Milkmaid*. One copy is undated but with advertisements on back cover of books by the same author which were first published in 1926, and another copy is dated 1929. The w-e. on cover-title was first used on a Rhyme-Sheet *Mary Sat A-Working* published by S. Dominic's Press in 1916 (no. 315b).

HORAE
BEATAE VIRGINIS MARIAE
JUXTA RITUM SACRI ORDINIS
PRAEDICATORUM

JUSSU EDITAE

TYPOGRAPHIA S. DOMINICI DITCHLING IN ANGLIA ANNO DOMINI MCMXXIII.

HORAE

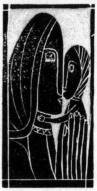

B. V. M.

[384. Title-page]   [384. Dust Jacket]

SONG OF THE   THE DRESSMAKER

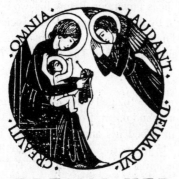   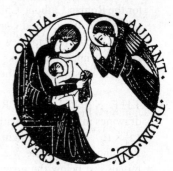

DRESSMAKER   AND MILKMAID

[386]

387 CHRISTMAS GIFTS. [By H. D. C. Pepler.] Ditchling: S. Dominic's Press. 1923. $5 \times 3\frac{7}{8}$. Printed from *Caslon O.F.* on hand-made paper. Contains w-e.'s *Christmas Gifts* (P83), p. [I] *Epiphany* (P84), p. [6] This is no. 9(c) of S. Dominic's Press publications. There is an undated and reset second edition, $4\frac{1}{2} \times 3\frac{3}{4}$, which also contains an initial letter *T* with *Woman and Child* (P234) on p. [I]. An edition dated 1928 was redesigned and contains only a w-e., not by Gill, on the cover. This entry must not be confused with the poem *Christmas* printed on a Christmas Card and showing w-e. *Christmas Gifts: Daylight* (P80) recorded in Cleverdon's list, cf. *The Fleuron*, no. VII under 1917. This small booklet was reprinted in 1925 wherein w-e. *The Manger* (P74) is substituted for *Christmas Gifts* (P83) and the *Imprint: S D P and Cross* (P145) appears on the back cover.

1924

387a THE DIAL. Edited by Scofield Thayer. Vol. LXXVI, no. 1, January 1924. New York: The Dial Publishing Co. The table of contents on the front wrapper lists 'Three Woodcuts' by Eric Gill as appearing between pp. 49 and 53. In fact they are on three unnumbered pages, one per page, after p. 52 and before p. 53. They are *Hair Combing* (P208), *The Money Changers (Christ and the Money Changers)* (P153) and *Christmas Gifts* (P83) and all three are enlarged. In Notes on New Contributors on the verso of the front wrapper the note on Gill reads: 'Eric Gill is a young English artist who devotes himself almost wholly to work for the Roman Catholic Church, of which he is a member. Before his two bold reliefs, *The Woman* and *Christ* were bought by the Contemporary Art Society, he was known only to a few and as a gifted master-carver of ornamental letters. His most important works are his bas-reliefs in marble, *The Stations of The Cross*, in Westminster Cathedral.'

387b THE NEW LEADER BOOK. London, 1924. Twelve woodcuts and drawings in a portfolio, with sketches, stories and poems from the new leader. $12\frac{1}{4} \times 10$. The fourth item in the List of Woodcuts and Drawings in the Portfolio [p. 2], is the w-e. *Clare* (P196). In the portfolio the w-e. has Gill's initials just below the image, 'Clare' in the lower left corner and 'Eric Gill' in the lower right.

LECTIONES
AD MATUTINUM
OFFICII DEFUNCTORUM
JUXTA RITUM SAC.ORD.PRÆD.
NECNON ORATIONES AD
PROCESSIONEM
POST MISSAM PRO
DEFUNCTIS

Typographia S. Dominici
Ditchling
A.D. Sussex 1925   [388*b*]

388*a* ST THOMAS AQUINAS CALENDAR 1925. Ditchling: S. Dominic's Press. 1924. $11\frac{1}{4} \times 3\frac{7}{8}$. A 'tear-off' calendar with a quotation from St Thomas Aquinas for each day of the year. Contains w-e.'s *Device: Chalice and Host with Candles* (P53). *The Manager* (P74). *St George and the Dragon* (P90). *Paschal Lamb* (P92). *Device: Spray of leaves* (variant of P108). *Device: Sacred Heart with Crown of Thorns* (P251). *Device: Crown of Thorns* (P252). *Device: Sacred Heart with Arrows* (P253), the first and only use made of this wood-engraving. *D P and Cross* (P64).

1925

388*b* LECTIONES AD MATUTINUM OFFICII DEFUNCTORUM, JUXTA RITUM SAC. ORD. PRAE. NECNON ORATIONES AD PROCESSIONEM POST MISSAM PRO DEFUNCTIS. Ditchling: S. Dominic's Press. 1925. $12\frac{1}{2} \times 10$. Printed in red and black from *Caslon O.F.* on hand-made paper. Printing: 200 copies. Full canvas boards. Copies are also known with blue or grey paper covered boards, linen spine. Light brown dust jacket, printed as per the title-page, in black and red. With fifteen wood-engravings by E. G.: The *S D P and Cross* (P145) on the title-page, followed by *The Last Judgment* (P107), then the first ten stations of the cross as found in *The Way of the Cross* (no. 268) and used here in the Officium Defunctorum section, then the last three stations (P104–6) in the Post Missam section. This series omits (P103).

CANTICA NATALIA

viginti hymni in honorem
Nativitatis Domini nostri
Jesu Christi

E Typographia S.Dominici
apud Ditchling Sussex
A.D. MCMXXVI

[391*a*]

The dust jacket also has the *S D P and Cross* (P145). The G L copy is inscribed 'No. 42 of 200 H.D.C.P.'. But G. F. Sims Catalogue 65, November 1966, item no. 148 lists a copy accompanied by an A.L.s. from Pepler (n.d., no recipient mentioned) from which this quote is provided: 'I much regret the delay (the binder's fault) in sending you this proof – Lectiones – of my good and bad work in one book. I have decided to withdraw it from my list and destroy all but about 20 copies. So this will have a scarcity value. . . .' 25*s*. This is no. 45 of S. Dominic's Press publications.

389 ST THOMAS AQUINAS CALENDAR 1926. Ditchling: S. Dominic's Press. Contains w-e. *Madonna and Child: with crucifix* (P113).

1926

390 PERTINENT AND IMPERTINENT. AN ASSORTMENT OF VERSE. By H. D. C. Pepler and others. Ditchling: S. Dominic's Press. 1926. $8\frac{1}{4} \times 5\frac{1}{4}$. Printed from *Caslon O.F.* on hand-made paper. 200 copies. $\frac{1}{4}$ linen grey paper boards, blue dust jacket printed in gold. [n.p.] [10*s*. 6*d*.] G L has a taller copy, $8\frac{7}{8}$, $\frac{1}{4}$ black cloth spine, black and white decorated paper boards, printed paper label on front. In both states the page numbers are in a larger type size and the pagination is corrected by hand in ink on pages 58–9, 62–3, 66–7. Contains w-e.'s *Lawyers Wig* (P150), p. 9. *St George and the Dragon* (P90), p. 28. This is no. 52 of S. Dominic's Press publications.

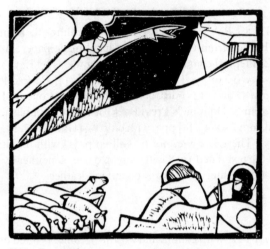

[391a. Page 24a]

391 THE COMMON CAROL BOOK. A COLLECTION OF CHRISTMAS AND EASTER HYMNS. Ditchling: S. Dominic's Press. 1926. $7\frac{3}{4} \times 4\frac{7}{8}$. Printed from *Caslon O.F.* on hand-made paper. 225 numbered copies. $\frac{1}{4}$ black cloth paper boards. G L copy has $\frac{1}{4}$ linen. 10s. 6d. Contains w-e.'s *Imprint: S D P and Cross* (P145) title-page. *The Shepherds* (P158), p. 3. *Ave Jesu Parvule* (P48), p. 13. This is no. 54 of S. Dominic's Press publications.

391a CANTICA NATALIA. VIGINTI HYMNI IN HONOREM NATIVITATUS DOMINI NOSTRI JESU CHRISTI. Ditchling, S. Dominic's Press. 1926. $20\frac{1}{4} \times 13\frac{3}{4}$. Printed from *Caslon O.F.* on hand-made paper, printed in black and red. [52] pp., numbered from 4–49. 95 copies, bound in brown sailcloth. G L copy is unbound in sheets. Contains ten wood-engravings, some hand coloured, including Gill's *Angel and Shepherds* (P269), on p. 24a, after a drawing by Elizabeth Gill. Physick, followed by Skelton, list the appearance of *The Shepherds* (P158) in this book but they have apparently confused it with P269. P158 was not used in *Cantica Natalia*. An enlarged version $(2 \times \frac{3}{4})$ of the *D P and Cross* (P145) appears below the colophon on p. [52]. Other wood-engravings are by David Jones, Desmond Chute and Philip Hagreen.
Note: This is the largest book printed by S. Dominic's Press. It was intended for use by a group of singers at a lectern, and was printed for use by the choir of St. Wilfrid's Church, Burgess Hill.

1927

392 ASPIDISTRAS & PARLERS. Ditchling: S. Dominic's Press. 1927. 5 × 3⅞. Printed from *Caslon O.F.* on hand-made paper. A Rhyme Booklet by H. D. C. P[epler] containing the following w-e.'s by E. G.: *Initial G with vetch and bee-hive* (P240), p. [1] *Gluepot* (P118), p. [4] *Parlers* (P85), p. [5] *Imprint: S D P and Cross* (P145) on back cover. This was one of the Rhyme Booklets (no. 9 [*d*] in S. Dominic's Press Book List [1930]) published at 6*d*. G L has an undated copy, 5 × 3⅞, [8] pp., with only two Gill w-e.'s, P240 on p. [2] and P85 on p. [5]. There is a w-e. not by Gill on p. [1] with the title. G L has another issue of the text dated 1928 with only two w-e.'s, neither by Gill. C L C also has a copy of this issue, dated 1929, bound in ¼ leather.

1928

392*a* VULGATA. With commentary by St. Jerome. Printed by the Cranach Press for Pressa-Austellung, Cologne. 1928. 13½ × 9. Edition limited to twenty copies, fifteen on Maillol-Kessler hand-made paper and five on vellum. Contains: an initial letter A from (P314) on p. [4] and an initial letter P (G41) on p. [5] ornamented by Aristide Maillol. RMK 44.

392*b* DER TOD DES TIZIAN. BRUCHSTUCK. By Hugo von Hofmannsthal. Printed by the Cranach Press for Insel Verlag, Leipzig. 1928. 10½ × 7. Edition limited to 231 numbered copies, 225 on Maillol-Kessler hand-made paper and six on vellum. Contains: an initial letter D on p. 2 and an initial letter S on p. 4 from (P314). RMK 46.

1930

392*c* THUCYDIDES. Translated into English by Benjamin Jowett, MA. Shelley House, Chelsea, Ashendene Press. 1930. Edition limited to 260 copies on handmade paper bound in white pigskin and twenty copies printed on vellum bound in full morocco. The initial letters used throughout were designed by Eric Gill. In the Ashendene Bibliography, Hornby states on p. 89 that, 'Each chapter begins with a 3-line red initial, designed by Graily Hewitt ... the opening line of each of the eight books was designed by Graily Hewitt.' It is clear, however, that Hornby was confused. A comparison of the initials shown in the bibliography as those by Eric Gill are the ones in fact used in the *Thucydides.* See *The Ashendene Press* by Colin Franklin, Dallas: Bridwell Library, Southern Methodist University, 1986, pp. 80–3.

1931

393 A BRADFORD PACKING SHOP. A pencil drawing in *Men and Memories: Recollections of William Rothenstein 1872–1900*. London: Faber and Faber, Ltd. 1931. This drawing, the original of which is in the Rutherston Collection of the Manchester Corporation Art Gallery, faces p. 7 where it is entitled *Packing room at my Father's warehouse*. The drawing was reproduced in *The Studio*, November 1931 and in *The Heaton Review* (London: Percy Lund & Humphries), V, 1932. Cf. no. 457.

394 UNCLE DOTTERY. A CHRISTMAS STORY by T. F. Powys. Bristol: Douglas Cleverdon. 1930. 8 × 5. Edition limited to 350 copies, numbered and signed by the author: of which nos. 1–50, bound in quarter vellum, contained extra prints of the engravings, at 30s., nos. 51–350, in patterned boards, at 10s. The two engravings are: *Device: Girl on Carpet* (P385), p. 7 and *Device: Girl in Leaves* (P386), p. [21] Note: Notwithstanding the date on the title-page (1930) quoted above, this book was not published until March 1931. Both states should have a laid-in note 5 × 4¾ concerning pricing, entitled SECOND THOUGHTS.

394a THE LONDON MERCURY. Vol. XXV, no. 145, November 1931. 8 pp. supplement on The Golden Cockerel Press using three Gill w-e.'s: P417, P535, P603.

1934

394b SERMONS BY ARTISTS. By Paul Nash et al. London: Golden Cockerel Press. 1934. 9½ × 6¼. Printed from Gill's *Perpetua* type on hand-made paper. Decorated black and white paper covered boards, brown leather spine, lettered in gold. 300 copies. Contains initial letters with leaves: 'H' on p. 41, 'T' on pp. 47 and 63 and 'B' on pp. 55 and 73, all from (G/B1). Unrecorded initials from the same alphabet are: 'F' on pp. [3] and 5, 'I' on pp. 11, 29 and 33 and 'G' on p. 21. See *Alphabet & Image* no. 7, p. 57.

394c LA BELLE SAUVAGE. *The Print Collector's Quarterly*. Vol. 21, no. 3, July 1934. Contains w-e. *La Belle Sauvage* (P623) on p. 258.

1938

395 JERUSALEM. *The Architectural Review*, Vol. LXXXIII, no. 495, February 1938. London: The Architectural Press. This issue contains (p. 87) two pencil drawings made in Jerusalem; a view from the roof of the Jerusalem Pottery Works in the Via Dolorosa and a view from a window in the Via Dolorosa.

Another (larger) drawing of Jerusalem was reproduced in *New English Weekly*, 18 March 1937. This is shown in *Letters of Eric Gill* (facing p. 388).

395a OUT OF DEBT OUT OF DANGER. By Jerry Voorhis. New York: Devin-Adair Company. 1943. Dust jacket has wrap-around photo of Eric Gill's bas-relief for Leeds University War Memorial. A note about the reproduced bas-relief, with several quotes by E. G., is on the back flap of the dust jacket.

1944

396 FIFTEEN POEMS. By Francis Meynell. London: The Nonesuch Press, Ltd. & J. M. Dent & Sons, Ltd. 1944. $6\frac{3}{4} \times 4\frac{1}{2}$. Printed under the direction of Ernest Ingham at The Fanfare Press, St Martin's Lane, London. Edition limited to 470 copies. 7s. 6d. Contains w-e. *Pegasus* (after P23) printed on title-page in red. This engraving was originally designed for a book-plate for Francis Meynell (P23). The blue dust jacket has a redrawn version of Gill's Pegasus, printed in white.

1947

396a ALL THE LOVE POEMS OF SHAKESPEARE. Privately printed for Sylvan Press, New York City. 1947. $10\frac{1}{2} \times 8\frac{1}{4}$. 166 pp. Design by Lewis F. White. 1499 copies for the United States and 1499 copies for the British Empire, plus ten unnumbered copies for reviewers. $25.00. Black leatherette, title and decorations stamped in front and spine in greenish yellow. Clear acetate jacket with tipped on upper inner paper flap. Contains numerous poorly reproduced Gill w-e.'s, mostly from *The Canterbury Tales* and *Troilus and Cressida*, published without permission.

1958

396b MAKING AND THINKING. ESSAYS. By Walter H. Shewring. Frontispiece (photo) shows 'Stone Tablet in Pigotts Chapel' with lettering by E. G. Buffalo, NY: Catholic Art Association. 1958. London: Hollis and Carter. 1959.

396c ROMAN LETTERING. ALPHABETS AND INSCRIP-TIONS. Victoria and Albert Museum. London: HMSO. 1958. Plate 7 – two alphabets by Eric Gill.

1986

396*d* WOOD-ENGRAVED INITIALS FOR THE GOLDEN COCKEREL PRESS BY ERIC GILL. Introduction by Sebastian Carter. [Cambridge: Rampant Lions Press] 1983, 50 copies.

396*e* BEREAVEMENT. STUDIES OF GRIEF IN ADULT LIFE. By Colin Murray Parkes. London: Penguin Books. Second edition, 1986. Cover design uses *Autumn Midnight* (P231).

IV

BOOKS, JOURNALS, &c., CONTAINING CRITICISM OF OR REFERENCE TO HIS WORK

Numbers 397 – 636.137

1911

397 POWER OF RELIGION, THE By William Temple (later Archbishop of Canterbury). *The Highway. A Monthly Journal of Education for the People.* Vol. III, no. 29, February 1911. Comments upon E. G.'s article 'Church and State' published in issue of December 1910. (Cf. no. 66.)

398 ENGLISH SCULPTOR, AN By Roger Fry. *The Nation,* 28 January 1911. Notice of an Exhibition of sculpture at the Chenil Gallery.

1912

398a FINE PRINTING IN GERMANY. *The Times.* 10 September 1912 (Printing number), p. 16. Mentions E. G.'s lettering for *Insel* and his 'new departure of personally cutting in wood all the capitals and headings of the first edition of a successful new translation of the "Odyssey"'.

1915

399 MEMORIALS AND MONUMENTS OLD AND NEW: TWO HUNDRED SUBJECTS CHOSEN FROM SEVEN CENTURIES. By Lawrence Weaver. 9 × 5½. 479 pp. Illustrated. London: Country Life and George Newnes, Ltd. 1915. Contains several references to E. G.'s work together with illustrations. As the Index is both inadequate and inaccurate these references are here listed: pp. 13, 14, 16, 18, 205, 268–71, 332, 338, 339, 367, 426, 458. Illustrations: Figs. 90, 132, 163, 173, 180, 188, 233, 236. Fig. 180 is only listed as a reference (p. 348) in Weaver's index.

1916

400 EXHIBITION OF WAR MEMORIAL DESIGNS. *Country Life.* 22 July 1916. With illustrations.

401 MODERN MEMORIAL TO OVERSEAS HEROES, A *The Graphic,* 29 July 1916. A description of the design submitted by E. G. and Charles Holden, architect under the auspices of the Civic Arts Association at the R.I.B.A. With illustrations. This design was awarded second prize. See also *The Builder,* 28 July 1916.

1918

402 ALPINE CLUB GALLERY. Foreword by D. P[epler] to Catalogue of Drawings & Engravings by Eric Gill. Alpine Club Gallery, 5–14 May 1918. 6*d.* (Cf. no. 364.)

403 MANUSCRIPT WRITING AND LETTERING: A HANDBOOK FOR SCHOOLS AND COLLEGES. By an Educational Expert. $8\frac{1}{4} \times 6\frac{1}{4}$. xiv + 180 pp. Illustrated. London: John Hogg. 1918. Fig. 2 on p. 11: *Alphabet of Roman Capitals—From Trajan's Column—Drawn by A. E. R. Gill.* Cf. *Portfolio of Manuscript and Inscription Letters, 1909* (no. 306).

1920

404 WESTMINSTER STATIONS, THE A letter from Laurence W. Hodson in *Blackfriars*, Vol. I, no. 9, December 1920.

405 SCULPTURE OF TO-DAY. By Kineton Parkes. Illustrated. London: Chapman & Hall. 1921. 2 vols. In Vol. I E. G. is mentioned on p. 28 and he is quoted concerning the definition of sculpture on p. 29. Gill's work is discussed on pp. 116–17 and p. 141. Plate, facing p. 116, is Gill's carving *Torso*. In Vol. II there is a reference on p. 250 to Gill's sculpture *Christ On The Cross* at the Victoria & Albert Museum.

406 SOCIETY OF WOOD-ENGRAVERS. *The Print Collector's Quarterly*, Vol. VIII, no. 3, October 1921. Contains a criticism of E. G.'s work as a wood-engraver and reproduces the w-e. *Crucifix, Chalice and Host* (P45) on p. [289].

406*a* DIE NEUE DEUTSCHE BUCHKUNST. By Hans Loubier. Stuttgart: Felix Krais. 1921. $10 \times 6\frac{1}{2}$. Pp. 122 and 157 plates. Gill is mentioned in chapter eight, 'Typographische Periode; Neue Kräfte' on p. 86 and the title page with Gill's lettering (G1–4) and page one with Gill's initial N (G11) from Vol. I of *Die Odyssee* (no. 308) are shown in plates 97–8.

1923

407 LEEDS UNIVERSITY WAR MEMORIAL. This Memorial is described in *The Yorkshire Post*, 18 May 1923. It was the subject of a leading article in that journal (issues of 23 and 30 May) and of a protracted correspondence in subsequent issues. E. G.'s *War Memorial, Welfare Handbook No.* 10 (cf. no. 9) was, to some extent, the outcome of this controversy. Cf. *The Manchester Guardian*, 28 May 1923 with photograph. See also *Outcry* (no. 632) and *Eric Gill: A Retrospect* (no. 634).

1924

408 DIABASIS AND MR. ERIC GILL. By Joseph Thorp. *Artwork*, Vol. I, no. 2, October 1924, pp. 93–7. Cf. issue for Feb.–April 1925 for E. G.'s reply (no. 91).

409 MODERN WOODCUT, THE: A STUDY OF THE EVOLUTION OF THE CRAFT. By Herbert Furst. With a Chapter on the Practice of Xylography by W. Thomas Smith. Illustrated. London: John Lane. 1924. Discusses E. G.'s influence, methods and results on pp. 128, 221–3 and 231. The book is copiously illustrated. Explaining the absence of any reproductions of E. G.'s work the author writes in a footnote (p. 223): 'Unfortunately I am unable to illustrate Gill's work, because he objects to what he calls the "pseudo-facsimile" of the photographic *line* block, whilst my aesthetic conscience will not allow me to mar the significance of his work by the half-tone process, which tends to reduce both black and white to grey, a deterioration to which, nevertheless, the artist would not appear to object.'

410 WOOD-ENGRAVINGS. BEING A SELECTION OF ERIC GILL'S ENGRAVINGS ON WOOD. THE FIRST (*Virgin and Child*) IS A WOOD-CUT, THAT IS CUT WITH A KNIFE ON THE LONG GRAIN OF THE WOOD INSTEAD OF WITH A GRAVER ON THE 'END' GRAIN. Ditchling: S. Dominic's Press. 1924. 12 × 10. Printed on hand-made paper in an edition limited to fifty copies. Contains thirty-seven engravings thus underlined and placed: Initial '*W*' (P237) and *Imprint:* (in red) *S D P and Cross* (P145), title-page. '*She loves me not*' (P179), p. [3] *Madonna for Poster* (*Madonna and Child*) (P154), p. 5. *Palm Sunday* (P86), p. 6. *The Holy Face* (P111), p. 7. *Money changers* (*Christ and the Money-Changers*) (P152), p. 8. *The Judgement* (*The Last Judgment*) (P107), p. 9. *The Divine Lovers* (P193), p. 10. *Mother and Child* (P219), p. 11. *S. Michael* (*S. Michael and the Dragon*) (P66), p. 12. *Adam and Eve* (P87), p. 13. *Petra* (*The Plait*) (P195), p. 14 (see note (2) below). *Silver Birches* (*New England Woods*) (P163), p. 15. *Madonna* (*Madonna and Child: The Shrimp*) (P209), p. 16. *Spoil Bank Crucifix* (P157), p. 17. *Westward Ho* (*Westward Ho!*) (P185), p. 18 (see note (3) below). *Bakery Bag* (*Device: Hog and Wheatsheaf*) (P31), p. 19. *Teresa and Winifred* (*Teresa and Winifred Maxwell*) (P255), p. 20. *Christmas Gifts* (*Christmas Gifts: Daylight*) (P81), p. 21. *Vesica* (*Madonna and Child in vesica*) (P143), p. 22. *Tennis Player* (P217), p. 23. *Portrait Mrs W.* (*Mrs Williams*) (P270), p. 24. *Autumn Midnight* (P231), p. 25. *Girl in Bath* (1) (P194), p. 26. *Girl in Bath* (2) (P218), p. 27. *Adeste Fideles* (four engravings: *Three Kings*—top left (P73), *Adeste Fideles*—top right (P72), *Cantet nunc lo*—lower left (P75), *The Manger*—lower right (P74), p. 28. *Sculpture* (P228), p. 29. *S. Angela* (*S. Angela Merici*) (P205), p. 30. *Crucifix* (*Crucifix, Chalice and Host*) (P45), p. 31. *Clare* (P196), p. 32. Bookplate, mitre printed in red (*S. Martin*) (P207), p. 33 (see note (3) below). Bookplate *T. & R. L.* (*S. Luke*) (P210), p. 34. *S. Christopher* – smoke from chimney printed in red (P220), p. 35. Bookplate (*Jesuit Martyr*) (P263), p. 36.

Note: (1) Where the title of the wood-engraving quoted above differs from that given to it in the authorized iconography (*Engravings by Eric Gill,*

Cleverdon, 1929) I have given the authorized title in parentheses immediately before the engraving number. This volume, which was prepared and published entirely without Gill's knowledge and consent, is no. 44 of S. Dominic's Press publications. (2) G L has a copy annotated and with the plates signed by Gill in which he drew a line through the title *Petra* and substituted it with the title *The Plait* and added 'This is not a portrait of Petra, E.G.' (3) In the same copy he identified *Westward Ho*, p. 18, and the bookplate, p. 33: 'These were engraved from designs by David Jones, E.G.' and signed each of them 'D.J. del.EG sc.'

411 FOUR CENTURIES OF FINE PRINTING. TWO HUNDRED AND SEVENTY-TWO EXAMPLES OF THE WORK OF PRESSES ESTABLISHED BETWEEN 1465 AND 1924. Compiled and with an Introduction by Stanley Morison. Illustrated. London: Ernest Benn. First published in a Limited Folio edition of 400 copies, 1924. Second (revised octavo) edition, 1949. 30s. There is a reference (p. 49) to E. G.'s calligraphic title-page designs for the Insel-Verlag series of German Classics. (Cf. no. 302.)

1925

412 PORTRAITS IN OIL AND VINEGAR. By James Laver. Illustrated. London: John Castle. E. G. is the subject of a 'portrait' (pp. 199–204) and his self-portrait drawing specially done for this volume is reproduced (facing p. 199). An American edition was issued the same year using the English sheets with a cancel title-page, New York: Lincoln MacVeagh The Dial Press. Dark green cloth, blue-grey dust jacket printed in red.

1926

413 PORTRAIT DRAWINGS OF WILLIAM ROTHENSTEIN, 1889–1925. With a Preface by Max Beerbohm and 101 Collotype Plates. London: Chapman & Hall. Contains the following drawings of E. G.: 1921. No. 562 Head, full-face. Black and white. Height $9\frac{1}{8}$ in. Width $8\frac{1}{2}$ in. Signed and dated 'W. R., 1921.' No. 563 Head, full-face. Pencil. Height $7\frac{5}{8}$ in. Width $4\frac{5}{8}$ in. 1922. No. 603. Half-length, three-quarters to right. Sanguine and white. Height $13\frac{3}{8}$ in. Width $9\frac{3}{4}$ in. Signed and dated 'W. R., 1922.' This last is Plate no. 74 in the book. Cf. *The Sphere* 11 October 1924 for notice of exhibition at the Redfern Gallery and reproduction of this drawing. See also *The Times* 26 March and 2 April 1936 announcing the presentation of Rothenstein drawings to the nation.

414 SUPERFLUOUS ARCHITECT, THE Leading article in *The Architects' Journal*, Vol. 63, no. 1619, 13 January 1926, p. 95. This commented upon E. G.'s article *Problems of Parish Church Architecture* published in *Pax*, Autumn 1925 (cf. no. 95). A second leader appeared in the issue of 17 February and correspondence arising out of the first leader appeared in the issues of 27 January, 3 and 10 February. (Cf. *Letters of Eric Gill*, pp. 195–209 where his two letters to the Editor are reprinted. See also no. 99.)

415 ON THE APPRECIATION OF THE MODERN WOODCUT. By Herbert Furst. *Artwork*, Vol. II, no. 6. January–March 1926, pp. 91–3, with reproductions of two wood-engravings by E. G.

416 MODERN ENGLISH WOOD ENGRAVING. By W. Gaunt. *Drawing & Design*, Vol. I, no. 1, July 1926, pp. 7–14 with reproductions of two wood-engravings by E. G.

417 TYPE DESIGNS OF THE PAST AND PRESENT. By Stanley Morison. Illustrated. London: The Fleuron, Limited. 1926. Speaks of E. G.'s collaboration with Edward Johnston and their joint influence on typography in Germany (p. 60).

417a JOHN QUINN 1870–1925. COLLECTION OF PAINTINGS, WATERCOLOURS, DRAWINGS & SCULPTURE. Huntington, New York: Pidgeon Hill Press. 1926. In the index, under Sculpture, is listed E. G.'s *The Dancer*, stone statue, height 17 in. and Plate 197 is a photo, presumably of this sculpture, captioned ' "Statuette": Eric Gill'.

1927

418 A REVIEW OF RECENT TYPOGRAPHY IN ENGLAND, THE UNITED STATES, FRANCE & GERMANY. By Stanley Morison. Illustrated. London: The Fleuron, Limited. 1927. Refers to the calligraphic half-titles E. G. designed for the Insel-Verlag publishing house (p. 48) and reproduces the title-page of the Golden Cockerel Press edition of *Passio Domini* (p. 13).

419 ERIC GILL. By J. K. M. R[othenstein] Illustrated. London: Ernest Benn, Ltd. 1927. One of the series of monographs of Contemporary British Artists published under the general editorship of Albert Rutherston. The Introduction by J. K. M. R. was the first published study of E. G. as a stone-carver. Contains a frontispiece portrait and thirty-three plates in half-tone of some of his stone-carvings and designs covering the period 1910–24. Reviews: *Illus-*

trated London News, 23 April 1927 and *The Times Literary Supplement*, 7 July 1927.

420 MODERN ENGLISH CARVERS. I.—ERIC GILL. By Kineton Parkes. London: *The Architectural Review*, April 1927. With ten illustrations of stone-carvings.

421 TROILUS & CRISEYDE. By John Rothenstein. *The Bibliophile's Almanack for 1928*, pp. 75–9. London, The Fleuron, Limited. A review-article of the Golden Cockerel Press edition of *Troilus & Criseyde* with illustrations and decorations by E. G. (cf. no. 279). One of the tail-pieces is reproduced on p. 77. In addition to the regular edition in wrappers, there are 120 copies on hand-made paper with paper-covered boards, cloth spine.

422 RECENT ETCHING AND ENGRAVING. By James Laver. *Artwork*, Vol. 3, no. 11, September–November 1927, pp. 144–52 with reproduction of a wood-engraving by E. G.

423 PRINTING NUMBER—THE TIMES LITERARY SUPPLE-MENT. 13 October 1927. The articles *Modern Typography* (pp. 3–10) and *Text and Illustration* (pp. 12–15) contain references to E. G. and there is a full-page reproduction of a page of *The Passion of Christ* (Golden Cockerel Press, 1926) showing the w-e. *The Carrying of the Cross* (P352), on p. 5.

1928

424 ERIC GILL. By John Gould Fletcher. *The Arts*, February 1928, pp. 92–6. Discusses Gill as a sculptor as opposed to a modeller. With five photographs of his stone-carvings.

424*a* MR ERIC GILL. ART EXHIBITS. *The Times*, 1 March 1928, p. 10. A review of an exhibit at the Goupil Gallery.

425 GOUPIL GALLERY EXHIBITION. *The Illustrated London News*, 10 March 1928 and *Sphere* of the same date. Each article contains five photographs of carvings.

426 ENGRAVINGS OF ERIC GILL, THE By R. A. Walker. *The Print Collector's Quarterly*, Vol. xv, no. 2, April 1928, pp. 144–66. With fifteen illustrations from wood-engravings. London: J. M. Dent & Sons, Ltd.

427 ERIC GILL: A RELIGIOUS SCULPTOR IN THE MODERN WORLD.
By R. H. W[ilenski]. *Apollo: A Journal of the Arts*, May 1928, pp. 206–12.
With seven illustrations from photographs of stone-carvings.

428 INTERIM PROOF OF AN ALPHABET OF SANS-SERIF
CAPITALS DESIGNED BY ERIC GILL FROM MATRICES CUT
BY THE LANSTON MONOTYPE CORPORATION LTD IN FIVE SIZES
FOURTEEN TO THIRTY-SIX POINT MCMXXVIII. $12\frac{1}{2} \times 9\frac{3}{4}$. Pp. 4 (unpagin-
ated). This folder was the first use of E. G.'s *Sans-Serif* type. It was distributed
at the Annual Conference of the Master Printers' Federation at Blackpool, in
June 1928. Accompanying it, as an inset, were 2 pp. of text 'The 2 Kinds of
Effectiveness', printed on a folded quarto sheet in the office of the Monotype
Corporation. Anonymous. In this (written by Stanley Morison) reference is
made to the programme for the Publicity and Selling Conference. Cf.
A Handlist of the Writings of Stanley Morison compiled by John Carter.
Cambridge: Printed at the University Press for private distribution. 1950,
entry no. 48, p. 16.

429 NEUBRITISCHE PLASTIK: JAKOB EPSTEIN UND ERIC GILL. By
Rom Landau. *Internationale Zeitschrift Die Böttcherstrasse*, I. Jahrgang, 4 Heft,
August 1928, pp. 35–8. Bremen: Angelsachsen-Verlag. With illustration of
Mankind.

430 MODERN BOOK PRODUCTION. London: The Studio, Ltd. 1928.
In the section devoted to Great Britain there are a half-page and two full-page
reproductions of wood-engravings for book illustration (pp. 51, 68 and 70).

431 PICTURE BOOK OF ROMAN ALPHABETS, A No. 32 of a
series of Picture Books published by the Victoria and Albert Museum under
the authority of the Board of Education. First published September 1928.
Revised edition January 1933. The third alphabet illustrated (pp. 20–3) was
cut by E. G. in Hoptonwood stone in 1927.

432 TWO SUSSEX HAND PRESSES. By Joan Firmin. *The Sussex County
Magazine*, October 1928, pp. 450–1. Contains a short account of S. Dominic's
Press, Ditchling.

433 SOME MODERN SCULPTORS. By Stanley Casson. Illustrated.
Oxford University Press. 1928 [27 November]. Chapter IV 'Eric Gill and
Gaudier-Brzeska. Two Independents' (pp. 88–100) with three full-page
photographs of carvings accompanied by descriptive notes (pp. 103–5). These
are: Fig. 30 *Stele*, Fig. 31 *Susan*, Fig. 32 *Mankind*.

1929

434 ART OF THE BOOK, The Golden Cockerel Press. By Robert Gibbings. *The Studio*, Vol. XCVII, no. 431, February 1929, pp. 98–101. A brief account of the aims and objects of the Press and of Eric Gill's collaboration as a type-designer. With reduced reproduction of pp. 2 and 15 from Vol. I of *The Canterbury Tales* (no. 281).

435 ERIC GILL. By Joseph Thorp. With a critical monograph by Charles Marriott. 11½×9. viii+28 pp. Illustrated. London: Jonathan Cape. 1929 [March] 25s. American edition: New York: Jonathan Cape & Harrison Smith. Buff dust jacket, printed in black and red. This book conerns itself chiefly (as the author says in his Preface) with E. G.'s sculpture though four of his pencil drawings have been reproduced in facsimile. There are thirty-eight plates in addition to a frontispiece portrait from a photograph by Howard Coster and a photograph entitled 'The Sculptor's Hands' (facing p. 6). There is also a list of books by E. G. 'relating directly or indirectly to the theory and practice of Art'. Reviews: *The Spectator*, March 1929. *Apollo*, April 1929. By Frank Rutter in *Sunday Times* 3 April 1929. *The Times Literary Supplement*, 18 April 1929. By Ronald Fraser in *Now and Then*, no. 31, Spring 1929. *The Studio*, June 1929. *The Times*, 22 June 1929. *The Observer*, 23 June 1929 and by 'E. M.' in *Artwork*, no. 18, Summer 1929. By G. F. A. *Burlington Fine Arts Magazine*, August 1929. (Cf. no. 456 *Friends and Adventures* by 'T' [Joseph Thorp] where this book is referred to at pp. 237–41.)

436 OPINIONS OF ERIC GILL. By N. Collins. *Commonweal*, New York. Vol. X, 15 May 1929, pp. 42–4.

436a TUNNELLING AND SKYSCRAPING. By Oliver P. Bernard. *The Studio*, Vol. 98, no. 437, August 1929, pp. 552–8. Discusses the new Head Offices for London Underground and commends 'a series of bas-reliefs which are distinctly related to one another without tiresome uniformity' but regrets 'that such excellent choice of sculptors should stop short of allowing them to function as more than incidental workmen'. E. G.'s sculptures, East, South and North Winds, illustrated.

437 ROSSALL SCHOOL WAR MEMORIAL. *Our King & Queen. A Pictorial Record of their Times* Edited by J. A. Hammerton. London: The Amalgamated Press [October 1929]. Photograph (p. 1017) thus underlined: 'Renascence of Byzantinism in Eric Gill's War Memorial Altar Piece.' There is a photograph of E. G. with a brief biographical note on the opposite page. Cf. *The Times*, 29 October 1927, *The Observer*, 30 October 1927 and *Burlington Fine Arts Magazine*.

438 ARCHITECTURE AS SCULPTURE: THE SAME SUBJECT FROM AN ARCHITECT'S POINT OF VIEW. By A. Trystan Edwards. *R.I.B.A. Journal*, Vol. XXXVI, no. 20, Third Series, 19 October 1929, pp. 783–4. Criticism of the lecture 'Architecture as Sculpture' delivered to the Liverpool Architectural Society, 21 November 1928, notes of which were published in this same issue of the *R.I.B.A. Journal* (pp. 779–83) (no. 122).

438a THE TEMPLE OF THE WINDS. By 'Myras'. *The Architectural Review*, Vol. 66, November 1929, pp. 240–1. Discusses the sculptures on the new Head Offices of the London Underground at St James's. Describes E. G.'s three carvings as 'the most emotional and the most decorative of the whole scheme'. Illustrations of the eight sculptures including E. G.'s.

1930

439 ERIC GILL. By Otto F. Babler. *Hollar*, Roenik II, Cislo 2, pp. 57–66. Prague. 1930. A full-length study (in the Czech language) of E. G.'s work as a wood-engraver illustrated by twelve examples taken in the main from *Troilus and Criseyde*, *The Canterbury Tales*, *Passio Domini*, *The Four Gospels* and *The Song of Songs*. The author writes with considerable knowledge and sympathetic appreciation of his subject.

440 ART AND MANUFACTURE. By Herbert Read. *The Listener*, 29 January 1930, pp. 192–3. A review-article, with one illustration (*The Serenade* (45)) from *The Song of Songs* (Golden Cockerel Press) of E. G.'s essay of this title (cf. no. 19).

441 RELIEF SCULPTURE—MEŠTROVIĆ AND GILL. By Stanley Casson. *The Listener*, 19 February 1930. The fourth of a series of talks under the general title *Modern Sculpture*. With one illustration, *A Tombstone* [*Stele*] This talk was broadcast on 14 February.

441a BRITISH WOOD ENGRAVING OF THE PRESENT DAY. By Maximilien Vox. *The Studio*, Vol. XCIX, no. 444, March 1930, pp. 155–72. *Belle Sauvage* III (P622) by E. G., illustrated.

442 ERIC GILL AND NO NONSENSE. By G. K. Chesterton. *The Studio*, Vol. XCIX, no. 445, April 1930, pp. 231–4. A review-article of *Art-Nonsense*. With six illustrations from wood-engravings. Reprinted in *A Handful of Authors*, London & New York: Sheed and Ward. 1953.

443 SENSE ABOUT ART. By A. K. Coomaraswamy. *International Studio*, New York. Vol. XCVI, no. 396, May 1930, p. 76. A review-article of *Art-Nonsense* with one illustration from a wood-engraving.

443*a* THE WESTMINSTER PRESS, ITS HISTORY AND ACTIVITIES. By Frank Sidgwick. *The Studio*, Vol. XCIX, no. 449, June 1930, pp. 438–42. Roman and italic capitals by E. G. from the Westminster Press type-specimen book, are illustrated. John Dreyfus on p. 14 of *A Book of Alphabets* (cf. no. 636.132) says that two alphabets commissioned by Gerard Meynell were made as line-blocks for use at the Westminster Press and were displayed in an undated type-specimen book completed in 1928.

444 MECHANISM AND CRAFT IN ARCHITECTURE. By Lionel Pearson. *Artwork*, Vol. VI, no. 22, Summer 1930, pp. 95–100. With illustrations.

445 THE ART OF MR. ERIC GILL. by George Bennigsen. *Blackfriars*, Oxford. Vol. XI, no. 124, July 1930, pp. 404–13.

446 A CENTURY OF BOOK ILLUSTRATION, 1830–1930. By Douglas Percy Bliss. *Artwork*, Vol. VI, no. 23, Autumn 1930, pp. 200–10. Contains a reference to E. G. (p. 209) and three illustrations from wood-engravings for *The Canterbury Tales* (pp. 220–1 and 228).

447 A CHRONICLE OF EXHIBITIONS. [Unsigned.] *Artwork*, Vol. VI, no. 23, Autumn 1930, pp. 222–6. There is a brief reference (p. 225) to E. G.'s carving *Chloe* shown at the Goupil Gallery. There is an article about David Jones on pp. 171–7 with several of Gill's w-e.'s shown on pp. 220–1 and p. [228].

448 ERIC GILL. By M. D. Z[abel] *Poetry*, Chicago. A MAGAZINE OF VERSE edited by Harriet Monroe. Vol. XXVII, no. 1, October 1930, pp. 41–4.

449 ERIC GILL: SCULPTOR OF LETTERS. By Paul Beaujon [Beatrice Warde] *The Fleuron. A Journal of Typography*. Edited by Stanley Morison. No. VII, pp. 27–51. Cambridge: The University Press. Garden City, N.Y.: Doubleday Doran & Co. This was the final and most sumptuous number of *The Fleuron*. Ordinary edition 21*s.*, *edition de luxe* (200 copies) 5 guineas. The photogravure frontispiece to Paul Beaujon's article, of E. G.'s stone-carving *Madonna and Child*, appeared in the *edition de luxe* only. There are in addition the following facsimile reproductions, etc.:

(*a*) in the text: half-title page from the Insel *Balzac* (Leipzig, 1908) [*sic.* see

250

Errata below], Fig. 1 (p. 28); lettering engraved in white on black, Fig. 2 (p. 32); initials and lettering, Fig. 3 (p. 33); title-page from *Die Odyssee* (Cranach Press, 1910) (p. 34); text-page from *Die Odyssee* (Cranach Press, 1910), (p. 35); title-page of *The Game* with a wood-engraving, Fig. 4 (p. 38), specimen of *Gill Sans-Serif Titling* (p. 40); E. G.'s *Sans-Serif* upper and lower case, Fig. 6 (p. 42); final Monotype cutting of the *Perpetua* type, Fig. 8 (p. 43); title-page showing 24 and 30 pt. *Titling Perpetua* capitals, Fig. 9 (p. 44); and first proof of *Perpetua* italic, Fig. 10 (p. 48).

(*b*) Outside the text: two folding collotype reproductions of inscriptions *J. S. Sargent* (p. 29) and *Sir Frederick Bridge* (p. 30); initial letters, etc. engraved for the Golden Cockerel Press—8 pp. (inset between pp. 40 and 41); *Passion of SS. Perpetua & Felicity* and specimens of *Perpetua* type—32 pp. (inset between pp. 50 and 51). With a List of Books with lettering and illustrations by E. G. compiled by Douglas Cleverdon (pp. 52–9). There are no Figs. 5 or 7 identified as such.

Reviews: *The Times* 2 December 1930. *The Times Literary Supplement*, 4 December 1930.

Errata: Contents, p. ix, for '1903' in reference to date of publication of the Insel *Balzac*, read '1908' and again on p. 28 of the text. P. xi. Collotype reproduction of inscription *Sir Frederick Bridge*, for '29' read '30'. List of Books: p. 52, Edward Johnston's *A Carol* is included in error as the 'formal lettering' referred to was not E. G.'s (see *Copy Sheets* no. 311). P. 53, *Concerning Dragons*, for 'D117' read 'D116'. P. 54, *Christmas Gifts* should be listed under the year 1916.

Notes: A version of this article appeared in *Arts et Métiers Graphiques Paris*, no. 25, 15 September 1931, pp. 357–64. There are in addition the following facsimile reproductions, etc.:

(*a*) in the text: the *Daily Herald Order of Industrial Heroism* (P220–3) in black and red and E R I C   G I L L in large *Gill Sans-Serif*, the G printed in red p. [357] (actually numbered IV); Gravestone in Memory of Florence Bradshaw, 1922 p. 358; a page of Gill's lettering, all examples of white lettering on black (Figs. 2 and 3 as above), being twelve initial letters from a roman alphabet for the Cranach Press (P314), lettering for the Cranach Press *Virgil* from (P399a), the lettering 'Fabian Tracts One Penny Each' from (P2), and the colophon lettering for the Cranach Press *Gedichte* of Paul Valery from (P310), all on p. 359; title-page from *Die Odyssee* Vol. II (G1, G2, G3) p. 360 (as found on p. 34 above); Eric Gill's *Sans-Serif* upper and lower case for 'His Holiness Benedict Pope XV' (Fig. 6 as above), and the initial letter N from Vol. I of *Die Odyssee* as well as the two-line chapter title lettering in red p. 361 (part of p. 35 above); *Mother and Child* (P219) and *Teresa and Winifred Maxwell* (P255), p. [362]; title-page for the 100 copies of the large-paper issue of *Art Nonsense* (no. 18) showing 24 and 30 pt. *Perpetua* titling capitals with (P622) p. [363] (Fig. 9 as above); a specimen of the final Monotype cutting of the *Perpetua* type p. 364 (Fig. 8 as above).

(b) outside the text: a specimen of *Gill Sans-Serif* titling inset between p. [362] and p. [363] (as found on p. 40 above); and a specimen of the first proof of *Perpetua* italic inset between pp. 363 and [365] (as found on p. 48 above).

A paragraph concerning *Perpetua* type from *The Fleuron* (p. 45 as above) was used in a pamphlet published by the Lanston Monotype Machine Co. of Philadelphia in 1953 entitled *Concerning Some Words by Beatrice Warde & Types by Various Hands*, quotations from the writings of Beatrice Warde now reprinted to commemorate a visit to the United States by Mrs. Warde during May of 1953. This excerpt appears on p. [23], a page designed by Arthur Rushmore of The Golden Hind Press of Madison, New Jersey. The excerpt was set in Monotype *Perpetua*.

450 ERIC GILL: THE SEARCHER FOR REALITY. A PERSONAL IM-PRESSION OF THE ARTIST. By John O'Connor. *The Bookman*, December 1930, p. 190.

450a SPECIMEN OF THE JOANNA TYPE. DESIGNED BY ERIC GILL CUT & CAST AT THE CASLON LETTER FOUNDRY. Printed by René Hague & Eric Gill at Pigotts, near Hughenden, Buckinghamshire, MCMXXX. Insert in *The Book Collector's Quarterly*, I, December 1930, one of 100 numbered copies printed on English hand-made paper. Only this special edition has the Joanna type specimen, a 4-page french fold on grey paper, $7\frac{5}{8} \times 4\frac{7}{8}$, as an inset facing p. 57, so noted at the bottom of the Contents page following the title page. The advertisement for the Lanston Monotype Corporation in the prelims shows a specimen of E. G.'s Monotype Perpetua and another prelim advertisement shows E. G.'s w-e. *La Belle Sauvage* (P606) used by Cassell & Co. Ltd. for La Belle Sauvage Editions.

1931

451 DECORATIVE INITIAL LETTERS. COLLECTED AND ARRANGED WITH AN INTRODUCTION BY A. F. JOHNSON. London: The Cresset Press. 1931. Plate CV (pp. 212–13) shows the initial letters engraved on wood for *Autumn Midnight* (here called *Autumn Nights!*).

452 DIE CRANACH-PRESSE IN WEIMAR. Mit 4 Textillustrationen, 2 Probeseiten im Text und 2 Beilagen. By Rudolf Alexander Schröder, Bremen. *Imprimatur Ein Jahrbuch für Bücherfreunde*. Zweiter Jahrgang 1931. Herausgegeben von der Gesellschaft der Bücherfreunde zu Hamburg, pp. 92–107. Reference is made at some length to E. G.'s work as a letter-cutter

(pp. 103 and 106) and to the initial letters he engraved for the Press. Two of these, for Rilke's *The Duinese Elegies*, are shown in the pages of that book, reproduced on pp. [100–1] A specimen leaf of *Das Hohe Lied* with the w-e. *Ibi dabo tibi* (P669) is inset at p. 104 and the w-e. *Dilecti mei pulsantis* (P668) is reproduced on p. 106.

453 VERZEICHNIS DER DRUCKE DER CRANACH-PRESSE IN WEIMAR GEGRUNDET 1913. By Harry Graf Kessler, Weimar. *Imprimatur* [as above], pp. 107–12. The list contains detailed descriptions of the following books for which E. G. designed initial letters, etc.: 1910, *Die Odyssee*; 1925, *In Memoriam Walther Rathenau 22 Juni* 1922; 1926, *P. Vergilii Maronis Eclogae & Georgica*; 1929, *Max Goertz: Zwei Novellen*; 1930, *William Shakespeare: The Tragedie of Hamlet Prince of Denmark*; *Rainer Maria Rilke: Gedichte*; 1931, *Rainer Maria Rilke: The Duinese Elegies* and *Das Hohe Lied*.

454 MODERNE ENGLISCHE PRESSEN. EIN BERICHT ÜBER IHRE ENTSTEHUNG UND IHRE TÄTIGKEIT IN NEUESTER ZEIT. By Anna Simons. *Imprimatur* [as above] pp. 135–67. A comprehensive survey of English printing and calligraphy with special reference to the work of William Morris, Emery Walker, Edward Johnston, Stanley Morison, Eric Gill and Graily Hewitt. Illustrated, where Eric Gill's work is concerned, by a reduced reproduction of a page from *The Four Gospels* (Golden Cockerel Press, 1931) (p. 140), specimens of *Gill Sans-Serif* and *Perpetua* types (p. 142) and *Joanna* type (p. 144), and pages from *The Canterbury Tales* (Golden Cockerel Press, 1929) and *Lamia* (Golden Cockerel Press, 1928) (inset). With a Bibliography of the following Presses (pp. 167–84): The Ashendene Press, The Golden Cockerel Press, The Gregynog Press, The Nonesuch Press, The Curwen Press, The Shakespeare Head Press, The Cresset Press and a list of books by Stanley Morison.

455 THE ART OF LETTERING AND ITS USES IN DIVERS CRAFTS AND TRADES. The Report of a Special Committee of the British Institute of Industrial Art. Oxford University Press. 1931. Contains a passing reference (p. 11) to E. G.'s *Sans-Serif* type (type-set illustration on p. 10) and to the alphabet he designed for W. H. Smith & Son, Ltd. (p. 38). Also reproduction of rubbings of two inscriptions (Plate III) and engraved brass tablet (Plate XI).

456 FRIENDS AND ADVENTURES. By 'T.' [of PUNCH]. London: Jonathan Cape, Ltd. 1931. Contains passing references to E. G. on pp. 42, 227, 230 and 256. The author [Joseph Thorp] writes of E. G. in the chapter *Artists and Craftsmen* on pp. 237–41. The w-e. *Imprint: Decoy Duck* (P35) cut for the Author, is reproduced on p. 241.

456*a* THE ART OF CARVED SCULPTURE. By Kineton Parkes. London: Chapman and Hall Ltd. 1931. Vol. 1, Western Europe, America and Japan. Discusses E. G. on pp. 13–21, 35, 58, 61, 81–3, 85, 118. The plate opposite p. 16 is *Mankind* and the plate opposite p. 85 is *The South Wind*.

457 MEN AND MEMORIES. RECOLLECTIONS OF WILLIAM ROTHEN-STEIN 1872–1900. London: Faber & Faber, Limited. February 1931. 2 Vols. (Vol. II published April 1932). Vol. I: Contains reproduction of pencil drawing *The Packing Shop* (facing p. 7) (cf. no. 393) and a reference to E. G. on p. 46. Vol. II: Contains references to E. G. on pp. 89, 189, 190, 195, 196–201, 225, 280, 290. Cf. Letter to *The Times*, 26 May 1932 reprinted in *Letters of Eric Gill* (pp. 262–3). Reviews: *The Times Literary Supplement*, 28 April 1932. *Daily Telegraph*, 28 April 1932. The pencil drawing referred to above was reproduced in *The Studio*, November 1931. See also no. 549*b*.

458 ERIC GILL'S PERPETUA. *The London Mercury. Special Printing Number*. Vol. XXIII, no. 137, March 1931, p. 492. A paragraph in *Book Production Notes* by B. H. Newdigate. Karel Capek's *An Ordinary Murder* on pp. 423–6 of this issue is set from this type. See also Sheed & Ward's advertisement (p. xl) announcing the forthcoming publication of E. G.'s *Essay on Typography*.

459 ERIC GILL AND TYPOGRAPHY. *This Publishing Business*. London: Sheed & Ward. October 1931, pp. 16–17. Describes E. G.'s book *Typography* and recalls 'certain values and facts' concerning the book and the press (Pigotts).

460 MODERNITY OF BROADCASTING HOUSE, THE ERIC GILL SCULPTURES FOR THE B.B.C. London: *The Illustrated London News*, 3 October 1931, p. 519. Reproduces the photographs by Howard Coster of models, unfinished and finished, of: *Ariel between Wisdom and Gaiety*, *Ariel and Children*, *Ariel hearing Celestial Music*, *The Sower* and *Prospero and Ariel*.

460*a* THE SCULPTURES ON BROADCASTING HOUSE. *The Listener*, 7 October 1931, pp. 569–70. Reproductions of Howard Coster's photographs as described in no. 460 (above).

461 STRIKING SCULPTURES FOR BROADCASTING HOUSE. ERIC GILL'S MODELS FOR THE SCULPTURES THAT WILL DECORATE THE GREAT NEW HEADQUARTERS OF THE B.B.C. London: *Radio Times*, 9 October 1931, p. 98. Reproductions of Howard Coster's photographs as described in no. 460, together with one of E. G.

461*a* GOLDEN COCKEREL PRESS. Supplement to *The London Mercury*, Vol. xxv, no. 145, November 1931, 8 pp., tipped inside front cover. Illustrated with three w-e.'s by E. G. On [p. 1] *Initial letter H, and Venus and Cupid with the Golden Cockerel* (P535), from p. 1, Vol. I of *The Canterbury Tales*, [p. 2] *The Nun's Priest's Tale*, (P603), from p. 166, Vol. II of *The Canterbury Tales*, and [p. 3] *Two Birds* (P417) from p. 18 and several additional locations in *Troilus and Criseyde*.

461*b* MODERN BOOK ILLUSTRATION IN GREAT BRITAIN & AMERICA. By F. J. Harvey Darton. London: The Studio Limited. 1931. Special Winter Number of *The Studio* edited by C. Geoffrey Holme. E. G.'s work appears on pp. 33, 89 and 135. He is referred to on pp. 34–5, 44, 58 and 64.

1932

462 BROADCASTING HOUSE. London: The British Broadcasting Corporation. 1932. This publication contains description of E. G.'s sculptures for Broadcasting House (pp. 13–14) and photographs (plates 10–12, 82).

463 ERIC GILL SANS-SERIF NULLI SECUNDUS SE NON E VERO E BEN TROVATO Modern Typography in Monotype Gill Sans-Serif produced by Students attending Classes at City of Birmingham School of Printing, Central School of Arts & Crafts, Margaret Street. 1932. A brochure.

464 PLUMED HATS AND MODERN TYPOGRAPHY. By B. L. Warde. *Commercial Art & Industry*, Vol. XII, no. 67, January 1932, pp. 10–11. London: The Studio, Ltd. The writer discourses upon the respective merits of *Gill Sans* as being 'the most generally useful sans-serif type' and of *Perpetua* roman as 'a classic letter . . . for which we have been waiting'.

465 INTRODUCTION TO THE ART OF EASTERN ASIA. By Ananda K. Coomaraswamy. The Open Court Publishing Co. March 1932. Reprinted from *The Open Court*. Cites E. G.'s *Art-Nonsense and Other Essays* with Maritain's *Art and Scholasticism* because the principles of Christian Art therein enunciated 'are so near to those of Asiatic art, that these books might be described as adequate introductions to the art of Asia, and may serve to make the latter more comprehensible'. Cf. *Letters of Eric Gill* (pp. 264–5).

466 PRINTING FOR PRINTERS. By Desmond Flower. *The Book-Collector's Quarterly*. No. VI: April–June 1932, pp. 75–8. A review-article of *Typography* (no. 21).

467 ERIC GILL, ARTIST-CRAFTSMAN. By J. N. C. *The Simmarian.* Organ of the Students of St Mary College, Strawberry Hill, Middlesex. No. 39, May 1932, pp. 12–13.

467a RECENT BUILDINGS AT CAMBRIDGE. By H. C. Hughes. *The Listener*, 23 March 1932. Gill is mentioned on p. 407 and there is a photo of his carving for Jesus College on p. 404.

468 A CHANCE FOR THE SCULPTOR. By 'Eric'. *Punch*, 22 June 1932, p. 692. An amusing contribution inspired by reading in Rothenstein's *Men & Memories* (Vol. II, p. 201) E. G.'s letter describing his and Epstein's scheme for 'a sort of twentieth-century Stonehenge'.

469 BROADCASTING HOUSE. By Robert Byron. *The Architectural Review*, Vol. LXXII, no. 429, August 1932, pp. 47–52. Plate 12 shows E. G.'s carving *Ariel hearing Celestial Music*.

470 PLAIN ARCHITECTURE. By A. Trystan Edwards, M.A., A.R.I.B.A. *Architectural Design & Construction*, Vol. II, no. 9, July 1932, pp. 383–5. Comments upon the Paper E. G. read at the R.I.B.A. Conference in Manchester, 16 June 1932. (Cf. no. 137.) See also leading article in this issue *The Sculptor Speaks* (p. 367) and issue of August 1932 for further letter from A. Trystan Edwards (p. 448) in reply to E. G.'s letter in the same issue (pp. 446–8). (Cf. no. 138.)

471 WOOD-ENGRAVING AND WOODCUTS. By Clare Leighton. NO. 2 OF 'HOW TO DO IT' SERIES. London: The Studio Ltd. 1932 [Oct.] Reprinted the same month. Black-and-white dust jacket. There are five reproductions of three engravings by E. G.: *Self-Portrait* (first stage), p. 25, with accompanying text on p. 24; *Self-Portrait* (final state), (P497), p. 27, with accompanying text on p. 26; *Naked girl with cloak* (P282), p. 39, shown two ways, as a surface print and as an intaglio print, with accompanying text on p. 38; and p. 91 from Vol. III of *The Canterbury Tales* which includes the initial letter 'T' and the illustration from *The Summoner's Tale* (P654), p. 57, with accompanying text on p. 56.

472 A HUGE TYPE SPECIFICATION. *Caxton Magazine*, Vol. XXXIV, no. 12, December 1932, pp. 565–6. Records the type standardization carried

out by the L.N.E.R. 'the largest scale typographic specification of modern times'. With photograph of E. G. affixing to the 'Flying Scotsman' a new name-plate painted by himself. The article also recalls the origin and first use of *Gill Sans-Serif* type.

437 PURPOSE AND ADMIRATION. A LAY STUDY OF THE VISUAL ARTS. By J. E. Barton. London: Christophers. December 1932. In his references to E. G. as a sculptor and engraver the writer (pp. 202–3) contrasts his work with that of Maillol. Plate 26 is a photograph of the XIVth Station of the Cross in St Cuthbert's Church, Bradford (facing p. 202). Reference is also made (p. 262) to E. G.'s writings.

473a THE TWO WORLDS. ERIC GILL'S ESSAY ON TYPOGRAPHY. By Noel Carrington. *Gutenberg-Jahrbuch*, 1932, pp. 292–4. Page 293 contains a reproduction of pages 68–9 from *Typography* (no. 21). The title on p. 292 uses the spelling Typographie. Carrington was the proprietor of the Kynoch Press, London.

1933

474 THE NEW SCULPTURE AT BROADCASTING HOUSE. By Whitaker-Wilson. *Amateur Wireless*, Vol. XXII, no. 554, 21 January 1933, p. 106. London: Bernard Jones Publications, Ltd. An interview with E. G. with a photograph of the original model of the *Prospero and Ariel* statue in the sculptor's workshop.

475 THE TECHNIQUE OF EARLY GREEK SCULPTURE. By Stanley Casson. Oxford University Press. 1933 [Feb.] References to E. G.'s carvings appear on pp. 79 and 142 and in an appendix (pp. 236–8) the Greek method of using the point in marble sculpture is discussed and a note on the subject, with a diagram, by E. G. is quoted. This book was reviewed by E. G. in *Architectural Design & Construction*, May 1933 (cf. no. 147). See also review by Bernard Ashmole in *The Listener* (cf. no. 483).

476 WHAT IS LETTERING? *Architectural Review*, Vol. LXXIII, no. 435, February 1933. Replies by Percy J. Smith and Graily Hewitt to an article by E. G. which appeared in the issue for January (cf. no. 142).

477 PROSPERO AND ARIEL. THE NEW SCULPTURE ON BROADCASTING HOUSE. *The Times*, 15 March 1933. With photograph. See issue of 26 April for a letter from Richard Sickert.

478 ERIC GILL 'FURNISHES' BROADCASTING HOUSE. By Christian Barman. *The Listener*, 15 March 1933, pp. 398–9. With three photographs. A companion article to that contributed to the same issue by E. G. *A Sign and a Symbol* (cf. no. 144).

479 PROSPERO: THE FOREFATHER OF THE B.B.C. By Archibald Haddon. *Radio Times*, 24 March 1933, p. 735. With a photograph.

480 EXPERIMENTAL APPLICATION OF A NOMENCLATURE FOR LETTER FORMS. By Joseph Thorp. *The Monotype Recorder*, Vol. XXXII, no. 1 (New Series), Spring 1933, pp. 15–20. A detailed description of the salient features of *Perpetua* roman and *Felicity* italic (p. 18) and an example of the *Perpetua* type on p. 25 (6) in the section entitled 'Pages from Typographic History, 1912–1932' in the same issue (cf. no. 646).

481 TYPE DESIGN: A LIVING ART. *The Monotype Recorder*, Vol. XXXII, no. 1 (New Series), Spring 1933, p. 21. An unsigned contribution concerning E. G.'s work for the Monotype Corporation. Under the title 'Contemporary Typographers who have acted as Advisors to the Monotype Corporation during the Formation of its Book Repertory' (p. 30) there is a brief sketch of E. G. together with a (reduced) reproduction of his w-e. *Self-Portrait* (P497).

481*a* PROSPERO AND ARIEL STONE GROUP BY ERIC GILL. By K[ineton] P[arkes]. *Apollo*, Vol. XVII, no. 101, May 1933, p. 224. With a photograph.

482 BLAIR HUGHES-STANTON. *The Times*, 11 April 1933. A notice, under 'Art Exhibitions' of an exhibition of wood-engravings at the Zwemmer Gallery in which Blair Hughes-Stanton's work as a wood-engraver is compared with that of E. G.

483 THE EARLY GREEK SCULPTOR AT WORK. By Bernard Ashmole. *The Listener*, 19 April 1933, p. 640. A review of *The Technique of Early Greek Sculpture* by Stanley Casson (cf. no. 475).

484 THIS MONTH'S PERSONALITY: ERIC GILL. By B. L. Warde. *Commercial Art and Industry*, Vol. XIV, no. 84, June 1933, pp. 213–16. London: The Studio, Ltd. With four illustrations, viz. a photograph of E. G. fixing a name board in his lettering to the front of the 'Flying Scotsman', hand-cut lettering and two reduced reproductions of wood-engravings.

484*a* ON ERIC GILL. By G. K. Chesterton. *Illustrated London News*, 10 June, 1933. Later reprinted in Chesterton's *Avowals and Denials*, London: Methuen Co., 1934.

485 AN ARTIST'S PHILOSOPHY. By G. B. Phelan. *Commonweal*, New York. Vol. XVIII, no. 14, July 1933, pp. 285–6.

486 GOOD-BYE TO SILK HAT SCULPTURE. By Herbert Read. *The Daily Mail*, 24 July 1933. With a photograph of E. G.'s carving *Prospero and Ariel*.

486*a* MORECAMBE HOTEL. *Architecture Illustrated*, September 1933. Gill's sculpture for the hotel is mentioned and there are photos of the sculpture. There was also a notice about the hotel in *Country Life*, 18 November 1933. A contemporary brochure for the hotel also shows Gill's sculpture.

487 WHAT IS 'TWENTIETH CENTURY TYPOGRAPHY'? *The Monotype Recorder, Modern Typography Special Number*, Vol. XXXII, no. 4, Winter 1933, pp. 3–5. An editorial foreword to the articles in this number which deal with historically recent problems of printers' designers. With a note on *sans-serif*.

488 THE L.N.E.R. REFORMS ITS TYPOGRAPHY. *The Monotype Recorder*, Vol. XXXII, no. 4, Winter 1933, pp. 7–11. A leading article, being an account of the L.N.E.R. type standardization, for which it chose *Gill Sans*. The inside cover of this number shows a fragment (actual size) of a large poster time table in *Gill Sans* 275, as issued by the L.N.E.R. On the last page there is a photo of E. G. at the ceremony at King's Cross when he affixed the name-plate of the 'Flying Scotsman' which he himself had painted, which marked the completion of the L.N.E.R.'s letter standardization.

489 ERIC GILL'S 'ART NONSENSE'. By D. H. Lawrence. *The Book-Collector's Quarterly*, no. XII, October-December 1933, pp. 1–7. A review-article of *Art-Nonsense and Other Essays*. In a foreword Frieda Lawrence writes: 'Lawrence wrote this unfinished review a few days before he died. The book interested him, and he agreed with much in it. Then he got tired of writing and I persuaded him not to go on. It is the last thing he wrote.' [Mrs Lawrence presented her husband's MS. to E. G.]

490 A SHORT HISTORY OF ENGLISH SCULPTURE. By Eric G. Underwood. London: Faber & Faber. 1933 [Nov.] Contains numerous references to E. G. and quotations from his writings, also a photograph of his stone-carving *Chloe* (facing p. 157).

491 ERIC GILL, T.O.S.D. By G. P. Dudley Wallis. *The Link Letter*. The Official Organ of the Link Society. Vol. I, no. 8, November 1933, pp. 128–9. Manchester.

491*a* MACHINES NOT MEN MAKE PRINT TODAY: ERIC GILL'S CRITICISM OF MODERN PAINTING. *The Caxton Magazine*, Vol. XXXV, no. 11, November 1933, pp. 456–7. An article on Gill's lecture to the Yorkshire Young Master Printer Conference, 9 October 1933.

492 ERIC GILL AS A DRAFTSMAN. A DISCUSSION OF THE BRITISH SCULPTOR'S VARIED TALENTS. By Kineton Parkes. *Pencil Points*, Vol. XIV, no. 12, December 1933, pp. 524–32. Stamford, Conn., U.S.A.: The Pencil Points Press, Inc. There are nine reproductions from pencil drawings. These are *Lettered Design for a Commemorative Tablet* (to Aubrey Beardsley), the Vth and XIVth *Stations* for Westminster Cathedral, SUSANNA, Design for a War Memorial (two drawings), sketches of *Ville de Madrid* and *Church of St Vincent at Salies-de-Béarn* and *Four Nude Studies*.

492*a* ERIC GILL, ONLOOKER. By Beatrice Warde. *The Three Ridings Journal*, Vol. 5, no. 1 [1933], pp. 6–7. Remarks on E. G.'s lecture to the Yorkshire Young Master Printers. On p. 6 there is a reduced reproduction of E. G.'s w-e. *Self-Portrait*, (P497).

1934
493 ERIC GILL: LO SCULTORE DELLA 'VIA CRUCIS' DI WESTMINSTER. By Gerald Vann, O.P., Vatican City: *L'Illustrazione Vaticana*, 16–31 Marzo 1934, pp. 263–5. With six illustrations of carvings: Rossall School Memorial, *Pastor*, the *Stations* in Westminster Cathedral (3) and one of the *Stations* in St Cuthbert's Church, Bradford. The same article appeared in the French edition of this publication at pp. 227–9 and also, it may be presumed, in the Spanish, German and Dutch editions.

494 THE BREAKDOWN OF MONEY. AN HISTORICAL EXPLANA-TION. By Christopher Hollis. London: Sheed & Ward. April 1934. 4*s.* 6*d.* On p. 213 E. G. is linked with Compton Mackenzie as an artist who has a clearer understanding of the nature of money than most business men of this country.

494*a* LETTERING ON MEMORIALS. *Monumental Architectural Stone Journal*, Vol. I, no. 3, March 1934. Gill is mentioned on p. 103.

495 THE AESTHETICS OF TOMBSTONES. By Herbert Read. *The Listener*, Vol. XI, no. 277, 2 May 1934, pp. 738–40. A brief survey of the tombstones of this country with eleven photographs which include one designed by E. G. to whom reference is made.

496 THE MASTER CRAFTSMAN. By Campbell Dodgson. *The Listener*, Vol. XI, no. 277, 2 May 1934, p. xi of Supplement. A review-article of *Engravings, 1928–1933* with two illustrations from *The Four Gospels*.

497 GILL AND EPSTEIN. By Dorothy Grafly. *American Magazine of Art*, Vol. XXVII, no. 6, June 1934, pp. 325–33. Washington: The American Federation of Arts. With six illustrations from photographs of stone-carvings by E. G.

497a MEN AND MACHINERY. Compiled by Peter Maurin. *Catholic Worker*, Vol. II, no. 2, 1 June 1934, p. 2. Selections from Gill's writings.

498 THE WORLD AT LARGE. A Correction. By Fr. John Baptist Reeves, O.P. *The Catholic Herald*, 23 and 30 June 1934. A criticism of review by Michael de la Bedoyere (*Catholic Herald*, 16 June 1934) of E. G.'s article *Morals and Money* in *The Colosseum*, June 1934 (no. 155).

498a THE LAST TEN YEARS OF WOOD-ENGRAVING. By Douglas Percy Bliss. *The Print Collector's Quarterly*, Vol. 21, no. 3, July 1934, pp. 250–71. E. G. is mentioned on pp. 253, 257, 259, 261 and 265. On p. 261 is the statement, 'The most distinguished engraver to do book-work in our time is, of course, Eric Gill.' *La Belle Sauvage* (P623) is shown on p. 258.

499 SCULPTURED MEMORIALS AND HEADSTONES DE-SIGNED AND CARVED IN SCULPTORS' STUDIOS IN BRITISH STONES. London: Sculpture and Memorials. This handbook was first published in November 1934 (second edition January 1937, third edition September 1938). The first edition contained no representation of E. G.'s carving. The second contains the following photographs: *Plaque in a Refectory at Mirfield* (p. 13), *Alphabet Incised and Coloured* (p. 14), *Sketch Design for Raised Ledger* (p. 16) *Headstones* (pp. 28, 36, 38, 41), *Sketch Design for Ledger in Portland Stone* (p. 42), *Alphabet in Stone* (designed by E. G., carved by Laurie Cribb, p. 56), *Sketch Design for Altar Tomb* (p. 58), *Part of Border of Alms Dish* (designed by E. G., engraved on silver by George Friend, p. 62) and a design by E. G. carved in oak by Donald Potter (p. 64). The design (p. 43), though not here attributed to E. G., was by him (cf. p. 41 of third edition).

Third edition. The designs shown on pp. 16, 28, 38, 41, 42, 43, 56 and 58 of the second edition are repeated on pp. 52, 36, 9, 11, 52, 41, 60 and 52 respectively of this edition with the addition of photograph of a raised ledger (p. 51). E. G.'s w-e. (P965), the letter 'S' above 'M', appears on the front cover of the second edition and on the title-page of the third (cf. no. 358*b*).

The aims and objects of 'Sculptured Memorials and Headstones' were fully set out in a letter to *The Times* of 13 August 1934, and warmly approved in a leading article in the same issue. See *The Designing of Tombstones* in *The Times*, 4 July 1936 and *The Beauty of Remembrance: In Memoriam Art* by C. B. Mortlock in *Church Times*, 24 March 1939.

It is perhaps worth mentioning that the *Headstone to a Sculptor with Incised and Coloured Lettering* worded: *Memento mei E. G. Lapidarii* MCMXXXVI *Heu mihi* (on p. 38, second edition; p. 9, third edition) was that which E. G. designed for his own grave.

The pictorial map facing the half-title in the third edition was drawn by E. G.'s brother Macdonald Gill, two of whose designs for tablets appear on pp. 54 and 58 of the same edition.

500 THE HAND PRESS. AN ESSAY WRITTEN AND PRINTED BY HAND FOR THE SOCIETY OF TYPOGRAPHIC ARTS, CHICAGO, BY H. D. C. PEPLER, PRINTER, FOUNDER OF ST DOMINIC'S PRESS. DITCHLING COMMON, SUSSEX, ENG. MCMXXXIV A.D. Edition limited to 250 copies on hand-made paper numbered and signed by the Author. Pp. 80. Some copies of the 'ordinary' edition were in blue cloth boards with white band, others were in brown paper wrappers with white band. These were sold at 15*s*. There were also a few copies in $\frac{1}{4}$ leather sold at 30*s*.

The book contains several references to E. G., notably to his collaboration with the author and Edward Johnston in *The Game*, and his early work as a wood-engraver. Three of E. G.'s wood-engravings are reproduced.

The text was reset and reprinted with facsimile reproductions from the 1934 edition, by the Ditchling Press Ltd. Sussex, 1952. Pp. 57. Blue cloth, stamped in gold. The grey dust jacket is dated 1953 and is printed in black and red.

501 THE ENGLISH ATTITUDE TOWARDS ART. By G. J. Renier. *The Studio*, Vol. CVIII, no. 500, November 1934, pp. 221–30. London: The Studio, Ltd. With illustrations from photographs of four of the Stations of the Cross in Westminster Cathedral.

1935

502 ERIC GILL—PRINTER. By Ernest Ingham. *Penrose's Annual*, 1935. Vol. XXXVII, pp. 28–31. London: Percy Lund & Humphries. With an inset being a specimen page from *Money and Morals* set in *Joanna* type.

503 WHAT ARE THE FRUITS OF THE NEW TYPOGRAPHY?
By J. C. Tarr, Typographer, Chief Instructor, Chiswick Polytechnic. *Penrose's Annual*, 1935. Vol. XXXVII, pp. 38–40. London: Percy Lund & Humphries. A commentary upon *Gill Sans-Serif* type.

504 MEDIAEVAL AESTHETICS. I. DIONYSIUS THE PSEUDO-AREOPAGITE, AND ULRICH ENGELBERTI OF STRASSBURG. By Ananda K. Coomaraswamy. *The Art Bulletin*, Vol. XVII, 1935, pp. 31–47. New York: The College of Art Associations of America. See note 5, p. 32, where E. G.'s understanding of the Scholastic Philosophy of Art is favourably contrasted with that of Maritain and De Wulf.

505 ARIES TYPE. A note on this type-face designed by E. G. for the Stourton Press in *Book-Production Notes* by B. H. Newdigate in *The London Mercury*, January 1935, p. 318. The book set from this type which prompted Bernard Newdigate's note was Marlowe's *Hero and Leander* (London: The Stourton Press, Dacre Street, Westminster. 200 copies. 15s.). Cf. no. 618, *The Type Designs of Eric Gill* by Robert Harling.

505a PROSPECT & RETROSPECT IN PRINTING. By Victor Clough. *Newspaper World*, 5 January 1935.

505b WHO IS A TYPOGRAPHICAL ARTIST, MR GILL? A QUESTION ASKED RESPECTFULLY by Pat V. Daley. *Publishers' Circular*, 23 March 1935.

506 THE MODERN TIME-TABLE AS SEEN BY THE TRAVELLER—THE COMPILER—THE MASTER PRINTER—THE COMPOSITOR. *The Monotype Recorder*, Vol. XXXIV, no. 1, Spring 1935, pp. 8–15. The third article of the series *Twentieth-Century Problems in Print*. This shows by illustrations the use of *Gill Sans-Serif* for wall time-tables, the 'Air Bradshaw' and other time-tables.

[This number of the *Recorder* is composed in various sizes of 'Monotype' *Perpetua*, a note concerning which appears on inside of front cover.]

507 PEACE PALACE OF THE LEAGUE OF NATIONS AT GENEVA. The first intimation that E. G. was to be commissioned by the British Government to execute the sculptural work which was to be Britain's contribution towards the decoration of the Palace of Peace at Geneva, appeared in the Press in April 1935. The Lord President of the Council (Mr Baldwin) replying to a question on the subject in the House of Commons on 15 April made an announcement to this effect. There are several references to this work

in letters published in *Letters of Eric Gill* (cf. no. 54), notably two to Mr Anthony Eden written in June/July 1935 (pp. 335–9) in which he outlines his hopes and fears, one to the Rev. Desmond Chute, August 1935 (p. 346) mentioning that 'the Geneva work had not yet been decided about' and one to Graham Carey, September 1938 (p. 407) in which he speaks of finishing the sculptures. See *The Bystander*, 8 September 1937, four double-spread photographs taken in E. G.'s workshop at Pigotts by Howard Coster and a description of the panels.

508 A GUIDE TO CONTEMPORARY SCULPTORS. THE WORK OF ERIC GILL. By Kineton Parkes. *Architectural Design & Construction*, Vol. V, no. 6, April 1935, pp. 185–7. With illustrations of *East Wind* (carving on the Underground Building, London), *Prospero and Ariel* (Broadcasting House), *Mother and Child* (relief carving), a wash and brush drawing of the XIVth Station of the Cross, Westminster Cathedral and *Line study for a decorative scheme* (pencil drawing).

509 RECIPES FOR LIVING. No. 7. ARTHUR GROOM INTERVIEWS MR. ERIC GILL. *The Rover World*, May 1935, pp. 49–50.

510 ARCHITECTURE AND SCULPTURE. THE HAND AND THE MACHINE. *The Manchester Guardian*, 5 June 1935. A letter to the Editor from Eric Newton in reply to one from E. G. under the same main heading published in the previous issue (cf. no. 171). See also a letter from Prof. C. H. Reilly, under the heading *Modern Buildings: A New Field for Sculptor and Painter*, also in issue of 5 June, commenting upon the same letter.

510a THE DESIGN OF A BOOK. By S. L. Dennis. *Publishers' Circular*, 8 June 1935, pp. 776–7.

511 A REPLY TO ERIC GILL. By Alick West. *Left Review*, Vol. I, no. 10, July 1935, pp. 410–11. Criticizes two letters from E. G. which were originally published in *Catholic Herald* and reprinted in the June issue of *Left Review* (cf. no. 170). See also the issue of *Left Review*, November 1935, for continuation of this correspondence, viz. a letter from the Organizer, London Management Committee, National Amalgamated Furnishing Trades Association (p. 78) and E. G.'s reply (pp. 79–80). Both letters appear under the heading: *Artist and Craftsman, Eric Gill & London Organiser of N.A.F.T.A.* and they are preceded by an editorial note—portion of which runs: 'What is, and what should be, the relation of the artist-craftsman working on commission to the wage-earning craftsman organised in a trade union?'

512 THE PALESTINE ARCHAEOLOGICAL MUSEUM, JERUSALEM. *The Architect & Building News*, Vol. CXLIII, nos. 3481–2, 6 and 13 September 1935. With a photograph (p. 263) of the tympanum over the main entrance and photographs (pp. 264 and 292) of the ten panels symbolizing the civilizations that have most affected the history of Palestine. See article with photographs in *The Times*, 13 January 1938, under the heading *Treasures of Palestine: A New Museum.*

512a ERIC GILL. By T. S. Wiebams. *The Terminal*, No. 2, Michaelmas Term, 1935, pp. 4–6. *The Terminal* was published by the University of London Catholic Society.

513a SANS V. SERIF: THE TREND OF PRESS TYPOGRAPHY. By Victor Clough. *British Press Review*, Vol. I, no. I, December 1936, pp. 34–5. London: Ludgate Publications, Ltd.

513b THE STORY OF GILL SANS, INSET: COMPOSED IN ALL THE DESIGNS AND SIZES OF THE GILL FAMILY. *The Monotype Recorder*, Vol. XXXIV, no. 4, Winter 1935–6. The inset comprises eight pages.

513c THE NATIVITY IN MODERN PAINTING. By Arthur B. Bateman. *Methodist Recorder*, 5 December 1935.

513d BOOK DESIGN THIS YEAR. By A. J. A. Symons. *Studio*, Vol. 110, December 1935, pp. 319–25. Praises E. G.'s design of the Aldine Bible.

1936

514 EXPERIMENTS AND ALPHABETS. By Robert Harling. *The Penrose Annual*, Vol. XXXVIII, 1936, pp. 60–4. London: Lund, Humphries, Ltd. With illustrations.

515 THE SOCIETY OF SCRIBES AND ILLUMINATORS EXHIBITION. A note by John M. Holmes in *The Architectural Association Journal*, Vol. LI, no. 589, March 1936, p. 373. One of the exhibits, an Alphabet designed and cut by E. G. is reproduced on p. [358]

516 ECCLESIASTICAL ORNAMENT. By Alan L. Durst. *Architectural Review*, Vol. LIX, no. 353, April 1936, pp. 194–9. With twelve illustrations from photographs two of which are of the Ist and XIIth Stations of the Cross in Westminster Cathedral.

517 L'APOSTOLAT D'ERIC GILL. By Fr. Hilary J. Carpenter, O.P., Blackfriars, Oxford. *L'Artisan Liturgique. Revue trimestrielle d'art religieux appliqué.* 10me—no. 42, Juillet–Août–Septembre. 1936, pp. 875–6. With six illustrations from photographs of stone-carvings by E. G. This article was reprinted in *Blackfriars*, December 1940 (pp. 690–3), with an editorial footnote recording his death.

518 TYPOGRAPHERS AT WAR. *The Times Literary Supplement,* 15 August 1936. A composite review-article of *First Principles of Typography,* by Stanley Morison and E. G.'s *An Essay on Typography* (second edition 1936) (no. 21).

519 NEW POSTAGE STAMPS OF KING EDWARD VIII. Following the issue (1 September 1936) of the King Edward VIII Postage Stamps of Great Britain and E. G.'s letter on the subject to *The Times* (22 September, cf. no. 191) there was considerable correspondence in *The Times*, commenting, both favourably and unfavourably, upon E. G.'s expression of opinion. See the following: From Edmund Dulac, 24 and 29 September. From Frank Pick, Charles Wheeler and Reginald Blunt, 25 September. From James Guthrie, 30 September and from Charles Knight and others, 8 October. A letter from E. G. to *The Manchester Guardian* (29 September) prompted a leading article in that journal and a letter from T. C. Dugdale (issue of 1 October), and the following further letters: from Harold Speed and Noel Carrington, 5 October, and a further leader and a letter from Arthur Rackham, 7 October. See also *New English Weekly*, 8 October for a further letter from T. C. Dugdale referring to E. G.'s letters to *The Times* and *Manchester Guardian*.

520 CHANTICLEER. A BIBLIOGRAPHY OF THE GOLDEN COCKEREL PRESS APRIL 1921—AUGUST 1936. INTRODUCTION BY HUMBERT WOLFE. FOREWORD & NOTES BY THE PARTNERS. ILLUSTRATIONS FROM THE BOOKS. Golden Cockerel Press. November 1936. Contains notes of the twenty-one books with which E. G. was either directly or indirectly concerned as author or illustrator. These are the following: nos. 25, 26, 29, 31, 33, 35, 37, 50, 61, 62, 63, 65, 66, 69, 74, 75, 78, 79, 92, 101, 111. His w-e. *The Single Bed* ('*Thanks*') (P875) is reproduced on p. [11] This is no. 116 of the Golden Cockerel Press publications. See the companion volume *Pertelote* (cf. no. 585). Review: *The Times Literary Supplement*, 20 February 1937.

520a PALESTINE ARCHAEOLOGICAL MUSEUM. *American Architect and Architecture*, October 1936, pp. 57–60. Shows E. G.'s ten sculptural panels placed between the arches of the cloisters and the *Africa and Asia* panel in the tympanum over the main entrance, pp. 58–9.

521 REASON AND TYPOGRAPHY WITH PARTICULAR REFERENCE TO TYPOGRAPHICAL LAYOUT: A DISCURSIVE ESSAY WITH EXAMPLES: BY RENÉ HAGUE. The examples set up and printed by Messrs Gill and Hague at their press at Pigotts, Buckinghamshire. *Typography*, no. 1, November 1936. London: The Shenval Press. Quarterly. 7s. 6d. The 'examples' (four) are inserted as insets and comprise: title-page of *An Essay on Typography*, front cover of *Unemployment*, a page from *Park* and a notice of a change of address. Also inserted, facing p. 36, is the first showing of *Kayo*, a type-face designed by E. G. for the Monotype Corporation.

522 THE FUNCTION OF THE BOOK JACKET. STRIKING CHANGES IN DESIGN. By Edward Young. *Daily Telegraph*, 14 December 1936. With a much-reduced reproduction of the jacket for Vol. 1 of The Aldine Bible. (Cf. nos. 162 and 292.)

523 VIEWS AND REVIEWS. I. ERIC GILL EPITOMISED. II. THE TESTAMENT OF AN ARTIST. By Holbrook Jackson. *The New English Weekly*, 31 December 1936 and 7 January 1937. A review-article of *The Necessity of Belief* and *An Essay on Typography* (second edition).

523a BEAUTY (IN ART) DOES NOT LOOK AFTER HERSELF. *The Artist*, Vol. XII, no. 4, December 1936.

1937

524 EVOLUTION IN PRINTING RAILWAY PROPAGANDA. By C. G. Dandrige. *The Penrose Annual*, Vol. XXXIX, 1937, pp. 50–3. London: Lund, Humphries, Ltd. With reduced reproductions of railway posters and time-table pages. This article, by the then Advertising Manager of L.N.E.R., deals with the adoption of *Gill Sans* in the L.N.E.R. type standardization. This issue of *The Penrose Annual* also contains no. 200 and no. 525.

525 NECESSITIES AND NOVELTIES. By Robert Harling. *The Penrose Annual* (as above), pp. 65–8. With illustrations of type-faces and references to *Jubilee* and *Kayo* type designs.

526 MODERN PAINTERS AND SCULPTORS AS ILLUS-TRATORS. Edited by Monroe Wheeler. New York: Museum of Modern Art. London: Allen and Unwin. Reviewed in *The Times Literary Supplement*, 2 January 1937, with a reduced reproduction of a page from the Golden Cockerel *Chaucer*.

527 THE CHURCH OF THE FIRST MARTYRS, BRADFORD. Architect J. H. Langtry-Langton, A.I.A.A. *The Parthenon, Journal of the Incorporated Association of Architects and Surveyors*, Vol. XI, no. 6, March 1937, pp. 195–8. Among the illustrations is one of E. G.'s statue of *Blessed John Bosco and his dog* which stands in the main porch. Cf. *The Builder*, 14 May 1937, pp. 1028–30.

528 PROSPERO AND AERIAL. By D. C. T. *The Oxford Magazine*, 4 March 1937, pp. 470–1. A light-hearted sketch prompted by E. G.'s carving in the entrance hall of Broadcasting House.

528a THE BIRTH OF A RATIONAL 'SANS'. *The British Printer*, Vol. XLIX, no. 293, March 1937, pp. 238–9. A discussion of Johnston's and Gill's contributions to sans-serif type.

529 SCULPTURE. By Richard Eurich. *Town Flats*, April 1937, pp. 354–8. With a photograph (p. 355) of E. G.'s carving of *Prospero and Ariel* in Broadcasting House.

529a R.A. ELECTIONS. *The Builder*, 30 April 1937, p. 919. Mentions E. G.'s election as Sculptor to the Royal Academy, with photos of three sculptures.

530 POSTAGE STAMPS OF KING GEORGE VI. The first postage stamps of the new reign were put on sale on Monday, 10 May in the denominations of $\frac{1}{2}d.$, 1$d.$ and 2$\frac{1}{2}d.$; other denominations followed later. E. G. collaborated with Edmund Dulac in the design of all the values from the $\frac{1}{2}d.$ to the 6$d.$ denominations, E. G. being responsible for the whole of the design with the exception of the King's head. The first Press announcements appeared on 5 May. The issue was the subject of a leading article in *The Times*, 6 May. See letter to me, dated 7 May, in *Letters of Eric Gill* (no. 54) under no. 275. See also *British Postage Stamp Design*, by John Easton (London: Faber, 1943), pp. 311–13.

531 CHRISTIAN SOCIAL IDEALS AND COMMUNISM. ERIC GILL'S POSITION. *Catholic Herald*, 21 May 1937. Letters from Victor White, O.P., Donald Attwater, Peter F. Anson and others following publication of E. G.'s letter on the subject in issue of 14 May (cf. no. 206b). The correspondence was continued in the issue of 28 May under the caption *Eric Gill Raises Hornet's Nest*. The subject was pursued in *Christus Rex*, Vol. VII, no. 3, 1937 (Mount Olivet Monastery, Frensham, Farnham, Surrey) in an article entitled *The Faith and Communism: Comment on a Controversy*, by M. G. S. Sewell, pp. 1–8. This was followed in the succeeding issue by an Editorial

Note, *Communism or—A Sane Corporative Order*, and an unsigned contribution on the subject (pp. 21–2, 25–6).

532 DITCHLING. By M. E. Christie and others. Ditchling: St Dominic's Press. 1937 [November]. Part III, 'Ditchling in our own Times' by Bridget Johnston contains a reference (pp. 84–5) to E. G.'s advent to the village. Part IV, 'Ditchling Common and Tenantry Down' by H. D. C. Pepler, Reeve, refers (p. [108]) to E. G.'s large wooden crucifix at Spoil Bank on Ditchling Common.

533 A BOOK OF PRINTED ALPHABETS. By David Thomas. London: Sidgwick & Jackson, Ltd. 1937 [December] Contains references to, and full-page specimens of, *Perpetua* and *Gill Sans* type faces.

533*a* ERIC GILL: HEWER OF STONE AND IDEAS. By Graham Carey. *Liturgy & Sociology*, December 1937. Also condensed by *Catholic Digest*, Vol. II, no. 3, January 1938, pp. 86–7.

533*b* SCULPTURE: PAINTING AS AIDS TO WORSHIP. By Sir Eric MacLagan. *The Listener*, 8 December 1937. Mentions E. G.'s work and one of the Westminster Cathedral Stations of the Cross is illustrated.

1938

534 MODERN ENGLISH ART. By Christopher Blake. London: George Allen & Unwin, Ltd. 1938 [February]

535 DESIGNER FOR INDUSTRY. CONFERMENT OF DISTINCTIONS ON INDUSTRIAL DESIGNERS. *Journal of the Royal Society of Arts*, Vol. LXXXVI, no. 4449, 25 February 1938. A report of the proceedings on 17 February when Diplomas to the first recipients of the R.D.I. distinction were presented by H.R.H. the Duke of Gloucester, K.G. With this issue of the journal was an inset relating to the Ordinance giving effect to this award, and a list of the first appointments. E. G. received the award 'for eminent services in Typography'. Photograph of E. G. p. 345.

536 THE RÔLE OF SCULPTURE IN CONTEMPORARY LIFE. By Stanley Casson. *The Studio*, Vol. 115, 4 June 1938, pp. 296–311. Contains references to E. G. and carvings by him, notably those for Broadcasting House one of which, *Ariel between Wisdom and Gaiety*, is here shown together with a photograph of *Chloe*.

537 **LEAVES OUT OF BOOKS.** BROUGHT TOGETHER AS EXAMPLES
OF 20 CLASSIC 'MONOTYPE' FACES AT WORK HELPING BRITISH
PUBLISHERS & PRINTERS TO ACHIEVE TYPOGRAPHIC DISTINCTION
IN TRADE MANUFACTURE. London: The Monotype Corporation, Ltd.
1938. As the title-page runs this is 'An album of leaves cut from eighty typical
current books the majority made to sell at or under 7*s*. 6*d*. net taken at random
and bound together for the Monotype Corporation, Ltd.' 11¼×9. Pp. 6 and
ten sections of specimen leaves. Spiral bound, clear acetate front cover. Section
V is devoted to 'Monotype' *PERPETUA 239* and comprises leaves from
seven different books. See also item 9 in Section VI showing 'Monotype'
BASKERVILLE combined with *Gill Sans Bold*. The Appendix consists of
pages from three 'Readers' Bibles', etc. one of which is Heinemann's
publication *The Bible Designed to be read as Literature* (cf. no. 654).

538 **MR. ERIC GILL IN IRELAND.** By Stephen J. Brown, S.J. *The Irish
Monthly*, Vol. LXVI, no. 781, July 1938, pp. 454–64. Cf. issue for October
containing a letter under the caption 'Echoes of an Article' and Fr. Brown's
comments at pp. 692–7.

538a **CHRISTIANITY, PEACE AND WAR.** By Michael de la Bedoyere.
The Dublin Review, July 1938, pp. 14–32. Review article of a number of books
including E. G.'s Pax Pamphlet 1, *And Who Wants Peace?*

539 **THE CATHOLIC ATTITUDE TO MACHINERY.** By D.
Marshall. Scotch Plains, N.J., U.S.A. The Sower Press. September 1938.
6¼×4⅜. Pp. 12. Stapled pamphlet, buff wrappers. Contains (p. 12) a reference
to E. G. and quotations from *Work and Property*. This booklet is printed from
Ludlow Tempo Medium type.

540 **THE ART OF THE BOOK.** By Bernard H. Newdigate. London: The
Studio, Limited. 1938 [Sept.] Special Autumn Number of *The Studio*. This
substantial volume contains the following references to E. G. and his work as a
book-illustrator and typographer:
In 'Book Production 1900–1928' at p. 5.
In 'Book Production 1928–1938' at pp. 6–9, showing decorations and
title-pages for the *New Temple Shakespeare* and the double title-page for *The
Green Ship*.
In 'Type-Design and Printing: England and America', p. [16] a page from
Sterne's *A Sentimental Journey*, printed by Hague and Gill at High Wycombe;
the first book to be set in the new Bunyan type designed for the Press by E. G.
His work as a type designer is discussed on pp. 17 and 19. There are also
passing references to him and his influence on printing in Germany on pp. 31

and 35. The Fontana device designed for Messrs Collins is reproduced on p. [40]

In 'Illustration and Text' at pp. 64 and 67, reproducing pages from *Work and Property* and *Park* (in *Joanna* type and *Joanna Italic* respectively), also his w-e. *S. Thomas' hands* (P889). An inset in this section reproduces two pages from the Cranach Press edition of *The Song of Songs*.

In 'The Work of the Presses' at p. 92 where mention is made of his work for the Golden Cockerel Press.

541 THE PRINTING OF BOOKS. By Holbrook Jackson. London: Cassell & Company, Ltd. 1938 [Novr.] Chapter x (pp. 140–54) is devoted to E. G., being a study of his philosophy, his book illustrations and his type designs. It contains the following illustrations:
Title-page and two other pages of the Golden Cockerel Press edition of Chaucer's *Troilus and Criseyde*, cover and first page of *The Game*, title-page of *The Temple Shakespeare* edition of *Sonnets*, cover of S. Dominic's Press booklet *The Dressmaker and Milkmaid*, two pages of Cassell's edition of Shakespeare's *Sonnets*, two pages of his own *Essay on Typography* and combined title-page and contents page for the second edition of the same. Other references to E. G. will be found at pp. 29, 54–5, 219 and 269. This book was reviewed in *The Times Literary Supplement*, 21 January 1939, in which issue the author was the subject of a leader entitled 'Type and Taste'. A second edition appeared in 1947.

542 THE HOUSE OF DENT 1888–1938. BEING THE MEMOIRS OF J. M. DENT WITH ADDITIONAL CHAPTERS COVERING THE LAST 16 YEARS BY HUGH R. DENT. London: J. M. Dent & Sons, Ltd. First published privately as *My Memoirs* in 1921, this book was reissued with an additional chapter under the title *Memoirs of J. M. Dent* in 1928. This edition was reissued with further additions in 1938. E. G.'s collaboration with the firm, notably in the *New Temple Shakespeare* and the *New Testament*, is described on pp. 274–5. Mention is also made (p. 275) of the association between Pigotts Press and the House of Dent.

543 TWENTIETH CENTURY SANS SERIF TYPES. By Denis Megaw. *Typography* edited by Robert Harling, no. 7, Winter 1938, pp. 27–35. London: The Shenval Press.

1939

544 AN APPROACH TO TYPE DESIGN IN THE TWENTIETH CENTURY. By P. B. *The Monotype Recorder*, Vol. XXXVIII, no. 1, Spring 1939, pp. 16–21. With twelve illustrations among which are E. G.'s drawings for *Gill Sans*.

545 PREPARING A RAILWAY TIME-TABLE. By Edwin Robinson, formerly assistant to Advertising Manager, London & North Eastern Railway. *The Monotype Recorder* (as above), pp. 24–6, with one illustration and an inset showing L.N.E.R. Monotype *Gill Sans-Serif* specimen of characters, figures, etc., standardized for the L.N.E.R. time-tables and (on verso), corrected page-proof of a time-table.

546 THE NOBLE SAVAGE REDIVIVUS. By E. P. Richardson. *The Examiner* (Bethlehem, Conn., U.S.A.), Vol. II, no. 2, Spring 1939. A review of certain pamphlets by Graham Carey and Ananda K. Coomaraswamy and Miss Ade de Bethune and of E. G.'s *Work and Culture (John Stevens Pamphlet*, cf. no. 39). See *Art, Reality, and Romanticism* in the Summer, 1939 *Examiner* for criticisms of this review by the first three named and Mr Richardson's rejoinder. Also the Autumn number (pp. 399–408) for letters from E. G., Margaret Townshend and Graham Carey on the same subject.

547 THE CHRISTIAN AND ORIENTAL OR TRUE PHIL-OSOPHY OF ART. By Ananda K. Coomaraswamy. A *John Stevens Pamphlet*. (Newport, R.I., U.S.A.) 1939. $9\frac{1}{4} \times 6\frac{1}{2}$. Pp. 38. 400 copies. Light orange wrappers. A Lecture given at Boston College, Newton, Mass., in March 1939. Frontispiece: E. G.'s w-e. *The Moneychangers* (P983). The author cites four books of E. G.'s in the bibliography (p. 37), viz. *Beauty Looks After Herself, Work and Leisure, Art,* and *Work and Culture*. This essay was reprinted in *Why Exhibit Works of Art?*

547a PAX PAMPHLETS. By Christopher Hollis. *The Tablet*, 29 April 1939, p. 554. Review of the Pax Pamphlets and criticises E. G.

548 SCULPTURE INSIDE AND OUT. By Malvina Hoffman. London: George Allen & Unwin, Ltd. On p. 29 in the chapter entitled 'A Brief Outline of Sculpture' E. G. as a sculptor is grouped with Bourdelle, Maillol and Despiau in France, Dobson and Epstein in England and others. Howard Coster's photograph of E. G. standing beside his bas-relief for the Palace of the League of Nations, Geneva, and *The Sower* in Broadcasting House, London, are reproduced on pp. 57 and 177 respectively.

549 THE LOVE OF GOD. AN ESSAY IN ANALYSIS. By Dom Aelred
Graham, Monk of Ampleforth. London: Longmans, Green & Co. E. G. is
mentioned as pointing out the disadvantages of the restricted viewpoint which
associates art solely with beauty and aesthetics, cf. p. 186. E. G. quotes a
passage from this book in his *Christianity and the Machine Age* (cf. no. 46), see
footnote on p. 26.

549*a* SOCIAL CLIMBERS IN BLOOMSBURY. By Count Potocki of
Montalk. London: *The Right Review.* 1939. Chapter Three is entitled
'Currying Favour, or, Pervasive Perversity.' Mentions meeting and speaking
with E. G. at a dinner at Anand K. Coomaraswamy's.

549*b* SINCE FIFTY. MEN AND MEMORIES 1922–1938.
RECOLLECTIONS OF WILLIAM ROTHENSTEIN. London: Faber & Faber.
1939. Contains references to E. G. on pp. 149, 227, 266.

1940

550 DESIGN OF A MODERN CHURCH. THE CHURCH OF ST.
THOMAS THE APOSTLE, HANWELL. Architect: Edward Maufe. *The Studio*,
March 1940, pp. 74–7. The photograph on p. 75 of the exterior of the East End
showing Crucifixion by E. G.

551 THE ELEMENTS OF LETTERING. By John Howard Benson and
Arthur Graham Carey. Newport, R.I., U.S.A.: John Stevens. 1940 [May]
There is a reference to E. G. on p. 116 where the authors speak of his
far-reaching influence in the twentieth century and as one who 'was realistic
enough to be willing to think of stone-cut letters in terms of cutting and stones,
as well as in terms of imagination and legibility'. Plate XXVII (p. 117) is a
rubbing of an alphabet cut in stone by E. G.

552 FRIENDS OF A LIFETIME. LETTERS TO SYDNEY CARLYLE
COCKERELL. Edited by Viola Meynell. London: Jonathan Cape. 1940 [Sept.]
a letter from T. E. Lawrence ('signed' T. E. S.) on p. 369 names E. G.
amongst other sculptors as one who might be invited to carve a statue of
Thomas Hardy.

553 COMMUNITY OF ARTISTS. SCULPTOR ERIC GILL'S HOME AT
PIGOTTS IN BUCKINGHAMSHIRE. *The Bystander*, 30 October 1940, pp.
142–3. A biographical sketch of E. G. with seven photographs of the interior
and exterior of Pigotts and the neighbouring workshops.

554 LET THERE BE SCULPTURE. AN AUTOBIOGRAPHY. By Jacob Epstein. London: Michael Joseph. 1940 [Nov.] E. G. is quoted (pp. 230–2) with special reference to the Hudson Memorial *Rima*.
Revised and extended edition EPSTEIN. AN AUTOBIOGRAPHY. London: Hulton Press. 1955. The E. G. quote (as above) is pp. 203–4. Ref. to E. G. p. 258. Third edition with an introduction by Richard Buckle, London: Vista Books. 1963.

555 ERIC GILL: Obituary Notices. Eric Gill died at Harefield House Sanatorium, Harefield, Middlesex, on Sunday 17 November 1940, aged fifty-eight. He was buried at Speen, Buckinghamshire, on 21 November. The following obituary notices and appreciations are noted:

19 November 1940   *The Times*, *The Manchester Guardian*, *The New York Times*.

21   „   „   *Daily Mail* ('Last Testament of an unusual man'), *World's Press News* ('Gill and Perpetua Inventor's Death'). *The Weekly Review*.

22   „   „   *Catholic Herald* ('Eric Gill, the Artist and Thinker' by Bernard Wall, and 'Gill the Christian' by a Priest Friend with reproduction of E. G.'s self-portrait), *Catholic Times* ('Mr Eric Gill, Artist and Author'), *The Universe* ('Mr Eric Gill, Craftsman and Author'), *Peace News*.

23   „   „   *The Tablet*.

28   „   „   *The Weekly Review* ('The Craft of Life', an editorial), *The Listener* ('Eric Gill: 1882–1940' by Charles Marriott, with four illustrations). *The New English Weekly*, *The New Age*, Vol. XVIII, no. 6.

29   „   „   *The Commonweal* (N.Y.) (under the title 'National Art Week' by H. L. B.), *Catholic Herald* ('Pigotts—Home and Workshop: To Eric Gill life and work were holy', with five illustrations).

30   „   „   *The Times Literary Supplement*, *The Tablet* (An Appreciation by David Jones), *Saturday Night*, Toronto.

December   „   *Print* (New Haven, Connecticut) Vol. 1, no. 3, pp. 43–6 ('Eric Gill 1882–1940' by Paul Standard, with two illustrations).

7   „   „   *Publishers' Weekly* (N.Y.), Vol. 138, pp. 2133–5 ('Eric Gill: Master Craftsman' by C. P. Rollins. Illus. portrait).

13   „   „   *Journal of the Royal Society of Arts*, Vol. LXXXIX, no. 4576, p. 54.

16 „ „ *Journal of the Royal Institute of British Architects.*
Christmas „ *Pax Bulletin*, no. 19, p. 13. (An unsigned appreciation by
Mark Fitzroy opening with the words 'Thou, Ruskin,
seest me'.)
January 1941 *The British Printer*, Vol. LIII, no. 316, p. 136, with a
full-page photograph by Howard Coster. *Members'*
Circular of the British Federation of Master Printers,
Vol. 40, pp. 7–8.
24 „ „ *The Commonweal* (N.Y.), Vol. XXXIII, no. 14, pp. 343–5
('In Memoriam; Eric Gill' by Donald Attwater).
25 „ „ *America* (N.Y.), Vol. LXIV, no. 16, p. 433 ('For Eric Gill:
May he have rest' by the Rt. Revd. Arthur Jackman).
March „ *L.S.P. Record*, The Magazine of the London School of
Printing, Vol. XVIII, no. 2, Session 1940–41, pp. 25–8
('Eric Gill 1882–1940' by Frederick Lambert, with
illustrations).

556 TOPICS. By Walter Shewring. High Wycombe: Hague & Gill, Ltd. 1940
[Dec.] The author makes reference to E. G.'s *Beauty Looks After Herself*
(cf. no. 24) in the essay entitled 'Book-learning and Education' (p. 82).

556a THE SYMBOLISM OF ORDINARY THINGS: A BED.
Christian Social Art Quarterly, Vol. IV, no. 1, Christmas 1940. Refers to and
shows an oak bedstead by E. G. with a quotation by E. G.

557 CATHOLIC ACTION AND INDUSTRIALISM. *Pax Bulletin*,
no. 19, Christmas 1940, p. 7. A note concerning E. G.'s *An Analysis of the*
Right to Private Property (cf. no. 187) originally published as a letter to the
Catholic Herald and here reprinted (pp. 8–9). On asking the author's
permission to reprint it, the Editor of *Pax Bulletin* received the following:
'I shall be very pleased for you to print the *Catholic Herald* letter—I had
entirely forgotten about it, and am agreeably surprised to discover that I had
written anything so good.'

558 ERIC GILL. By M. P. [Max Plowman] *The Adelphi*, Vol. XVII, no. 3,
December 1940, pp. 75–9. An appreciation together with two letters from E.
G. (not subsequently published in his *Letters*) which reveals his interest in the
Adelphi Centre at Langham, near Colchester.

559 BLUNDELL'S SCHOOL. THE CHAPEL ALTERATIONS. A leaflet,
printed for private distribution, by the Headmaster (the Rev. Neville Gorton,
now Bishop of Coventry) describing the extensive alterations made in the

School Chapel largely by the boys themselves but inspired by and with the 'advice and moral support of Mr Eric Gill' and working from his designs.

559*a* THE COLLECTION OF DESIGNS IN GLASS. By twenty-seven contemporary artists. New York: Steuben Glass Inc. *c*. January 1940. The tenth artist is Gill. On the right-hand page is a photo of a pair of vases designed by Gill, described in no. 636.12 as *Adam and Eve*. They are done in the style of the w-e. border illustrations for *The Canterbury Tales*, 1929 (no. 281). The height of the vases is given as 14 inches, priced at $800. The verso of the title page states that 'Steuben will make six pieces from each of these twenty-seven designs of which one will be retained by Steuben for its permanent collection. The remaining five are thus available for sale.' The GL copy has laid in a 4-page single fold list of the artists in the exhibit which was held January 10 – February 19, 1940 at Steuben Glass Inc. 718 Fifth Avenue, New York. Cf. nos. 610, 636.12.

1941

560 ERIC GILL. AN APPRECIATION. By Thomas McGreevy. *The Studio*, Vol. CXXI, no. 574, January 1941, pp. 2–9. With fifteen illustrations: *Prospero and Ariel stone-carving for Broadcasting House*. Three w-e.'s *Babe on Bough* (P874), *Bookplate for Austen St Barbe Harrison* (P887) and *Bookplate for A. H. Tandy* (P839). Stone-carvings *Chloe* and *Ariel between Wisdom and Gaiety* (the latter for Broadcasting House). Title-page for *Hamlet* (P838). Page from *The Four Gospels* showing w-e. *THERE, The Visitation* (P791).

561 IN MEMORIAM: ERIC GILL. NOVEMBER 17, 1940. By Donald Attwater. *The Commonweal*, Vol. XXXIII, no. 14, January 24, 1941, pp. 343–5.

562 FOR ERIC GILL: MAY HE HAVE REST. By the Rt. Rev. Arthur Jackman. *America*, Vol. LXIV, no. 16, 25 January 1941, p. 433.

563 ERIC GILL: MEMORIAL NUMBER. *Blackfriars*, Vol. XXII, no. 251, February 1941. Contains the following: 'Eric Gill' (editorial). 'Appreciations' by F. Lockyer, J. Middleton Murry, M. C. D'Arcy, S.J., Neville Gorton, Bernard Delany, O.P., Hilary Pepler, Donald Attwater and Anthony Foster. 'Eric Gill as Sculptor' by David Jones. 'Created Holiness' by Kenelm Foster, O.P. 'Eric Gill's Social Principles' by Bernard Kelly. 'Eric Gill and Eastern Thought' by Walter Shewring. 'A Personal Memoir' by René Hague. These contributions are followed (pp. 95–100) by reviews of the following books: *Autobiography* by *Viator*, *Drawings from Life* by Ivo Thomas, O.P. *Topics. Ten Essays by Walter Shewring* by A. E. H. Swinstead. The w-e.

JESUS, Christ crowned (P822), in reduced form, is reproduced as frontispiece.

564 ERIC GILL: MEMORIAL NUMBER. *Pax Bulletin*, no. 20, February 1941. This issue, comprising ten stencilled f'cap. leaves, contains appreciations by: Dr Cecil Gill, Fr. Gerald Vann, O.P., The Rev. T. Brock Richards, Prof. Harold Robbins. There are also extracts from other appreciations: By Kevin Williams in *The Catholic Worker*, January 1941. By David Jones in *The Tablet*, 30 November 1940. By Carl Purington Robbins, Printer to Yale University, in *The Publishers' Weekly* (N.Y.). By Max Plowman in *Peace News*, 29 November 1940. 'Eric Gill as Carver', being an extract from Charles Marriott's monograph in Joseph Thorp's *Eric Gill* (Cape, 1929). A review of E. G.'s *Autobiography* by Donald Attwater. A list of books by E. G. This issue closes with *The First Step*, an extract from an article in *Peace News* and *Finis Operantis*, being an extract from his *Autobiography*.

565*a* ERIC GILL—ANARCHIST. By Herbert Read. *War Commentary*, Vol. II, no. 4, February 1941, pp. 7–9. A review-article of E. G.'s *Autobiography*. Reprinted as 'Eric Gill' in *A Coat of Many Colours*, London: Routledge. September 1945. A much longer extensively revised version appeared in *Retort. A Quarterly of Social Philosophy and the Arts*, Bearsville (N.Y.), Vol. II, no. 4, Spring 1945, pp. 12–20. This revised version was reprinted in 1963 as *Eric Gill An Essay*, printed by The Oriole Press, Berkeley Heights, New Jersey, in an edition of 100 copies for private distribution.

565*b* ERIC GILL: TRIBUTE. By T. Barry. *Commonweal* (N.Y.), Vol. XXXIII, 7 February 1941, p. 400.

566 ART, CRAFT, AND COMMON SENSE. By Ivor Brown. *The Manchester Guardian*, 15 February 1941. See also letters under the general heading 'Industrial Life and Art', 'The Myth of Progress' from Harry Norris (17 February) and 'Political Action?' from F. H. Amphlett Micklewright (25 February).

567 ERIC GILL: NEGATIVE-POSITIVE. By Ralph Velarde. *The Beda Review*, Vol. IV, no. 5, March 1941, pp. 32–4. A review-article of E. G.'s *Autobiography*.

568 MEMORIES OF ERIC GILL. By Peter F. Anson. *Pax. The Quarterly Review of the Benedictines of Prinknash*, Vol. XXXI, no. 218, Spring 1941, pp. 27–36. In the same issue (pp. 40–2) there is an appreciation of E. G. under 'Prinknash Notes'.

569 WILLIAM MORRIS, ERIC GILL AND CATHOLICISM. By Nicolete Gray. *The Architectural Review*, Vol. LXXXIX, March 1941.

570 THE AUTOBIOGRAPHY OF ERIC GILL. By Dom Alphege Shebbeare. *The Downside Review*, Vol. LXIX, no. 178, April 1941, pp. 205–24. A review-article of E. G.'s *Autobiography*.

571 WOMAN OF STONE: AUTOBIOGRAPHY. *Commonweal* (N.Y.), Vol. XXXIV, 13 June 1941, pp. 175–7.

572 ERIC GILL AND LITURGICAL WORSHIP. By Donald Attwater. *Orate Fratres* (U.S.A.), June 1941, pp. 199–203. An appreciation.

573 ERIC GILL, T.O.S.D. By Rev. Michael Kelly. *Art Notes*, Vol. V, nos. 3 and 4, Double Summer Number, pp. 29–32. An appreciation with w-e.'s *THE, The Baptism of Jesus* (P780). *JESUS, Christ crowned* (P822). *AND, The Nativity* (P795). Three photographs of the Church of St Peter's, Gorleston and one of the stone-carving: *Annunciation*.

574 NOTES ON THE PLANNING OF A CHURCH. EXTRACTS FROM AN UNPUBLISHED BOOK ON CHURCH PLANNING AND FURNISHING. By Peter Anson. *Art Notes* [as no. 573 above], pp. 33–4. The writer quotes E. G.'s *Sacred and Secular* and the essay *Mass for the Masses* in that volume in support of his plea for the placing of the High Altar in a church. Illustrated with a sketch of the High Altar in the Church of the First Martyrs, Bradford. (Cf. nos. 218 and 527.)

575 EX-PATRIATE OF THE GOTHIC AGE. By F. S. Berryman. *Magazine of Art* (U.S.A.), Vol. XXXIV, October 1941, p. 438.

575a A POCKET BOOK CONTAINING TWELVE OF THE MOST DIS-TINGUISHED SERIES OF PRINTING TYPES CUT BY THE MONOTYPE CORPORATION LIMITED LONDON, ENGLAND OFFERED TO DIS-CRIMINATING PRINTERS IN AMERICA. By the Lanston Monotype Machine Company Philadelphia. 1941. *Gill Sans Extra Heavy* 321 is shown on pp. 19 and 20 in a range of sizes from 72 point to 6 point. In a double-ruled border on the front wrapper the title 'XII Type Faces From England XCMXLI' is printed. Around the box a variant wording of the title page is given.

1942

576 ERIC GILL: ARTEFICE E APOSTOLO. By Desmondo Chute. *L'Osserva-tore Romano*, 28 Febbraio 1942, p. 3. An appreciation by the Rev. Desmond Chute with two illustrations: w-e. *The Good Shepherd* (P489) and of the ninth of the Stations of the Cross in Westminster Cathedral *Jesus Falls a Third Time*. An English version by Chute entitled 'Eric Gill: Apostolic Craftsman', appeared in *The Catholic Art Quarterly*, Vol. XVII, no. 1, Christmas 1953, pp. 17–22. Gill's w-e. *Three Kings* (P73) appears on p. 18 and *Cantet Nunc Lo* (P75) on p. 19. Chute's note concerning the article in English is as follows: 'The present article was originally written in Italian to introduce a translation of *Social Justice and the Stations of the Cross*. It also embodies a previous and briefer notice printed in the *Osservatore Romano*, Feb. 28, 1942 . . .'

577 THE SIGNIFICANCE OF ERIC GILL. *The Socialist Christian*, Vol. XIII, no. 3, May–June 1942, pp. 7–8. An unsigned contribution, being the first of several articles on the life and thought of some contemporary Christian social thinkers.

578 ERIC GILL. [By A. Phillips (Harold David Phillips).] *Air Mail Magazine*, no. 40, June 1942, p. 782. Published by A. Phillips, 4 and 5 Dock Street, Newport, Mon. A biographical sketch with special reference to lettering and typography. This issue of the magazine was set in Monotype *Gill Sans*.

579 GERMANY IN PERIL. By Erich Meissner. Oxford University Press. In his discussion of the 'destruction of handicraft' Dr Meissner writes in recognition of the work of E. G.

580 COMING DOWN THE WYE. By Robert Gibbings. London: J. M. Dent & Sons, Ltd. The author writes (pp. 80–2) of E. G. at Capel-y-ffin and of the origins of his stone-carving *Mankind* now in the Tate Gallery.

581 ERIC GILL 1882–1940—THE LAST YEARS. [By Ralph S. Stokes.] *Staples Digest. Mirror of English Life and Letters.* December 1942, pp. 7–9. An unsigned review-article of E. G.'s *Autobiography* preceded by a brief biographical sketch.

1943

582 THE POLITICS OF THE UNPOLITICAL. By Herbert Read. London: George Routledge & Sons, Ltd. This collection of Essays contains references to E. G. It was extensively reviewed in *The Times Literary Supplement*, 17 April 1943, under 'Menander's Mirror' [Charles Morgan]

583 WHY EXHIBIT WORKS OF ART? By Ananda Coomaraswamy. London: Luzac & Co. Collected Essays on the traditional or 'normal' view of Art. E. G. is quoted on pp. 14–15 and cited in the bibliography (p. 60). A slip pasted on the front of the wrapper quotes an extract from E. G.'s *Autobiography* concerning the author. The volume contains the essay 'The Nature of Mediaeval Art' to which E. G. makes reference in a letter printed in *Letters of Eric Gill* under no. 320.

584 ERIC GILL, CATHOLIC PACIFIST. By Stormont Murray. *Pax Bulletin*, no. 34, July 1943, pp. 1–2.

585 PERTELOTE. A SEQUEL TO CHANTICLEER. BEING A BIBLIOGRAPHY OF THE GOLDEN COCKEREL PRESS OCTOBER 1936–1943 APRIL. FOREWORD & NOTES BY THE PARTNERS. ILLUSTRATIONS FROM THE BOOKS. London: The Golden Cockerel Press, 10 June 1943. Item no. 136 describes *The Travels & Sufferings of Father Jean de Brébeuf* for which E. G. engraved the double title-page. The w-e. *The Attack* (P972) is reproduced on p. 33. (Cf. no. 520.)

586 ENGLISH PRAYER BOOKS. AN INTRODUCTION TO THE LITERATURE OF CHRISTIAN PUBLIC WORSHIP. By Stanley Morison. Cambridge: The University Press. 1943 [24 Nov.] This is the first of a series entitled 'Problems of Worship' edited by the Very Rev. W. R. Matthews, Dean of St Paul's, and the Very Rev. F. W. Dwelly, Dean of Liverpool. In this (the first) edition reference is made (p. 95) to the new edition of the *Ordo Administrandi Sacramenta* published by Burns and Oates in 1915 for which E. G. engraved a half-title: *Three Martlets* (P28). Also (pp. 96 and 102) to the *Horae Beatae Virginis Mariae* ... MCMXXIII printed at S. Dominic's Press, Ditchling, and for which E. G. cut wood-engravings (see no. 384 above). The latter is described as 'the best example I have seen of English liturgical-music printing'. A second edition of this book was published in 1945. A third, and considerably enlarged, edition appeared in 1949. In this the references to the two publications mentioned above appear on pp. 171 and 172. Reviews: *The Times Literary Supplement*, 25 December 1943 and 25 November 1949. *The Church Times*, 21 January 1944.

587 ERIC GILL. By John Middleton Murry. *Pax Bulletin*, no. 36, Christmas 1943, pp. 5–6. This article appears in what is described as 'Special Eric Gill Number' of the *Bulletin*.

588 DESIGN FOR PEACE. A TALK ON THE LIFE AND TEACHING OF ERIC GILL. By Olive Wilson. *Pax Bulletin*, no. 36, Christmas 1943, pp. 6–8.

The same issue contains an article 'William Richard Lethaby, 1857–1937' by Mark Fitzroy which cites E. G. and quotes from his *Autobiography*.

1944

589 ERIC GILL, A.R.A.—1882–1940. Notes by Walter J. Roberts. *Builders and Makers: A Scheme of Study for the Year 1944 for Adult Schools*, pp. 74–8. London: National Adult School Union. A brief but very comprehensive biographical sketch covering the major aspects of E. G.'s life and work with a short list of books by and concerning him.

590 BRIDGE INTO THE FUTURE. LETTERS OF MAX PLOWMAN EDITED BY D. L. P[LOWMAN] London: Andrew Dakers Ltd. 1944. Contains references to E. G. in letters on pp. 706, 708, 715, 741, 751, 754, 758, 760, 765, 768 and a letter to him, p. 726. The letters on the pages mentioned cover the period from April 1940 to May 1941. They are chiefly concerned with the writer's and E. G.'s common interests in the Peace Pledge Union and E. G.'s *Autobiography*. The letter on pp. 714–15 describes a visit to Pigotts.

591 GILBERT KEITH CHESTERTON. By Maisie Ward. London: Sheed & Ward. 1944. Quotations from two letters of E. G. to G. K. C. appear on pp. 422 and 423. These concern *G.K.'s Weekly* for which E. G. had been invited to 'become the chief contributor on art'. There are further references to him on pp. 554 and 563 and, facing p. 537, a photograph of the monument he designed for G. K. C.'s grave at Beaconsfield.

591*a* WHAT IS MAN? Arranged by Peter Maurin. *The Catholic Worker*, Vol. XI, no. 2, February 1944.

592 THE MACHINE MENTALITY. By S. Sagar. *The Weekly Review*. London: 9 Essex Street, W.C. 2, 17 August 1944.

592*a* REMEMBERING ERIC GILL: GILL AND THOREAU. By Ridley Hughes. *America*, Vol. LXXI, no. 23, 9 September 1944, pp. 556–7.

592*b* GILL THE MAN. By Theodore Yardley. *America*. Vol. LXXI, no. 23, 9 September 1944, p. 557.

593 A CATHOLIC APPROACH TO THE PROBLEM OF WAR. A Symposium edited by Hubert Grant Scarfe. Published by *Pax* (Hon. Sec. Stormont Murray, Radnage nr. High Wycombe, Bucks.). E. G.'s influence on

the direction of 'Pax', of which Society he was the third Chairman (1939), is referred to in the Editor's Introduction (p. 8). (Cf. nos. 237, 255 and 594.)

594 A CATHOLIC CONSIDERS COMMUNITY. By Stormont Murray. *A Catholic Approach to the Problem of War* (see no. 593 above). This is reprinted from *Community in a Changing World*, second edition.

595 CONSIDERATIONS ON ERIC GILL. By Walter Shewring. *The Dublin Review*, October 1944. A lengthy study of the man and his work as exemplified in the two volumes of his published Essays, viz. *Last Essays* and *In A Strange Land* (published in U.S.A. in one volume as *It All Goes Together*). This article was revised and reprinted in *The Catholic Art Quarterly*, Vol. VIII, no. 2, Easter 1945, pp. 13–27. The revised article was later included in the collection of Shewring's essays, *Making and Thinking*, pp. 88–103. (Cf. no. 636.16.)

596 BREAD AND ROSES. AN UTOPIAN SURVEY AND BLUE-PRINT. By Ethel Mannin. London: Macdonald & Co. [7 Dec. 1944] Contains several references to E. G. notably to his books *Sacred and Secular* and *Work and Property*. See pp. 14–15, 18, 63, 67, 88, 90, 97, 102.

1945

597 THE GUILD OF MEMORIAL CRAFTSMEN. London: The Central Institute of Art and Design. National Gallery, W.C. 2. First Series 1945. A brochure. Contains photographs of the following designs by E. G.: p. 6, Memorial to Dorothea Beale (designed in collaboration with his brother Macdonald Gill); p. 9, Memorial to Michael George Herbert (designed in collaboration with L. Cribb). Also reproduced are designs by the following who were pupils of E. G.: Joseph Cribb, Denis Tegetmeier, L. Cribb and Donald Potter.

598 FIFTEEN CRAFTSMEN ON THEIR CRAFTS. Edited and with an Introduction by John Farleigh. London: The Sylvan Press. [May] 1945. There are references to E. G. on pp. 55, 58, 65, 116 and 117.

599 ERIC GILL: Workman. By Donald Attwater. London: James Clarke & Co. [Sept. 1945] This was the first of a series of 'studies in the thought of some outstanding Christian thinkers' edited by Donald Attwater under the general title *Modern Christian Revolutionaries*. With a list of books by E. G. The author's aim in this book was 'to give a summary exposition of E. G.'s ideas and the convictions that lay behind them'. Reviews: *The Times Literary*

Supplement, 17 November 1945, *Expository Times*, June 1946. This, with four other studies, was published by The Devin-Adair Company, New York in 1947 under the title *Modern Christian Revolutionaries*. Reissued New York: Books for Libraries, 1971.

1946

600 FIGURES OF SPEECH OR FIGURES OF THOUGHT. COLLECTED ESSAYS ON THE TRADITIONAL OR 'NORMAL' VIEW OF ART. Second Series. By Ananda Coomaraswamy. London: Luzac & Co. 1946. Cf. the essay 'The Mediaeval Theory of Beauty' [originally published as 'Mediaeval Aesthetic' in *Art Bulletin* (N.Y.), Vols. XVII (1935) and XX (1938)] Also 'The Nature of Buddhist Art'. Note 5 (p. 68) refers to the writings of E. G. E. G. refers to these Essays in letters published in *Letters of Eric Gill* under nos. 238 and 286.

601 ART IN CHRISTIAN PHILOSOPHY. By Walter Shewring. Plainfield, New Jersey: The Sower Press. 1946. Edition limited to 500 copies. The writer cites E. G. (p. 15) and includes in his Bibliography (p. 21) E. G.'s *Art* (1934), *Christianity and the Machine Age* (1940), *Sacred and Secular* (1940) and *Work and Property* (1937).

602 ERIC GILL AND 'THE NEXT STEP'. *Pax in Terra News Sheet*. Edited by Stormont Murray, Radnage, High Wycombe. No. 1, February 1946. A publication of seven stencilled pages. This article appears on pp. 6–7 and is signed 'S. M[urray]'.

603 MAKERS OF ALPHABETS. *Alphabet and Image*, no. 1, Spring 1946, pp. 74 and 76. London: The Shenval Press, 58 Frith Street, Soho. Appreciations of E. G. and Edward Johnston and of their influence as type designers.

604 OPENING BARS. BEGINNING AN AUTOBIOGRAPHY BY SPIKE HUGHES. London: Pilot Press, Ltd. March 1946. The statement that 'there was an interminable nightly performance of compline around a spinet with Eric Gill taking the part of cantor and plainsong singing in *an unmusical voice*' (the italics are ours) may be taken as a measure of the importance to be attached to the author's description (pp. 68–71) of life with the Gill family at Ditchling in 1919—E.R.G.

605 THE CHURCH AND WORK. By Dorothy Day. *Catholic Worker*, September 1946. This was reprinted in *Pax Bulletin*, no. 50, Christmas 1946, pp. 2–6, with quotations from letters written to the *Catholic Worker* by E. G.

606 THE EARLY ALPHABETS OF ERIC GILL. By Robert Harling. *Alphabet and Image*, no. 3, December 1946, pp. 61–7. With three folding reproductions of lettering. An important and valuable outline of E. G.'s work and influence first as a letter-cutter and later as a designer of type-faces.

607 THE BODY OF WOMAN. By Oliver Hill. *Christmas Convoy*. London: Richards Press, Ltd. With six illustrations from drawings by E. G. first published in *Twenty-Five Nudes* (no. 38).

1947

608 AM I MY BROTHER'S KEEPER? By Ananda K. Coomaraswamy. New York: The John Day Company. [1947] Contains (p. xvi) a reproduction of E. G.'s w-e. *Progress* (P41) to which reference is made on p. 67 and there are quotations from E. G.'s *Autobiography* on pp. 1 and 57. On the dust-jacket is printed the reference to Coomaraswamy E. G. makes in his *Autobiography* wherein he acknowledges the influence Coomaraswamy's writings and teaching have had upon him (p. 174—U.S. edition, p. 179).

608a RICH AND POOR IN CHRISTIAN TRADITION. Writings of many centuries chosen, translated and introduced by Walter Shewring. London: Burns Oates & Washbourne. [1947] The dedication is 'In remembrance of Eric Gill' and the frontispiece photo shows St Martin of Tours from a sculpture by E. G. at Campion Hall, Oxford. The same is also reproduced on the dust jacket. E. G. is mentioned on p. 23 as having said that secular social reformers desire the poor to become rich, but Christ desires the rich to become poor and the poor holy.

609 THE VISION OF THE FOOL. By Cecil Collins. London: The Grey Walls Press, Ltd. 1947. In a footnote on p. 15 the author in a tribute to E. G. speaks of him 'as one of the few great men of conviction, whose deep integrity and life-long work for the cause of Art in contemporary society commands from all artists a respect and admiration'.

610 STEUBEN GLASS. With an Introduction by Sidney Waugh. New York: Steuben Glass, 718 Fifth Avenue. A handsomely gotten up pamphlet reviewing the recognition that has come to Steuben Glass since 1934; p. 38 shows a pair of vases designed by E. G. See also *Country Life*, 15 February 1941, pp. 150–1, 'Modern American Glass. Distinguished Designs by British Artists' by C. H. No. 5 of the accompanying illustrations is of the same pair of vases here described as *Bud vases*. See also *The Connoisseur*, January 1940.

611 A HANDBOOK OF PRINTING TYPES WITH NOTES ON THE STYLE OF COMPOSITION AND GRAPHIC PROCESSES USED BY COWELLS. Ipswich: W. S. Cowell, Ltd. Distributed by Faber and Faber, Ltd., London, 1947. There is a reference (p. 13) to the *Gill Sans* family. Pp. 66–70 are set in *Gill Sans* and pp. 55–60 in *Perpetua*; each design is accompanied by descriptive notes. Second, enlarged, edition 1948.

612 A STUDY IN INTEGRITY. THE LIFE AND TEACHING OF ERIC GILL. By Conrad Pepler, O.P. *Blackfriars*, Vol. XXVIII, no. 326, May 1947, pp. 198–209. This was reprinted in *The Catholic Art Quarterly*, vol. XI, no. 2, Easter 1948, pp. 87–96.

613 REJECTION (THOUGHTS FOR MEDITATION). Compiled by Stanley Vischer. Easton, Pa.: David Hennessy, Maryfarm Bookstall. Hand-set and limited to 475 copies, June 1947. A little booklet of nine unnumbered pages containing 'sayings' of five different writers of whom E. G. is the first quoted.

614 THE MONKEY. By Brynhild Locock. *The Ark. Bulletin of The Catholic Study Circle for Animal Welfare*, no. 31, August 1947, pp. 47–9. A Poem 'dedicated to St Thomas More, Eric Gill, Fr. Martindale, Robert Speaight, and all others who see as they do'. This poem was inspired by the action the Westminster Cathedral authorities took when they caused the figure of the monkey, in E. G.'s carving for the altar-piece in the Chapel of the Martyrs there, to be removed. This action was the subject of a protracted correspondence in the *Catholic Herald* in 1947 (see issues of February 7, 14, March 7, 14, 21).

615 ERIC GILL: WORKMAN AND ARTIST. By Stormont Murray. *The Adelphi*, Vol. XXIV, no. 1, October–December 1947, pp. 13–20. This is an adaptation of a paper read to The International Arts Centre, London.

616 ERIC GILL: *Boghaandvaerkeren, Skrifttegneren, Mennesket 1882–1940*. Af Erik Lassen. Kobenhavn: *Bogvennen*, Aarbog for Bogkunst og Boghistorie, udgivet af Foreningen for Boghaandvaerk, under Redaktion af Svend Dahl. Ny Raekke, Bind 2, 1946. Fischers Forlag, MCMXLVII. [ERIC GILL: *the book craftsman, the type designer, the man, 1882–1940*. By Erik Lassen. Copenhagen: *The Book Friend*, Annual for Book Art and Book History, published by The Bookcraft Society, edited by Svend Dahl. New Series, Volume 2, 1946. Fischer's Publications, 1947] With the following illustrations: *Self-portrait* (1927). Lettering in relief carving (1909). Pencil drawing of

Chartres Cathedral (1907). Half-title from the Insel Verlags *Balzac* (1903) [*sic*][1]
Example of E. G.'s sans-serif upper and lower case. Title-page of *Art-Nonsense*
showing 24 and 30 pt. *Titling Perpetua* capitals (1929). Specimens of *Perpetua*
type. Half-title of *The Passion of SS. Perpetua and Felicity* (1929). Publication,
notwithstanding the dates quoted above, was actually delayed until the end of
1947.

1948

617 DE HOUTGRAVURE IN DE HEDENDAAGSE ENGELSE
BOEKKUNST. Deer Johan Schwencke. Met 76 afbeeldingen. 'S-
Gravenhage. A.A.M. Stels Uitgever. 1948. Contains an account of the Golden
Cockerel Press (pp. 27–32) and E. G.'s work for it with reproductions of one of
his w-e.'s for *Troilus and Criseyde* and of the book-plate he engraved for Freida
& Kemp Waldie (P886). E. G. as a writer is also discussed (pp. 32–4). The
book is printed from *Perpetua* type.

618 THE TYPE DESIGNS OF ERIC GILL. By Robert Harling.
Alphabet and Image, no. 6, January 1948, pp. 55–69. A valuable study
illustrated by numerous specimens including one of the *Aries* type which was
designed for the exclusive use of the Stourton Press for use in one book,
A Catalogue of Chinese Pottery and Porcelain (1934). Cf. no. 505 for reference to
Aries type in *Book-Production Notes*, *London Mercury*, January 1935.

619 WER IST WER? ERIC GILL. *Schweizer Graphische Mitteilungen*.
Heft v, 67. Jahrgang, Mai 1948, pp. 230–1. St Gallen: Verlag Zollikofer & Co.
A biographical sketch with a list of his published writings and mention of some
of his carvings together with a reduced reproduction of w-e. *Self-portrait*
(P497).

620 THE LETTERS OF ERIC GILL. AN EDITORIAL. *Blackfriars*, Vol.
XXIX, no. 338, May 1948, pp. 209–15. A review-article of *The Letters of Eric
Gill*. The 'opposite view of Gill's thought', an article by Fr. Ralph Velarde,
appeared in the following issue of *Blackfriars* under the title 'The Mind of
Middle Age' (pp. 283–7). Walter Shewring replied to this 'attack' in the
August issue (pp. 385–7) under the title 'Eric Gill: A Reply'.

621 POVERTY AND THE WORKERS. By R. P. Walsh, Editor of *The
Catholic Worker*. *Blackfriars*, Vol. XXIX, no. 340, July 1948, pp. 320–3. Quotes
several passages from E. G.'s writings.

[1] The Insel Verlag edition of Balzac's *Menschliche Komödie* was published in 1908 not in
1903. (Cf. no. 449.)

622 LETTERS OF ERIC GILL. By Dr Cecil Gill. *Pax*, Vol. XXXVIII, no. 247, Summer 1948, pp. 78–84. A review-article of *Letters of Eric Gill* written by his brother.

623 A DOMESDAY AND 18TH CENTURY HOUSE. *Ideal Home & Gardening*, Vol. LVIII, no. 5, November 1948, pp. 26–7. A description of E. G.'s home at Pigotts, High Wycombe, illustrated by eight photographs.

1949

624 DAVID JONES. By Robin Ironside. Penguin Books, Ltd. One of a series published under the general title *The Penguin Modern Painters* under the editorship of Sir Kenneth Clark. In this study of David Jones frequent mention is made of his association with E. G. both at Ditchling and at Capel-y-ffin and of the latter's influence in his development.

625 ERIC GILL'S DEVOTIONS. By James E. Walsh. *New York Times Book Review* 6 March 1949. A review-article of *The Letters of Eric Gill* (American edition New York, The Devin-Adair Company, 1948). (See no. 54.)

626 WOOD-ENGRAVING IN MODERN ENGLISH BOOKS. The Catalogue of an Exhibition arranged by Thomas Balston, October–November 1949. Cambridge: Cambridge University Press for the National Book League. Frequent mention of E. G. as a wood-engraver and his influence in this sphere is made in the Introduction. Plate 4 is a reproduction of his w-e. *St Paul* (P894) in Vol. III of *The Aldine Bible* (no. 292). The Exhibition contained twenty-four books illustrated with wood-engravings by him. The issue of *Image* (no. 5, Autumn 1950, edited by Robert Harling, Art and Technics, Ltd.) consisted almost wholly of this Introduction in a greatly extended and more elaborate form under the title *English Wood-Engraving 1900–1950*. This, again, was reprinted with alterations by Art and Technics, Ltd., in 1951. Review: *The Times Literary Supplement*, 25 August 1950.

627 ERIC GILL. Contribution by Walter Shewring to *The Dictionary of National Biography 1931–1940*, edited by L. G. Wickham Legg. Oxford: The University Press.

628a THE WOOD-ENGRAVINGS OF ROBERT GIBBINGS. By Thomas Balston. London: Art and Technics, Ltd. 1949. Several references are made to E. G. and his association with Robert Gibbings, notably in their work together for the Golden Cockerel Press.

628*b* TRADITION IN SCULPTURE. By Alec Miller. London: The Studio Publications. 1949. In the chapter 'The Twentieth Century: Actions and Reactions' the author deals at some length (pp. 153–4) with E. G.'s methods with special reference to the torso *Mankind* of which Plate 202 is a full-page photograph. There is also a reference to him and Epstein (p. 152) and their break away from the Rodin school of sculpture.

628*c* TWENTIETH CENTURY SCULPTURE. By E. H. Ramsden. London: Pleiades Books. 1949. E. G. is discussed on pp. 16–17 et passim. Plate 1 shows Gill's *Crucifixion*, 1910 and plate 2 shows Gill's *Flying Angel*, *c.* 1928.

628*d* COCKALORUM. A SEQUEL TO CHANTICLEER AND PERTELOTE. BEING A BIBLIOGRAPHY OF THE GOLDEN COCKEREL PRESS JUNE 1943 – DECEMBER 1948. Foreword and Notes by Christopher Sandford. Illustrations from the Books. [London: The Golden Cockerel Press. n.d.] The w-e. of one of the double-opening title pages from *The Green Ship* (P898) is shown reduced on p. 84. (Cf. no. 520 and no. 585.)

628*e* MAKING A BOOKPLATE. By Mark F. Severin. London: The Studio Publications. 1949. How To Do It Series Number 39. E. G.'s w-e. bookplate for Desmond Flower, 1932 (P848) is reproduced on p. 50, for Miriam Rothschild, 1932 (P834) on p. 55, and for Elizabeth Foster and Arthur Graham Carey, 1928 (P501) on p. 59. There are three references to E. G. On p. 35 in a discussion of the cost of a bookplate, Severin says, 'I should like to quote an amusing – and categorical – answer I had from the late Eric Gill, that great engraver, when once I asked him what he was going to charge for my own plate: 'From five to fifty guineas, according to the amount of work', he said. Under the principal types of bookplates on p. 83 is the category 'Renovation. E. Gill, etc.' with a reduced reproduction of E. G.'s w-e. bookplate for Austen St Barbe Harrison, 1935 (P887). E. G.'s bookplates are referred to as classics on p. 84. (Cf. no. 636.128.)

628*f* FIGURE DRAWINGS, VICTORIA AND ALBERT MUSEUM. London: HMSO. 1949. Plate 24 reproduces a reduction of a pencil drawing ($11\frac{3}{4} \times 5\frac{1}{2}$) of a female nude by E. G. dated 9.12.27, number E.875–1936. (Cf. no. 548.)

1950

629 IN MY VIEW. By Eric Newton. London: Longmans, Green & Co. 1950. Contains an Essay: 'Eric Gill: Artist & Craftsman' (pp. 121–3). This is a commentary written in January 1941 upon a contemporary Exhibition, held at the Victoria and Albert Museum, of E. G.'s books, drawings, typography and carved lettering together with a stone-carving.

630 A LETTER FROM SUSSEX BY H. D. C. PEPLER ABOUT HIS FRIEND ERIC G. Chicago: Cherryburn Press and The Society of Typographic Arts. $7\frac{1}{2} \times 4\frac{1}{2}$. Sixteen (unnumbered) pages. 1950. [The half-title reads: A LETTER ABOUT ERIC GILL] Extract from the Foreword: 'On February 11, 1949 an exhibition of graphic work by Eric Gill opened at The Newberry Library, Chicago, under the sponsorship of The Society of Typographic Arts and The Newberry Library. It consisted of seventy-four wood engravings and three drawings selected by H. D. C. Pepler and loaned by the artist's widow, Mary Gill. ... R. H. M. Chicago, Illinois, January 16, 1950.' Hilary Pepler was prevented by illness from attending the opening of this exhibition; his letter was accordingly printed as 'an S. T. A. keepsake'. Printed from *Perpetua* type by Greer Allen. The 'Eric G' on the title-page is in facsimile of E. G.'s signature. E. G.'s w-e. *The Constant Mistress* (P867) is shown on the front of the grey wrappers. [It might here be recorded that Hilary Douglas Clark Pepler died at Ditchling, Sussex, 20 September 1951. R.I.P.] A 4-page, single-fold $10\frac{1}{2} \times 4\frac{1}{4}$ checklist of the prints exhibited was issued.

631 FIFTY YEARS OF TYPE-CUTTING. A POLICY REVIEWED AND RENEWED. *The Monotype Recorder*, Vol. XXXIX, no. 2, Autumn 1950. A survey of the history of the Monotype Corporation's activities over the fifty years 1900–50. Several references are made to the types E. G. designed for the Corporation; these are 'illustrated' by pp. 21–2 for *Gill Sans* and pp. 23–4 for *Perpetua*.

632 OUTCRY. By Tim Evens. *The Gryphon. The Journal of the University of Leeds*. October 1950, pp. 24–30. A summary of the controversy aroused by E. G.'s bas-relief *The Money-changers* outside the Great Hall of Leeds University. With a scraper-board illustration and a short list of the chief sources of information for the article. (Cf. no. 407.)

633 ERIC GILL: A SPECIAL KIND OF ARTIST. By Kerran Dugan, C.S.C., of the Brothers of Holy Cross. *The Catholic Worker*, Vol. XVII, 5 November 1950, pp. 4 and 7. The writer made a correction to a certain passage in this article in the issue for March 1951.

634 ERIC GILL: A RETROSPECT. By Desmond Chute. *Blackfriars*, Vol. XXXI, no. 369, December 1950, pp. 572–82. The Rev. Desmond Chute's study of E. G. was continued in the following issue (January 1951) which contains a photograph of the stone carving *The Glastonbury Madonna* (facing p. 5) and a reproduction of w-e. *Christ and the Money-Changers* (P152), p. 23.

634a HEDENDAAGSE ENGELSE EXLIBRIS. By Johan Schwencke. 'S-Gravenhage: Nederlandsche Exlibris-Kring. 1950. 10×7. Pp. 38. Stiff wrappers. Contains references to Gill on pp. 12–15, 17 and 21 and reproductions of Gill's w-e.'s: the *Decoy Duck* (P35) pressmark for the Decoy Press on p. 24 and the bookplates for Miriam Rothschild (P835) and for Scott Cunningham (P758), both on p. [25]

634b TYPOGRAPHICALLY SPEAKING. By Harry A. Bollinger. *Typographer*, the student publication of the Publishing and Printing Department, Rochester Institute of Technology Rochester, New York, Spring 1950, pp. 11–14. An overview of E. G.'s career with specific reference to the designing of the *Perpetua* typeface used in this issue of *Typographer*. *Perpetua* is described as, 'probably the first original twentieth-century type design of any real typographic value'. A redrawn and reversed portrait of E. G., unsigned, occupies p. 12, based on E. G.'s *Self-portrait* (P497).

634c ERIC GILL. By Jean Charlot. This is chapter 23 in his book, *Art-Making from Mexico to China*. New York: Sheed & Ward. 1950, pp. 256–62. Page 256 shows E. G.'s w-e. *Crucifix*, 1919 (P151).

1951

635 ERIK GILL: LA GIUSTIZIA SOCIALE E LA VIA CRUCIS. *Humanitas. Rivista Mensile di Cultura*. Brescia: Anno VI, N. 3, marzo 1951, pp. 221–5. This is an incomplete and unauthorized publication of translations from *Social Justice and the Stations of the Cross* (cf. no. 40) and other material supplied by the Rev. Desmond Chute. There is a bad reproduction of w-e. *Jesus dies upon the Cross* (P104) on p. 221.

636a ERIC GILL. By Bōn Blake Kelly. *Youth*, The Official Organ of the Catholic Action Girls' Organisation. London: 22 Bramham Gardens, S.W. 5. Vol. X, no. 5, April–June 1951, pp. 5–7 and 10. A biographical sketch with photographs of three stone-carvings: *St Martin* (p. 5), a plaque for Campion Hall, Oxford, *The Immaculate Conception* (p. 6) and *The Sacred Heart* (p. 7). The last two, which are at Ratcliffe, Leicester, though carved from E. G.'s designs are nearly all the work of his pupil Anthony Foster.

636*b* THE MAKING OF BOOKS. By Seán Jennett. London: Faber and Faber. 1951. Contains references to E. G. both as a wood engraver and type designer, see pp. 110, 212, 215, 300 and 370. Fig. 113 shows twelve varieties of the *Gill Sans* family of related type faces. *Perpetua* type is shown and described (p. 250). A page from *The Four Gospels* (p. 271), an initial designed by E. G. (fig. 145) and the title-page of *Troilus and Criseyde* (p. 355). The American edition of the same year was issued by Pantheon Books Inc. in New York.

636*c* THE ILLUSTRATION OF BOOKS. By David Bland. London: Faber and Faber. 1951. There are references to E. G. on pp. 84–6, 93 and 122 with special reference to the books he decorated for the Golden Cockerel Press and the Cranach Press. The American edition of the same year was issued by Pantheon Books Inc. in New York.

636*d* PUBLIC LETTERING. A Design Folio prepared by the Council of Industrial Design. London: Tilbury House, Petty France, S.W. 1. November 1951. Pp. 34. 14½×17. This is Book R of the Second Series of six Design Folios. Subscription for the series (containing seventy-two plates) 25*s*. This folio comprises two pages of text, twelve plates and five pages of notes on the plates, 'Books to Read', etc. In the introduction to the folio E. G. is described as one of England's three greatest type designers (with Caslon and Baskerville). Examples of his lettering are shown in plates 6, 8 and 10, together with the following alphabets designed by him: *Gill Bold Condensed, Perpetua Bold, Gill Sans-Serif* (roman and italic), *Perpetua Titling, Gill Extra Bold* and *Perpetua Italic*.

636.1 THE LOST CHILDHOOD AND OTHER ESSAYS. By Graham Greene. London: Eyre & Spottiswoode. 1951. E. G. discussed pp. 132–4 'out of his gritty childhood and his discovered faith a rebel should have been born ... but something went wrong'.

636.2 AS I KNEW HIM: ERIC GILL. By James Laver. *London Calling* [Magazine of the BBC External Services] No. 606, 3 May 1951, p. 13. Keeper of Prints and Drawings at the Victoria and Albert Museum, the author discusses E. G.'s work, beliefs and recalls his personal memories of E. G.

1953
636.3 BIBLIOGRAPHY OF ERIC GILL. By Evan R. Gill. London: Cassell & Co. Ltd. 1953. Foreword by Walter Shewring. Colophon: OF THIS BOOK | ONE THOUSAND COPIES WERE PRINTED | IN ERIC GILL'S PERPETUA

TYPES | AT THE | UNIVERSITY PRESS | CAMBRIDGE | THIS IS COPY NO.
[...] 10 × 7. Pp. 223. Blue cloth, spine lettering stamped in gold, top edge gilt.
Light grey dust jacket, printed in black and red. Subtitle on dust jacket:
A RECORD OF ALL ERIC GILL'S | WRITINGS &
ILLUSTRATIONS | WITH A LIST OF THE MAJOR |
CRITICISMS OF HIS WORK | AND 96 FACSIMILES OF |
TITLE-PAGES. 63s., $12 in the United States. There is a four-page pros-
pectus. The book was reprinted in 1974 in an edition of 500 copies with the
imprint Folkestone: Dawsons of Pall Mall, 1973. An American reprint also
appeared in 1973, published by Rowman and Littlefield of Totowa, New Jersey.
In 1983 St Paul's Bibliographies entered into an agreement with the heirs and
assignees of Evan Gill to publish the revised edition.
   REVIEW: By James Moran, *The British and Colonial Printer*, Vol. 153,
no. 6, August 7 1953, pp. 162 & 166.

636.4 ERIC GILL'S PILGRIM (NÉ BUNYAN) TYPE. By Robert
Harling. *The Penrose Annual* Vol. 47, 1953, pp. 53–4 with 4 pp. inset of the
type.

636.5 PORTRAIT DRAWINGS. VICTORIA AND ALBERT
MUSEUM. London: HMSO. 1953. Plate 25 reproduces a pencil portrait
by E. G. of Aristide Maillol, dated 1930, (14 × 10), reduced, number
E. 572–1941.

636.6 SCULPTURE: THEME AND VARIATIONS. TOWARDS A
CONTEMPORARY AESTHETIC. By E. H. Ramsden. London:
Lund Humphries. 1953. Discusses E. G. on pp. 2, 5, 7, 29–31, 51. Plate 5b is
Prospero and Ariel, Plate 52 is *The Deposition* and Plates 53 a & b *St Sebastian*.

636.7 LINOTYPE ANNOUNCE AN ADDITION TO THEIR
RANGE OF FACES FOR TEXT COMPOSITION. THE TYPE,
A RECUTTING OF A FACE DESIGNED BY ERIC GILL IS NAMED PILGRIM.
Linotype Matrix, no. 15, January 1953. 1 photograph of E. G. taken c. 1930 by
Howard Coster. 'This issue of Linotype Matrix is designed as a specimen of the
type face and contains notes on the artist, an account of the production of the
face and a description of its characteristics.'

636.8 A NOTE ON ERIC GILL'S PILGRIM TYPE. By Walter Tracy.
The Book Collector, Vol. 2, no. 1, Spring 1953, pp. 50–3. Illustrated.

636.9 MEMORIES OF ERIC GILL. By Robert Gibbings. *The Book Collector*, Vol. 2, no. 2, Summer 1953, pp. 95–103. Three illustrations.

1954

636.10 FIRST NUDES. By Eric Gill. With an introduction by Sir John Rothenstein. London: Neville Spearman. 1954. New York: Citadel Press. 1954. 24 plates. A printed note states: 'Paris 1926 May (Sketch book No. 1) for Gordian Gill (because it was begun on his birthday & it's the first time I did any life drawing).'

636.11 CATALOGUE OF AN EXHIBITION OF ERIC GILL. FROM THE COLLECTIONS OF ALBERT SPERISEN & OTHERS. With an introduction by Evan R. Gill. Stanford University Library November 7th to December 11th 1954. $9\frac{1}{2} \times 6\frac{1}{4}$. 23 pp. Grey-green wrappers with Eric Gill 1882–1940 and Gill's monogram signature on the front. Five hundred copies of the catalogue were printed at the Greenwood Press in San Francisco by Jack Werner Stauffacher. This was the first major West Coast exhibition of E. G.'s work.

636.12 BRITISH ARTISTS IN CRYSTAL. New York, Steuben Glass Inc. [1954] Two vases, entitled *Adam and Eve*, designed by E. G., are reproduced on p. [18]. Cf. no. 559a.

1956

636.13 ERIC GILL 1882–1940. By Albert Sperisen. San Francisco: Black Vine Press. 1956. [12 pp.] There are three issues, each with different colophons: A regular edition, one for the 1956 joint meeting of the Roxburghe Club of San Francisco and the Zamorano Club of Los Angeles, and one for The Typophiles in New York. The text was first printed as a broadsheet for the Gill exhibition at the Stanford University Library November 7 – December 11, 1954. There is a photo of E. G. used on the title page. Of it, Evan Gill wrote, 'I can't date the photograph but it was taken in his workshop at Ditchling and it would be somewhere about 1912 when he was 30.'

1958

636.14 A KEEPSAKE FOR THE GUESTS AT THE OPENING ON OCTOBER 14TH 1958 OF AN EXHIBITION OF THE WORK OF ERIC GILL MASTER OF LETTERING HELD AT MONOTYPE HOUSE, FETTER LANE, LONDON UNDER THE AUSPICES OF THE MONOTYPE CORPORATION LIMITED. London: Monotype Corporation Ltd. 250 copies. 16 pp. inc. 8 pp. of plates.

636.15 COMMEMORATING AN EXHIBITION OF LETTERING AND TYPE DESIGNS BY ERIC GILL HELD AT MONOTYPE HOUSE LONDON IN OCTOBER 1958. *The Monotype Recorder*, Vol. 41, no. 3, 1958. Photographs of the exhibition at Monotype House included.

636.16 CONSIDERATIONS ON ERIC GILL in MAKING AND THINKING. ESSAYS. By Walter H. Shewring. Buffalo, NY: Catholic Art Association. 1958. London: Hollis and Carter. 1959. Pp. 88–103.

1959

636.17 EDWARD JOHNSTON. By Priscilla Johnston. London: Faber and Faber. 1959. Contains references to E. G. on pp. 105, 127–30, 134, 144–6, 170, 182–3, 189, 196–204, 216–17, 225, 232, 276–8, 288–9. Second edition published by Barrie & Jenkins Ltd., 1976 with the following note by Priscilla Johnston about the addition of 'a few minor corrections and alterations in the text and some new notes. It has also been possible to include more illustrations.'

636.18 EPOCH AND ARTIST. SELECTED WRITINGS BY DAVID JONES. Edited by Harman Grisewood. London: Faber and Faber. 1959. Contains 'Eric Gill as Sculptor' [Cf. no. 563] pp. 288–95 and 'Eric Gill. An Appreciation' [Cf. no. 555] pp. 296–302.

636.19 DITCHLING. A COMMUNITY OF CRAFTSMEN. By Father Conrad Pepler O.P. *The Dublin Review*, Vol. 233, no. 482, Winter 1959–60, pp. 352–62. Publication of *Edward Johnston* by Priscilla Johnston prompts another child from that community to describe the life there, E. G.'s part in it, the schisms and E. G.'s departure to Wales.

1960

636.20 FOUR ABSENTEES. By Rayner Heppenstall. London: Barrie and Rockliff. 1960. Author's reminiscences of four men: Eric Gill, 'George Orwell', Dylan Thomas, J. Middleton Murry. References to E. G. pp. 7, 9, 2–13, 15–20, 97–105 (a visit to Pigotts in 1936). Set in Perpetua.

636.21 ERIC GILL 22 FEBRUARY 1882 – 17 NOVEMBER 1940. SEIN LEBEN, SEINE ANSCHAUUNGEN, SEIN WERK. By Paul Heuer. *Typographische Monatsblätter*, No. 12, December 1960, 79 Jahrgang, pp. 652–74.

1961

636.22 ERIC GILL, MEISTER DER SCHRIFTKUNST. By Prof. Johannes Boehland. *Archiv für Druck und Papier*, No. 4, 1961, pp. 352–8. Eight illustrations including six of the Monotype Corporation exhibition in 1958.

636.23 ERIC GILL ALS SCHRIFTKÜNSTLER ZUR GESCHICHTE DER ENGLISCHEN TYPOGRAPHIE ZWISCHEN DEN BEIDEN WELTKRIEGEN. By Wolfgang Kehr. *Börsenblatt für den Deutschen Buchhandel*, Frankfurter Ausgabe, Nr. 77a, 28 September 1961, pp. 1543–1626, bibliography pp. 1620–26. This article also appeared in *Sonderdruck aus dem Archiv für Geschichte des Buchwesens*, Band IV, Lieferung 2/3 [1962] columns 453–620.

636.24 ERIC GILL'S COIN DRAWINGS. By Graham Carey. *Good Work*, Vol. XXIV, no. 1, Winter 1961, pp. 11–20.

636.25 ERIC GILL: 20th CENTURY BOOK DESIGNER. By Sister Elizabeth Marie Brady, I.H.M. *Print*, Vol. 15, November 1961, pp. 41–3. Adapted from her book of the same name published in 1962 (no. 636.27). Three examples of books designed by E. G. are shown: p. 131 of the *Four Gospels* with *The Visitation* (P791) on p. 42, and the title page of *Art Nonsense* with *La Belle Sauvage* (P623) and p. 132 of Vol. I of *The Canterbury Tales* with *The Reeve's Tale* (P543) on p. 43.

1962

636.26 WILLIAM ROTHENSTEIN. THE PORTRAIT OF AN ARTIST IN HIS TIME. By Robert Speaight. London: Eyre & Spottiswoode. 1962. References to E. G. on pp. 187, 246–7, 252, 256, 263, 285–9, 312, 314, 362, 386–7.

636.27 ERIC GILL: 20th CENTURY BOOK DESIGNER. By Sister Elizabeth Marie Brady. Metuchen, New Jersey: Scarecrow Press, Inc. 1962. Revised edition, 1974.

1963

636.28 THE ENGRAVED WORK OF ERIC GILL. By J. F. Physick, Victoria and Albert Museum. London: Her Majesty's Stationery Office. 1963. A catalogue of Mrs Mary Gill's gift of E. G.'s personal reference file of his engraved work. This has since become a standard reference work and 'Physick' numbers are used in the present volume.

636.29 THE ENGRAVED WORK OF ERIC GILL. Victoria and Albert Museum. London: Her Majesty's Stationery Office. 1963. Large Picture Book No. 17. 94 pp. 206 wood-engravings illustrated. Issued in conjunction with no. 636.28 (above). Second edition, 1977, with 221 wood-engravings.

636.30 TWO FRIENDS. JOHN GRAY & ANDRÉ RAFFALOVICH. Essays Biographical & Critical with three letters from André Raffalovich to J-K Huysmans. Edited by Father Brocard Sewell. [Aylesford]: Saint Albert's Press. 1963. Reference to E. G. on pp. xii, 39, 45, 119, 139. E. G. drawing of Father John Gray opposite p. 118 and of André Raffalovich opposite p. 142. (Cf. no. 636.49.)

636.31 DESMOND CHUTE 1895–1962. By Walter Shewring. *Blackfriars*, Vol. XLIV, no. 511, January 1963, pp. 27–36. E. G. is mentioned throughout. Reprinted in *Good Work*, Vol. XXVI, no. 2, Spring 1963, pp. 45–53, with a few changes in the text and with the addition of illustrations, including Chute's pencil and ink portrait of E. G. done in 1926.

1964

636.32 THE INSCRIPTIONAL WORK OF ERIC GILL. By Evan R. Gill. London: Cassell & Co. Ltd. 1964. (Cf. no. 636.63.)

636.33 A NOTE ON THE LATIN PREFACE TO ERIC GILL'S INTRODUCTION FOR HIS ENGRAVINGS 1929. By Walter Shewring. San Francisco: The Black Vine Press. 1964.

636.34 ERIC GILL HIS SOCIAL AND ARTISTIC ROOTS. By Edward M. Catich. Iowa City, Iowa: The Prairie Press. 1964. [36 pp.]
    Note [p. 34]: 'An earlier draft of the foregoing text was delivered by Father Catich several years ago as a talk at the opening of a comprehensive showing of the work of Eric Gill at the Newberry Library, Chicago ... sponsored by the Society of Typographic Arts.' Colophon [p. 35]: 'This book has been designed and printed by Carroll Coleman ... The body type is Joanna, the large letters on each page of text are Perpetua Titling Capitals, and the two decorative letters on the title page are Floriated Capitals, all types designed by Eric Gill ...'

636.35 THE MODERN BRITISH PAINTINGS, DRAWINGS AND SCULPTURE. By Mary Chamot, Dennis Farr & Martin Butlin. Volume I Artists A–L. Tate Gallery Catalogues. London: The Oldbourne Press by order of the Trustees of the Tate Gallery. 1964. E. G. occurs on pp. 229–32 with short biography and details of the following sculptures in the collection: *Crucifixion* (1910), *The East Wind* (1928), *Prospero and Ariel* (1931), *Mankind* (1927–8), *Saint Sebastian* (1919–20), *Eve* (1928).

636.36 THE ERIC GILL DESIGN FOR THE COVER OF THE JOURNAL. By J. R. Swain. *Saint Bartholomew's Hospital Journal*, Vol. LXVIII, no. 5, May 1st 1964, pp. 181–3. Two illustrations. (Cf. no. 359.)

636.37 ERIC GILL. AN INTRODUCTION TO HIS WORK. By W[alter] S[hewring]. Chichester City Museum. 1964. Produced for an exhibition of E. G.'s work 24 June – 29 August 1964. In a letter from Shewring to Albert Sperisen (G L) dated 26 June 1964 he states that the Lanston Monotype Corporation did the printing and, 'very handsomely shouldered the expenses of this tract' and that 2000 copies were printed. Copies were sold at 1*s*. 6*d*. or twenty-five cents for the benefit of the Eric Gill collection. Exhibition reviewed in *The Observer* 3 July 1964 by Bernard Price. (Cf. no. 636.96.)

636.38 ERIC GILL: THE MAN AND THE MAKER. By Desmond Chute. *Good Work*, Vol. XXVII, no. 1, Winter 1964, pp. 21–32. Taken from the unfinished preface to a projected book on the sculptures and drawings of Eric Gill and arranged for publication by Walter Shewring. Illustrated with six examples of E. G.'s sculpture, *The East Wind* (study), *Mankind in the Making*, *Holy Water Stoup*, *Deposition of Christ*, *Prospero and Ariel* (study) and *The Foster Father*, as well as a 7″ painted plaster statuette *Madonna and Child*, an oak panel bas-relief *Death-Bed*, an alphabet stone carved in 1939 and a chalk drawing on stone (study for Station Twelve for St Cuthbert's church in Bradford). One of E. G.'s compasses and his square, hammer and chisel are also shown. The initial 'T' on p. 3 is a reduction of (P770).

1965

636.39 GOODNESS AND EFFORT. By Elizabeth Abraham. *Good Work*, Vol. XXVIII, no. 1, Winter 1965, pp. 9–13. An English economist, Miss Abraham responds to the text of a lecture given by W. R. Lethaby in 1922 which was printed in *Good Work*. She considers Lethaby and Gill to have had an 'attitude of denial rather than welcome for the modern world' and Gill is mentioned throughout her article.

636.40 GOODNESS & JUDGEMENT. By Graham Carey. *Good Work*, Vol. XXVIII, no. 2, Spring 1965, pp. 41–2. A response to *Goodness and Effort* by Miss Elizabeth Abraham (no. 636.39) concerning her points of disagreement with 'the school of Lethaby and Gill'.

1966

636.41 MY DEAR TIME'S WASTE. By Brocard Sewell. Aylesford: Saint Albert's Press. 1966. 500 copies. Numerous references to E. G.

636.42 ERIC GILL AND TODAY'S PROBLEM. By Roger Smith. *Good Work*, Vol. XXIX, no. 1, Spring 1966, pp. 23-5. A discussion of E. G.'s concern with 'the place of the artist-craftsman, the designer and the workman in the industrial society'.

636.43 ERIC GILL. By H. D. C. Pepler. *The Aylesford Review*. Vol. VII, no. 1, Spring 1966, pp. 37-9. A short article chiefly remembering E. G.'s work for the St Dominic's Press. The editorial on [p. 1] mentions that the essay, 'has not been published in this country until now'. On the cover a subheading for this issue is 'Hilary Pepler and The Saint Dominic's Press'. There are five articles on Pepler, three of which mention Gill. These are: 'Hilary Pepler: 1878-1951' by Fr Brocard Sewell, O. Carm., pp. 2-18; 'Douglas Hilary Pepler' by Fr Walter Gumbley, O.P., pp. 27-31 and 'Hilary Pepler, Printer' by Edward Walters, pp. 31-2. 'Memories of Ditchling' by David Lawson, O.P., pp. 33-7 also mentions Gill frequently. 'H. D. C. Pepler: Select Check-list of Writings', p. 41, lists several books illustrated by Gill. 'Saint Dominic's Press: Check-list of Printed Books', pp. 42-3, lists 'only the more typographically distinguished, or otherwise specially interesting, of the some two hundred items listed by Will Ranson in his *Selective Check Lists of Press Books*, New York: Duschenes. 1946. The present selective list has many books written or illustrated by Gill for the Press.'

636.44 ERIC GILL. By Sir Herbert Read. *Good Work*, Vol. XXIX, no. 3, Summer 1966, pp. 69-73. A review-article of Robert Speaight's *The Life of Eric Gill* and touching on E. G.'s fundamental ideas of life and art which, as Read points out, were 'categories which Gill did not distinguish'. The editorial entitled 'The Word "Artist"', pp. 67-8, aims 'to attempt here some conceptual and verbal examination of Gill's thought ...' The full page frontispiece photographic portrait of E. G. on [p. 66] is by Howard Coster.

636.45 DITCHLING CRUSOES AND CRAFTSMEN. By Fiona Mac-Carthy. *The Guardian*, 24 September 1966. A look at the Ditchling Community in E. G.'s time and at the present (1966).

636.46 THE LIFE OF ERIC GILL. By Robert Speaight. London: Methuen. 1966.

1967

636.47 MR ERIC GILL. RECOLLECTIONS OF DAVID KINDERSLEY. [New York:] The Typophiles. 1967. Typophiles Chapbook 44. [San Francisco:] Book Club of California. 1967.These recollections were reprinted, with a new preliminary essay, as *ERIC GILL: Further Thoughts by an Apprentice* and published London: Wynken de Worde Society, Lund Humphries Publishers Limited. 1982. New York: The Sandstone Press. 1982. A facsimile of the 1967 edition was published by Cardozo Kindersley Editions, Cambridge, 1990, with the addition of the 1982 preliminary essay – 'an attempt to provide an appreciation of the validity of Gill's views and work today'. This edition was entitled *MR ERIC GILL: Further Thoughts by an Apprentice.* (Cf. no. 636.79.)

636.48 THE LIFE AND WORKS OF ERIC GILL. Papers read at a Clark Library Symposium, 22 April 1967, by Cecil Gill, Beatrice Warde and David Kindersley. Introduction by Albert Sperisen. Los Angeles: William Andrews Clark Memorial Library, University of California. 1968. Los Angeles: Dawson's Bookshop. 1968.

1968

636.49 FOOTNOTE TO THE NINETIES. A MEMOIR OF JOHN GRAY AND ANDRÉ RAFFALOVICH. By Brocard Sewell. London: Cecil and Amelia Woolf. 1968. References to E. G. pp. 57–8, 87.

636.50 ERIC GILL—A PORTRAIT. By G. W. Sadler. *Print*, Vol. 5, no. 4, April 1968, p. 6.

636.51 The ISSUED STAMPS OF KING EDWARD VIII. By Marcus Arman. *Philatelic Bulletin*, Vol. 6, no. 4, December 1968, pp. 8–10.

1969

636.52 HARRY GRAF KESSLER UND DIE CRANACH-PRESSE IN WEIMAR. By Renate Müller-Krumbach. Mit einem Beitrag von John Dreyfus und einem Verzeichnis der Drucke der Cranach-Presse. Hamburg: Maximilian-Gesellschaft. 1969. References to E. G. on pp. 17, 20, 25, 27, 28, 40, 42–5, 49, 50–3, 56, 58–61, 63, 64, 67, 68, 72, 75, 79, 93, 111. E. G. is also mentioned in the following numbers of the checklist of the press: 7, 10, 16, 17, 17a, 19, 38, 40, 42, 44, 46, 47, 48, 52, 53, 54, 55, 56, 57. The checklist provided seven new entries and information about other editions for another four entries in the present volume. (Cf. no. 452.)

636.53 STANLEY MORISON 1889–1967. A radio portrait compiled by Nicolas Barker and Douglas Cleverdon. Ipswich: W. S. Cowell Ltd. 1969. 800 copies of which 550 for sale. It includes quotations from a 1961 interview with Morison about E. G.

636.54 A CELL OF GOOD LIVING. THE LIFE, WORKS AND OPINIONS OF ERIC GILL. By Donald Attwater. London: Geoffrey Chapman. 1969. 16 pp. of plates.

636.55 THE STOURTON PRESS (FROM 1930–1935). By Fairfax Hall. *The Private Library*, Second series, Vol. 2, no. 2, Summer 1969, pp. 54–63. Fairfax Hall, the proprietor of the press relates the involved story of the creation of *Aries* type by Gill and the first use of the type. In contradiction to the note in no. 505, Hall states on p. 58 that Sir Percival David, 'paid for Eric Gill's designs, and for the punches, matrices and the casting of the types, giving them all to me provided the 'Aries' types were used for the first time in his catalogue. While the catalogue was being set and the colour plates were being printed at Barnet by John Swain, it was a problem for me not only to pay but to find work for Gage-Cole. He printed three short pieces for me, two of which – being set in Aries – were not to be issued until after the catalogue.' In Hall's checklist of the books printed at the Stourton Press the first book listed as printed in *Aries* type is no. 3, *A Catalogue of Chinese Pottery and Porcelain in the Collection of Sir Percival David, Bt., F.S.A.* by R. L. Hobson, C.B., 1934. The two other titles set in *Aries* type in 1934 were Marlowe's *Hero and Leander*, no. 4 and *Bitter Memory*, by Fairfax Hall himself.

636.56 ERIC GILL 1882–1940. DRAWINGS & SOME CARVINGS. London: The Piccadilly Gallery. Catalogue of exhibition held 16th October – 8th November 1969. Preface by Robert Pincus-Witten. 66 items. Eight illustrations.

1970

636.57 DAS SCHRIFTSCHAFFEN ERIC GILLS UND DESSEN GESTALTERISCHE ANWENDUNG. By J. J. de L. Meyer. *Form und Technik*, January 1970, pp. 25–9. Illustrated.

636.58 ERIC GILL AND EDMUND DULAC ARTISTS AND MEN OF LETTERS. By Marcus Arman. *Philatelic Bulletin*, Vol. 7, no. 10, June 1970, pp. 3–6.

636.59 ERIC GILL, MASTER OF LETTER FORMS. By William R. Holman. *The Library Chronicle* of the University of Texas at Austin. New Series, No. 2, November 1970, pp. 14–25. Illustrated.

1971

636.60 LLANTHONY MONASTERY & ERIC GILL. By C[ecil] G[ill]. [Llanthony?] 1971. Two illustrations.

636.61 THE DIARIES OF A COSMOPOLITAN. COUNT HARRY KESSLER, 1918–1937. Translated and edited by Charles Kessler. Originally published as *Tagebücher 1918–1937* (Insel 1961). London: Weidenfeld & Nicolson. 1971. Contains references to E. G. on pp. 245, 256, 260, 262, 330–1, 352, 394–5.

1972

636.62 STANLEY MORISON. By Nicolas Barker. London: Macmillan. 1972. Cambridge, Massachusetts: Harvard University Press. 1972. Copious references to E. G.

636.63 ADDENDUM AND CORRIGENDA TO THE INSCRIPTIONAL WORK OF ERIC GILL. Compiled with an introduction by David Peace. San Francisco: The Brick Row Book Shop. 1972. 275 copies. (Cf. no. 636.32.)

636.64 ERIC GILL'S METHOD OF TYPE DESIGN AND BOOK ILLUSTRATION. By John Dreyfus. *The Record* of the Gleeson Library Associates, University of San Francisco, No. 9, June 1972, pp. 3–11. This is the edited version of an address delivered before the Gleeson Library Associates on November 7, 1971.

1973

636.65 ERIC GILL. THE MAN WHO LOVED LETTERS. By Roy Brewer. The Ars Typographica Library. London: Frederick Muller Ltd. 1973. Totowa, New Jersey: Rowman and Littlefield. 1973.

1974

636.66 THE STORY OF JOANNA. By J[ames] M[oran]. *Printing World*, Vol. 194, no. 18, 2 May 1974, pp. 292–4, 298. Three illustrations.

1975

636.67 WILLIAM MORRIS AND ERIC GILL. By Peter Faulkner. London: William Morris Society. 1975. 1750 copies. This essay discusses the resemblances and the contrasts between the outlooks of the two men in relation to the different times in which they lived.

636.68 ERIC GILL AND CHICHESTER. By John Skelton. *Chichester 900*, pp. 48–52. Chichester: Chichester Cathedral. 1975.

1976

636.69 MEN OF PRINTING. Edited by John J. Walsdorf. Wood engravings by Barry Moser, Easthampton, Massachusetts: Pennyroyal Press. 1976. 300 copies. E. G. is one of the eight subjects. The text is obituary material.

636.70 THE LETTER FORMS AND TYPE DESIGNS OF ERIC GILL. Notes by Robert Harling. Westerham, Kent: Eva Svensson. 1976. These notes were first published in *Alphabet & Image* and now revised and expanded (cf. no. 618). Second revised edition, 1978. Third edition Westerham: Hurtwood Press. 1979. Boston: D. R. Godine. 1978 (revised edition).

1977

636.71 COOMARASWAMY. 3: HIS LIFE AND WORK. By Roger Lipsey. Princeton University Press. 1977. Bollingen Series LXXXIX. E. G. met Coomaraswamy through William Rothenstein about 1910 and the ensuing friendship was important to both men. E. G. is mentioned on pp. 33n, 117–20, 123, 154, 173, 219, 221–2, 287, 291. On p. 119 is Coomaraswamy's second book plate, an engraving by E. G. (P173), 1920.

1978

636.72 ENGLISH ART 1870–1940. By Dennis Farr. Oxford: Oxford University Press. 1978. Contains references to E. G. on pp. 196, 202, 220–3, 250–1, 253, 292, 303, 321. Plates 80 b and c show a preliminary drawing for *Gill Sans* and Station of the Cross I, Jesus is condemned to death.

636.73 THE MALE NUDE. A NEW PERSPECTIVE. By Margaret Walters. London: Paddington Press Ltd. 1978. On p. 268 the author discusses E. G.'s 'private' drawings in comparison to his bland public nudes.

1979

636.74 THE MAN WHO BUILT LONDON TRANSPORT. A BIOGRA-
PHY OF FRANK PICK. By Christian Barman. Newton Abbot: David &
Charles. 1979. E. G. mentioned on pp. 43 and 128 in connection with his
sculptures on the London Underground HQ building.

636.75 BRITISH BOOKPLATES, A PICTORIAL HISTORY. By
Brian North Lee. Newton Abbot: David & Charles. 1979. References to E. G.
on pp. 7, 14, 17. E. G.'s bookplates nos. 193 and 194. References to E. G. in
captions for bookplates nos. 197 and 261.

636.76 A CHECK LIST OF BOOKS, PAMPHLETS, BROAD-
SHEETS, CATALOGUES, POSTERS, ETC. PRINTED BY
H. D. C. PEPLER AT SAINT DOMINIC'S PRESS DITCH-
LING, SUSSEX BETWEEN THE YEARS A.1916 AND
1936D. Compiled by Brocard Sewell. Ditchling: Ditchling Press. 1979.
There are 143 numbered items and twelve pages of miscellanea chronologically
arranged. E. G. is mentioned in the Foreword and his illustrations are
mentioned for the appropriate items.

636.77 TYPE DESIGNS OF ERIC GILL. By Roy Brewer. *Baseline*, International Typographics Magazine, Issue Two, 1979, pp. 14–15. Illustrated.

636.78 ERIC GILL, HILARY PEPLER AND THE DITCHLING
MOVEMENT. By Barbara Wall. *The Chesterton Review*, Vol. V, no. 2,
Spring-Summer 1979, pp. 165–87.

636.79 MY APPRENTICESHIP TO MR ERIC GILL. By David Kindersley. *Crafts Magazine*, No. 39, July/August 1979, pp. 40–4 (part 1), No. 40,
September/October 1979, pp. 40–4 (part 2).

636.80 ERIC GILL. STONE CARVER. WOOD ENGRAVER.
TYPOGRAPHER. WRITER. Three essays to accompany an exhi-
bition of his life and work. A Dartington Cider Press/Kettle's Yard Exhibition.
Dartington Cider Press Centre 17 July – 27 August 1979. Kettles Yard,
Cambridge 20 October – 18 November 1979. 'An Introduction & Memoir' by
David Kindersley, 'The Sculptor' by Sir John Rothenstein, 'The Engravings
of Eric Gill' by Douglas Cleverdon. Seven illustrations.

1980

636.81 TO BE A PRINTER. By Brooke Crutchley. London: The Bodley Head. 1980. References to E. G. pp. 51, 61, 70–1, 85, 87, 112, 129, 138, 166, 185.

636.82 DAI GREATCOAT. A SELF-PORTRAIT OF DAVID JONES IN HIS LETTERS. Edited by René Hague. London: Faber & Faber. 1980. References to E. G. on pp. 11, 21, 28, 29, 40, 54, 56, 63, 104, 117, 124, 184, 192, 211, 227, 232.

636.83 MY TIME WITH ERIC GILL: A MEMOIR. By Donald Potter. Kenilworth, Warwickshire: Walter Ritchie. 1980. 500 copies. Ten illustrations.

636.84 BRITISH WOOD ENGRAVING OF THE 20th CENTURY. A PERSONAL VIEW. By Albert Garrett. London: Scolar Press. 1980. E. G. discussed pp. 22–8. Fourteen illustrations.

636.85 STRICT DELIGHT. THE LIFE AND WORK OF ERIC GILL 1882– 1940. Manchester: Whitworth Art Gallery. 1 March – 26 April 1980. Contains chapters on the following: Biography, Lettering, Typography, Graphic Art, Sculpture, Book Design. Thirty-nine illustrations.

1981

636.86 ERIC GILL. MAN OF FLESH & SPIRIT. By Malcolm Yorke. London: Constable. 1981. New York: Universe Books. 1982.

636.87 ERIC GILL. By George Allen. Hove: Chichester Diocesan Fund and Board of Finance. [1981]

636.88 A SEARCH FOR RIGHT RELATIONSHIPS: THE TWENTIETH-CENTURY MEDIEVALISM OF ERIC GILL. By Maureen Corrigan. *English Literature in Transition*, Vol. 24, no. 3, 1981, pp. 117–30.

636.89 BRITISH SCULPTURE IN THE TWENTIETH CENTURY. Edited by Sandy Nairne and Nicholas Serota. London: Whitechapel Art Gallery. 1981. References to E. G. on pp. 10. 20, 63, 77, 91, 92, 95, 97, 101, 103, 254. Illustrations on pp. 20, 68, 78, 92, 93.

636.90 THE GATES OF MEMORY. By Geoffrey Keynes. Oxford: Clarendon Press. 1981. References to E. G. pp. 119–22, 165, 246.

1982

636.91 THE ERIC GILL COLLECTION OF THE HUMANITIES RESEARCH CENTER: A CATALOGUE. Compiled by Robert N. Taylor with the assistance of Helen Parr Young. Humanities Research Center, The University of Texas at Austin [1982]. Issued as a) The Eric Gill Collection Humanities Research Center, The University of Texas at Austin b) The Library Chronicle of the University of Texas at Austin New Series Number 18. Introduction by John Dreyfus. Seventy-two illustrations.

636.92 LIKE BLACK SWANS. SOME PEOPLE AND THEMES. By Brocard Sewell. Padstow, Cornwall: Tabb House. 1982. 500 copies. E. G.'s association with H. D. C. Pepler discussed pp. 131–47.

636.93 THE DOROTHY DAY BOOK. A SELECTION FROM HER WRIT-INGS & READINGS. Edited by Margaret Quigley & Michael Garvey. Springfield, Illinois: Templegate Publishers, 1982. Day quotes E. G. on p. 33 and E. G. quotes are found on pp. 45, 48, 57 and 99.

636.94 LOOKING BACK AT ERIC GILL. By Brian Keeble. *Temenos* 3, [1982] pp. 175–83. A review-article of Malcolm Yorke's *Eric Gill: Man of Flesh and Spirit*. Cf. no. 636.86. One illustration.

636.95 ERIC GILL. STAMP DESIGNER MANQUÉ. By David Rutt. *Typos* 5 (London College of Printing, 1982), pp. 29–32. Illustrated.

636.96 THE ERIC GILL COLLECTION AT CHICHESTER. A CATALOGUE. Second, revised and enlarged edition edited by Timothy J. McCann. Chichester: West Sussex County Council. 1982. Contains 'The Eric Gill Collection at Chichester' by Walter Shewring first published as 'Eric Gill: An introduction to his work' (cf. no. 636.37) and reprinted here with a few alterations. Also 'Eric Gill and Chichester' by John Skelton (cf. no. 636.68) reprinted here with a few alterations. 300 items. 4 pp. of plates.

636.97 LEGIBILITY GILL. ERIC GILL (1882–1940). By Francis Watson. *Country Life*, Vol. CLXXI no. 4409, 18 February 1982, pp. 438–9. Illustrated.

636.98 ERIC GILL: 'FIRST I THINK, THEN I DRAW MY THINK'. By Francis Watson. *The Listener*, Vol. 167, no. 2749, 25 February 1982, pp. 6–7. Illustrated.

636.99 ERIC GILL—ARCHITEKT, BILDHAUER UND SCHRIFT-KÜNSTLER. By R. Herold. *Schweizerische Buchdruckerzeitung*, Vol. 107, no. 10, 11 March 1982, pp. 579–80. Two illustrations.

636.100 ERIC GILL 'MATTER AND SPIRIT'. London: Gillian Jason Gallery. 12 March – 30 April 1982. Introduction by Monica Bohm Duchen. 313 items. Five illustrations.

636.101 ERIC GILL 1882–1940. PRINTS AND DRAWINGS. A CENTENARY TRIBUTE. London: Blond Fine Art. 25 March – 24 April 1982. Introduction by Douglas Cleverdon. 136 items. Forty-four illustrations.

636.102 ERIC GILL 1882–1940. DRAWINGS & CARVINGS. A CENTENARY EXHIBITION. London: Anthony d'Offay. 12 May – 18 June 1982. Introduction by Richard Cork. Fifty-three drawings, thirteen carvings. Twenty illustrations.

636.103 ERIC GILL AND THE ARTIST'S CONNECTION WITH SOCIETY. By William Webb. *Lithoprinter Week*, Vol. 4, no. 24, 16 June 1982, pp. 16–19. Illustrated.

636.104 ERIC GILL: MAN OF SUSSEX. By Michael Renton. *Sussex Life*, Vol. 18, no. 6, June 1982, pp. 40–1. Four illustrations. Survey of E. G.'s life stressing the Sussex connections.

636.105 ERIC GILL CENTENARY ISSUE. *Fine Print: A Review for the arts of the book*, Vol. VIII, no. 3, July 1982. Contains 'On Type – Eric Gill's Perpetua Type' by James Mosley, pp. 90–5 (the article is set in Monotype *Perpetua*) and Gill's *The Artist & Book Production* which is set in Monotype *Joanna*. Alan Fern's review of *A History of the Nonesuch Press* by John Dreyfus, pp. 87–9, has several lengthy references to Gill. A pencil portrait of Sir Francis Meynell is shown on p. 92 and Gill's sketch for (P18), a trial design for the cover of the catalogue for which it was used in 1914, and the cover as issued, are shown on p. 110. The cover depicts the w-e.'s *Tree and Dog* (P733) and *Flames for Tree and Dog* (P733a), the latter printed in red.

636.106 'YOUR AFFECTIONATE SON IN ST DOMINIC ERIC GILL T. S. D.' By Bede Bailey O.P. *New Blackfriars*, Vol. 63, nos. 745/746, July/August 1982, pp. 298–304. Also contains the following: 'Eric Gill and Workers' Control' by Adrian Cunningham pp. 304–11. 'Eric Gill and the Contemporary' by Michael Kelly pp. 311–17.

36.107 ERIC GILL CENTENARY. By Timothy J. McCann. *West Sussex History*, Journal and Newsletter of the West Sussex Archives Society, No. 23, September 1982, pp. 27–9.

36.108 REMINISCENCES OF UNCLE ERIC. By Andrew Bluhm. *Lithoweek*, Vol. 4, no. 41, 13 October 1982, pp. 31–2.

36.109 THE CHESTERTON REVIEW. Ian Boyd, Editor. Vol. VIII, no. 4, November 1982. The whole number is a special Gill issue. The contents are: G. K. Chesterton, 'Eric Gill and No Nonsense', pp. 283–9. The essay first appeared in *The Studio* in 1930 and was reprinted posthumously in *A Handful of Authors* in 1953 (cf. no. 442). Chesterton's monument designed by Gill appears on p. 285. E. G.'s letter to Chesterton dated 26 March 1930, pp. 289–90 in response to the above essay. The letter is number 175 in the *Letters of Eric Gill*, 1947 (no. 54). G. K. Chesterton, 'On Eric Gill', pp. 290–4. The essay first appeared in the *Illustrated London News* on 10 June 1933 and was reprinted in Chesterton's *Avowals and Denials*, London: Methuen Co., 1934 (cf. no. 484a). Brocard Sewell, 'Aspects of Eric Gill, 1882–1940', pp. 295–310. The text was a paper read to the Newman Association at Whitefriars School, Cheltenham, England. There are showings of E. G.'s three principal type-faces, *Perpetua, Joanna* and *Gill Sans* on pp. 311–12. Mary Ellen Evans, 'Man Out of Balance: Some Problems with Gill and the new Gill Biography' pp. 313–20. A review-article of *Eric Gill: Man of Flesh and Spirit* by Malcolm Yorke, 1982. (The author made corrections to this article in Vol. IX, no. 1, February 1983, pp. 71–2.) Sir John Rothenstein, 'Eric Gill: Some Recollections', pp. 321–31. A photograph of an oil portrait painted by William Rothenstein entitled *Eric Gill and the Wife of the Artist* is reproduced on p. 323. It had never been published before and the photograph was provided by Sir John Rothenstein. Several unpublished letters from Gill are printed. There is a photograph on p. 332 of the war memorial at the University of Leeds finished by Gill in 1923. Conrad Pepler, 'In Diebus Illis: Some Memories of Ditchling', pp. 333–52. The essay was first presented as a paper at the Eric Gill centenary celebration held at Spode House, Hawkesyard Priory on Sunday 30 May 1982. There is a review by J. M. Purcell on pp. 353–5 of the reprint of E. G.'s *Beauty Looks after Herself*, 1933 (no. 24), New York: Arno Press. Brocard Sewell, 'Eric Gill: Some recent publications' pp. 356–8. Reviews of *My Time with Eric Gill: A Memoir* by Donald Potter (no. 636.83); *Eric Gill: Man of Flesh and Spirit* by Malcolm Yorke (no. 636.86); *Eric Gill: Further Thoughts by an Apprentice* by David Kindersley (no. 636.47); and *Eric Gill, 1882–1940: Catalogue of the Exhibition at the Anthony d'Offay Gallery* (no. 636.101).

636.110 ERIC GILL, MAN AND MAKER. Report on the Chichester Colloquium held to mark the centenary of Eric Gill. By Roy Brewer. *British Printer*, December 1982, pp. 32–3. Illustrated.

636.111 ERIC GILL AND THE GOLDEN COCKEREL TYPE. By James Mosley. *Matrix* 2, Winter 1982, pp. 17–22 with an insert on p. 16 of E. G.'s design for the *Golden Cockerel* type. This issue also contains 'A Note on the Golden Cockerel Type' by Christopher Sandford on pp. 23–5 with an insert at p. 28 of 'A Type Specimen of the Golden Cockerel Type 1982 with an initial by Gill printed from the wood. Printed at the Rampant Lions Press for Matrix by Sebastian Carter'. (Cf. no. 396*d*.)

636.112 RENÉ HAGUE AND THE PRESS AT PIGOTTS. By Christopher Skelton. *Matrix* 2, Winter 1982, pp. 75–81 with an insert of a Hague & Gill poster.

1983

636.113 THE ENGRAVINGS OF ERIC GILL. Wellingborough: Christopher Skelton. 1983. 545 pp. 1350 copies of an ordinary edition. Eighty-five special copies printed on St Cuthbert's Mill archival rag paper and bound in two volumes, together with a portfolio containing eight prints taken from the original wood-blocks. In the Publisher's Preface it says, 'This present book is largely an illustrated companion to the V&A Catalogue' (cf. no. 636.28). A trade edition entitled *Eric Gill: The Engravings* (minus the Appendices, Douglas Cleverdon's memoir, Sources and Translations of Inscriptions), 480 pp., was published in 1990 by The Herbert Press, London and David R. Godine, Boston. Printed from artwork supplied by Christopher Skelton.

636.114 A HOLY TRADITION OF WORKING. PASSAGES FROM THE WRITINGS OF ERIC GILL. Introductory essay by Brian Keeble. Foreword by Walter Shewring. Ipswich: Golgonooza Press. 1983. West Stockbridge, Massachusetts: Lindisfarne Press, 1983. 139 pp. Selections concerning E. G.'s thoughts on the nature of art, beauty and workmanship.

636.115 STANLEY MORISON AND ERIC GILL, 1925–1933. By Douglas Cleverdon, Privately Printed. 1983. '230 copies of this book were printed for the subscribers and for presentation to Douglas Cleverdon on his eightieth birthday, 17 January 1983. The text is based on a talk given to the Double Crown Club, the Wynkyn de Worde Society, and on several other occasions.' It was also printed in *The Book Collector*, Vol. 32, no. 1, Spring 1983, pp. 23–40.

636.116 IN THE DORIAN MODE. A LIFE OF JOHN GRAY.
By Brocard Sewell. Padstow, Cornwall: Tabb House. 1983. References to
E. G. on pp. ix, 32, 135, 156, 157, 165, 185, 194, 210n.

636.117 A REVIEW OF ERIC GILL'S LIFE AND WORK. By Michael
Renton. *Printing World*, Vol. 209, no. 1, 5 January 1983, pp. 10–12. Six
illustrations.

636.118 GILL, CHESTERTON AND RUSKIN: MEDIAEVALISM
IN THE TWENTIETH CENTURY. By Maureen Corrigan. *The
Chesterton Review*, Vol. IX, no. 1, February 1983, pp. 15–30. Two illus-
trations.

636.119 BRITISH WOOD ENGRAVING OF THE 20's AND 30's.
Catalogue of an exhibition held at Portsmouth City Museum and Art Gallery
7 October – 27 November 1983, Kimberlin Exhibition Hall, Leicester
Polytechnic 9–26 January 1984. References to E. G. in 'British Wood
Engraving: The Heroic Age' by Yvonne Deanne and 'British Wood Engrav-
ing: The "Printer's Flower"' by Joanna Selbourne.

1984

636.120 INNER NECESSITIES. THE LETTERS OF DAVID
JONES TO DESMOND CHUTE. Edited and introduced by Thomas
Dilworth. Toronto: Anson-Cartwright Editions. 1984. References to E. G. on
pp. 12, 25, 34, 51, 86.

636.121 A MAN OF MANY PARTS. By Peter Fuller. *New Society*, Vol. 67,
no. 1103, 12 January 1984, pp. 50–1. Illustrated.

636.122 ERIC GILL AND HIS FAMILY. By George Sims. *Antiquarian Book
Monthly Review*, Vol. XI, no. 5, issue 121, May 1984, pp. 172–7 and no. 6,
issue 122, June 1984, pp. 216–21. There are a number of illustrations and the
cover for the May issue features *The Plait* (P195) a portrait of Petra, E. G.'s
daughter. The author's book, *The Rare Book Game*, Philadelphia: Holmes
Publishing Co., 1985 contains the same material in Chapter 12, pp. 147–61,
also entitled 'Eric Gill and his family'. Describes visits to Pigotts and recounts
the purchase of E. G. material for sale to the William Andrews Clark Memorial
Library.

636.123 TYPOGRAPHIC MILESTONES—ERIC GILL. By Allan Haley.
Upper and Lower Case, The International Journal of Typographics, Vol. 11,

no. 3, November 1984, pp. 16–19. Illustrations from *The Letter Forms and Type Designs of Eric Gill* (cf. no. 636.70).

636.124 ERIC GILL: MAN OF FLESH & SPIRIT. Review-article by Karla Huebner. *Yellow Silk*, Issue 13, Winter 1984, pp. 7–9. Issue illustrated throughout with w-e.'s and original erotic drawings by E. G. E. G.'s work mentioned in the editorial by Lily Pond, p. 4. The entire issue set in *Gill Sans*. Although it is not so stated, most of the original drawings are at the Harry Ransom Humanities Research Center, University of Texas, Austin, and copies of most of the wood-engravings that were used in the issue were found in the Gleeson Library, University of San Francisco.

636.125 THE MAKING OF THE ENGRAVINGS OF ERIC GILL. By Christopher Skelton. *Matrix* 4, Winter 1984, pp. 93–9. Page 97 is blank and is used as the place to tip in a page from *The Engravings of Eric Gill*.

636.126 ST. DOMINIC'S PRESS: A SUPPLEMENT TO THE 1979 CHECK-LIST. By Brocard Sewell. *Matrix* 4, Winter 1984, pp. 135–44. Gill is referred to throughout the text. (Cf. no. 636.76.)

1985
636.127 ERIC GILL: A CONTINUING INFLUENCE. By David Peace. *Churchscape*, No. 4, 1985, pp. 30–6. Three illustrations. Discussion of E. G.'s inscriptional work.

1986
636.128 THE ENGRAVED BOOKPLATES OF ERIC GILL 1908–1940. Compiled by Christopher Skelton with an introduction by Michael Renton and an afterword by Albert Sperisen. Private Libraries Association. San Francisco: The Book Club of California. 1986. A collection of reproductions of all fifty-three bookplates in their actual size. $8\frac{3}{4} \times 6$. 79 numbered pages. Printed in black and red in Linotype *Joanna* at the September Press, Wellingborough. Red cloth, title stamped in gold on spine. Reddish-grey dust jacket printed in black and red. Shows bookplate for Austen St Barbe Harrison (P887) in black on front. 1000 copies, 600 for The Book Club of California, 400 for The Private Libraries Association, England.

636.129 SCULPTURE IN BRITAIN BETWEEN THE WARS. By Benedict Read and Peyton Skipwith. London: The Fine Art Society. 1986. Catalogue of an exhibition 10 June – 1 August 1986. References to E. G.

on pp. 6, 7, 8–9, 10, 12, 13, 18, 19, 21, 50, 76. Fourteen illustrations. Ten items.

636.130 LESSONS IN FORMAL WRITING. By Edward Johnston. Edited by Heather Child and Justin Howes. London: Lund Humphries. 1986. Reference to E. G. pp. 11, 31, 50, 54, 74, 81, 87, 88, 107, 109–12, 204, 231. The five plates done by E. G. for Johnston's *Manuscript & Inscription Letters* (London, 1909) are illustrated pp. 124–8.

636.131 EYE FOR INDUSTRY: ROYAL DESIGNERS FOR IN-DUSTRY 1936–1986. By Fiona MacCarthy and Patrick Nuttgens. London: Lund Humphries in association with The Royal Society of Arts. 1986. Published on the occasion of the exhibition 'Eye for Industry' held at the Victoria & Albert Museum, London 26 November 1986 – 1 February 1987. Mentions E. G., one of the first of R D I s, on pp. 17, 18, 29, 75.

1987

636.132 A BOOK OF ALPHABETS FOR DOUGLAS CLEVERDON DRAWN BY ERIC GILL. With a foreword by Douglas Cleverdon and an introduction by John Dreyfus. Wellingborough: Christopher Skelton at the September Press. 1987. Limited edition of 550 copies. A reproduction of the alphabets drawn by E. G. in October 1926 in a Nonesuch Blank Book.

636.133 TWENTIETH CENTURY TYPE DESIGNERS. By Sebastian Carter. London: Trefoil Publications Ltd. 1987. E. G.'s work is discussed pp. 72–81 and referred to elsewhere throughout the book.

1988

636.134 HERBERT READ'S *ART AND INDUSTRY:* A HISTORY. By Robin Kinross. Journal of Design History Vol. 1, no. 1. 1988, pp. 35–50. Discusses Read's and E. G.'s views on art and industry.

1989

636.135 ERIC GILL. By Fiona MacCarthy. London: Faber and Faber Limited. 1989. New York: E. P. Dutton. 1989. 338 pp. with 129 plates and fifty-eight illustrations in the text. Paperback edition – London: Faber and Faber Limited. 1990. 338 pp. with the same illustrations as in the hardback edition.

636.136 THE PRIVATE WORLD OF ERIC GILL. By Fiona MacCarthy. *The Independent* Magazine, 21 January 1989, pp. 38–41. Article by author of the Gill biography (no. 636.135) concentrating on the new revelations about his sexual habits. In *The Independent* Magazine, 4 February 1989, p. 7 Elizabeth Roots (E. G.'s niece) and Christopher Skelton (nephew) complained 'against the tone and substance of Fiona MacCarthy's article'. In *The Sunday Times* (Books G4), 5 February 1989, Fiona MacCarthy responded to criticism of her revelations. Also discussed by Elizabeth Grice in *The Sunday Times*, 5 March 1989.

1990

636.137 A TYPOGRAPHICAL MASTERPIECE AN ACCOUNT BY JOHN DREYFUS OF ERIC GILL'S COLLABORATION WITH ROBERT GIBBINGS IN PRODUCING THE GOLDEN COCKEREL PRESS EDITION OF 'THE FOUR GOSPELS' IN 1931. San Francisco: The Book Club of California. 1990. 105 pp. Illustrated. 450 copies.

V

MISCELLANEA

Numbers 636.138 – 664.40

1924

36.138 SOCIETY OF WOOD ENGRAVERS EXHIBITION. London:
St George's Gallery. December 1924. Eight works by E. G. are listed. CLC
has Gill's own annotated copy, recording how many copies were sold of his
wood-engravings.

1926

637 SAPPHO. Two fragments, in Greek capitals, written into a copy of the
Bremer Press *Sappho* for Walter Shewring. This copy, which also contains a
letter from E. G. to Mr Shewring, dated from Capel-y-ffin, 8 November 1926,
is now in the Bodleian Library (Ref. 29361 d. 14). The following is a copy of
the letter:
'Dear Shewring: Herewith I return your Sappho; I hope I have done what
you wished with it. I do not profess to be able to write with a pen. I took it
that you wanted the words just written in and I have done it straight off as
naturally as possible. P'raps I ought to have done it bigger and with a
narrower pen. I didn't leave spaces between the words. I think inscriptions
all in caps shouldn't descend to trivialities of that sort. Yours sincerely,
Eric G. t.s.d.'
Cf. *Letters of Eric Gill*, p. 225, and illustrations on the opposite page for
evidence of E. G.'s interest in the Greek alphabet.

638 THE STATIONS OF THE CROSS. Two sets of post-cards
numbered 1–7 and 8–14, being collotype reproductions after the original
sculptures in Westminster Cathedral. London: The Medici Society, Ltd.
August 1926. 1*s*. each set. These reproductions were re-issued as one set of
post-cards by the same publishers in 1951. 2*s*. 6*d*. the set.

1927

639 PICTURE POST CARDS. In their *Spring List*, 1927, the Golden
Cockerel Press announced a series of picture post-cards printed from the
various engravings in their publications. In two sets of twelve cards each, price
2*s*. each set. Cards with wood-engravings by E. G. were as follows: Series A:
no. 3 *Young Fawn* (P333). Series B: no. 13 *The Kiss of Judas* (P351), no. 15
Mary Magdalen (P349), no. 18 *My Love among the Lilies* (P327) and no. 21
Let us fare forth into the fields (P330).

1928

640 FRY, J. S. & SONS. THE ROYAL MINT. Fifty-eighth Annual Report of the Deputy Master and Comptroller of the Royal Mint, 1927. Reference is here made to the designs E. G. submitted for a medal to be produced for J. S. Fry & Sons in celebration of their bicentenary. E. G.'s design is illustrated in *Artwork*, no. 10, Summer 1929.

641 ERIC GILL. *The London Mercury*, Vol. XVIII, no. 107, September 1928, p. 459. A pen and ink drawing of E. G. by Powys Evans.

1929

642 THE BRITISH MUSEUM. A CATALOGUE OF AN EXHIBITION OF BOOKS ILLUSTRATING BRITISH AND FOREIGN PRINTING, 1919– 1929. London: British Museum. The following were exhibited in the British Section: no. 22 *The Future of Sculpture*, no. 52 *Passio Domini* and no. 53 *Canterbury Tales*. A page from *Passio Domini* showing w-e. *The Carrying of the Cross* (P352) is reproduced on p. 19. 10 × 7$\frac{1}{2}$. Pp. 60. Price: 2s. 6d.

1930

643 JOANNA TYPE. *This Publishing Business*. London: Sheed & Ward. Vol. III, no. 3, December [1930] contains a specimen of the *JOANNA* type designed by E. G. (p. 19) to which reference is made on p. 11. Cf. *A Specimen of Three Book Types* (no. 30).

644 NOTICES OF BOOKS TO BE PRINTED BY RENÉ HAGUE AND ERIC GILL At Pigotts, near Hughenden, Buckinghamshire. No. 1, January 1931. A prospectus of *TYPOGRAPHY* AN ESSAY BY ERIC GILL. On front cover is the w-e. *Letters: E. R.* (P723). 7$\frac{1}{2}$× 5. Pp. 16. 1s. Printing: 300 copies. 29 December 1930. The type (12 pt. *Joanna*) and paper are the same as used for the book. A leaflet of four pages bearing the same title as above, also described as 'No. 1' but dated April, 1931, was issued by Sheed & Ward. This is likewise mainly a prospectus of *TYPOGRAPHY* but carries some notes entitled *The Press at Pigotts*. (Cf. nos. 648 and 655.)

644a ENFANTS TERRIBLES. By Jean Cocteau. New York: Brewer & Warren Inc. 1930. Note [p. 177]: 'This book has been set in twelve point . . . Gill Sans-serif, designed by Eric Gill for the Lanston Monotype Corporation of London and specially imported by the Plimpton Press. As far as the publishers are aware, this is the first time in America that this type has been used completely throughout a book.'

1931

645 GOLDEN COCKEREL TYPE. The first book to be printed from this type (14 pt.) was *The Hundredth Story of A. E. Coppard*. The Golden Cockerel Press. January 1931. $9\frac{1}{2} \times 6$. Pp. 58. One guinea. No. 74 of the Golden Cockerel Press publications.

646 PERPETUA TYPE. *The Monotype Recorder*, Vol. XXX, no. 241, 1931. This number is printed from *Monotype Perpetua roman* which type is described on inside of front cover. Cf. no. 480, *The Monotype Recorder*, Vol. XXXII, no. 1, Spring 1933.

1932

647 VICTORIA & ALBERT MUSEUM. Review of the principal acquisitions during the year 1931. London: Published under the Authority of the Board of Education. 1932. 2*s*. 6*d*. Mention is made (p. 6) of three panels of lettering in Hoptonwood stone carved by E. G. in 1909 and presented by him. Fig. 1, p. 1, shows two of these panels.

648 NOTICES OF BOOKS printed by René Hague & Eric Gill at Pigotts, near Hughenden, Buckinghamshire. No. 2, May 1932. An eight-page prospectus of *Bishop Blougram's Apology* by Robert Browning with a copperplate by Denis Tegetmeier. $5\frac{3}{4} \times 4$. (Cf. nos. 644 and 655.)

649 PERPETUA CAPITALS. *The Times*, 27 September 1932. Speaking of the change over to *Times New Roman* designed for the newspaper by Stanley Morison: 'Only two elements in the old material have survived. The 'Perpetua' capitals, cut from a design by Mr Eric Gill and adopted from December 28, 1929, for the main heading of the picture page, could not be surpassed.' The other 'element' is the clock above the Contents column.

650 THE MOUNTAINEERING JOURNAL. Vol. 1, no. 2, December 1932. Birkenhead: Carl K. Brunning, 62–68 Chester Street. The text of this magazine is printed throughout from *Gill Sans-Serif* concerning which type there is an editorial note on p. 82. $9\frac{3}{4} \times 7\frac{1}{2}$. 2*s*. 6*d*.

650*a* NOTICES OF BOOKS printed by René Hague and Eric Gill at Pigotts, near Hughenden, Buckinghamshire. No. 3, May 1932. A four-page frenchfold prospectus of *Park a fantastic story* by John Gray with a copperplate by Denis Tegetmeier. $7\frac{1}{2} \times 5$. (Cf. nos. 644, 648 and 655.)

1933

651 THE ROYAL SOCIETY MOND LABORATORY, CAM-
BRIDGE. A brochure with nine illustrations and a sketch-plan published on
the occasion of the opening of the Laboratory, 3 May 1933. One of the
illustrations is of the stone-carving of a crocodile by E. G. See *The Manchester
Guardian*, 3 February 1933, for description and photographs of the building.
See also 'Peter Kapitza, Soviet Scientist' by Ritchie Calder in *Compass*, no. 2,
1946, p. 1067.

1934

652 BRISTOL MUSEUM AND ART GALLERY. Report for the year
ending 31 December 1933. Reference is made (p. 6) to an exhibition of the
work of E. G., including sculpture, books, lettering, wood-engraving and
book illustration with a photograph of the exhibition—Plate 4 (facing p. 28).

652*a* A CATALOGUE OF CHINESE POTTERY AND PORCE-
LAIN IN THE COLLECTION OF SIR PERCIVAL DAVID,
BT., F.S.A. By R. L. Hobson, C.B. Westminster: Stourton Press. 1934.
16 × 12. Decorated blue Chinese silk boards. In no. 636.55 Fairfax Hall states
that there were: '650 copies on Aries paper, of which about 300 were sold
before the war at £12 12*s*., and the remainder after the war at £14 14*s*.; 30
copies on Imperial Japanese paper, signed by the author, sold on publication at
£31 10*s*.', p. 61. 'This [the *David Catalogue*] was dated 1934 but was not issued
until 1935', p. 57. 'David made a generous arrangement. He paid for Eric
Gill's designs, and for the punches, matrices, and the casting of the types,
giving them all to me provided the "Aries" types were used for the first time in
his catalogue', p. 58.

652*b* HERO AND LEANDER. By Christopher Marlowe. Westminster:
Stourton Press. 1934. The fourth book of the press, as listed by the proprietor,
Fairfax Hall, in no. 636.55, but apparently the first use of Aries type (p. 58):
'*Hero & Leander*, was rightly criticized by Hornby and Eric Gill for its heavy
three-line initials, so that I only gave away a few copies and put off selling the
rest until 26 years later' – 100 to Quaritch in October 1961 at 10*s*. each.

1936

653 REPRODUCTIONS OF LETTERING BY ERIC GILL.
Victoria and Albert Museum, South Kensington. (See 'List of Publications'
issued under the Authority of the Board of Education.) These reproductions
are in sheet form ($22\frac{1}{2} \times 15$) and comprise:

    1. *Panel of Hoptonwood stone, carved with Roman capitals.*

2. *Panel of Hoptonwood stone, carved with alphabets and numerals.*
3. *Panel of Hoptonwood stone, carved with words from Saint Thomas Aquinas.*
4. *Wooden panel, painted with words from Saint Thomas Aquinas (French and English translations).*

Price (1936) 6*d.* each or 2*s.* the set.

1937

654 THE BIBLE DESIGNED TO BE READ AS LITERATURE. Edited and Arranged by Ernest Sutherland Bates. London: William Heinemann, Limited. 1937 [Dec.] The type face used throughout is *Perpetua* which is referred to in 'A Note on the Production of this Book' on p. [1238] (Cf. no. 540 *The Art of the Book*, p. 45.)

654*a* PERPETUA LIGHT TITLING. COMMENTS ON THE TYPE WITH ALPHABET AND FIGURES. By S.G.R. *Typography* 4, Autumn 1937, p. 27 (Type Supplement).

1938

655 HAGUE & GILL LTD. A FIRST LIST OF BOOKS, 1938. London: J. M. Dent & Sons, Ltd. A pamphlet, printed by Hague & Gill, Ltd., of books published for them by J. M. Dent & Sons, Ltd. and of books printed by them and published for them by other publishers. $6\frac{1}{2} \times 4$. Pp. 16. (Cf. nos. 644 and 648.)

656 TYPE DESIGNED BY ERIC GILL and printed by Hague & Gill, Ltd., High Wycombe. A type specimen book showing: *Perpetua, Perpetua Titling, Perpetua Bold, Solus, Jubilee, Gill Sans, Gill Sans Titling, Bunyan, Joanna, Gill Sans Bold, Gill Woodletter* and *Gill Bold Condensed.* $11\frac{1}{2} \times 8\frac{3}{4}$. Pp. 12. n.d. [*c.* 1938] (Cf. no. 657.)

657 BOOKS. SPECIMEN PAGES FROM BOOKS PRINTED BY HAGUE & GILL LTD., HIGH WYCOMBE. All the books shown, with one exception, were printed in types designed by E. G. The pages shown are from the following books: *In Parenthesis*, by David Jones (13 pt. and 11 pt. *Perpetua*), *A Sentimental Journey Through France & Italy*, by Laurence Sterne (14 pt. *Bunyan*), *The Aldine New Testament* (12 pt. *Joanna*), *Greek and Latin Versions*, by Walter Shewring (12 pt. *Joanna* and 12 pt. *New Hellenic*), *The Minute Book of the Monthly Meeting of the Society of Friends for the Upperside of Buckinghamshire*, 1669–1690 (13 pt. *Perpetua*), *Work and Property*, by Eric Gill (12 pt. *Joanna*), *The Song of Roland* (12 pt. *Joanna*), *Charister*, by Violet Clifton (12

pt. *Bembo*), *The Holy Sonnets of* John Donne (14 pt. *Bunyan*), *Poems*, by Ann Lyon (12 pt. *Joanna*), *The Lessons and Gospels for the Season of Lent* (11 pt. and 12 pt. *Joanna*), *Park*, by John Gray (12 pt. *Joanna italic*) and *Hoelderlin's Madness*, by David Gascoyne (12 pt. *Joanna*). $9\frac{3}{4} \times 12\frac{1}{4}$. Pp. 30 (unpaginated). n.d. [*c.* 1938] Spiral wire binding. The colophon (p. [29]) shows w-e. *Three-leaved clover* (P897). (Cf. no. 656.)

657*a* ENGLISH PRESENT-DAY CALLIGRAPHY & ILLU- MINATION. AN EXHIBITION LENT BY THE SOCIETY OF SCRIBES AND ILLUMINATORS OF LONDON. New York: American Institute of Graphic Arts, February 2 to 26, 1938. 12 pp. pamphlet, stapled. Under 'Engravings on Wood & on Copper' E. G. is listed at number 108, described as Title Page, *Hamlet*; at number 109, described as Title Page, *Troilus and Cressida*; and at number 110, described as Title Page, *Henry VIII*. Under 'Inscriptions in Wood & Stone', E. G. is listed at number 119 which is described as Alphabet in Light Hopton Wood Stone.

657*b* TYPE SUPPLEMENT. Gill Sans Medium Condensed and Gill Bold Extra Condensed. *Typography*, No. 5, Spring 1938, p. 44.

1940
658 THE ERIC GILL WORKSHOPS. Pigotts, North Dean, High Wycombe. A Statement by Gordian Gill and others, dated 5 December 1940, expressing their intention to carry on the spirit and tradition of E. G.'s work at Pigotts. The w-e. *S. Thomas' hands* (P889) is printed on front cover.

1948
659 OPEN AIR EXHIBITION OF SCULPTURE. At Battersea Park, May–September 1948. Organized by the London County Council in associa- tion with the Arts Council of Great Britain. E. G.'s *Mankind*, a photograph of which appears on p. 27, is no. 11 in the list of sculpture shown. $8\frac{1}{2} \times 5\frac{1}{2}$. Pp. 12. 6*d*. (Cf. no. 661.)

659*a* GILL SANS IN USE. By Edward Paxton. *Advertising and Marketing Review*, July 1949, pp. 36–8. With six illustrations.

1951

660 BOOKS OF OUR TIMES. 100 CHOSEN TO ILLUSTRATE THE
RENASCENCE OF BOOK DESIGN IN GREAT BRITAIN & 100 CHOSEN TO
EXPRESS THE CONTEMPORARY BRITISH ACHIEVEMENT IN LITERA-
TURE. London: The British Council in association with the National Book
League. This is the catalogue of an exhibition which was shown in Canada
under the auspices of the British Council. The selectors of the first group were
Sir Francis Meynell and Desmond Flower; of the second group, V. S.
Pritchett, Rose Macaulay and C. Day Lewis. The following books by, or
illustrated by, E. G. were shown: no. 20 *Troilus and Criseyde* (Golden Cockerel
Press), no. 27 *Art Nonsense* and no. 33 *The Four Gospels* (Golden Cockerel
Press). The description of each book is accompanied by a comment which, in
the items here mentioned, was by Sir Francis Meynell. Reference to E. G. is
also made in the comments upon the following items: nos. 12, 39, 48, 73, 74,
78 and 86. $7\frac{1}{4} \times 4\frac{1}{4}$. Pp. 100. n.p. n.d. [1951]

661 SCULPTURE. An open-air exhibition organized by the London County
Council in association with the Arts Council of Great Britain at Battersea Park,
May to September 1951. This catalogue is accompanied by a Foreword by
Ruth Dalton and 'The Sculptor's Problems' by Nikolaus Pevsner. Exhibit no.
16 was E. G.'s *The Deposition* carved in Black Hoptonwood Stone in 1925
(Plate 5 in the catalogue). There is a reference to this in Prof. Pevsner's survey.
$8\frac{1}{2} \times 5\frac{1}{2}$. Pp. 16. 6*d.* Post-card photographs of this sculpture were also on sale at
the exhibition. (Cf. no. 659.)

662 THE FESTIVAL OF BRITAIN—EXHIBITION OF
BOOKS. Catalogue of the exhibition arranged by the National Book League
at the Victoria and Albert Museum, 5 May to 30 September 1951. London:
Published for the National Book League by the Cambridge University Press.
This catalogue was compiled by John Hadfield. Each entry is accompanied by
a descriptive note. Exhibit 20 was *The Four Gospels* (Golden Cockerel Press),
with decorations by E. G. No. 771 was his *Autobiography*. $8\frac{1}{2} \times 5\frac{1}{2}$. Pp. 224.
1*s.* 6*d.* Review: 'Books and the Festival', *The Times Literary Supplement*,
11 May 1951.

663 A TRIBUTE TO THE PIONEERS OF THE WRITTEN
WORD. London: G. S. Royds, Ltd. 160 Piccadilly. A folder showing a
carved mural sculpture representing twenty men 'who, in the past 500 years,
have helped to shape the history of the printed word'. The carving, by Arthur
Cousins, is in Austrian oak and measures 5 ft. by 7 ft. It was exhibited at the
International Advertising Convention, Central Hall, Westminster, 7–14 July
1951. The folder also contains an Introduction to the carving and brief

biographical sketches of those depicted, of whom E. G. is one.

664 LE LIVRE ANGLAIS. TRÉSORS DES COLLECTIONS ANGLAISES. Paris: Bibliothèque Nationale. 1951. Catalogue of the Exhibition of English Books held in the Galerie Mazarine of the Bibliothèque Nationale in Paris, November–December 1951. Preface by M. Julien Cain, administrateur général de la Bibliothèque nationale. Avant-propos by F. C. Francis, Conservateur des Imprimés, British Museum. Exhibit 364; Chaucer's *Troilus and Criseyde* with wood-engravings by E. G. (Golden Cockerel Press, 1927). Exhibit 365: 'Un des blocs de bois gravés pour le *Chaucer* exposé sous le n° 364.' With a note concerning the Golden Cockerel Press and E. G.'s connexion with it.

664.1 LETTERING. A SOURCE BOOK OF ROMAN ALPHABETS. By John C. Tarr. London: Crosby Lockwood & Son, Ltd. 1951. Page 7 shows *Gill Sans Light* in an upper-case alphabet and numbers and a lower-case alphabet. Page 8 displays *Gill Sans Medium* similarly and page 10, *Gill Sans Italic*. Pages 26 and 27 show Roman capitals, lower-case and italic letters cut in stone by E. G.

1952
664.2 THE HOLY PLACES. By Evelyn Waugh with wood-engravings by Reynolds Stone. London: The Queen Anne Press. 1952. 950 copies. The first book to be set in Linotype *Pilgrim*.

1953
664.3 LINOTYPE 'PILGRIM'. By Peter Mytton-Davies. *Caxton Magazine*, Vol. 55, no. 3, March 1953, pp. 22–4.

664.4 PILGRIM. AN ADDITION TO THE RANGE OF LINOTYPE FACES FOR TEXT COMPOSITION. *The British Printer*, March/April 1953, pp. 48–9.

664.5 LINOTYPE'S PROGRESS WITH PILGRIM. By Stuart Rose. *Society of Industrial Artists Journal*, No. 32, April 1953, p. 13.

664.6 LINOTYPE'S NEW FACE PILGRIM, A RECUTTING OF A FACE DESIGNED BY ERIC GILL. *Print in Britain*, Vol. 1, no. 1, May 1953, p. 7.

664.7 TYPOGRAPHY FOR SCREEN PRINTERS. GETTING TO KNOW A FACE—GILL SANS. By Peter Mytton-Davies. *International Screen Printer and Display Producer*, Vol. 3, no. 3, May 1953, pp. 10–13. Illustrated.

664.8 THE INTRODUCTION OF LINOTYPE PILGRIM IS RE-GARDED AS AN IMPORTANT TYPOGRAPHIC EVENT. *Linotype Matrix*, 16 June 1953, p. 2. Eight photographs of those attending a reception to introduce 'Pilgrim'.

664.9 TYPOGRAPHY FOR SCREEN PRINTERS. GETTING TO KNOW A FACE—PERPETUA. By Peter Mytton-Davies. *International Screen Printer and Display Producer*, Vol. 3, no. 6, August 1953, pp. 9–11. Illustrated.

664.10 A STONE-CARVING, ORIGINAL WOOD-BLOCKS, ENGRAVINGS AND AUTOGRAPH LETTERS FROM VARIOUS SOURCES INCLUDING THE COLLECTION FORMED BY MR DOUGLAS CLEVERDON. Catalogue 131. Elkin Mathews Limited, Takeley, Bishop's Stortford [1953?].

1954

664.11 ABOUT PERPETUA. *Print in Britain*, Vol. 2, no. 3, July 1954, p. 91 plus 4 pp. specimen sheet between pp. 80–1.

1957

664.12 ERIC GILL'S FIRST SANSERIF. *The Jobbing Printer*, Vol. 9, no. 1, January 1957, p. 24.

1958

664.13 THE STORY OF JOANNA. By James Moran. *Book Design and Production*, Vol. 1, no. 3, Autumn 1958, pp. 24–9. Five illustrations.

664.14 JOANNA: A NEWLY RELEASED MONOTYPE TEXT SERIES DESIGNED BY ERIC GILL. *The British Printer*, Vol. LXXI, no. 12, December 1958, pp. 68–9.

1963

664.15 ERIC GILL: A CATALOGUE OF MANUSCRIPTS, BOOKS, ENGRAVINGS, DRAWINGS AND SCULPTURE IN THE COLLECTION OF MR AND MRS S. SAMUELS. Roger Smith. Liverpool. 1963.

1966

664.16 GILL AND THE GOSPELS. By 'Peterborough'. *The Daily Telegraph*, May 23 1966. Mentions sale of E. G. material by bookseller G. F. Sims.

1967

664.17 THE ERIC GILL MEMORIAL COLLECTION. A CATA-LOGUE. Edited by Noel H. Osborne. Chichester Papers No. 51. Issued by the West Sussex County Council. [1967]

1971

664.18 BRITISH MODERN PRESS BOOKS, A DESCRIPTIVE CHECK LIST OF UNRECORDED ITEMS. By William Ridler. London: Covent Garden Press. 1971. Pp. 139–41 list Hague & Gill items. New and revised edition Folkestone: William Dawson and Sons Ltd., 1975. (Cf. no. 54*a*.)

1974

664.19 ERIC GILL 1882–1940. ENGRAVINGS AND DRAWINGS. Mercury Gallery, London, 8 May – 4 June 1974. 105 engravings (three illustrated) and seventeen drawings (three illustrated).

1976

664.20 ERIC GILL. Broadside with a wood-engraving of E. G. by Barry Moser and a quotation from E. G. on 'the advantage of wood engraving'. Published in an edition of 200 by J. P. Dwyer, Northampton, Massachusetts, 1976. Also an edition of fifty of just the portrait signed by Jack Coughlin who placed the drawing on the wood-engraving block and Barry Moser who engraved the block.

664.21 A TRIBUTE TO ERIC GILL. Betty Clark, Studio One Gallery, Oxford. 22–30 November 1976. Seventy engravings and drawings, twenty-one additional exhibits.

664.22 AN EXHIBITION OF THE WORK OF THREE PRIVATE PRESSES. Devised and presented by Brocard Sewell. National Book League 14 July – 4 August 1976. The presses were Saint Dominic's, Ditchling; Edward Walters, Primrose Hill; Saint Albert's Press, Aylesford.

664.23 THREE PRIVATE PRESSES. SAINT DOMINIC'S PRESS, THE PRESS OF EDWARD WALTERS, SAINT ALBERT'S PRESS. By Brocard Sewell. Wellingborough, Northamptonshire: Christopher Skelton. 1979. An enlarged and illustrated version of the booklet produced to accompany the exhibition for the 1976 exhibition of the work of these presses held at the National Book League in London. $10\frac{1}{4} \times 7\frac{1}{4}$. 54 numbered pages. Printed in black and red in Monotype Baskerville by Skelton's Press, Wellingborough on St Cuthbert's Mill mould-made paper. Decorated $\frac{3}{4}$ paper-covered boards on front, spine and back cover in green buckram. Title stamped in gold on spine and on front. Thin plain plastic jacket. Decorated red endpapers. Pocket inside lower cover contains a folded $18 \times 7\frac{1}{2}$ reproduction of a poster for the 98th annual Ditchling Horticultural Show, 28 July 1920, printed originally at the S. Dominic's Press. 250 numbered copies signed by the author. Saint Dominic's Press chapter is on pp. 11–29. Gill is mentioned throughout and four pages of *Autumn Midnight* (no. 273) are reproduced.

1978
664.24 THE ILLUSTRATORS OF THE GOLDEN COCKEREL PRESS. Foreword by Christopher Sandford. Catalogue of exhibition, at Studio One Gallery, Betty Clark, Oxford, 9–21 October 1978.

1979
664.25 ERIC GILL 1882–1940. DRAWINGS & SOME OTHER WORKS. London: The Piccadilly Gallery. 15 March – 21 April 1979. Sixty-seven items with eight illustrated.

664.26 LANDMARK IN THE SUCCESS OF GILL SANS. *The Monotype Recorder*, New Series, No. 1, December 1979, p. 16. May 1978 marked the Golden Jubilee of Monotype *Gill Sans* appearing on the printing scene and the range is listed here.

1980
664.27 ERIC GILL EARLY WORK. Catalogue of exhibition at Manor Gallery, Wimbish Manor, Shepreth, Royston, Herts, 30 March – 26 April 1980.

664.28 POETRY MAGAZINE: A GALLERY OF VOICES. Catalogue of an exhibition from the Harriet Monroe Poetry Collection at the Joseph Regenstein Library, University of Chicago, May–October 1980. $8\frac{1}{4} \times 5\frac{1}{2}$. Pp. 94 (unnumbered). On p. 94 is the note: 'The typeface of this catalogue is

Gill Sans, chosen because of Eric Gill's association with the magazine.' Gill had specified that *Gill Sans* should be used with the *Pegasus* (P727a) he had designed for the cover of *Poetry*. (Cf. no. 345.)

1981

664.29 SOTHEBY'S SALE 9 November 1981. Catalogue of books, manuscripts, prints and drawings by Eric Gill, David Jones and their associates. The property of the late Joan and René Hague. The property of Mrs. A. M. Stanley. Collections of books printed at the St. Dominic's Press, 1916–33, and by Hague and Gill, 1930–48; drawings, sketches, and wood-engravings by Eric Gill. 214 E. G. items.

1982

664.30 THE FINE-PRINTING COLLECTION: AN OVERVIEW AND A GLANCE AHEAD. By John Bidwell. *The Clark Newsletter*, No. 2. William Andrews Clark Memorial Library, Los Angeles, 1982, p. 6 describes the E. G. collection.

664.31 ERIC GILL: 1882–1940. A handlist of an exhibition at Cambridge University Library. March–May 1982. 166 items mostly from the Library.

664.32 PRINTED BY HAGUE AND GILL. A Checklist prepared in conjunction with the exhibit 'A Responsible Workman' observing Eric Gill's centenary at UCLA Library 26 April – 16 July 1982. Compiled by Jim Davis. [Los Angeles]: Regents of the University of California. 1982.

664.33 ERIC GILL 1882–1940 DRAWINGS OF THE NUDE. London: The Piccadilly Gallery [8 June – 3 July 1982]. Thirty-five items including seven drawings from E. G.'s sketchbook, Paris, May 1926. One illustration.

664.34 ERIC GILL 1882–1940. Centenary Exhibition. Chichester: Pallant House Gallery. 4 September – 30 October 1982. 120 items. Four illustrations.

664.35 ERIC GILL 1882–1940. A centenary exhibition of drawings and designs at the David Paul Gallery, Chichester, 6 September – 3 October 1982.

664.36 TONY APPLETON CATALOGUE 34. Brighton. [1982] Anti-quarian bookseller's catalogue. E. G. is the subject of the first ninety-eight items, of a total of 150 items in the catalogue. Eighteen of E. G.'s wood-engravings are reproduced in the catalogue and additional examples are shown on the front and back wrappers of the catalogue.

1983

664.37 A FORAGER IN THE GILL COLLECTION. By Christopher Skelton. *The Clark Newsletter*, No. 5, pp. 4–5. Los Angeles: William Andrews Clark Memorial Library. 1983. Discusses working with the E. G. collection to gather material for his book *The Engravings of Eric Gill* (cf. no. 636.113).

1984

664.38 HAROLD BERLINER'S TYPEFOUNDRY. Special Casting, Eric Gill issue, Summer 1984. Harold Berliner's Typefoundry, 224 Main Street, Nevada City, CA 95959. [8 pp.] red wrappers.

1985

664.39 RARE PROOFS AND UNUSUAL PRINTS. Catalogue of N. W. Lott & H. J. Gerrish Ltd. The Old Rectory, Froxfield, Marlborough. [1985] pp. 18–22. The reference nos. are P137, P294, P411, P576 and P878 and are all illustrated.

1986

664.40 PENCIL PEN & BRUSH. MODERN BRITISH DRAWING. London: Gillian Jason Gallery. 10 January – 14 February 1986. Five E. G. items of which four are illustrated.

VI

POSTERS AND RELATED ITEMS
ILLUSTRATED BY ERIC GILL

Numbers 664.41–664.49

CHRISTMAS GIFTS

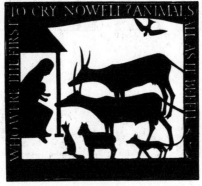

ENGRAVINGS & BOOKS
AT THE
DRYAD SHOWROOM
S. NICHOLAS St. DAILY 10 to 5. [664.42]

1918

664.41 EXHIBITION OF WOOD ENGRAVINGS BY ERIC GILL AT THE GOUPIL GALLERY. Quad crown. Text in black and red. Shows *Animals All* (P51). Sewell, p. 39.

664.42 CHRISTMAS GIFTS. Reproduced. Shows *Animals All* (P51). $29\frac{1}{2} \times 22\frac{1}{2}$. Printed in black and red on hand-made paper. Imprint: Printed by Douglas Pepler at Ditchling Sussex A.D. MCMXVIII.

664.43 THE FORTY HOURS PRAYER. Shows lettering by E. G. (P146a – Skelton). Done for the Diocese of Westminster. Sewell, p. 38: 'Quad crown. A two-column list of churches where the devotion was to be held, with the relevant dates. The arms of the Cardinal Archbishop, Dr. Francis Bourne, at the top, in red and black, from a wood-engraving by Eric Gill. This poster, which was displayed in the porch of all churches in the diocese, was reprinted, with the necessary adjustments, each year, down to 1936 or thereabouts. There is no copy in the Westminster Cathedral archives. Shown at the Three Private Presses exhibit held at the National Book League, summer 1976 [no. 664.22]'.

331

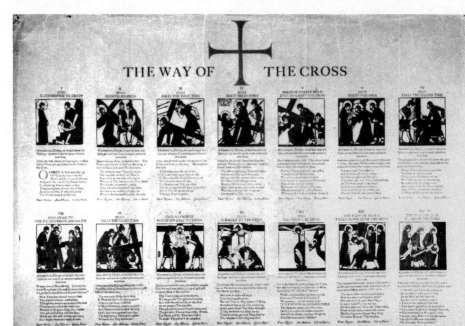

[664.44]

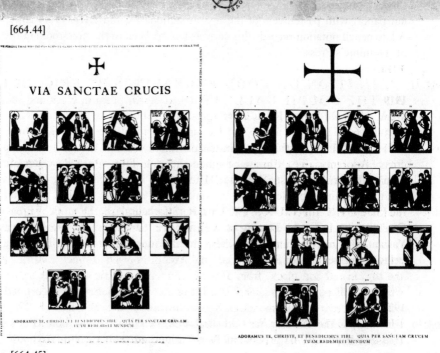

[664.45]

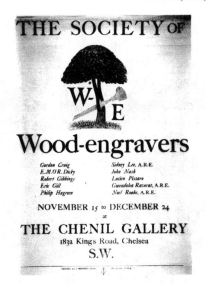

Wood-engravers

Gordon Craig	*Sidney Lee*, A.R.E.
E.M.O'R. Dicky	*John Nash*
Robert Gibbings	*Lucien Pissaro*
Eric Gill	*Gwendolen Raverat*, A.R.E.
Philip Hagreen	*Noel Rooke*, A.R.E.

NOVEMBER 15 to DECEMBER 24
at
THE CHENIL GALLERY
183a Kings Road, Chelsea
S.W.

[664.46]

664.44 THE WAY OF THE CROSS. Reproduced. Shows *Cross* (P112), *The Way of the Cross* (P93–P106), and *Paschal Lamb* (P92). $17\frac{1}{2} \times 22\frac{1}{2}$. No date but Physick suggests *c*. 1918. Note: G L has a copy printed in black and red on stiff tan paper, with paste-overs of the text at stations IX and XIII. Proof copy? A late pencil notation records this copy as having been in the pressroom of the St. Dominic's Press.

1919

664.45 VIA SANCTAE CRUCIS. Reproduced. Shows *The Way of the Cross* (P93–P106). The cross at the top has not been identified as E. G.'s work. $18\frac{1}{2} \times 12\frac{1}{2}$. Printed in black on thin tan paper. Text below the stations of the cross: Adoramus Te, Christe, Et Benedicimus Tibi. Quia Per Sanctam Crucem/Tuam Redemisti Mundum. The Lord's Prayer runs along the sides and top, forming a border. At the bottom: 'Wood engravings by Eric Gill after the Stations of the Cross in Westminster Cathedral. S. Dominic's Press. Ditchling. A.D.1919.' The D in A.D. is printed backwards. Proof copy. Variant. G L has another version, also probably a proof, $18 \times 13\frac{1}{2}$. The *Cross* (P112) is printed in red. Reproduced.

1920

664.46 THE SOCIETY OF WOOD ENGRAVERS. Reproduced. Shows *Tree and Burin* (P176) printed in green, blue and orange, plus a red dot.

333

Posters, etc., illustrated by Gill

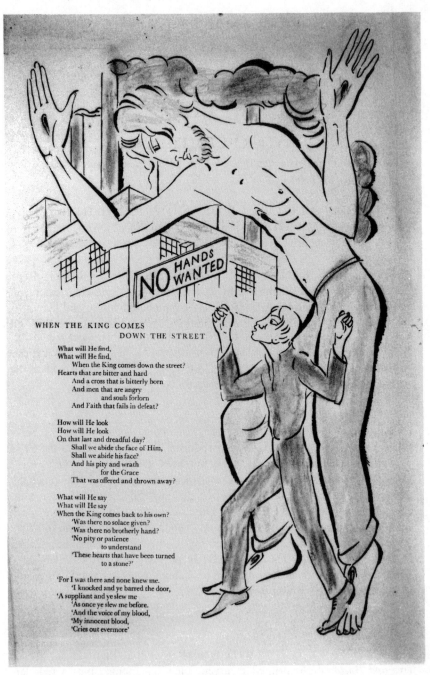

WHEN THE KING COMES
DOWN THE STREET

What will He find,
What will He find,
   When the King comes down the street?
Hearts that are bitter and hard
   And a cross that is bitterly born
   And men that are angry
          and souls forlorn
   And Faith that fails in defeat?

How will He look
How will He look
On that last and dreadful day?
   Shall we abide the face of Him,
   Shall we abide his face?
   And his pity and wrath
        for the Grace
   That was offered and thrown away?

What will He say
What will He say
When the King comes back to his own?
   'Was there no solace given?
   'Was there no brotherly hand?
   'No pity or patience
        to understand
   'These hearts that have been turned
        to a stone?'

'For I was there and none knew me.
  'I knocked and ye barred the door,
'A suppliant and ye slew me
  'As once ye slew me before.
  'And the voice of my blood,
  'My innocent blood,
  'Cries out evermore'

[664.4

334

30 × 20. Printed in black and red on smooth white paper. Imprint: Printed at S. Dominic's Press [device of a cross with the initials J.M.J.D.] Ditchling, Sussex.

1923

664.47 DAILY HERALD ORDER OF INDUSTRIAL HEROISM. CERTIFICATE. $7\frac{3}{4} \times 9\frac{1}{2}$. Contains *St. Christopher and Chimney Smoke* (the smoke printed in red) (P220), printed in red (P224). Certificate printed in black and red. E. 1056–1952 in the V&A. *A Rose-Plant in Jericho* (P221), *Wave* (P222), and *The Holy Ghost as Dove* (P224).

664.48 DAILY HERALD ORDER OF INDUSTRIAL HEROISM. As above, but with *The Holy Ghost as Dove* (P224) replaced by *Star*, printed in red (P223). Certificate printed in black and red. E. 1055–1952 in the V&A.

664.49 WHEN THE KING COMES DOWN THE STREET. Reproduced. Reproduces a drawing by E. G. $17\frac{1}{2} \times 11\frac{1}{4}$. Line cut, text printed letterpress. No imprint. n.d. CLC copy is numbered 76/100 and signed Eric G. GL copy is unsigned but the illustration is hand-coloured in yellow, grey and red.

CROSS REFERENCE LIST
OF ENGRAVING NUMBERS

DITCHLING/GILL NUMBERS *TO* PHYSICK
(V. & A. Catalogue) NUMBERS

Includes those print numbers inserted in the V. & A. Catalogue and those added to
The Engravings of Eric Gill *(1983) and given the prefix P which have no*
Ditchling/Gill equivalent

DI	PI	D31	P49	D63	P66	D95	P102
D2	P2	D32	P33	D64	P67	D96	P103
D3	P3	D33	P34	D65	P68	D97	P104
	P3a	D34	P35	D66	P69	D98	P105
–	P3b	D35	P36	D67	P70	D99	P106
D4	P4	D36	P37	D68	P72	D100	P107
D5	P5	D37	P38	D69	P73	D101	P108
D6	P6	D38	P39	D70	P74	D102	P109
D7	P7	D39	P40	D71	P75	D103	P110
D8	P8	D40	P41	D72	P76	D104	P111
D9	P9	D41	P42	D73	P77	D105	P112
D10	P11	D42	P43	D74	P78	D106	P82
D11	P12	D43	P44	D75	P79	D107	P113
D12	P13	D44	P45	D76	P80	D107A	P114
D13	P10	D45	P46	D77	P81	D107B	P116
D14	P14	D46	P47	D78	P83	D107C	P117
D15	P15	D47	P30	D79	P84	D107D	P119
D16	P16	D48	P48	D80	P85	D107E	P120
D17	P18	D49	P50	D81	P86	D107F	P115
D17A	P17	D50	P51	D82	P87	D107G	P129
D18	P19	D51	P52	D83	P89	D107H	P121
D19	P20	D52	P53	D83A	P90	D107I	P123
D20	P21	D53	P54	D84	P91	D107J	P124 / P124a
D21	P22	D54	P55	D85	P92	D107K	P125
D22	P23	D54A	P56	D86	P93	D107L	P130
D23	P24	D55	P57	D87	P94	D107M	P127
D24	P25	D56	P58	D88	P95	D107N	P118
D25	P26	D57	P59	D89	P96	D107O	P126
D26	P27	D58	P60	D90	P97	D107P	P131
D27	P28	D59	P61	D91	P98	D107Q	P122
D28	P29	D60	P62	D92	P99	D107R	P128
D29	P31	D60A	P63	D93	P100	D107S	P132
D30	P32	D61	P145	D94	P101		
		D62	P64				

Cross reference list

D107T	P133	D143	P172	D184	P215	D226	P212
D107U	P134	D144	P173	D185	P216	D227	P257
D108	P135	D145	P174	D186	P217	D228	P258
D109	P136	D146	P177	D187	P218	D229	P259
D110	P138	D146A	P175	D188	P219	D230	P260
D111	P139	D147	P178	D189	P220	D231	P261
D112	P71	D148	P179	D190	P221	D232	P262
D113	P140	D149	P180	D191	P222	D233	P263
D114	P137	D150	P181	D192	P224	D234	P264
D115	P141	D151	P182	D193	P223	D235	P265
D116	P142	D152	P183	D194	P225	D236	P266
D117	P143	D153	P184	D195	P226	D237	P267
D118	P144	D154	P185	D196	P227	D238	P268
–	P146	D155	P186	D197	P228	D239	P269
–	P146a	D156	P187	D198	P229	D240	P270
–	P147	D157	P158	D199	P230	D241	P271
D119	P150	D158	P176	D200	P231	1	P272
D120	P151	D159	P188	D201	P232	2	P273
D121	P152	D160	P189	D202	P233	3	P274
D122	P153	D161	P190	D203	P234	4	P275
D123	P88	D162	P191	D204	P235	5	P276
D124	P154	D163	P192	D205	P236	6	P277
D125	P155	D164	P193	D206	P237	7	P278
D126	P156	D165	P194	D207	P238	8	P279
D127	P157	D166	P195	D208	P239	9	P280
D128	P148	D167	P196	D209	P240	10A 10B	P281
–	P149	D168	P197	D210	P241		
D129	P149a	D169	P198	D211	P242	11A 11B	P282
D130	P159	D169A	P199	D212	P243	12	P283
D131	P160	D170	P200	D213	P244	13	P284
D132	P161	D171	P201	D214	P245	14	P285
D132A	P162	D172	P202	D215	P246	15	P286
D133	P163	D173	P203	D216	P247	16	P287
D134	P164	D174	P204	D217	P248	17	P288
D135	P165	D175	P205	D218	P249	18	P289
D136	P166	D176	P206	D219	P250	19A 19B	P290
D137	P167	D177	P207	D220	P251		
D138	P168	D178	P208	D221	P252	20A 20B	P291
D139	P169	D179	P209	D222	P253		
D140	P170	D180	P210	D223	P254	21	P292
D141	P65	D181	P211	D224	P255	22	P293
D142	P171	D182	P213	D225	P256	23	P294
		D183	P214			24	P295

25	P296	61	P338	102	P382 / P383	139	P421
26	P297	62	P339	103	P384	140	P422
27	P298	63	P340	104	P385	141	P423
28	P299	64	P341	105	P386	142	P424
29	P300	65	P342	106	P387	143	P425
30	P301	66	P343	107	P388	144	P426
31	P302	67	P344	108	P389	145	P427
32	P303	68	P345	109	P390	146	P428
33	P304	69	P346	110	P391	147	P429
34	P305	70	P347	110A	P392	148	P430
35	P306	71	P349	111	P393	149	P431
36	P307	72	P350	112	P394	150	P432
37	P308	73	P351	113	P395	151	P433
37A	P309	74	P352	114 / 114A	P396	152	P434
37B	P310 / P311	75	P353	115	P397	153	P435
		76	P354	116	P166 (2nd state)	154	P436
37C	P312 / P313	77	P355			155	P437
37D	P314	78	P356	117	P398	156	P438
38	P315	79	P357	–	P399	157	P439
39	P316	80	P358	–	P399a	158	P440
40	P317	81	P359	118	P400	159	P441
41	P318	82	P360	119	P401	160	P442
42	P319	83	P361	120	P402	161	P443
43	P320	84	P362	121	P403	162	P444
44	P321	85	P363	122	P404	163	P445
45	P322	86	P364	123	P405	164	P446
46	P323	87	P365	124	P406	165	P447
47	P324	88	P366	125	P407	166	P448
48	P325	89	P367	126	P408	167	P449
49	P326	90	P368	127	P409	168	P450
–	P326a	91	P369	128	P410	169	P451
50	P327	92	P370	129	P411	170	P452
51	P328	93	P371	130	P412	171	P453
52	P329	94	P372	131	P413	172	P454
53	P330	95	P373	132	P414	173	P455
54	P331	96	P374	133	P415	174	P456
55	P332	97	P375	134	P416	175	P457
56	P333	98	P376	135	P417	176 / 176A	P458
57	P334	99A	P377	136	P418	177 / 177A	P459
58	P335	99B	P378	137	P419	178	P460
59	P336	99C	P379	138	P420		
60	P337	100	P380				
		101	P381				

179	P461	219	P502	259	P543	296	P584
180	P462	219A	P503	260	P544	297	P585
181	P463	220	P504	261	P545	298	P586
182	P464	221	P505	262	P546	299	P587
183	P465	222	P506	263	P547	300	P588
184	P466	223	P507	264	P548	301	P589
185	P467	224	P508	265	P549	302	P590
186	P468	225	P509	266	P550	302A	P591
187	P469	226	P510	267	P551	303	P592
188	P470	227	P511	268	P552	304	P593
189	P471	228	P512	269	P553	304A	P594
190	P472	229	P513	–	P553a	305	P595
191	P473	230	P514	270	P554	306	P596
192	P474	231	P515	271	P555	307	P597
193	P475	232	P516	271A		308	P598
194	P476 P477 P348	233	P517	272	P556	309	P599
		234	P518	272A	P557	310	P600
195	P478	235	P519	273	P558	311	P601
196	P479	236	P520	274	P559	312	P602
197	P480	237	P521	275	P560	313	P603
198	P481	238	P522	276	P561	314	P604
199	P482	239	P523	277	P562	315	P605
200	P483	240	P524	278	P563	316	P606
201	P484	241	P525	279	P564	317	P607
202	P485	242	P526	280	P565	–	P608
203	P486	243	P527	281	P566	–	P609
204	P487	244	P528	282	P567	–	P610
205	P488	245	P529	283	P568	–	P611
206	P489	246	P530	284	P569	–	P612
207	P490	247	P531	285	P570	318	P613
208	P491	248	P532	286	P571	319 319A 319B	P614
209	P492	249	P533	287	P572		
210	P493	250	P534	288	P573	320	P615
211	P494	251	P535	289	P574	321	P616
212	P495	252	P536	289A	P575	322	P617
213	P496	253A 253B	P537	289B	P576	323	P618
214	P497	254	P538	289C	P577	324A	P619
215	P498	255	P539	290	P578	324B	P620
216	P499	256	P540	291	P579	325	P621
217	P500	257	P541	292	P580	326	P622
218	P501	258	P542	293	P581	327	P623
				294	P582		
				295	P583		

–	P623a	368	P665	408	P707	444	P744
328	P624	369	P666	409	P708	445	P745
329	P625	370	P667	410	P709	446	P746
330	P626	371	P668	411	P710	447	P747
330A	P627	372	P669	412	P711	448	P748
331	P628	373	P670	413	P712	449	P749
332	P629	374	P671	414	P713	450	P750
333	P630	375	P672	414A	P714	451	P751
334	P631	376	P673	415	P715	452	P752
335	P632	377	P674	416	P716	452A	P753
336	P633	378	P675	417	P717	452B	P754
337	P634		P676	418	P718	452C	P755
338	P635	379	P677	419	P719	452D	P756
339	P636	380	P678	420	P720	453	P757
340	P637	381	P679	421	P721	454	P758
341	P638	382	P680	422	P722	455	P759
342	P639	383	P681	423	P723	456	P760
343	P640	384	P682	424	P724	457	P761
344	P641	385	P683	425	P725	458	P762
345	P642	386	P684	426	P726	459	P763
346	P643	387	P685	427	P727	460	P764
347	P644	388	P686	–	P727a	461	P765
348	P645	389	P687	–	P727b	462	P766
349	P646	390	P688	428	P728	463	P767
350	P647	391	P689	429	P729	464	P768
351	P648	392	P690	430	P730	465	P769
352	P649	393	P691	431	P731	466	P770
353	P650	394	P692	432	P732	467	P771
354	P651	395	P693	432A	P732a	468	P772
355	P652	396	P694	432B	P732b	469	P773
356	P653	397	P695	–	P732c	470	P774
357	P654	398	P696	433	P733	471	P775
358	P655	399	P697	434	P734	472	P776
359	P656	400	P698	435	P735	473	P777
360	P657	401	P699	436	P736	474	P778
361	P658	402	P700	437	P737	475	P779
362	P659	403	P701	438	P738	476	P780
363	P660	403A	P702	439	P739	477	P781
364	P661	404	P703	440	P740	478	P782
365	P662	405	P704	441	P741	479	P783
366	P663	406	P705	442	P742	480	P784
367	P664	407	P706	443	P743	481	P785

482	P786	523	P827	559	P869	600	P911
483	P787	524	P828	560	P870	601	P912
484	P788	524A	P829	561	P871	602	P913
485	P789	524B	P830	562	P872	602A	P914
–	P789a		P831	563	P873	603	P915
486	P790	525	P832	564	P874	604	P916
487	P791	526	P833	565	P875	605	P917
488	P792	527	P834	566	P876	606	P918
489	P793	528	P835	567	P878	607	P919
490	P794	529	P836	568	P877	608	P920
491	P795	530	P837	569	P879	609	P921
492	P796	531	P838	570	P880	610	P922
493	P797	532	P839	571	P881	611	P923
494	P798		P840	572	P882	611A	P924
495	P799	533	P841	573	P883	612	P925
496	P800		P842	574	P884	613	P926
497	P801		P843	–	P884a	614	P927
498	P802	534	P844	575	P885	615	P928
499	P803	535	P845	576	P886	616	P929
500	P804	536	P846	577	P887	617	P930
501	P805	537	P847	578	P888	618	P931
502	P806	538	P848	579	P889	619	P932
503	P807	539	P849	580	P890	620	P933
504	P808	540	P850	581	P891	621	P934
505	P809	541	P851	581A	P892	621A	P935
506	P810	542	P852	582	P893	622	P936
507	P811	543	P853	583	P894	623	P937
508	P812	544	P854	584	P895	624	P938
509	P813	545	P855	585	P896	625	P939
510	P814	546	P856	586	P897	626	P940
511	P815	547	P857	587	P898	627	P941
512	P816	548	P858	588	P899	628	P942
513	P817	549	P859	589	P900	629	P943
514	P818	550	P860	590	P901	630	P944
515	P819	551	P861	591	P902	631	P945
516	P820	552	P862	592	P903	632	P946
517	P821	553	P863	593	P904	633	P947
518	P822	554	P864	594	P905	634	P948
519	P823	555	P865	595	P906	635	P949
520	P824	556	P866	596	P907	636	P950
521	P825	557	P867	597	P908	637	P951
522	P826	558	P868	598	P909	638	P952
				599	P910		

639	P953
640	P954
641	P955
642	P956
643	P957
644	P958
645	P959
646	P960
647	P961
648	P962
649	P963
650	P964
651	P965
652	P966
653	P967
654	P968
655	P969
656	P970
657	P971
658	P972
659	P973
660	P974
661	P975
662	P976
663	P977
664	P978
–	P978a
665	P979
666	P980
667	P981
668	P982
669	P983
670	P984
671	P985
672	P986
673	P987
674	P988
675	P989
676	P990
677	P991
678	P992
679	P993

I. TITLES

[The references are to entry numbers. The figures in bold type indicate
editiones principes]

Eric Gill: Man of Sussex, 636.104
Eric Gill: Master Craftsman, 555
Eric Gill, Master of Letter Forms, 636.59
Eric Gill 'Matter and Spirit', 636.10
Eric Gill, Meister der Schriftkunst, 636.22
Eric Gill Memorial Collection, The, 664.17
Eric Gill: Memorial Number of 'Blackfriars', 563
Eric Gill: Memorial Number of 'Pax Bulletin', 564
Eric Gill: Negative-Positive, 567
Eric Gill: Obituary Notices, 555
Eric Gill on Art and Propaganda, 170
Eric Gill, Onlooker, 492a
Eric Gill—Printer, 502
Eric Gill—Sans-Serif—Nulli Secundus, 463
Eric Gill, Sculpteur du 'Chemin de la Croix' de Westminster, 493
Eric Gill: Sculptor of Letters, 449
Eric Gill. Stamp Designer Manqué, 636.95
Eric Gill. Stone Carver. Wood Engraver. Typographer. Writer. 636.80
Eric Gill, T.O.S.D., 491, 573
Eric Gill, the Artist and Thinker, 555
Eric Gill: The Man and the Maker, 636.110
Eric Gill, The Man Who Loved Letters, 636.65
Eric Gill: The Searcher for Reality, 450
Eric Gill: 'Thou, Ruskin, seest me', 555
Eric Gill: Tribute, 565b
Eric Gill: 20th Century Book Designer [Article], 636.25
Eric Gill: 20th Century Book Designer [Book], 636.27
Eric Gill 22 February 1882 – 17 November 1940, 636.21
Eric Gill: Workman, 599
Eric Gill: Workman and Artist, 615
Eric Gill Workshops, 658
Eric Gill's 'Art Nonsense', 489
Eric Gill's Coin Drawings, 636.24
Eric Gill's Devotions, 625
Eric Gill's First Sanserif, 664.12
Eric Gill's Method of Type Design and Book Illustration, 636.64
Eric Gill's Perpetua, 458
Eric Gill's Pilgrim (né Bunyan) Type, 636.4
Eric Gill's Social Principles, 563
Erik Gill: La giustizia sociale e la Viá Crucis, 635
Essay in Aid of a Grammar of Practical Aesthetics, An, 18, **82**
Essays by Eric Gill, 53
Essential Perfection, 4, 18, **69**
European Mediterranean Academy, 351
Evolution in Printing of Railways Propaganda, 524
Evolution of Peace, The, 237
Exhibition of the Work of Three Private Presses, An, 664.22

Exhibition of War Memorial Designs, 400
Exhibition of Wood Engravings by Eric Gill at the Goupil Gallery, 664.41
Ex-Patriate of the Gothic Age, 575
Experimental Application of a Nomenclature for Letter Forms, 480
Experiments and Alphabets, 514
Eye for Industry, 636.131
Eyeless in Gaza, 190

Fabian Essays in Socialism, 305a
Fabian Tracts, 305
Factory System and Christianity, The, 50, 52, **69**
Failure of the Arts and Crafts Movement, The, 61
Faith and Communism, The, 531
Festival of Britain—Exhibition of Books, 662
Fifteen Craftsmen and their Crafts, 598
Fifteen Poems, 396
Fifty Years of Type-Cutting, 631
Figure Drawings, 628f
Figures of Speech or Figures of Thought, 600
Fine Printing in Germany, 398a
Fine Printing Collection, The, 664.30
First Edition Club [Liverpool], 129
First Edition Club [London], 146
First Nudes, 636.10
First Step to Peace, Stop False Thinking, The, 241
Five Hundred Years of Printing, 50, 52, **256**
Five on Revolutionary Art, 167
Fleuron, The, 332, 346a
Fools and Beasts, 222
Footnote to the Nineties, 636.49
Forager in the Gill Collection, A, 664.37
For an Arts and Crafts Exhibition, 189
For Eric Gill: May he have rest, 562
For Reconciliation, 253
Forty Hours Prayer, The, 664.43
Four Absentees, 636.20
Four Centuries of Fine Printing, 411
Four Gospels, The 285
Francis Meynell, 350
Friends and Adventures, 456
Friends of a Lifetime, 552
Fry & Sons, J. S., 640
Function of News Type, The, 179
Function of the Book Jacket, The, 522
Functionalism, 205
Future of Sculpture, The, **16**, 18, 113

Gallery, The, 226
Game, The, 69, 263
Gates of Memory, The, 636.90
Gauguin, Paul (see Paul Gauguin), 302b
Gazette, St George's Hospital, The, 355a
Gedichte: Paul Valéry, 326
Gedichte [Rainer Maria Rilke], 342

Titles Index

Taking of Toll, The, 258
Technique of Early Greek Sculpture, The, **147**, 475
Temple of the Winds, The, 438*a*
Testament of Beauty, The, 340
'The Times' Coat of Arms, 140
This Month's Personality: Eric Gill, 484
Three Book Types (*see* Specimen of Three Book Types, A), 30
Three Poems [Ananda Coomaraswamy], 271
Three Poems [H.D.C.P.], 367
Three Private Presses, 664.23
Thucydides, 392*c*
To be a Printer, 636.81
Tod des Tizian, Der, 392*b*
Tony Appleton Catalogue, 664.36
Topics, 556
Town Child's Alphabet, The, 94*a*
Tradition and Modernism in Politics, 208
Tradition in Sculpture, 628*b*
Transeamus Usque Bethlehem (*see* Three Poems by H.D.C.P.), 367
Travels & Sufferings of Father Jean de Brébeuf . . ., The, 297
Tribute to Eric Gill, A, 664.21
Tribute to the Pioneers of the Written Word, A, 663
Tristram Shandy, 337
Troilus & Criseyde, **279**, 421
Trousers, 35
True Philosophy of Art, The, 245
Tunnelling and Skyscraping, 436*a*
Tuppence Plain, Penny Coloured, 24, **117***a*
Twentieth Century Sans Serif Types, 543
Twentieth Century Sculptors, 344
Twentieth Century Sculpture, 628*c*
Twenty-Five Nudes, 38
Twenty-Four Portraits, 81
Twenty-Three Carols, 346*b*
Twopence Plain, Penny Coloured (*see* Tuppence Plain, Penny Coloured), 24, **117***a*
Two Friends, 636.30
Two Sussex Hand Presses, 432
Two Worlds, The, 473*a*
Two Worlds of Typography, The (*see* Typography), 21
Two Worlds: There are Two Worlds . . ., 246
Type Design: A Living Art, 481
Type Designed by Eric Gill and Printed by Hague & Gill, Ltd., 656
Type Designs of Eric Gill, 636.77
Type Designs of Eric Gill, The, 618
Type Designs of the Past and Present, 417
Type Supplement, 657*b*
Typographers at War, 518
Typographic Milestones – Eric Gill, 636.123
Typographical Masterpiece, A, 636.137
Typographically Speaking, 634*b*
Typography, 21

Typography for Screen Printers [Gill Sans], 664.7
Typography for Screen Printers [Perpetua], 664.9

Ulysses, 357
Uncle Dottery, 394
Unemployment, 25
Unholy Trinity, 37
Union of Work and Culture (*see* Work and Culture), 45, **217**
Utopia [Ashendene Press], 303
Utopia [Golden Cockerel Press], 336

Valéry, Paul: Gedichte (*see* Paul Valéry: Gedichte), 326
Value of the Creative Faculty in Man, 33, **174**
Verzeichnis der Drucke der Cranach-Presse in Weimar, 453
Via Sanctae Crucis, 664.45
Victoria and Albert Museum, 647
Views and Reviews: Eric Gill Epitomised . . ., 523
Vision of the Fool, The, 609
Viśvakarmā: Examples of Indian Architecture, Sculpture . . ., 67
Vulgata, 391*a*

W. E. Campbell's Utopia, 134*a*
War and Economics, 230*a*
War and Peace, 202
War, Conscience & the Rule of Christ, 238
War Graves, 73
War is not Romance, 251
War Memorial, **9**, 18
Way of it, The, 69
Way of the Cross, The [Book], 268
Way of the Cross, The [Poster], 664.44
We are Persons, 232
Wer ist Wer?, 619
Westminster Cathedral, 18, **76**
Westminster Press, its History and Activities, 443*a*
Westminster 'Stations', The, 404
What are the Fruits of the New Typography?, 503
What is Lettering?, **142**, 476
What is Man?, 591*a*
What is Sculpture?, 154
What is Truth?, 128
What is 'Twentieth Century Typography'?, 487
What should Art mean?, 119
What's it all bloomin' well for?, 92
What's the use of Art anyway?, 210
When Body holds its Noise, 178
When the King comes down the street, 664.49
Who is a typographical artist, Mr Gill? 505*b*
Why Exhibit Works of Art?, 583
Why I Designed 'Jubilee', 182

354

II. AUTHORS AND TITLES

DALEY, Pat V., *Who is a typographical artist, Mr Gill?*, 505*b*
DANDRIDGE, C. G., *Evolution in Printing of Railway Propaganda, The*, 524
D'ARCY, M. C., S.J., *Appreciation*, 563
DARTON, F. J. Harvey, *Modern Book Illustration in Great Britain and America*, 461*b*
DAVIS, Jim [Compiler], *Printed by Hague and Gill*, 664.32
DAWSON, Christopher
    Christianity and Sex, 131*a*
    Religion and the Modern State, 354
DAY, Dorothy
    Church and Work, The, 605
    Dorothy Day Book, The [Ed. by M. Quigley and M. Garvey], 636.93
DEGERING, Hermann [Introduction by], *Lettering*, 121
DE LA BEDOYERE, Michael, *Christianity, Peace and War*, 538*a*
DELANY, Bernard, O.P., *Appreciation*, 563
DENNIS, S. L., *Design of a Book, The*, 510*a*
DENT, J. M. and Hugh R., *House of Dent, 1888–1938, The*, 542
DILWORTH, Thomas [Editor], *Inner Necessities*, 636.120
DOBSON, Frank, *Sculpture*, 183
DODGSON, Campbell, *Master Craftsman, The*, 496
DONNE, John, *Holy Sonnets, The*, 298
DREYFUS, John
    Book of Alphabets for Douglas Cleverdon drawn by Eric Gill, A [Introduction], 636.132
    Eric Gill Collection of the Humanities Research Center: A Catalogue, The [Introduction], 636.91
    Eric Gill's Method of Type Design and Book Illustration, 636.64
    Typographical Masterpiece, A, 636.137
DUCHEN, Monica Bohm [Introduction], *Eric Gill 'Matter and Spirit'*, 636.100
DUGAN, Kerran, C.S.C., *Eric Gill: A Special Kind of Artist*, 633
DUNCAN, Ronald, *Complete Pacifist, The*, 201*a*
DURST, Alan L., *Ecclesiastical Ornament*, 516

EASTON, John, *British Postage Stamp Design*, 530
'EDUCATIONAL EXPERT', *Manuscript Writing and Lettering*, 403
EDWARDS, A. Trystan
    Architecture as Sculpture, 438
    Plain Architecture, 470
EPSTEIN, Jacob, *Let There be Sculpture*, 554
'ERIC', *Chance for the Sculpture, A*, 468
EURICH, Richard, *Sculpture*, 529
EVANS, Powys, *Eric Gill*, 641
EVENS, Tim, *Outcry*, 632

FARJEON, Eleanor
    Country Child's Alphabet, The, 94
    Town Child's Alphabet, The, 94
FARLEIGH, John, *Fifteen Craftsmen on Their Crafts*, 598
FARR, Dennis
    English Art 1870–1940, 636.72
    Modern British Paintings, Drawings and Sculpture, The [in part], 636.35
FAULKNER, Peter, *William Morris and Eric Gill*, 636.67
FIRMIN, Joan, *Two Sussex Hand Presses*, 432
FITZROY, Mark, *Eric Gill: 'Thou, Ruskin, seest me'*, 555
FLETCHER, John Gould, *Eric Gill*, 424
FLOWER, Desmond, *Printing for Printers*, 466
FLOWER, Margaret [Editor], *Sonnets of Shakespeare, The*, 288
FOLEY, Helen, *Poems*, 360
FOSTER, Anthony, *Appreciation*, 563
FOSTER, Kenelm, O.P., *Created Holiness*, 563
FRANCIS, F. C. [Foreword], *Livre Anglais, Le*, 664
FRY, Roger, *English Sculptor, An*, 398
FULLER, Peter, *Man of Many Parts, A*, 636.121
FURST, Herbert
    Modern Woodcut, The, 409
    On the Appreciation of the Modern Woodcut, 415

G., C. [Cecil Gill], *Llanthony Monastery & Eric Gill*, 636.60
G., C. [Rev. Albert Gille], *Evolution of Peace, The*, 237
GARRETT, Albert, *British Wood Engraving of the 20th Century*, 636.84
GARVEY, Michael [part editor], *Dorothy Day Book, The*, 636.93
GAUNT, W., *Modern English Wood-Engraving*, 416
GIBBINGS, Robert
    Art of the Book, The, 434
    Coming Down the Wye, 580
    Memories of Eric Gill, 636.9
GILL, Dr Cecil, *Letters of Eric Gill*, 622
GILL, Eric [Writings]
    A. R. Orage, 159
    Abolish Art and Teach Drawing, 250
    Actus Sequitur Esse, 69
    All Art is Propaganda, 167
    All That England Stands For, 44
    Analysis of the Right to Private Property, An, 187
    And Who Wants Peace?, 36
    Appeal for assistance in the erection of a crucifix . . ., An, 74*a*
    A Propos of Lady Chatterley's Lover, 133
    Architect, The, 64
    Architects and Builders, 168